18
1

GREAT MEN AND MOVEMENTS
IN ISRAEL

THE MACMILLAN COMPANY
NEW YORK · BOSTON · CHICAGO · DALLAS
ATLANTA · SAN FRANCISCO

MACMILLAN & CO., Limited
LONDON · BOMBAY · CALCUTTA
MELBOURNE

THE MACMILLAN COMPANY
OF CANADA, Limited
TORONTO

SET UP BY BROWN BROTHERS LINOTYPERS
PRINTED IN THE UNITED STATES OF AMERICA
BY THE FERRIS PRINTING COMPANY

Great Men and Movements in Israel

BY

RUDOLF KITTEL

PROFESSOR AT THE UNIVERSITY OF LEIPZIG

AUTHORIZED TRANSLATION BY

CHARLOTTE A. KNOCH

AND

C. D. WRIGHT

New York

THE MACMILLAN COMPANY

1929

TO MY SONS

THEODOR KITTEL, LL.D.

*Member of the Board of Directors and the
Board of Managers of the German
National Railroad Company
in Berlin*

AND

GERHARD KITTEL, D.D.

*Professor at Greifswald of the New
Testament and of the Philosophy
of Late Judaism*

PREFACE

For more than two thousand years Judaism has interested and influenced humanity. Some people admit this fact with pride and joy; others, with regret; none deny it. A country, located as a bridge between Asia and Africa, and between the great centers of culture of Babylon, Assyria, and Persia on the east, and the Mediterranean countries on the west, was of necessity a center of history throughout the centuries. A people worthy of the natural gifts of this favored country must indeed have something to contribute to the world, provided that the people have developed in close harmony with the destiny of their native soil.

The highest purpose of history is not to relate what battles have been fought, or what kings have been set upon thrones or deposed, not even to state the accomplishments of the arts and sciences as such, but in all things to try to learn to understand the soul of individuals and great peoples, and thus the history of humanity. To approach this goal is the object of this book. The statements on this subject included in the chapter called "Great Narrators" are only suggestive. The whole book attempts to open a new path as yet untrod. In the early pages of my introductory chapter, I have tried to show of how great significance to history are the lives of great men. With this thought in mind, and in contrast to former presentations of Israelite history, I have tried to present Israel's development from the human side, that my book may be considered a sketch of Israelite-Jewish characters. A central idea is followed, namely, that with all due deference to the democratic idea, history must be understood as a purely aristocratic phenomenon. History

PREFACE

is really made by its heroes, its leading minds. Although the masses seem to make history and may believe that they do make history, they do not realize that they are under the dictatorship, either physical or mental, of a few individuals. In the following pages I hope that much new light may fall upon the development and the inner life of the most remarkable of all civilized peoples. The book is intended for the educated general public; I hope it may be valuable also to the scientist.

From the epilogue, the reader may see that the author had a secondary purpose. With the aid of an important chapter in the world's history, he would like to help dispel an illusion which, through a long lifetime, he has observed as an unwholesome influence upon the thoughts and deeds of many peoples, especially among philosophers, politicians, and statesmen.

THE AUTHOR.

Leipzig, October, 1925.

INTRODUCTION

PROFESSOR RUDOLF KITTEL needs no introduction to an American audience. For a generation his books have commanded the attention and stimulated the thought of our scholars. This is evidenced by the fact that a considerable number of his books have appeared in English dress. His first important work, *The History of the Hebrews,* published in Germany in 1888 (Volume I) and 1892 (Volume II) made such an impression that it was published in English only three years later, in 1895, and in the same year appeared his edition of *Chronicles* in *The Sacred Books of the Old Testament* (the "Rainbow Bible"). His smaller but interesting monograph, *The Babylonian Excavations and Early Biblical History,* was brought out in Germany in 1903, was almost immediately translated into English and went through three editions in its English form (1904-1908). This was followed by *The Scientific Study of the Old Testament* in 1911 and after a long interval, within which fell the War, by *The Religion of the People of Israel* (1925). Almost all of these translated works have had interest for a larger audience than the comparatively small group of scholars and specialists in Old Testament study. But the present book is addressed especially to this larger company of readers. To them it may prove helpful to say a word upon its origin and viewpoint, and upon the character of the man who wrote it.

Professor Kittel will probably be remembered longest for his *Biblia Hebraica* (the text of the Hebrew Bible) with its admirably convenient critical apparatus, which has become a *vade mecum* for all students of the Old Testament, and for his *History of the Hebrews* (in later editions with the title, *History of the People of Israel*). The history of this *History* is interesting and significant and furnishes the background for understanding the present volume. The first edition of the *History* appeared, as has been pointed out, in 1888 and 1892. This was just about ten years after the appearance of Wellhausen's famous *History of Israel*. The brilliance of Wellhausen's work had captured the imagination of most of the abler scholars in Germany, and what may be called the Wellhausen school was at that time carrying everything before it. In the *History of the Hebrews* Kittel, though a young man and still comparatively unknown, ventured to attack Wellhausen's hypothesis at one of its most vital points and to defend a view which the reigning School regarded as unduly conservative. He knew at the time that this would tend to injure his reputation and check the sale of his book. As a matter of fact it did both. On presenting in person the first copy of his book to his friend, Kautzsch, one of the foremost exponents of Wellhausen's views, Kautzsch "made a wry face," he tells us, and said: "I am sorry for this; since Wellhausen we have gone ahead much further." As to the fate of the *History,* a second edition of Volume II was not called for until seventeen years later (1909) and of Volume I, in which the criticism of Wellhausen was especially elaborated, not until 1912, twenty-four years after the first edition! But in this long interval the situation in Old Testament research had changed. Wellhausen and his followers had elaborated their theories almost exclusively on the basis of the data furnished by the Old Testament books themselves. But in the meanwhile the discovery and decipherment of the inscriptions in Egypt (especially the Tel el Amara tablets) and in Mesopotamia had yielded a vast amount of material in the light of which the religion of Israel was to be reëxamined. Just how far this material corroborates the Wellhausen hypothesis or justifies its critics is still a matter of dispute among Old Testament scholars. At any rate, Professor Kittel was the first to write an exhaustive history of Israel in which the results of the inscriptions and excavations were systematically woven into the thread of the narrative and utilized to reënforce his earlier positions. The result for the fortunes of the *History* was astonishing. The third edition of the very important first volume was called for in 1916, a fourth in 1921, and a fifth and sixth in 1923. Meanwhile, the second volume was keeping pace with the first and reached its sixth and seventh editions in 1925. The significance of this change of attitude toward Professor Kittel's work can hardly be overestimated. It is unquestionably a reflection of the change of attitude in Germany, especially since the war, toward the older critical positions. Whether there will be, in the future, a swing back to these earlier views no one can foretell. But in any case it must be a great satisfaction to Professor Kittel to feel that the positions he adopted early in life and steadfastly adhered to in spite of all opposition, have become so widely recognized and approved.

Another main feature of the *History* in addition to its more cautious critical viewpoint, and a feature which has undoubtedly contributed very largely to its widening influence, appears in the fact that the various editions show a steadily lessening interest in the merely literary side of the work, the critical analysis of documents, which absorbed so much attention in the first edition, and an ever increasing interest in the life that lies back of these documents. Professor Kittel's journey to Palestine in his later life was of very great influence upon his thinking in this regard. In a brief autobiographical sketch he tells us that before this journey he looked on the Old Testament as only a literary product, as a book. But during his travels through Syria and Palestine "the scales fell from his eyes; the conviction came that it was not primarily a book which we have in the Old Testament, nor must we try to understand it as only a book, but rather as a reflection of a *life,* a rich historical, cultural and religious life, full of movement and vitality." In agreement with this conviction the author sought, in the multiplying editions of the *History,* to push personalities to the front. For him as for Carlyle, great personalities are the decisive factors in history and it was the heroes in the Old Testament that gripped his imagination.

Out of this conviction and out of the labor of a lifetime which Kittel's *History of the People of Israel* represents has arisen the present volume. In it the majestic characters of Israel are drawn for us upon the background of the crises in Israel's history in which they appeared. It thus represents the quintessence of Professor Kittel's work upon the history of Israel adapted to the interests of the general reader. Such a work grows naturally out of the character of the man himself.

It is often difficult for readers to separate an author from his books, especially if the author happens to be a foreigner. Names such as Wellhausen, Kittel, Kautzsch are too apt to stand simply for this or that critical tendency or scientific monograph. We forget the man behind the book. Professor Kittel comes of an ancient Swabian family. He grew up in a home of devout piety. His youthful ambition was to be a country pastor, and though his life for the larger part of it has been that of a teacher, "a friendly, idyllic pastorate," he tells us, "such as often existed in earlier days was ever my happy dream." He is himself a specialist but he knows the dangers of specialization, particularly for a theologian. He believes that the duty of a theological teacher is to remember that he is training pastors and preachers. He has always been deeply interested in the practical side of his work and has shown his administrative abilities as rector at the Universities of Breslau and Leipzig. At Leipzig he was elected to this office two successive years, the last year of the war and the year of the revolution, a most noteworthy recognition of his capabilities. It was during the Red riots in Leipzig in the winter and spring of 1919 that Professor Kittel saved the University from pillage and probable destruction. The Reds were very suspicious of the University. Rumors had gone abroad that on several occasions shots had been fired from the University upon Red parades. On March 8th an armed guard appeared and, covering the Rector with their guns, demanded to search the students for arms and propaganda literature. Professor Kittel is a tall man, dignified in appearance, altogether an impressive personality. He looked steadily at his assailants and calmly invited them to fire if they dared. They hesitated. After waiting for them to act, the Rector, with a quick gesture thrusting their guns aside, suggested that they confer together as reasonable men. A parley followed and the episode ended in their peaceful withdrawal. The University was not further molested. The courage and endurance of the ancient heroes of Israel in their crises did not fail the lifelong student and admirer of them in his own.

The work of translation has been in the hands of two very competent women, Miss Charlotte A. Knoch, of Leipzig, Germany, and Miss Carrie D. Wright, of Stockton, California. Miss Knoch, upon whom the major part of the labor has fallen, is a native of St. Louis and a graduate of Leland Stanford University. After graduation, she became Vice-principal in the Pasadena High School where she taught modern languages for many years. From 1915-19 she was a member of the German Department in Leland Stanford, first as instructor and then as Assistant Professor. In 1920 she went to Germany to do relief work among German students. In 1922 she became Professor Kittel's secretary, and from that time to the present has assisted him in the publication of his various books. Miss Wright is a native of

INTRODUCTION

Vermont, a graduate of Smith College, and has been teaching English for some years in the Stockton High School. The reader may rest assured that in the present instance he will be spared the hackwork which translations of foreign scientific treatises are so apt to be, and which only too often stand as a barrier rather than as an interpretative medium between himself and the original author.

KEMPER FULLERTON.

CONTENTS

GREAT MEN AND MOVEMENTS
IN ISRAEL

GREAT MEN AND MOVEMENTS
IN ISRAEL

INTRODUCTION

DAVID, the general and statesman of divine choice, founded a kingdom—an extraordinary achievement for his time and his surroundings. But what was this kingdom compared with the achievements of Alexander and of Napoleon? What, compared with the great nations surrounding Israel on the Nile, on the Tigris, or on the Euphrates? Solomon built a temple and a capital, long unparalleled in Israel. He adorned them with such splendor that they became proverbial. But what were Solomon's creations compared with the temples of Thebes and the palaces of Nineveh or of Babylon? What were his artists compared with Phidias and Praxiteles? Had Israel nothing more to offer the world than what great men gave as their best accomplishments, we, in the light of the great deeds and achievements of history, should have no reason to praise Israel.

Rome gave the world both the law and the state; Hellas taught the world to drink at the fount of wisdom and of art. In these fields, Israel offers no parallel. It taught, however, something higher. "For what shall it profit a man if he gain the whole world and lose his own soul?" Of greater value than state and law, than art and worldly wisdom, is the power to concentrate the mind on the eternal depths from whence all life springs. Of greater value than all the stores of wisdom is the one treasure that on earth provides peace for the soul, and when the hour of death comes, eases its pangs by confidence in the Deity. Israel's chief accomplishment was in religion. Israel produced a faith in God and passed it on to the world: this, itself, was a great historical achievement, greater than all that preceded it and all that followed it. Judaism, Christianity, and Islam are the products of Israel. To this day we gather our spiritual food from what Israel gave the world. Even where faith in God seems long to have been cast aside, and where with shortsighted abnegation we seek to deny all that is apparently foreign to the inheritance of Israel, even there we draw from it, often unconsciously.

In the age of democracy, individuals with insight (their number is always limited) realize that nothing is more aristocratic than history. To be sure, true democracy should consider the will of the majority. In no time or place, however, have the masses been able to rule themselves. The more they believed themselves able to do so, the less were they really capable of it. The community, the state, and the world have always been guided by a few gifted leaders. Even where nominally the masses ruled, they were merely tools in the hands of superior personalities. A personality, to be sure, is nothing more than the product of the whole of which it is a part, in which it lives, and from which it springs. The contrast of individual and masses finally disappears in the higher union.

This law of the rule of strong personalities is very apparent in the history of Rome. From the days of the elder Scipio, a long unbroken line of superior leaders guided the ship of state with a firm hand, and stamped their will and personality upon the people. In Hellas we find the same condition. The leaders of Athens and Sparta—Miltiades, Themistocles and Pericles, Plato and Socrates, Pisistratus and Epaminondas, Thucydides and Demosthenes, and many others—really created the Hellas that we respect and honor in history. Thus Hellenic spirit is nothing other than the accomplishment of the great men of Hellas.

So it was in Israel. What was best and permanent in Israel was its religion. The soul of the nation is grateful to its leaders in this field of religious life and thought. As the body is the dwelling place and the tool of the soul, so the state and society are the dwelling place of the national soul. They, too, are not created and cared for by the whole nation. Those who devote themselves to the nation and thus serve to develop and advance it are the natural leaders and great personalities, as are also those heroes of religious life. Here appear men like Saul, David, Solomon, Joshua; as contrasting figures with them or their successors, Jeroboam, Jehu, Athaliah, and spiritual men like Isaiah and Jeremiah; the great nameless ones like Second Isaiah; and, in earlier times, the great narrators and great lawgivers, who were partly their contemporaries, partly their successors. The names of neither the narrators nor of the lawgivers are recorded, but intellectual greatness and its effects upon history do not depend upon names but upon the mentality of the man and the greatness of his achievement. Men like Moses and Samuel, who represent both the soul and the body of national life, are coördinating links.

To bring before the reader this most remarkable of all civilized peoples of history, we shall not follow the usual presentation. Instead of a continuous narrative of events, national life will be presented in the words, thoughts, and deeds of its great personalities. That this life did not consist merely of material things, mere wars and political events, as we so frequently find in the histories of nations, is from our point of view obvious. We hope that our method will have the advantage of teaching facts and ideas associated with persons. This frequently is not the case with the other method. As in life, attainments are the outgrowth of personality, so here we shall consider history from the standpoint of words and deeds which are immediately associated with individuals.

The earliest beginnings of all nations are hidden in obscurity. These beginnings were among peoples who lived only in the present. Only after they had long passed away, the desire awakened among their descendants to cherish what legend and recollection reports of former days and their heroes. Thus it was in Israel. Israel's origin and ancestors we do not know and, in all probability, shall never know with certainty. Yet we see that through all the centuries, down to Mohammed and the awakening of Islam, and in a lesser degree to our own day, the desert lands of the east, northeast, and southeast of Palestine have contributed and do still contribute to the population of the fertile lands of Syria and Palestine.

Arabia and the steppes north of it, as far as the central and the upper Euphrates, have few oases and little productive land. Wars and feuds for the possession of the few rich pastures or land capable of producing fruit and grain have occurred throughout the ages.

Tribes and groups of tribes whose inherited pastures and fields became incapable of supporting and feeding the increased population, crowded upon other weaker tribes. There was constant motion, encroaching upon others or being encroached upon. The result was invariably that the weaker were pushed toward the edge of the fertile district: in the east, toward the plain of the Tigris and Euphrates; in the west, toward Syria and Palestine.

This process occurred repeatedly from earliest times in the far north and northeast. The people of the Caucasus, Armenia, and the surrounding territory were repeatedly subjected to similar influences. Great overpowering numbers came from without, usually from the east, and pushed them

[4]

forward. In this way the Amorites reached the western country; the Hittites, Asia Minor; the Hyksos, by way of Syria and Palestine, Egypt; and an Aryan wave, Asia Minor and Syria. For the most part these peoples, it seems, were not mere Bedouins or real nomads. Many of them were tribes that had had a settled abode who now migrated with all their belongings, including their flocks. Such was the case of Abraham in Genesis. He migrated from Ur in the Chaldean country to Harran on the Euphrates, and from there to Canaan, apparently a settled or semi-settled herdsman.

At a very early time, Palestine, the country later occupied by Israel, and which we often call Canaan, became in this way not only the scene of great migrations but a great mixture of races. From the older stone age, there were people in different parts of the country whose origin and race we cannot determine. Nor can we tell how they came into the country. In time, they were followed by people of Arabian blood from the peninsula of Sinai, i.e., from the south and from the eastern Arabian desert. The Amurru, or Amorites, were pushed into the country from the north by way of Syria. Soon after them came hosts of Hyksos, who pushed on to Egypt, but many of their clans remained in Canaan until later. In 1580 the Hyksos surged back again from Egypt through Palestine and once more left many of their number in the country.

It is possible that in these repulsed Hyksos people we have the so-called Canaanites, who, together with the Amorites, according to the tradition of later Israel, were the principal pre-Israelite inhabitants of Canaan. Although the Hyksos may have much Semite blood, they doubtless also had a large admixture of blood from Asia Minor and from farther Asia. To these were added inhabitants of Hittite origin, or those usually called Hittite, for the kingdom of Hittites or Chatti in Asia Minor consisted of no single race but of a number

[5]

of different races of peoples from Asia Minor, from farther Asia, and especially of Indo-Germanic Aryan blood.

Considering all this, we see how correct is the biblical tradition that emphasizes the fact that Israel, on its entrance into Canaan, had to battle with a great number of races. To-day we are inclined to consider the enumeration of the Canaanites, Amorites, Hittites, Perizzites, Jebusites, Chiwites, or Hevites and however else they may be called, as a purely schematic invention of later unhistoric conception. The enumeration may be schematic, but it reflects the true fact that when Israel entered Canaan there were many races present. In the middle of the thirteenth or the end of the fourteenth century B.C., besides the Arabic or purely Semitic people, there were mixed Semitic races and people from Asia Minor, Armenian or Caucasian, as well as Indo-Germanic Aryan races. Added to these was a constantly decreasing remnant of the original inhabitants; and again under the Egyptian rule, there were many pure Egyptians and blacks from Central Africa who came as slaves and then remained.

From the above we can judge how erroneous is the conception that Israel found a single closely bound or even a pure Semitic population. Even before Israel's coming, the admixture of races and population had reached an advanced stage. In the post-Mosaic period when Israel entered Canaan, many Israelites intermarried with the Canaanite population (as we assume and for which we have some proof), and so then we clearly see how little in early centuries may it be considered a race of pure blood with the stamp of an ethnographical unity. We may assume that all the different races who were in the country then and in former times (and were also much intermixed) offered the newcomers an opportunity for intermingling. The admixture may have occurred in varying degrees with the different nations; earlier with some, and later with others.

Accordingly, we must not imagine an Israelite in David's

and Solomon's time, and even less in Isaiah's and Jeremiah's time, as a racially pure Semite, as were the pure-blooded Bedouins of the Arabian peninsula, although there always were such types in Israel and especially in the south. The Israelites were by no means alone, among them dwelt also different types: some were a mixture of Hittite-Asia Minor; others, the Assyrian-Babylonian type.

During the Hyksos rule in Egypt, we find for the first time, in the name of a Hyksos king, the name Jacob which later, together with the name Israel, designated the nation itself or at least one of its tribal patriarchs. We might consider the name as accidental; at least, we should not need to attach special significance to it, did it not appear in Palestine itself as a district or tribal name in combination with a second name which a few centuries later (about 1500 B.C.) we may probably construe as Joseph. There must be a connection. Jacob and Joseph are good Semitic names that can be explained in the Hebrew or Canaanite language: the former, in its fuller form Jacob-el, signifies "God rewards," perhaps also "God outwits"; the latter, Joseph-el, "God increases," "God enriches." When in Egypt we find Jacob as a Hyksos name and in Palestine as a tribal or district name, the assumption is well grounded that the tribe that later gave the territory its name was merely the name of a Hyksos tribe that had remained in Palestine and became Canaanite, i.e., it belonged to those ᵔeoples that Israel found when it entered Canaan.

We do not know when this happened for the first time, but we have an inscription dated 1230 in the reign of the Egyptian Pharaoh, Meneptah, in which we read of a tribe or a small nation called Israel in Central Palestine. Together with other districts, this territory was subject to the Pharaoh. The inhabitants here were not the people of Israel who had migrated from Egypt. Although this opinion naturally finds many champions, it is probably unsound because the

Exodus from Egypt could not have taken place before the time of Pharaoh Meneptah. If, however, this was the case, and it is probable, the people were Israelites who had entered Canaan independent of those of the post-Mosaic time, and who had settled in Canaan at an earlier time.

This would assume a tribe of Jacob and a tribe of Israel in Canaan in the pre-Mosaic period. The former was the offshoot of a Hyksos branch; the latter came into the country from elsewhere. Thus we now understand how it might happen that the people of Israel were occasionally called Jacob and, above all, that the patriarch Jacob, the ancestor of the twelve tribes, also bears the name Israel. If the two tribes who dwelt side by side in Canaan, even though separated, were closely related in language and nationality, then by marriage and other ties they gradually intermingled and were sooner or later completely fused. Then Jacob-Israel formed a unit, and Jacob may be called Israel, and Israel, Jacob. This condition is reflected in the old legend that the tribal father had formerly been called Jacob, but God himself renamed him Israel. "Hereforth shalt thou be called Israel." In this we also have reflected the memory that the older united group was called Jacob; the later, Israel. We do not know when the union took place. It is probable that it occurred before the people of Israel, led by Joshua, entered the country.

Legend reports that Jacob-Israel had twelve sons, each one of whom founded a tribe of the later people of Israel. The fact is that later Israel believed itself to have been built up of twelve principal tribes, but the division into twelve is not always reported. From this we see that it was probably a later and an artificial division. But in spite of this, the principal tribes must have existed at a relatively early period. It is quite probable that before Moses appeared with his people at the gates of Canaan, a greater or lesser number of subtribes in Canaan considered themselves part of Israel.

[8]

INTRODUCTION

In the above transcribed sense, we may also call them "Canaanite." They are better described as Canaanite-Israelite tribes. They help in solving a problem that otherwise might trouble us greatly; namely, how does it happen that in spite of its strong enmity toward the people in Canaan, post-Mosaic Israel intermingled so much with the Canaanite people? The answer to the question calls for consideration as to whether there were Israelites or tribes of Israel in Canaan who were Israelites, but who, because they had long lived in Canaan and intermixed with the Canaanites, themselves half-Canaanites, were naturally the tie between the Canaanites and Israelites. They could suppress enmity and lead the way to peaceful alliances, as well as knit closer ties by occasional marriage bonds.

In considering the Israelite tribes of 1230 in Palestine, we went a step in advance of our story. We must go back. In the winter of 1888 and 1889, the political archives of the Pharaoh, Amenophis III and IV, were found in central Egypt near El Amarna. They contain the correspondence of the Pharaohs with their foreign friends and vassals, especially the subjugated lesser kings and territorial rulers of Palestine and southern Syria. Through this correspondence, for the first time we gain a clear picture of the conditions in the country.

After Thutmoses III, in a number of campaigns, had driven the Hyksos from the country, he conquered the whole of Syria as far as the Euphrates, and annexed it to his kingdom. This made Palestine an Egyptian province. In the commercial cities of the Syrian and Phœnician coast and in various places of the interior, even more Egyptian colonies than formerly settled for trade. The Pharaoh's governors and officials ruled the country. Fortified cities, that had been fitted up as Egyptian strongholds, contained Egyptian garrisons. The native population paid rich tribute to Thebes. Even Egyptian temples were erected, and a great wave of the Egyptian religious spirit and of Egyptian cultural influences spread over the country, but these were only of secondary influence. The Babylonian spirit and Babylonian influences had long had the upper hand. Thus it happens that this important correspondence of and with the Pharaohs was not in the Egyptian but in the Babylonian language and characters. This fact does not reflect the Babylonian importance at this period but at an earlier one. The use of the Babylonian language, apparently, had long been customary and still was so in this so-called Amarna period.

The Amarna letters that interest us most are those written by and to the lesser kings and Canaanite district princes. It seems Canaan had long been in possession of real city organizations. Everywhere we find city states, i.e., city communities which formed independent little states usually with a very limited territory about them. This form of government already seemed common in the Amarna period. We nowhere find an account of its origin, or a statement that it had been recently introduced. Thus we may conclude that it was an institution of long standing.

The same is true of the many subdivisions in the country. Aside from the Pharaoh as the overlord, there are no traces of one or several centralized powers. Almost every city and every larger district was a political unity. This large number of political divisions, which later proved detrimental to this as well as to many other states (Greece for example), did not originate at this time, but apparently had long existed and, therefore, was firmly rooted.

We must go back to the Hyksos period if we would seek the origin of this phenomenon. We are told that the Hyksos dwelt near Tanis in the Delta of the Nile. In the book of Numbers we hear that this Tanis was built seven years after Hebron. We cannot interpret this other than that Tanis in Egypt and Hebron in South Palestine were in close touch with each other from the beginning. In fact, it is probable that they both were important centers of the Hyksos government; indeed, the Hyksos may be looked upon as the ones who originated city organization and city states.

The fortified cities ruled by petty kings may have originated thus. The natives fled before the Hyksos to the numerous fastnesses and the conquerors built fortresses for themselves against the natives. Hebron may have been the first and strongest one in Southern Canaan. We may readily assume that the real rulers in the cities, the ruling nobility with the petty kings at their head, were for the most part not natives, but belonged to the Hyksos who at this time were still foreigners. The native Amorites and true Canaanites were subject to them and lived, for the most part, outside of the cities. The foreign-sounding names of the governors in the Amarna period agree with this. Presumably the overlords gave the army leaders certain territory as fiefs. This would satisfactorily explain the petty kingdoms in the Amarna period, and, especially, the many subdivisions already mentioned.

Even the Hyksos destroyed a state that had previously existed and of which there are still traces. It was replaced by their feudal system. This government in turn was destroyed by the Egyptians, who founded new small city states on the ruins. Close examination proves that the most foolish thing that Thutmoses III and his successors could have done was to continue this system of minute subdivision even as a support for their sovereignty. Whenever the Egyptian government was busy with Egyptian affairs or for any reason was absent from Palestine, then it was dependent upon the good will of its vassals in Palestine. We shall soon hear of the nature of this good will.

All this development occurred long before the Amarna time. The real Egyptian power was also a thing of the past. Thutmoses III had introduced a firm, harsh government. This strict government continued for a time after his death.

Gradually the Pharaohs loosened the reins. When Amenophis IV, a great man from a mental and religious point of view but politically entirely insignificant, removed the capital to Thebes and devoted himself to religious speculation and his noble but entirely unpolitical interests, events took their own course. The Egyptian power and the Pharaoh's authority were completely ruined. No one concerned himself about Egypt's power and the good man on the throne at El Amarna.

The Palestine vassals sound scornful and perhaps are so when they write the Pharaoh letters overflowing with deference, meanwhile merrily doing as they please and treating the commands and threats of the Pharaoh as a joke. Such expressions as I am the "king's dog" or the "overlord's lackey" or the "footstool of thy feet," or the "throne upon which thou sittest" or the "dust of thy feet" flow from their lips. Even expressions such as "at the feet of my Lord, the King, the Son of Heaven have I thrown myself upon my back and my belly seven times and again seven times" belong to the devotional scheme of these faithful ones. When the overlord demanded anything of them or even reminded them of the duty of obedience, then poor excuses, too dainty subterfuges were their mildest replies. They knew all too well that they might do all this without being punished.

What wonder that the Egyptian government was illtreated on all sides. It seems as if all whom it concerned knew that they could strike at the government without being punished. Then each hastened to outdo the other.

In northern Palestine there were the Hittites, and they behaved the worst. In his day Thutmoses had conquered the strong Hittite fortress at Kedes on the Orontes, captured northern Syria from the Hittites, and advanced as far as the Euphrates and into the Mitanni country. As long as the Hittites and the Mitanni felt the power of the Pharaoh, they did not venture to resist. Now the time came to become aggressive. For a long time, especially during the Hyksos period, they had held certain outposts in Syria and southern Palestine. All these long lost places they hoped to regain. The princes of Syria and Phœnicia sent heartrending complaints to the Pharaoh. Ribaldi of Byblos (Gebal), the celebrated old seaport, complained that the Hittites were already devastating the environs of their thriving city. No action was taken. "I have repeatedly written (to the Pharaoh) but no answer came." The incendiaries and plunderers camped round about them. The poor man sent constant appeals for help to the Pharaoh but not a hand was turned, not even an answer came.

Even now we can understand how severely the vassals' fidelity was put to the test and how depressing, indeed embittering, was the absolute indifference of the court to their trials. The King of Byblos was not the only one, nor was he an exception. The King of Tyre fared no better, and in Köle-Syria and in the district about Damascus conditions were the same. In addition, the Babylonians and the Mitanni were as uncongenial neighbors as were the Hittites.

At this time the country about Lebanon and Anti-lebanon was called Amurru. It was ruled by a governor called Abdi Ashrat (Ashirta), and after his death, by his son Aziru. They, too, went to great excesses. It seems that Abdi Ashirta, as Pharaoh's regent, at first did his duty honestly against the invading Hittites, but when the Pharaoh made no effort to help him, he seems to have become weary and, although the confidant of the king, became an accomplice of the insurgents. The example of the Hittites, whom no one dared attack, was indeed alluring. He, therefore, followed their example, and seems to have fared well. After his death, his son Aziru continued this policy. This bold vassal even ventured to halt and to plunder the Pharaoh's caravans. Unscrupulously he attacked governors and captured their cities by force of arms. When they appealed to the Pharaoh, the suave hypocrite drew himself out of the affair with fine phrases. He greatly oppressed Rib Abdi of Byblos, of whom we have already spoken, until when no help came, he was forced to capitulate to Aziru.

Then came one of those grim jokes of history such as have occurred from time to time. In the Moroccan affairs of our day there was a hardened bandit, the very clever and energetic rebel leader, Raisuli, who finally was appointed governor, apparently as a reward for his rebellion. Aziru's experience was similar. After he had succeeded in circumventing all of Pharaoh's efforts against him by stout denials and clever evasions he, in triumph, was finally appointed royal governor and thus became the actual ruler of the Amurru. Since they could not conquer him by force of arms, Thebes or El Amarna made the best of a bad matter.

What wonder if Palestine proper was in mad confusion. Almost every city had its prince, and each one was at sword's points with his neighbor. None of the complaints and pleas to the Pharaoh for help and protection found a listening ear. The governors were forced to resort to helping themselves, and the country resounded with the clang of arms in the many-sided feuds. Conditions were similar to those in the darkest days of mob law in certain periods of German and Central European history. Conditions in Jerusalem and in the territory of a certain Lapaja were especially typical. Jerusalem, which we know as a very ancient settlement, was ruled by an Egyptian vassal king, with the strange name Abdi-chiba, probably referring to an Indo-Germanic Mitanni goddess. His letters, which are preserved to us, are very interesting testimony of the many complaints he made to the Pharaoh, and also the real distress with which the poor man had to struggle in this trying time. In the country about Gezer and farther on in central Palestine, a petty king and adventurer, named Lapaja, behaved shamelessly at the expense of his neighbors and of the Pharaoh.

[14]

It seems he had conceived the bold idea of building up a kingdom, or at least an independent government within the Pharaoh's kingdom. He even went farther than Aziru, who had been satisfied with outwitting the Pharaoh's government, to gain his nomination as governor. Lapaja disregarded the Pharaoh entirely, and straightway followed his own ends. He is a forerunner of Abimelech, Gideon's son. In the same region, where several centuries later the latter appeared as ruler, he reigned over a territory that reached at least from Sunem to Shechem. After his violent death, the kingdom was broken up and again fell to Egypt.

In all the territory in northern, southern, and central Palestine, conditions could not have reached this stage but for the interference of a new enemy, the Habiru, whose mission it was to spread confusion. They took part in the troubles in the region about Jerusalem; Gezer, Shechem, and Hazor went over to their side; Ashirta joined forces with them. In innumerable letters they appear as the phantom of terror, before which the country trembled, and it was they who most threatened Egypt's rule.

Who were the Habiru? If we call them "Hebrews," we do not go far astray. Only we must not forget that this designation should have a far more general significance than we usually give it. The word means simply those who travel through, or the wanderers. It, therefore, designated wandering nomads, tribes, or hordes of a definite race and of a certain group of languages—those in whose dialect the word *abar* signifies to wander and *brm* or *oberim,* the wanderers. This language, spoken in Canaan later, is called Hebrew. Perhaps it did not have its origin in Canaan but was brought there by the Habiru tribes. There were Habiru long before the Amarna time. We hear of them in much older texts, but at this time their hordes advanced against Canaan with increased strength and great violence. We know for some time that they bore the name of *sagaz,* rob-

[15]

bers, plunderers. Would-be saviors of the German nation, led by the unfortunate Frederich Delitzsch, seized this equation, saying, "Here we have it; the Hebrews forced their way into Palestine as robbers and plunderers, and they have continued this occupation to the present." Whatever the truth may be about the latter assertion, the former, i.e., that they came as robbers and plunderers, was certainly invented for an all-too-modest demand upon human intelligence. Have other conquerors and victors up to those of the present day applied the golden rule to their booty?

We do well to return from the confusion and unsatisfactory present to antiquity. It does not distress us to the same degree because it is so remote. These wandering tribes came as conquerors and invaders from the East, and forced an entrance in several places. Although they are not "the Hebrews" in the sense of the Israelites, they belonged to the same large circle of people or tribes and groups of tribes. To be more definite, Israel and what we usually call the Hebrews were probably a certain single branch of this great tribe which we find there and called Habiru or Hebrews in the broader sense.

But how are the Habiru connected with those Israelites who were in Canaan in 1230? Probably the Amarna period (about 1370), about a century and a half before this time, was not the first of the greater invasions of the Habiru into Canaan. It is probably an accident that we know nothing of them before this time. The invaders now seem to have reached their main goal. They were settled in and about Shechem and in various places in Palestine, especially in central Palestine. There, as we have already heard, the Israelites of Pharaoh Meneptah's time were settled. Since Israel later, doubtless, considered itself part of the Hebrews, it almost seems that the Israelites of 1230 were a single branch of the greater Hebrew tribes, bearing a special name of Habiru, which attacked Palestine in 1370. Accordingly the relationship of Jacob, Israel, and the Habiru was probably thus: Jacob was an old Hyksos tribe in Canaan, perhaps descended from the Habiru of an earlier time (perhaps eighteenth century B.C.). At the time of the great invasion of the Habiru into Palestine in the fourteenth century, a smaller tribe or clan of Habiru, named Israel, settled in central Canaan and, on the basis of its relationship with Jacob, was fused with it.

The patriarchal legend in the first book of Moses speaks of Jacob as well as Abraham, Isaac, and others, as real persons. Is this correct? At any rate, the fact that Israel never appears in older texts as the name of an actual person is worth considering. Therefore Israel was probably always used as the designation of a tribe. Jacob, however, appears as the name of a person as early as the Hyksos period. There is nothing, therefore, to prevent us from assuming that at the head of the tribe was a man named Jacob, a man like that Hyksos king whose name became the heritage of the tribe. This has happened and is still happening in thousands of cases in the Semite world of the past and present. This we may accept as the historical nucleus of the biblical Jacob legend.

With Abraham, too, we can at least surmise a similar process, for Abraham actually appears in olden times in Babylon as the name of a person. To this the biblical legend that he migrated from the far East, the region of the Euphrates, fits admirably. He, too, once with special emphasis, was called the "Hebrew." This may suggest a surmise that at the time when Jacob and Israel were wandering, an independent tribe of Habiru, with an unknown name, led by one called Abraham (the tribe itself was never called Abraham), came from the East. Yet we cannot go beyond surmises.

How the tribes that migrated into Canaan lived in Canaan, we can determine with a degree of probability from different narratives in the first book of Moses. The tribes adapted

themselves to the inhabitants as best they could. Wherever
they found pasture land, there they grazed their flocks of
sheep, goats, sometimes cattle and camels. Occasionally,
they contracted for or bought the land. Thus Jacob is said
to have had an agreement with the inhabitants of Shechem,
and Abraham bought a piece of land in Hebron from the
Hittites. Elsewhere they dug wells and erected places of
worship. All these stories, whatever may be their individual
historical merit, were at least typical of the relations that
existed between the immigrants and those who were already
settled inhabitants.

The life of peoples of such different qualities in a country
without a central government is never without quarrels,
jealousies, and disagreements. New immigrants pushed forward, or the land became insufficient to support the older
inhabitants because of drought or crop failures. Then some
were pushed south. The great steppes had room for all of
them, even if bread was scarce. If there were no book to
tell us of this process, we should surmise it, but we have
written evidence of this fact,

II

MOSES

FROM earliest times in Israel, generation after generation has told the story of the great man who, even before the Israelites could be called a nation, led them from Egypt, the house of bondage, into freedom and a new life. He broke the Egyptian yoke, led his hosts into the desert where he gave them the God whom they ever afterwards worshiped, gave them the code of laws of their God, and finally led them through the desert to the land which they had learned to look upon as their own. Through all the ages Moses has been honored as the helper in need, the leader, the founder of the nation, but most revered as the messenger of the new God and His laws.

Thus Moses appears to posterity which, although it has gilded and enlarged his image as it has done to all great men of antiquity, has preserved on the whole the fundamental characteristics of the real Moses. Wherever and whenever Israel's great past is mentioned, his name will be praised as one of the greatest in Israel.

We have no clear portrait of Moses. Many a trait has been blurred with time, but the tall and powerful frame, the well-poised head, the sharp penetrating eyes of the leader, of the victor over man and obstacles, the firm hand of the ruler ever alert and faithful to his duty, the keen insight of the man who found God and who dwelt in him, the insight which penetrated even the divine being and saw deeply into the heart of man, we may still recognize despite the faded colors and retouching of the ages.

We left Israel, or the clans and tribes that were later included under this name, as shepherd tribes in Canaan where possibly the land was overpopulated. Legend tells us that famine came to Canaan, forcing the sons of Jacob to make a pilgrimage to the south to procure grain from Egypt. Legend also tells us of dissension among Jacob's sons with the result that one of them, Joseph, drifted to Egypt and rose there to high honors. Later he sent for his brothers and established them in the region of Goshen near the eastern delta of the Nile. In the course of time the great increase in their numbers made them a burden to the Egyptians and they were oppressed with statute labor.

There were, indeed, in Egypt certain tribes who considered themselves a part of Israel. Not all of the twelve sons of Jacob with their father, as present legend has it, gathered in Egypt, but a part of them were there under the name of Joseph. Doubtless they consisted of families and clans who had lived in southern Canaan or who had been pushed southward from their homes in the north. At first they tried to gain a living on the southern steppes, and from there, as frequently happened among the people of the steppes, they entered Canaan.

The sojourn of the Israelites in Egypt has been questioned, because Egyptian inscriptions furnish no direct evidence of their presence in Egypt. We must remember how little this silence signified in connection with a few unimportant shepherd tribes, especially when there were neither great deeds nor victories, but only painful experiences to relate. The belief that all Israel migrated to Egypt has long been questioned. The fact that we find a people in Egypt in 1230, at a time when the exodus could hardly have taken place, is good evidence against this theory. But if we dismiss the theory that all of Israel was in Egypt, we may also dismiss the doubt as to the presence of separate tribes of Israel in Egypt. We have points of evidence that certain Israelite tribes were present in Egypt.

The following proofs may be considered. In the second book of Moses we read that the Pharaoh who oppressed the Israelites forced them to statute labor in Pithom and Rameses, cities founded by Pharaoh. There are inscriptions that tell us that this very Pharaoh, Rameses II, who for other reasons we suspect of having been Israel's oppressor, actually built these cities. Indeed, there were members of Semite tribes who can only be designated by the general term "Hebrew," who were forced to statute labor, in the building activities of this very Pharaoh. If they were Hebrews, they belonged to the great group of tribes to whom the Israelites also belonged. Those Hebrews (they were the Apuriu or *pr*-people) were in Egypt in an earlier time and later were found not only in Egypt but elsewhere. Thus we see that the Apuriu evidently included the Israelites in their numbers. It is probable that the Israelites were not the only ones oppressed by the Pharaoh. All the Semites in that region seem to have shared this fate. These points all coincide with the general impression which other sources give of the course of events of this time.

As further evidence, we may mention that in the story of Moses we find Egyptian proper names. The name Moses itself has long been recognized as Egyptian. It occurs frequently in Egyptian names of persons such as Thutmoses, Ach-moses, Ra-moses, and means child. Probably the biblical name, Moses, is only the abbreviation of a former fuller compound. Beside the name Moses itself, we have such names as that of the priest Phinehas or of a prominent man among the contemporaries of Moses, who had the name of the Egyptian God Horus; the father-in-law of Aaron's son was called Putiel. After the Babylonian captivity we find among the Jews many Babylonian proper names acquired in Babylon. This same process, even though it cannot be definitely proven, is probably the cause of these Egyptian names.

A document especially important both for Israel's sojourn in Egypt and also for their exodus, is the Song of Victory after their passage through the Sea of Reeds, and is found in the second book of Moses, chapter fifteen. The twentieth verse states that after the Israelites had successfully escaped from the Egyptian pursuers, Miriam, Aaron's sister, the prophetess (this means the singer by the grace of God) seized a timbrel. "And all the women went out after her with timbrels and with dances." Miriam answered them, singing

> Sing ye to the Lord for he hath triumphed gloriously,
> The horse and his ruler hath he thrown into the sea.

We are familiar with the custom of antiphonal singing. Often the women praised the returning victors or glorified their victory immediately after the battle. Thus Jephtah's daughter met her father "with timbrels and with dances," i.e., with a festive dance of the women. Thus Saul and David were greeted on their return by choruses of women chanting in praise of their bravery. So, too, the song mentioned in the fifth chapter of Judges is an antiphonal song chanted by Deborah and Barak, a song that was the immediate outgrowth of recent experiences in battle. Everything favors the belief that Miriam's song in its original form was simply the usual women's song of victory arising from and following the victory. Thus in this song we have a contemporary document from the Mosaic period.

History provides several witnesses to tell us how the immigration of such shepherd tribes from the peninsula of Sinai and the steppes of southern Palestine took place. Even in the Amarna period we read that under pressure from the *Kh*abiru many Canaanites preferred to leave the country and to seek protection in Egypt, and that this practice was not new at that time, but dated back to ancestral times. A general of Amenhotep IV, who later became Pharaoh Harmhab, wrote the following about them:

They are demolished; their city destroyed; their lands are barren; they live like mountain goats. Some of the Asiatics, unable to exist elsewhere, have come (here we must supply to petition for a dwelling place in the lands) of the king, as the fathers of thy father (the king) did from the beginning. Now the king places them in thy hands to protect thy borders.

We see that these are the instructions which the general gave his subordinates concerning foreign Asiatic fugitives.

It is especially interesting that the region about Goshen and places like Pithom are prominent. A papyrus document tells of a customs officer in Meneptah's time who reports the following to his superior officer.

We have permitted the Bedouin tribes of Edom to pass through Meneptah's fortress at Zeku (Succotto) to the swamps of Pithom of Meneptah in Succotto in order to save their lives and their flocks within the territory of the king, the good sun of every country.

This proves that the movement goes back even to Menaptah's time and that the causes were dissension at home and the great difficulty in securing a living. Frequently both causes may have been at work.

Although we have no definite statement that in any of the cases here cited our Israelites were meant, the examples show that such conditions were common and that what is reported of Israel coincides with what was constantly occurring.

The fact that they were fully prepared shows clearly how common such occurrences were in Egypt. We have documents giving the names of those who desired admission, exact statements of the purpose and business causing the traveler to cross the border. Thus even in Meneptah's time there were a careful border inspection and close examination of passports, as we would say to-day.

If we ask when those Israelite tribes emigrated, we may choose between the period after the days of the fathers of Meneptah IV and the time of Meneptah himself. It is most natural to turn to the confusion of the Amarna period, but the period after Amenhotep IV offered favorable opportunity for emigration. When Amenhotep IV died in 1358, after ruling seventeen years, his two sons-in-law, Sakire and Tutenkaton, succeeded him. Neither of them was able to regain the great respect and power in Syria which Amenhotep IV and his father before him had carelessly lost. Tutenkaton broke away from the El Amarna tradition and moved the capital back to Thebes. He again assumed the name of Tutanch-amon, "living image of Amon." By this name, because he was buried with splendor, he recently gained fame far beyond his merits. Soon after him the dynasty of Thebes disappeared, after having established its fame by repulsing the Hyksos and founding the Egyptian empire. The new dynasty, the nineteenth of Manetho, was begun by Harmhab, the former general of Amenhotep IV. He brought a new spirit to Thebes. He revived the old form of worship which again elevated polytheism to a state religion. He was a great organizer and a wise and just lawgiver, but he could not prevent the loss of the Egyptian power in Syria.

His second successor, Seti I (1313), ventured to attack Syria. Again, as in the time of the Amarna kings, the nomad tribes of the East invaded Palestine, following the example of the Habiru. In the bas-reliefs of the temple of Karnak, Seti himself reports concerning them. It was announced to his majesty:

The miserable Bedouins (*shasu,* i.e., robber band) are planning an uprising. Their tribal leaders have joined forces and are gathered on the heights of Charu, the highlands of southern

Palestine. They have begun to quarrel, each one is slaying his neighbor, and they disregard the laws of the palace.

We see that conditions were similar to those of the Habiru, and the people also seem similar to them. Seti made war upon them and conquered the whole of Palestine and Transjordania. To this day we have monuments that bear witness to the victory.

His son, Rameses II, who ascended the throne in 1292, continued his work. He gathered a large army, consisting chiefly of Nubian and Sardian (Sherden) hirelings. With them he sought to regain Syria, but the Hittites captured his permanent camp, whereupon Syria as far as southern Palestine joined the rebellion. Still Rameses succeeded in conquering Palestine and Transjordania, and in forcing Hattushil, the king of the Hittites (1272), to make a treaty or "eternal bond" with him. The text of this treaty is preserved in several copies and in two languages—Babylonian and Egyptian. Peace was sealed by the marriage of the somewhat aged Pharaoh with the daughter of the Hittite king. We may mention, however, that the vassal-state of the Amurru or Amoretes, familiar to the reader from the quarrels of the Amarna period, still existed, partly under Egyptian and partly under the Hittite rule. Once more taking advantage of the unsettled condition, this vassal-state extended its border at the expense of Babylonia which was now reduced to a minor kingdom and established new settlements in various places.

Rameses II died at ninety years of age after reigning sixty-seven years. Of his many sons twelve had died before him. The thirteenth, Meneptah, ascended the throne of the Pharaohs. According to now usual reckoning of time, he ruled from 1225-1215 B.C., but there is a possibility, significant for the history of Israel, that these figures may be pushed forward and that he may have begun his reign in 1250 B.C. His father had a brilliant reign, but its pomp and splendor could not conceal the fact that the Syrian power was not restored to its former status. In Palestine proper the restless vassals were restrained only with difficulty, while in the north they were recognized as equals by a treaty.

These conditions offered serious dangers for the new ruler, and they were greatly increased by the appearance of a new insurgent. Hardly had the main wave of these eastern nomads or Habiru begun to recede, when new claimants appeared at the borders of the Egyptian kingdom. Pushed and pressed by others crowding from behind, the people of the northern Mediterranean country and with them those of central Asia Minor and Libya were set in motion. They are called Maritime Peoples. Of course, Egypt's old enemies, led by the allied Hittites, did not stand idly by. The former could at least depend upon their encouragement, in part, even upon their help. In the third year of Meneptah's reign the fires of rebellion burned brightly throughout the whole Asiatic province of Egypt. The allied Hittites also took part, but Meneptah succeeded in conquering them. On the monument of victory already mentioned, after telling of subjugating the Hittites and plundering Canaan, he boasts

> Carried off is Askalon;
> Seized upon is Gezer;
> Yenoam is made as a thing not existing;
> Israel is desolate, her seed is not;
> Palestine has become a (defenseless) widow for
> Egypt.

This is the important inscription considered above as first mentioning Israel.

It may be worth while to pause and look backward. When we attempt to determine the time when the Israelite tribes emigrated to Egypt (dependent upon this, is of course the date of the exodus) we may choose, first, the confusion of the Amarna period; then, the advance of the nomads in the latter part of the fourteenth century, just described; and

lastly, the unrest in Meneptah's time. We have already
stated that the last (although preferred by some scientists)
was scarcely probable. We cannot definitely decide between
the other two possibilities. If it could be proven that under
Amenhotep IV, the governor called Yanachamu was the biblical Joseph, as Hugo Winckler believed, the question would
be solved. Even without the equation, i.e., Yanachamu is
Joseph (for which there is no deciding evidence) we give
the preference to the Amarna period or a time near it, because of a longer intervening period. Besides the three
periods we have just mentioned, there may have been a great
many similar ones which accident has not disclosed. Should
we accept the Amarna period or the decades following it as
the time of the emigration, it would have been about the
middle of the fourteenth century. If we may interpret the
suggestion of a "new king" in Egypt, who knew nothing of
Joseph, as a faint recollection of a change of dynasty, then
the oppression of the Egyptian Israelite tribes must be understood as beginning with the nineteenth dynasty, that of
Harmhab. During this dynasty, Rameses II was evidently
the Pharaoh who oppressed the Israelites. We may believe
this because of the statement in the Book of Exodus that
Israel took part in the building of the cities of Pithom and
Rameses which Rameses II founded. Then the Pharaoh
under whom the exodus occurred would naturally be Meneptah. In fact if the exodus occurred at all, there was scarcely
a more favorable opportunity for it than during the tempes-
tuous, at times exceedingly critical, reign of this Pharaoh.
We shall speak of this later.

Let us return to the people migrating into Egypt. We do
not know definitely which tribes took part in the migration:
certainly the tribes of Joseph, i.e., the clans later called
Ephraim, Manasseh, and Benjamin, although Benjamin immigrated later, probably also Levi and Simeon, and perhaps
Judah. We know nothing of how they fared in Egypt ex-

d has told us of the increasing oppression
l the desire to leave the country.

y true that they left the country sooner or
oppression had reached its climax. The Song
which we have already heard testifies to the
net with resistance, at least that the Egyptians
ly permit them to depart. The song is also
the best evidence for the main facts of the story of the passage through the Sea of Reeds and definite proof of the exodus itself. No one will deny that the catastrophe that befell
the Egyptians occurred, as it is recorded in the biblical narrative, or that the conflict between the two parties can be
explained in any other way than by the secret flight of the
valuable laborers.

Now we meet the man who influenced the whole period—
Moses. The meager reports do not permit us to-day to
portray him in such sharp outlines as to reproduce every
single trait. But we know his principal characteristics.
This is certain. Without Moses we should know nothing
of the exodus, nothing of Israel's experiences in the desert,
nor of its immigration into Egypt. Probably history would
not even know of the existence and of the fate of the people
of Israel were it not for him.

Without Moses there would have been of course certain
tribes of Israel in Egypt and in Canaan. Whether they
would have united and become a nation without him;
whether the Israelites in Egypt would later have found the
way out of the "House of Bondage" as the Israelites called
Egypt; and if so, whether they would have found their way
out of the desert; nay, more, whether the people of Israel
would have gained the form of government, code of laws,
and a religion in Canaan that would enable them to stand
effectively aloof from the Canaanites and thus to assert
their own national and religious life; these are all questions
which we have every reason to ask.

They answer the oft-repeated question as to whether Moses is an historical character. It is not necessary to point to his non-Israelite name, although we may safely assume that a Hebrew legend would surely have given its hero a Hebrew name—as it actually did attempt to do in its narrative of the child rescued from the water. This and other proofs vanish under the greater consideration that without a superior leader, an achievement such as leading the tribes out of Egypt and through the dangers and terrors of the desert with its hostile people and hostile forces of nature, added to all the obstacles and difficulties in their own ranks, would be an impossibility.

Entirely apart from the revelation of God on Mt. Sinai, only a man of genius could lead this multitude unharmed into the desert and out again to their goal. If tradition did not give us Moses, the historian would be forced to demand such a character as soon as he accepted the fact of the exodus from Egypt, of the passage through the Sea of Reeds and through the desert, and above all, of the manifestation of God on Sinai. The name is of no importance. Whether his name is Moses or anything else, he who could help the Israelite tribes to accomplish all this must have possessed elemental genius that raised him far above average human beings. Only a person of truly superhuman power in whom the fire, indeed the fervency and the volcanic nature of a Luther combined with the iron will of a man of action like Bismarck, could accomplish this. Although Moses is still half merged in legend, from the legend clearly gleams the power of one of the very greatest men in history.

We know nothing of Moses' youth except what legend tells us. Like Sargon of Agade, Alexander, and many other great men, legend makes him a youthful prodigy whose origin and remarkable fate as a child announced that he was destined to accomplish great things, an dthat he, therefore, grew up under the special favor of the deity. Moses first actually appears to us as a shepherd in the Kenite steppes. In the silent loneliness of the endless desert he came to know his God. Among the terrifying paroxysms of the devastating desert storm, or from lightning, thunder, cloudburst, and torrent, the word "God" gained an entirely new meaning. Destructive powers often reveal in a moment to the desert inhabitants, both to man and his flocks, the impotence of all creatures before natural forces. He had always known the word God. The bright sky, the fertile meadowlands, and valleys of the district of Goshen had long ago interpreted it to him in the same way as the bright sunshine and the ministering springs and streams of the meadows of Canaan had taught it to the patriarchs. But here he was taught by the grandeur which inspires man with shrinking terror before the omnipotence of nature, by the eternal oppressive silence, by the gigantic mountains towering heavenward, by flashing lightning, by columns of mist, perhaps even by giant mountains shrouded in volcanic vapors, and by the sky with its brazen splendor that hung over all; by all these he had been overpowered. In them a new God had revealed himself, a consuming fire that shot out toward him from the spear-shaped, fingerlike thorns of the desert bramble.

With this God in his heart he came to Egypt. He longed to tell his enslaved tribesmen of the new but ancient God. "The God of your fathers hath appeared with me saying, I have surely visited you and seen that which is done to you in Egypt.¹ I will bring you up out of the affliction of Egypt." It was clear to him that this God would have no slaves. If this was the God of our fathers, what had this great, free, strong ruler in common with slavish chains and slavish souls? Only his servants, even though they were slaves, might acknowledge him, none other, be he god or man.

Then it was clear to him and to his people that they must leave. Thus from the very beginning he had a double purpose: to depart from Egypt, the house of bondage; and to go into the desert for the new revelation of God and to worship the new God. "Let my people go, that they may hold a feast unto me in the wilderness." Thus he approached the Pharaoh. We do not know whether Moses and his fellow-tribesmen and related tribesmen already had Canaan in mind, nor do we know whether from the beginning they even had a definite plan in mind. Their object was to get away from the fetters and on to the God of their fathers. His ways are manifold and His strength is ever great.

It is evident that gradually Moses turned his thoughts more and more to the land of his fathers. It is also evident that as soon as he did this, his great spirit was no longer satisfied with what the desert seemed to offer him. When we consider how quickly reliable news from the outer world often penetrates to the remotest sections of the desert, how one caravan calls to another and every wide-awake sheik hails caravans and strangers that pass through his territory with "What news in the world?" we know how easily and how safely Moses could gain information of what was happening or had happened in Canaan and in Egypt.

That the Eastern nomads were again in motion, that the Maritime Peoples were everywhere vigorously rapping at the gates of the vast empire, that the Pharaohs, Seti I and Rameses II, had gone north and sometimes returned without a complete victory, how could all this be unknown in the desert and particularly in Goshen? If Moses and his people were eager to leave Egypt, or if he had already left and, from the desert he sought a place where they might live, what place was more natural than the home of their fathers? Conditions seemed more favorable than they had long been because of the confusion and unrest in the country. The Israelites may have had encouragement from Canaan, for by no means all the people who considered themselves part of Jacob-Israel had migrated to Egypt with Joseph. Only a few days of rapid travel for couriers were necessary to take messages hither and thither. Thus the tribal kinsmen must have been in touch with each other, and those in Canaan may have promised their kinsmen in the desert a helping hand in Canaan itself in time of need.

It is probable that the Pharaoh, as legend reports, objected to the departure of his statute laborers. Why should he be willing to lose these valuable laborers? It is equally probable under these conditions that sooner or later there would be conflicts. For the children of Israel there was no other way out of Egypt than by the desert of Sinai, as a glance at the map of the region and a mere reminder of the strong fortification of the lower eastern border of Egypt will show. Thus an engagement could take place only in the desert east of Egypt.

We know that the engagement took place at the "Sea of Reeds" and that it led to the catastrophe of the Egyptians who were in pursuit. This is well established by Miriam's Song of Victory. It may not be superfluous to state that the death of the Pharaoh himself is not mentioned in the older accounts. The enlarged account seems to have substituted the Egyptian army led by the Pharaoh for a division of the army of the border troops of the eastern delta. They are reported to have been swallowed up by the Sea of Reeds, either while pursuing the fleeing Israelites as they crossed a shallow place in the sea or in some other way. This reminds us of the very critical position of Napoleon's troops in the Bay of Suez during the Egyptian campaign. The story of the passage of the Sea of Reeds in the simple form does not seem improbable, even though we may never know all the details, but there is greater difficulty when we seek the place where it occurred. This difficulty is increased by the fact that we are uncertain of the location of Mt. Sinai, one of the principal goals of their desert wanderings.

The Bible designates the Sea of Reeds (as far as the words reproduces the meaning of the Hebrew word *jam suf*) as both the western and the eastern arm of the Red Sea, or the Bay of Suez and the Gulf of Akaba. From the early Christian era, tradition connects Mt. Sinai with the great group of mountains in the southern part of the peninsula at whose base the famous old Sinai monastery had long stood. If the fugitives wished to go there, the greater part of their journey lay along the shore of the Bay of Suez. Then the Sea of Reeds must mean the Bay of Suez or one of its northern projections. But this Mt. Sinai is not a volcano and never was one. In recent times scientists believe they have discovered that the description of the lawgiving does not presuppose a volcano.

We cannot deny that we like to imagine a volcano in action when we read that the mountain trembled, that it was enveloped in smoke as of a smelting furnace; indeed that "the mountain burned with fire unto the heart of heaven." There are numerous extinct volcanoes on the eastern coast of the Red Sea in Arabia proper on the road to Mecca and Medina. For this reason, many modern scientists believe that Moses led his hosts to Sinai in this section and are unconcerned about the improbable distance and many other difficulties thus imposed upon Moses and his people. I cannot agree to invite my readers to this quixotic excursion into uncertainty, and prefer to remain on the peninsula of Sinai itself.

The present Sinai with its immediate surroundings certainly has a very old tradition in its favor. We can trace not only the pilgrimage of the Abbess Æthera who was there in the year 530 A.D., and earlier that of the Emperor Julian (360-363 A.D.) but the numerous Nabataic-Arabian inscrip-

tions in the *wadi firan* prove that in the first century A.D.
perhaps even at the time of Christ this region was often
visited by pious pilgrims, who of course believed the Sacred
Mountain of Moses to be there.

We see that active volcanoes were not unusual to the
Israelites of old. There were occasional eruptions in historic
times, especially in Transjordania. Therefore the speeches
of the prophets contain many figures of speech apparently
taken from such experiences. If this be true and if the
figures of speech based on experiences from volcanic eruptions were common among Hebrew poets and narrators,
then there is no reason why they might not be interwoven
in this narration of the revelation of God on the sacred
mountain without the mountain's necessarily having been
a volcano. The most powerful and most thrilling impression
that Israelite imagination was capable of was a severe
thunderstorm in the high mountains and flames shooting
from the crater of a volcano. They felt that both phenomena
must necessarily have been present when the God of Israel
revealed himself for the first time, at the birth hour of this
chosen people. Thus both must have acted together here
on Sinai (wherever it may be) as an accompaniment to
Moses' work. The peninsula has several stately mountains,
some near the oasis of Kadesh-Barnea that might claim consideration as the place of the wondrous meeting with God.
Without ever having been volcanoes, the mountains may
have been given these attributes in the legend of the Seat
of God. The place might have been Mt. Araif, or Mt. Al-
Makra, the southern section of which is also called Mt.
Faran and whose name recalls to this day the desert Paran.
One mountain may formerly have been designated a Mt.
Horeb; the other, the real Mt. Sinai.

The reasons that lead us to seek the sacred mountain in
this northern region of the Sinai desert are two: First,
a remark in an old narrative that the place in the desert

where Israel wished to offer sacrifice to its new God could
be reached in three days' journey as would be the case with
these mountains. Second, there was an important desert
station, Kadesh-Barnea, whose location is definitely known.
If Sinai were near Kadesh-Barnea, then many difficulties
would be removed.

However this may be, it is true that the essential part
of Moses' work, so important to his people, took place at
Sinai and at Kadesh-Barnea. We cannot tell how long the
Israelites remained at either place nor where else Moses
led them or drifted with them. Tradition gives us a long
list of desert stations, but we do not definitely know their
location, nor whether they really were stations of Mosaic
Israel and not merely halting places for later desert trav-
elers. Tradition tells of forty years of wandering in the
desert. This is clearly a round number created for chronol-
ogy. We can only surmise the time. The only thing
certain seems to be that much of the desert period was spent
at Kadesh-Barnea and at Sinai. At any rate, there the
important events took place.

These events were not important from a political standpoint but rather from a religious one for the future of the
people. As Moses himself was primarily the prophet and
spiritual leader of his people, so his people, who after all
were his work, bore his characteristics not outwardly but
in their innermost souls.

To be sure, the old Israelite people were a rough, uncouth,
and energetic race. We shall hear more of its qualities.
But whenever the soul of the people was expressed in its
great men, and the more it was done, the more striking
appeared a characteristic which differentiated it from other
peoples. Its thoughts turned inward, and its leaders were
not rulers and men of action but men of words and thoughts.
They were not philosophers like the Hellenes, but were
mentally related to them, in the form, however, in which

only Israel could produce them,—i.e., as prophets. Moses was resurrected in them. He was their prototype. He stamped his image and the prophetic type upon the nations. "Ye shall be unto me a kingdom of priests and an holy nation," [2] Moses, in a later text, says to his people. He might have said, "Ye shall be a people of prophets and men of God."

Amid the thunders of Sinai, to the people waiting at the foot of the mountain, was revealed the same Yahweh who had previously appeared to Moses alone in the fire of the burning bramble bush. Moses brought the people the will of his God written upon tablets.

I, Yahweh, am thy God. Thou shalt have no other gods beside me.
Thou shalt make thyself no image of God.
Thou shalt not take in vain the name of thy God Yahweh.
Thou shalt keep the Sabbath holy.
Thou shalt honor thy father and thy mother.
Thou shalt not kill.
Thou shalt not commit adultery.
Thou shalt not steal.
Thou shalt not bear false witness against thy neighbor.
Thou shalt not covet thy neighbor's house.

We may wish to make some changes in these sentences. For example, in the last sentence it is not certain whether Moses spoke to his compatriots, who dwelt in tents, of "a house," or whether he used some other word. Nor can there be a doubt that the so-called Ten Commandments, as we read them to-day, are an elaboration of the original form. But if we eliminate the explanatory and expanding additions as we have done above and state the ten sentences in their original lapidary form, they are a real monument to Moses' greatness. Because the Sabbath and the image of God are mentioned, these laws have been attributed to a much later period. However, there is increasing evidence to the contrary, and the most critical scientists are dropping the earlier view.

Because these laws indicate exalted prophetic morality, it was believed that they belong to a much later period than do those very ancient laws that decree that one must celebrate feasts and bring gifts to Yahweh and not seethe the kid in his mother's milk. People did not realize that those laws, important as they may have been for the everyday life of the people, were after all insignificant to a man like Moses, mere minor matters which the people could regulate for themselves. Only the ten sentences do justice to a man of Moses' gigantic mind. Each one of them is a brazen pillar upon which the structure of the future rests; each one, a granite cornerstone hewn from the native rock of true humanity.

The spirit that inspired the ten laws of Moses is the spirit of the God who revealed himself to Moses in the fire of the bramble bush and in the roar of Sinai. "I, Yahweh, am a jealous God"; a jealous, indeed a demoniacal God as well as the God of the ethical laws and of the ethical will; this is the nature of the Mosaic Yahweh.

In the book of Genesis we have a plausible story of the patriarchs which tells that they sometimes worshiped their deity as El-eljon or the highest god, sometimes as El-olam or the god of eternity, sometimes also El-roi or the god who has mercy. This god gave us the impression of a kindly, friendly, gentle master, who ruled quietly, who rejoiced in giving happiness and blessing and was seldom roused to anger—much as our children and many older good people imagined the "dear God" as a good man, who, even if they had forgotten him for a long time, in time of need would still be well disposed toward them. Thus the Israelites of Moses' time may have imagined God. It is only very seldom that another sort of God appeared. Once the god that Israel worshiped was called the "terror" of

Isaac.[3] Beyond the Jordan at the Jakkob stream we suddenly find a god with Jacob who seized him like a grim, raging river demon and would kill him, until finally Jacob overpowered him. Thus twice a deity appeared to the patriarchs who, as compared with their usual god, seemed like a being from another world.

And he was of another world. In both cases he was like a Yahweh or like a part of Moses' conception of Yahweh. Like the god who appeared at the Jakkob, Yahweh appeared to Moses in the desert to kill his child in the inn at night, but Zippora appeased him with the boy's circumcision blood. When later in Canaan the people came too near the ark, he was again angered; he might then break forth in wild rage and strike them down unexpectedly. His origin was there in the desert where Moses felt his power.

We do not know just what Yahweh means, although we have no dearth of conjecture. "I am that I am" is the phrase by which the Jews usually interpret the Eternal One; we others interpret it as the "effectively active one"; but we do not know how the name of God was understood in Israel in the post-Mosaic time. We know that the god had his origin in the desert, and his character was in keeping with the terrifying powers of nature that control desert life. As he appeared in the burning bramble bush or in the flashing lightning or roaring thunder of Mt. Sinai, so he was in truth and so he remained throughout the centuries in Israel; not primarily a friendly and kindly god, but an uncanny, all-powerful, jealous, wrathful, and revengeful lord and master.

We may not conclude, however, that Moses' god originated in the desert and was simply a desert god or a desert demon. Nothing is more erroneous. Yet those impetuous, undependable, and distinctly irrational characteristics appeared for the first time and most clearly in the desert as characteristics of God for all true religion. The grandeur

[38]

of nature was the most appropriate place for the revelation of the true God.

He was, therefore, an exclusive, consciously one-sided and negative god; this was his peculiarity and his greatness. He rejected, indeed he violently repelled all other gods, refused their imagery, would have nothing of their satellites, the demons. This is the meaning of the first three norms.

"No other God and no image of God, for I am a jealous God"; not to use his name in vain, not to utter it or call it "in vain," i.e., in a curse or for magic, "for Yahweh will not hold him guiltless that taketh his name in vain." [4] This is the meaning of the three first sentences. The "other gods" did not mean primarily those of the great heathen religions. They were first of all the gods of their fathers, who were more closely related to Israel. They should not vanish, but nothing might stand "beside" Yahweh; they must, therefore, be merged with him. Much less might the demons and the spirits of the dead by whom the gods of all those religions were vanquished exist beside him. Magic and conjuration are the characteristics of nature religions. God was a power of nature, and every power could be conquered by a greater one. Conjuration served this purpose. If a mortal had offended the god and roused his anger, then sacrifice and burnt offering or the conjuration of the magician priest must appease this anger. There might be no magic, no placating Yahweh; he would accept only the fulfillment of his commandments. Therefore images were forbidden. Every image of the god made him a creation, a being of the senses and of visible creation; therefore, every image was a challenge to conquest by magic power.

The Mosaic Yahweh rejected all this with uncanny severity. Not that the secret powers and forces that control nature and human life and that frequently cause man to fear and tremble were suddenly denied and abolished;

they existed and continue to exist to this very day. We may close our eyes to them; we may deafen ourselves in blind intoxication, for a time. Then that uncanny, intangible, gruesome something suddenly breaks forth all the more appalling in man's terrible deeds, in illnesses, the furies of war that bring destruction to the country, or in devastating hurricanes and earthquakes. What mortals need in all times is not only knowledge of God's loving kindness but above all of the serious character of the deity.

Even Moses knew this. This characteristic is present, and if it is not associated with God, the uncanny and fearful is associated with superstition, magic, astrology, theosophy, and the occult sciences. This was always the case and will remain so as long as man continues to exist. Therefore, Moses did not abolish these things but retained them, not outside of God but in God. All was included in him, even the uncanny, gruesome, and the demoniacal in man and nature. Only then the way was opened to a universal, all-embracing idea of God—a terrible God before whom "all the world trembles" [5] and yet a God who teaches us to overcome all the fearful and gruesome in the world, and to whom past and future belong. The acceptance of the demoniacal and the terrible in the conception of God means the overcoming of them.

This does not mean that the terrible was suddenly eliminated from Moses' world or that of post-Mosaic Israel. This will never happen as long as the world stands. In this conception of God there is a second power, a counterbalance for the evil, thus excluding magic and demons, which gives understanding and mental control over fate. This is God as the ethical will. If everything comes to us from a single source, both destructive destiny and ethical will, then there must be justice; life and death, reward and punishment, terror and consolation, must come from the same source. Its action may be difficult to understand in particular cases, but as a whole it must be explained as wisdom and sacred justice.

In the most highly developed Oriental religions, the ethical power vanished because man possessed magic to free himself from the ethical and to force his will upon the gods. By cutting the very roots of magic and conjuration in Israel, ethical justice could flourish. The springs at the oases of Kadesh-Barnea were also called *enmich pat,* springs of justice. Probably the peninsular tribes gathered there from ancient times to seek justice from the priest of the holy place and to have their disputes settled. The name Kadesh-Barnea means "sanctuary." The place probably was protected by an El of Kadesh-Barnea in whose name the priest spoke justice. This presupposes that the tribes who made a pilgrimage to the place to seek an oracle of the god first dropped their feudal disputes. Thus this Kadesh-Barnea became a place of the covenant and its El a god of the covenant, in whose worship certain covenant rites were included.

It is probable that such a union of tribes for the joint celebration of feasts had already become habitual to the Egyptian Israelites; also this accounts for Moses' request to the Pharaoh to permit them to journey to the desert to celebrate a feast there. The Levites, an old clan of Leah (Leah was the name of one of Jacob's wives), seem to have been the connecting link. So the Levite Moses came to the priests of Kadesh-Barnea and learned the form of worship of the God of Kadesh-Barnea from them. Perhaps he learned the name Yahweh there also. At any rate tradition tells us that Yahweh gave his people "statute and ordinance in Kadesh-Barnea." We can easily surmise what they contained. Posterity later ascribed to Moses the whole of the large book of laws that we have to-day in a part of the second one, all of the third, fourth, and fifth books of Moses. For many reasons this assumption is out of the question, yet the book would not have been ascribed to him, if in some way it were not fundamentally connected with him. In the name of the god newly revealed at Sinai, who probably became a god of the covenant for Israel similar to the El of Kadesh-Barnea, he pledged his people to the service of this god in the sense of the laws that are contained in the ten sentences of Sinai.

This is the oldest tora, the foundation of all the later torot or codes. Thus Moses became the lawgiver for his people; not primarily for the rites and ceremonies, although they, too, must have been included, but for living according to the will of Yahweh. This will is ethical living. Moses neither wished nor knew another kind of Yahweh. Since the natural and fatalistic elements were still a part of the god of Israel, a great task remained for the future.

The question has often been asked: what was left for the prophets of Israel to do, once given this or a similar conception of Yahweh? The purpose of this question was to minimize the power of the prophets in the interest of wholesome development. The above presentation shows (and the delineation of the prophets will verify this) that there was enough left to be done. Moses' deeds for his people and for humanity may be stated as follows: he cleared away polytheism, demonism, and magic by amalgamating with Yahweh all godlike and spirit beings to whom the people paid homage, and he opened the way for real morality by interpreting Yahweh's will as purely ethical. What was left to do was to sever the tie between the two characteristics, or at least to loosen it. The natural, the violent, and the irrational in God must gradually give way to the moral and purely spiritual. Attempts in this direction were made very early. Harmful activity was attributed to a special angel, the angel of destruction, *maschchit,* instead of to Yahweh. Instead of seeing Yahweh in earthquakes and storms, Elijah found him in gentle breezes. More and more the great prophets sought to explain great catastrophies from the ethical standpoint.

So the moral elements were emphasized. If the prophets of Israel did not succeed entirely in eliminating the irrational, the fault was not theirs, nor was it that of Moses. It is in the character of true religion, i.e., in the being of the deity itself after which true religion seeks. By understanding this trait in the being of the deity, Moses did his people and humanity great service; and equally great, perhaps even greater, service by emphasizing the underlying ethical principle. He taught that religion has the endless task of relating the two elements. Once for all he started religion on this path, which it cannot leave without denying itself. Whenever we speak of the greatest men who were instrumental in elevating and purifying religious life and thought, men like Zarathustra, St. Paul, St. Augustine, Luther, and Calvin, we shall always speak of Moses.

III

DEBORAH

The story of Moses ends with Sinai and Kadesh-Barnea. His armies or at least a part of them did, indeed, make an attack from the south to force an entrance into Canaan from that side, but they were repulsed. This seems to have decided Moses to venture an attack from the east. With this attack the conquest of the country began, but Moses had no active part in it.

Before the real attack across the Jordan began, Moses is lost to our view. He died in sight of the Promised Land. Every one who ascends Mt. Peor, the place from which Moses saw the wonders of this land, and who looks as he did at the fields beyond the Jordan to the mountains about Hebron and to Mt. Hermon can join with the narrator in entering into the feeling of the departing leader. Before and behind the mountain are dolmens, graves that date back to dusky antiquity. Among these Moses is believed to be buried. Certainly, many a leader and captain of ancient time rests among the nameless dead. We are told that Yahweh himself buried Moses, "but no man knoweth of his sepulchre unto this day." [1] These strange words show us that a mystery shrouds his death, and even those people little removed in time from him did not venture to lift the veil. From this fact, certain scientists have recently concluded that Moses did not die a natural death, but that he was murdered by an enemy within his own ranks. This may or may not be true. Who can tell?

Joshua of the tribe of Ephraim is considered his successor.

We do not at all get the impression that his personality, even in the slightest degree, approached that of his master. Nevertheless the tribe succeeded, either with or without his help (many times writers would eliminate him entirely), in gaining a foothold in different places in Canaan. Of course, this could not be called a "conquest" of Canaan. A few generations after Moses' death, we find Judean and related clans settled in the South, and clans of Ephraim and probably also that of Benjamin, in the mountains of the central country and on their southern slopes. The tribe of Dan took possession of the western slopes of the southern mountains, and the tribe of Manasseh of the northern slopes of the central mountains. The tribe of Asser settled in the region of Ascho; Zebulon and Naphtali in the region north of the plain of Jezreel, where Dan soon followed them.

Almost everywhere they failed to get control of the military and economic centers of the country. Neither the fertile plains nor the strongly fortified walled cities fell into their hands, for in the former they could not compete with the iron war chariots nor with the walls and bastions of the latter. Not in vain had Canaan been under Egyptian rule for centuries. The Israelites equaled only in mountain warfare an enemy who was superior in the military art and technique of an old civilization. Thus the Israelites had to be satisfied with penetrating here and there the pasture lands and fields of the rural population in mountainous regions. Wherever they could, they forced the former masters into their service. As semi-serfs the conquered ones were obliged to till the soil either as tenants with a certain share in the crops, or as farm hands. When the latter grew powerful, it sometimes happened that the Israelites in their turn performed the statute labor or were semi-serfs. This difference, of course, worked out later in the real founding of the nation of Israel. For the most part the Israelites were not admitted to the cities. When admitted, they were there on suffrance, until gradually by intermarriage, or by the influence of certain families or by occasional clever strokes, they gained prominence and a foothold.

A few cities, such as Jericho, Bethel, and Ajah, seem to be exceptions. These they gained in their first attack. Treason played a noticeably important rôle. Two of the above cities came into their possession in this way. Perhaps a circumstance previously mentioned explains the reason for it. As we have already heard, by no means all the people who belonged to Jacob-Israel in Canaan had migrated to Egypt. Many clans remained in Canaan and became bastard clans, half Israelite and half Canaanite: the former, because of their past; the latter, because of their present state. When the Israelites invaded Canaan, the Canaanites felt the call of the blood. Thus may have felt the clan of Rahab in Jericho and that man or those people in Bethel who delivered the city over to the Israelites. The people of Asser, who presumably had long dwelt in the section, may have felt it their duty to find a dwelling place in the country but outside of the cities for the newcomers.

We must imagine the old tribe of Israel in this condition. From former discussions we know that under the Pharaoh Meneptah, i.e., at the time when Israel forced its entrance into Canaan, there were people in Canaan called Israelites. It seems that Meneptah oppressed them greatly because they were a part of those who rebelled against the Egyptian overrule. This is probably the historic nucleus of the Pharaoh's boast that Israel was destroyed. The insurrection occurred because of the political disorder in the country; perhaps the Israelites in Canaan joined the insurrection because their own tribesmen were entering the country and were anxiously waiting the result in Goshen or in the desert. Many of the oppressed Canaanite-Israelites must have extended to the newcomers the cordial welcome of old friends, indeed of helpers in time of need, when first Moses, and later Joshua appeared at the border of Canaan. Perhaps this explains not only the almost effortless surrender of those cities to the Israelites but also the quick settlement in Canaan. The end came in the mountains of Ephraim. What could be accomplished for the time being was done quickly, probably favored by circumstances.

Astonished, we may ask about the Egyptian overrule. Why, in the whole book of Joshua and everywhere where this Israelite invasion into Canaan is discussed, with the single exception of Judges ten and eleven, are the Egyptians not mentioned? Neither Joshua nor any of the tribes had a struggle with them. The Israelites fought with the Canaanites, or the Amorites, and made agreements with the cities and the city kings of these peoples, but we hear nothing of the Egyptians or their governors. If we did not hear of them through Egyptian sources, it would never occur to us that the Pharaoh was still a power with whom the new-comers who struggled for control in the cities and the country districts had to deal. How can this strange circumstance be explained? Had Egypt actually lost its authority, or had the Israelite narrators forgotten their importance, or did they deliberately fail to mention them? Each one of these interpretations has its champions.

We remember that Meneptah boasted that in the fifth year of his reign he again subjugated all of Palestine. Although his hymn of victory may be exaggerated, he did have great success. If, before this time, the governors had been driven out of the country or killed, and their garrisons scattered, they now seem to have returned. Their present success, however, was short lived, a one-day success. With Meneptah's death, at a single blow all that he had gained was lost. In Egypt first came confusions of party struggles, and soon anarchy reigned. A foreign Syrian ascended the throne of the Pharaohs. All joined hands to plunder Egypt's possessions.

Under these circumstances Egypt's authority was soon destroyed. We can readily understand that at this particular time the Israelites who entered the country from the east had no cause to show much consideration toward Egypt, its city governors, and its troops. They simply ignored them. If we assume that Joshua's time and the invasion of Israel into Canaan coincide with the time from Meneptah's death to the coming of Rameses III (1215-1198 or perhaps 1235-1218), the question is solved for this period.

To be sure, Egypt rallied for a time. A new attack of the Maritime Peoples roused Rameses III to action. The enemy came in great numbers by land and by sea from the north and advanced as far as the delta. They seem to have overrun all of Syria, at least in the coast regions. Although they seem even to have demolished the Amorite kingdom, Rameses III conquered them at sea, and with the aid of his Sardish hirelings, on land. This brought Palestine and southern Syria once more under the Egyptian rule. The Pharaoh rebuilt fortresses, filled them with garrisons, and boasted that the Syrian princes paid their tribute to the temple of Ammon. Indeed the Egyptian temple of Ammon in Thebes, according to the statement of Rameses III, is said to have possessed nine cities of Syria and Kusch. Even Thutmoses III presented it with three Syrian cities.

To be sure, control again weakened after the death of Rameses III. Of the Pharaohs who succeeded him, none seems to have possessed the power to enforce obedience upon his Palestine vassals, who failed in their duties. The reign of Rameses III lasted, in round numbers, thirty years. This was presumably just after Israel's first invasion or a generation after Joshua. We cannot verify Rameses' statement concerning the tribute of the Palestine dynasty to the temple of Ammon. Stone inscriptions, like the newspaper of to-day, are not always trustworthy. An example of this will appear later concerning the Philistines. It may be that the Pharaoh was satisfied that there was no open revolt, and was, therefore, willing to overlook much.

That he did not interfere with the feuds in the country, which are reported in Judges, is a matter of course. For centuries the Pharaohs were accustomed to seeing the Canaanite vassals at sword's points with each other. Thus the only question is why our biblical reports are silent about Egypt. They also do not mention the Maritime Peoples to whom the Philistines belonged. We do not hear that the Philistines came or how they came. Suddenly we find them in the country and causing trouble. Only at the time when they oppressed Israel are they mentioned; before that time they did not interest the narrator, which fact proves that the narrator was interested only in Israel and the people of Israel. The horizon was limited to the narrator's own country; he did not see beyond. From this we may not conclude that they no longer knew of the Egyptian power and the demands of the Pharaohs or of the tribute demanded and the various tribute payments, or that they deliberately remained silent concerning them. Nor did they deny the bondage in Egypt. Occasionally there may have been Egyptian governors and divisions of troops there, but they apparently were not prominent and, therefore, made no great impression. The narrations in the book of Joshua are for the most part of too late a date to clearly recall the Egyptian rule, and those of the book of Judges, many of which are older, pay no attention to the Egyptians because they seemed unimportant.

Thus we, too, may be unconcerned about Egypt and turn our attention toward Israel's welfare. The position which Israel had gained by its first invasion was unstable. In one place the Israelites had the upper hand; in another, the old inhabitants. Each did his utmost to gain territory. This struggle was a silent one, which, apart from a few exceptions and hints, is realized only by its effects. There were other reasons why Israel was not content with what it had gained. The Canaanites and the Amorites, hard pressed first by the Maritime Peoples, and later by the Israelites, could not possibly be satisfied with the present conditions. They were obliged either to regain their lost territory or to repair their fortunes in some other way. Even less could the Eastern nomads forsake their old custom of making raids in the west; they always looked longingly toward the fertile lands. Thus there was no lack of conflict and struggle.

Perhaps one of the first of these conflicts concerned the little tribe of Dan. It had settled on the western slopes of the Judean mountains when the Philistines, together with the Maritime Peoples, invaded the country. In spite of the victory of Rameses III they succeeded in establishing themselves in the country and caused Israel great annoyance for a long time. From this we see how carefully must be considered such reports as Rameses' message of victory. At first, as the story of Samson proves, the Danites seem to have offered stubborn resistance. The struggles in this setting can be understood because of the conditions. In time the Philistine oppression of Israel itself as well as of the Amorites living in the desert plain along the coast increased to such a degree that the Amorites were pushed back toward the mountains, and thus they in turn pressed against the Danites who dwelt there. Thus the hilly country of Aijalon and Shaalbim, which doubtless the Danites had once taken from the Amorites, again became Amorite territory, and presumably remained so until Saul's time. The six hundred armed men whom Dan could summon were insufficient to protect the territory. They, therefore, made a raid upon the other end of the country. They attacked a territory called Laish, near the region of Sidon and the springs of the Jordan, settled there, and called the place Dan after their tribe.

Of far greater importance for the nation than the vicissitudes of this single tribe is what is reported of Deborah. She is one of the few examples of a truly heroic woman in Old Israel. In Israel, woman was very dependent upon man and too much restrained by custom to play a prominent part in public life, yet ever and anon a woman ventured to break through the barriers, whether to Israel's misfortune, as in Jezebel's and Athaliah's cases, or to her weal, as in Deborah's case. Here it was her special gifts that helped her. She was justly called a prophetess, for she was both a seer and a poet. This gift of prophecy was a gift of God; she, therefore, was a woman of God and was, therefore, raised above the limitations of ordinary women.

In the northern part of the country, in Harosheth of southern Galilee, a government was established, ostensibly under a king named Jabin and his general Sisera, but in reality probably under General Sisera. The name Sisera is probably a Hittite or related word, and this government may have attempted to unite the scattered and much-decimated remnants of the old Hittite state and the Canaanite-Amorite provinces of that region. The latter still possessed most of the fortified cities, especially in the plain of Jezreel. A close union, the concerted action of the cities, and the wise use of their superior weapons and war chariots made a victory seem certain. If they succeeded, the country at least as far as the mountains of Ephraim, i.e., Galilee, and part of the fertile valley that they possessed would be taken from Israel.

The very announcement of their plan seems to have had a depressing effect upon Israel. A paralyzing fear overcame them. "Was there a shield or spear seen among the forty thousand in Israel?" [2] The blow seemed already to have succeeded in part, and the Israelites must thus early have met with serious reverses. They felt Yahweh had deserted them. Farm labor ceased. Whoever was obliged to leave home and hearth and cross the open country went by secret paths in order to evade the enemy's army which was already in the country. Attempted resistance failed, for before a new battle took place, whole tribes failed, through fear, to obey the summons to battle.

Then help came from the woman favored of God. Although Barak stood aloof in discouragement, she inspired him with courage to act by reminding him of the disgrace and injury done him; the wavering tribes, who hesitated and remained aloof, she inspired with new strength. It seems that since the days of the heroic invasion of the country, a weak unwarlike spirit had come over Israel. The comforts of peaceful rural life had succeeded the hard struggle for life's needs on the desert. Thus the old heroic spirit weakened. The enervating Baal religion, with which they came in closer contact as time progressed, did its part. Yahweh was a strong, jealous, and severe God. Baal and Ashtart favored effeminate, enervating, and sensual pleasures.

Thus Deborah had to recreate in her people two things, or at least awaken them from their slumber: an understanding of and faith in Yahweh, and in addition to this a courage to act. She succeeded in this, and thus led them to victory. All her deeds were performed in the name of Yahweh. In this respect her people had failed. Scarcely fifty or sixty years had elapsed since Moses had left them. The fathers had known him and could tell the children, who gathered about the hearth fire in the hut, of the great man and the great deeds of the desert day. They could tell how the great Yahweh had appeared to Moses in the fire of the burning bush and to his people in the storm of Sinai; how in the Sea of Reeds he had greatly helped his people against the mighty and well-equipped enemy. But the sons and grandsons had already begun to prefer to listen to the sensual music of the noisy Baal feasts rather than to the serious tales about the stern Yahweh. This attitude had been their ruin, and if help did not come, would cause the ruin of the entire nation. Even without oppression from the enemy, they would be brought to the abyss of lost nationality and thus to serfdom or annihilation.

What the voices announced to the Maid of Orleans in her ecstatic devotions, the heavenly voice also announced to this woman of God. In Israel, inspired women who proclaimed victory and acted as heralds, and praised the victor, were not uncommon. Among them were Miriam, Jephthah's daughter, and the women who proclaimed David's fame. Among the Arabs such women also served as passionately excited companions in battle, mingling in the ranks of the combatants, spurring the warriors on to courage and battle fury with wild calls and excited gestures of ecstatic rage. Deborah was greater than these. With a stirring song and an appeal to Barak to sound anew the summons to battle, she combined prophet and zealot in urging her people to battle for Yahweh. As with Joan of Arc so with Deborah, the battle to which she summoned her people was for God and his cause, and not primarily to favor men.

Deborah had not forgotten Moses and his work. Mt. Sinai, the Sea of Reeds, and all Yahweh's deeds were vital to her. The heavenly voice announced to her that the Yahweh of Hosts would give Israel victory if she wished it. To Deborah all centered about Yahweh. She would have nothing of the "new gods," Baal and Ashtart. The whole thundering song of victory in the fifteenth chapter of the book of Judges, whether composed by her or by one who shared her sentiments, is a powerful song of praise of Yahweh and his deeds. It begins with Yahweh's praise and ends with the fame of the friends of Yahweh. His honor was at stake. She sings of Yahweh, and again of Yahweh. Her song tells us that the Israelite peasants recount Yahweh's deeds, and his leaders praise him to make the men, as they gather among the women drawing water at the wells of the shepherds' fountains and in the cities, willing to follow the call to arms. They tell of the deeds that Yahweh had once done for their fathers. They now must protect Yahweh's honor. If his people were ruined, who would serve Yahweh in future and proclaim his deeds to the world? It was not only Yahweh, but the Yahweh of Moses, the Yahweh of Sinai for whom she struggled.

> Lord, when Thou wentest out of Seïr, when thou marchedst out of the field of Edom, the earth trembled, and the heavens dropped, the clouds also dropped water.
> The mountains melted from before the Lord, even that Sinai from before the Lord God of Israel.[3]

This is clearly the God of Hosts, the God of Battles, the God coming from Seïr and Edom, i.e., from Sinai to battle for his people. For Deborah, his seat was still on Mt. Sinai; for Elijah, on Mt. Horeb.

This was the faith to which this woman again turned her people, and in it she carried the masses with her. Thus the faith of a weak woman became for her people both the spark that revived the dying flame of faith in Yahweh and the bond that reunited the tribes that had become discordant and enervated. Yahweh, the God of Sinai, the God of Hosts, who helped Moses, now carried his banner before the people. This banner was the banner of both unity and strength and, therefore, of victory.

So they came in great numbers, the tribal lords, "appearing willingly before the people," and hosts of armed peasants, who "as the people of the Lord went down to the gates." [4]

> Then he made him that remaineth have dominion over the nobles among the people: the Lord made me have dominion over the mighty.
> Out of Ephraim was there a root of them against Amalek; after thee, Benjamin, among thy people; out of Machir came

down governors, and out of Zebulun they that handle the pen of the writer.

And the princes of Issachar were with Deborah; even Issachar, and also Barak; he was sent on foot into the valley. For the divisions of Reuben there were great thoughts of heart.

Zebulun and Naphtali were a people that jeoparded their lives unto the death in the high places of the field.[5]

Yahweh kept his word. Because they found him and with him found themselves and their power, they gained the victory. The God of Sinai left Seïr and set off with his heavenly hosts. As the archangel Michael supported Joan of Arc, as the spirits of the air fought with the Christian hosts in the battle with the Huns, so here fought the spirit of the stars.

They fought from heaven; the stars in their courses fought against Sisera.

The river of Kishon swept them away, that ancient river, the river Kishon. O my soul, thou hast trodden down strength.[6]

Thunder and cloudburst, perhaps accompanied by hail and earthquake, were the heavenly messengers of Yahweh's and Israel's allies. The usually sluggish brook of Kishon, that crosses and recrosses the plain near Tanaak and Megiddo, became a raging torrent whose destructive waters carried off the enemy's hosts together with their horses and chariots (Sisera is said to have had nine hundred iron war chariots) as the wind drives the stubble before it. The outcome of the battle was decided.

The kings came and fought, then fought the kings of Canaan in Taanach by the waters of Megiddo; they took no gain of money.

Then were the horsehoofs broken by the means of the prancings, the prancings of their mighty ones.[7]

They pursued and destroyed the enemy's army in its wild flight. Those that were not carried away by the rushing

torrent were killed in their flight by Barak. Deserted by
his knights, weary and on foot, Sisera himself sought safety
in flight. Exhausted he sought food and rest in the nomad
tent of a Kenite named Heber. The Kenites were a branch
of an old desert tribe that in Moses' time, obeying the ties
of friendship and fraternity, had followed the Israelites thus
far in their wanderings. In this day lesser Bedouin tribes
still pitched their tents on the edge of the plain of Jezreel
and in parts of Galilee. Heber's wife, Jael, was alone in
the tent. She recognized the fleeing general. Perhaps the
shining armor betrayed the great warrior. With enticing
words she invited him into the tent. "Enter, my lord, thou
hast nothing to fear." He entered and lay down to rest;
she covered him with a cloth. Thirsty, he asked for a drink
of water.

He asked water, and she gave him milk; she brought forth
butter in a lordly dish.
She put her hand to the nail and her right hand to the work-
men's hammer; and with the hammer she smote Sisera, she
smote off his head, when she had pierced through his temples.
At her feet he bowed, he fell, he lay down; at her feet he
bowed; where he bowed, there he fell down dead.[8]

Passion of battle and the hatred of the oppressed loosened
all bonds. This deceitful woman overstepped even the ever-
sacred law of hospitality that offered the enemy protection
and safety when once he had entered his host's tent; but
both her contemporaries and posterity forgave her, nay more,
they praised her even after centuries. "The wife of Heber
the Kenite, blessed shall she be above women in the tent."
Instead of the water he asked for she gave him a dish of
milk from the milk in the goat skins.
Sisera, completely exhausted, readily believed her assur-
ances and, suspecting nothing, permitted her to cover him
with the cloth. Should anyone come and ask, "Is anyone

there?" then answer, "No one." With this he lay down at her feet to sleep. He intended to continue his flight at nightfall. Scarcely had she heard his quiet breathing when with her left hand she seized a tent peg. Every Bedouin tent is protected against the stress of the wind by ropes that are fastened to great pegs rammed into the ground. With her right hand she grasped the work hammer used for hammering the pegs into the ground when the tent is set up. Stealthily creeping up, she bent over the unsuspecting warrior, held the sharp nail over the temple of the sleeper, whose head was turned to one side. With terrible blows of the heavy hammer she drove the nail through his brain and on into the ground. This was the real course of events. The legend, although of a later date, has kept more faithfully the entirely repulsive perfidy of the deed than has the song. The song idealized the act and thus made it more acceptable to our natural feeling. Instead of by carefully planned assassination, Sisera was killed by suddenly roused passion. After he entered the tent and was still standing, he drank the milk. Then patriotic rage seized the woman. With quick determination, hammer in hand, she approached the warrior from behind as he stood drinking, and crushed his skull so that he reeled and fell dead at her feet.

The peasants and shepherds in the huts and tents were not tender-hearted. The tent woman's deed was told them in all its hideous gruesomeness. Sisera was the hated ruler. He deserved neither consideration nor loyalty. Treason was strategy. Even at that time, however, there was a different attitude in the circles of the poets and among the bards of Israel, to whom characters like Deborah belonged, and in the company of those for whom her song was first intended. At the lesser court or in the castles of the tribal princes like Barak, in the manor houses of the knights and the nobility, the laws of hospitality and chivalry were upheld even toward an enemy. The passion of the victor's honest revenge and his frank joy over the fine booty, even the mourning and disappointment in the enemy's palace, not the blessing on cunning and murder, are well suited to the fine work of art which we may frankly call this poem. After the deed was done, Barak, Israel's leader, suddenly appeared before the tent of Heber in search of the fugitive. Jael came out of the tent. "Come and I will show thee the man whom thou seekest." [9] Then Barak saw Sisera lying in his blood with the tent peg bored through his head. This is improbable, unless in rapid pursuit Barak had reached the hostile capital at the western edge of the plain and again returned to search for the missing one. There was scarcely time for this before nightfall. But those who listened to the splendid tale, that doubtless long went the rounds of all the villages and the cities and kept listeners in breathless suspense, liked this sonorous and rounded close. After the battle their own general found the much-feared enemy lying in his blood, murdered by a woman's hand. What a triumph, what a picture, what splendid material to pass on to their children and children's children!

Barak played only a subordinate part in the whole drama here enacted. Decorative as he appears in the closing scene, he is not really the actor. Whether the expression was uttered by Deborah or not, "I shall surely go with thee, notwithstanding the journey thou takest shall be for thine honor; for the Lord shall sell Sisera into the hand of a woman," [10] signifies little. It contained the truth. The fame of having captured and slain the enemy belonged to Jael. The honor of defeating him in battle was Yahweh's, for Barak's greatest help was the good fortune that Yahweh sent him. The praise finally for having called the people and Barak to battle and of having encouraged them belonged to Deborah. This was far more than Jael's fame.

Deborah deserved it. We know nothing of her youth

or her later life, but this one deed has made her immortal. She belongs to the few great women of the early history of humanity. The victory over Sisera, in reality entirely Deborah's victory, had a far-reaching effect upon Israel. The Canaanites who had united under Sisera never again ventured to join forces for serious resistance against Israel. The victory must, therefore, have been final and the destruction of the enemy complete. Even the fortified cities which, on the whole, still remained in the enemy's hands were insufficient to give them the necessary courage and strength for a renewed attack. This explains clearly the significance of what had just occurred.

To be sure, new struggles awaited Israel. It was a long time before it was destined to enjoy this fine country; but the main enemy, the one they had fought since Moses' death, the one who had a right to call the country his own, was so cast down that he could not venture to raise his head. This achievement was hardly the result of the victory as such; other influences worked together with it. Israel had power to conquer because of the union of the tribes and the inner vital strength. The enemies' alliance had counted upon the old civil strife and the enervation of the Canaanites. Thus far these qualities in Israel had been the enemy's best ally. Now it was evident that the union of only a large part of the nation sufficed to make Israel a powerful enemy. Certain it was that the reproachful and threatening appeal which the song directed to all the tardy ones had helped to bring many of the laggards to the ranks of duty. What would be the result if a new war should bring those who still stood aloof to the side of those faithful to Yahweh? Then it would infallibly prove that the unity of Israel made them invincible. This was the consideration which led the companions and successors of Sisera, when the Canaanite city princes did not venture to annoy Israel by a new attack. That they refrained from it and that, as far as they were concerned, Israel was the uncontested master in the country, is the second service, far more important than the single victory, of Deborah, the woman of God.

Deborah who has much in common with Joan of Arc had one advantage over her. The latter had first to be burned at the stake to become a saint. During her very lifetime Deborah had the honor of being called a "Mother in Israel,"

IV

JERUBBAAL-GIDEON

THE eastern Bedouins were never at rest. What the Khabiru and the Israelites, and later, in the Islam period, the Moslem hordes attempted, has been done for thousands of years and is still being done on a small scale by innumerable bands. Drought and crop failure in the central desert, the advance of tribes with tents pitched farther inland, who were pushed forward by others, and the erratic whim of certain groups who moved forward or were pushed by others, occurred periodically on the borders of the fertile lands. Security for these lands could come only by means of a strong government in Palestine and in Syria. When it was lacking, the desert sons, who ever cast longing glances at the fertile lands, mounted their swift camels, broke forth from the desert, and took from these lands whatever they offered, only to disappear again into the trackless desert as swiftly as they had come.

To understand these conditions, read what an eye-witness (still living) tells of the conditions in that region during the Turkish rule.

In June and July they (the Bedouins of the Arabian Desert) came northward from the desert half dead with thirst. The largest "birke" (pool) is not sufficient to quench their thirst. Then the tens of thousands of camels with half naked riders mounted on their select delules (riding camels) break through the thin ranks of soldiers, and woe unto the fields over which the hungry hordes first scatter! Not a stem, not a blade of grass is left, for what they do not devour is trampled under the broad hoofs of their camels.

[61]

Israel was freed from the Canaanite city governor's control and seemed safe against renewed invasions, but the union of the important tribes was insufficient to replace a central power strong enough to protect the country from the Bedouin robber bands, who at this time were the Midianites. In Moses' time they had had their abode farther south in the region where Moses, while still a shepherd, pastured his sheep. They must have been closely related to the Kenites, for the region into which Moses fled after he had slain the Egyptian is sometimes called Media in the Old Testament, and the kinsfolk of Moses, elsewhere called Kenites, are here called Midianites. It is possible that the close relation with Israel impelled them as well as the Kenites, whom we found in the plain of Jezreel in the story of Deborah, to push slowly northward. In the story of the later Mosaic period we actually find the Midians in the back country of the Dead Sea and along the mouth of the Jordan near Mt. Peor where Moses had his farewell view into the Promised Land. We hear that the Midianites there became a great danger to the Israelites who were unable to withstand the temptation to worship the very obnoxious Baal Peor.

If legend be true, the Israelites were soon lured into the Canaanite Baal worship, or at least occasionally fell into its meshes. Doubtless, originally the Baal Peor was a Canaanite god who dwelt on Mt. Peor near the present Madaba, the ancient Medeba. But we do well not to consider this narrative, because in its oldest form it does not seem to deal with the Midianites but with Moabite women and a Moabite god. Since the region belonged to Moab, this version seems entirely probable. It makes the presence of the Midianites in this region as early as Moses' time very questionable, and we must admit ignorance concerning the time of their shifting northward.

It is a fact that at this time those nomadic hordes were

within reach of Palestine, and that they were a grave danger to its inhabitants, especially to the Israelite peasants who dwelt outside of the fortified cities. The narrator sounds truthful when he tells us that each year before the harvest the nomads came on their swift camels riding at full speed to invade the country.

They attacked them, destroyed the increase of the earth till thou come into Gaza and left no sustenance in Israel, neither sheep nor ox nor ass. For they came with their tents, they came in as locusts for multitude; both they and their camels were without number. and they came into the land to destroy it.

As developments show, the next region to suffer was the country inhabited by Manasseh and the plain of Jezreel. Manasseh had its seat south of the plain on the heights of Ephraim extending toward Shechem. A large part of the fertile plain also belonged to them, in fact all that was not claimed by Canaanite fortresses. They may have crossed the Jordan at the great estuary of Bethshean, the Besan of to-day. From there they could spread unhindered over the rich plain. They plundered all the grain that had been threshed and all the crops that had been garnered; also all they found of flocks and domestic animals. Their countless camels consumed the grain and fodder that was still in the fields. The frightened peasants left hearth and home and sought to escape with their lives by fleeing for refuge to the remotest rifts and caves in the mountains and into the walled castles. When a section was sacked, the unwelcome guests rode on. At Mt. Carmel they turned south and entered Sharon, the second fertile plain to lure them. They are reported to have reached Gaza, the southernmost Philistine city, near the southern border of the country. When this land was grazed over, their swift animals bore them back to the desert, only for them to repeat their wicked game the following year.

A generation, perhaps more, may have elapsed since the splendid forward movement which Deborah brought to Israel. It was near the turning of the twelfth century B.C., about the years 1130 to 1125. The peaceful development of the tribes may have made good progress under the wholesome influence of the respect which Israel's victory at Tanaach had forced from the Canaanite communities. Agriculture and probably commerce flourished. Then for a number of years the peasants' lives were in danger, and each year within a few days the fruits of hard labor were wrenched from them.

The real danger was not that the Midianites wished to conquer the land and expel the Israelites from their holdings, as a few scholars believe. Had the Midianites been shepherd nomads then it might have been so, but they were genuine Bedouins with herds of camels. What did the Midianites want of the people of Palestine, unless they first completely changed their mode of living? In truth the method they pursued was far more convenient for them. The Israelite peasant worked hard during the entire year to set a good table for them. They ate all he provided, and then went their way only to return as often and as long as the peasant was long suffering. Yet a serious danger threatened. What would become of the peasant if these conditions continued? What was to become of the country? There was danger that the peasant would desert the land, lose interest in agriculture, in fact in all kinds of work, and would thus bring about the ruin of national life and orderly living which had just begun to develop so satisfactorily. Israel, now well on the road to become a nation, was seriously threatened with dropping back into the lower state of civilization of the time of its entrance into Canaan. The tribal union that Deborah had brought about and the other gains from the past would be lost. Under the paralyzing influence of this continued danger much was already lost. During the long comfortable years of peace, Baal had so gained the upper hand that the formerly strong and victorious tribes of Manasseh and Ephraim could no longer gather the necessary strength to withstand the invasions of the nomadic hordes, much less of the other tribes. A state of decline had already appeared. Conditions could hardly grow worse.

The Midian hordes that had not crossed the Jordan at Bethshean and from there invaded the plain of Jezreel, found a second estuary of the Jordan at Adam (now Tell-ed-damie) at the confluence of the Jakkob and the Jordan. From there through the Wadi Fara, which extends northwest in the direction of Shechem, they advanced toward the interior mountain region. Perhaps the town of Ophrah is named from this wadi. At any rate we may look for it to be in this region. It also seems to have suffered greatly. In this town dwelt the Abiezrite clan. At the time of the Bedouin invasion, the head of the clan was a certain Joash. His youthful son Gideon, or as he was now called, Jerubbaal, was destined to become Israel's help in need.

The word Gideon means the smiter or the grim warrior. Jerubbaal probably means Baal fights, perhaps, also, Baal is strong. At any rate the name put the bearer under Baal's protection. According to this the young man's original name probably was Jerubbaal, and Gideon was an added name of honor. The Arabs call such a name a man's *kunja,* the name that is given him by virtue of his deeds.

Legend tells us that one day under his father's turpentine tree the young man was threshing wheat into the wine press in order to hide the grain from the Midianites. Yahweh appeared to him and greeted him as a brave warrior. He answered, crestfallen and bitter: "Oh, my lord, if the Lord be with us, why then is all this befallen us?" Yahweh then promised him his strength to conquer the Midianites "as one man." For he who felt so deeply the distress of his people would prove himself a man of deeds. Whether or not

[65]

the above really took place as here related, it at least describes the conditions perfectly. Wheat was threshed on the barn floor, the doors being open so that the wind would carry off the dust and chaff. Either beasts of burden trampled over the grain to free the kernels, or a threshing sled was driven over the grain. Only grain that had small kernels or the little owned by the poor man with no beast of burden was threshed with flails. Why did Jerubbaal not thresh his father's grain? And what was he doing at the wine press where the wine was usually made?

The object seems to be to bring Israel's great distress once more vividly before us. Either the enemy was already in the country or might appear at any time. His first act would be to search the threshing floor for the threshed grain. Therefore Jerubbaal fled to the wine press with his father's harvest. Here no one would search for grain, especially when he did not thresh in the usual way but with a flail. For the little that was to be gathered from the downtrodden and impoverished country this manner of threshing sufficed. Thus the image of the unfortunate country and of the downtrodden nation so cruelly tortured was reflected in the soul of the unfortunate young man, the youngest of his father's sons. The picture of the misery about him and the rebellious rage of the people tyrannized over by their torturers decided him to follow the inner voice.

With his decision made, as soon as opportunity offered, he acted. Soon the Bedouins again invaded the plain of Jezreel and conducted themselves in their usual manner. This was Jerubbaal's time to act. He did not call upon the tribal leaders or the nobility of his own tribe (Manasseh), nor did he turn to Ephraim for help. He understood the situation and knew that he had little to expect from them or from others. All depended upon quick action. He sounded the bugle call in his own district and called his vassals to arms.

Ophrah seems to have been the center of the clan of Abiez-rite, and Jerubbaal's father, Joash, was the clan leader. Three hundred armed men answered his call. This was a modest following, not even a third of a thousand; a thousand men were considered the least number for a normal tribe. Yet they were a determined group, enraged at wrong doing. The leader was courageous, strong, and wise, guided by God himself. Two factors may replace an army. Legend ex-presses the same thought when it has Jerubbaal first gather a stately army, then voluntarily reduce it to the three hun-dred with whom he set out.

Jerubbaal and his three hundred clansmen were stationed at the spring of Harod which probably was on the slope of the Gilboa range. The Midianites encamped opposite him on the plain. On the eve of battle Jerubbaal with his armor bearer crept close up to the enemy's camp. Here he heard a warrior tell another of a dream of disaster. He dreamed that a cake of barley bread rolled against the camp and on the chieftain's tent, and overthrew it. In this he saw a bad omen for the battle. Jerubbaal joyously accepted the omen. Confident and sure of God's help, he returned to his camp. "Arise for the Lord hath delivered into your hands the host of Midian." [2] He divided his soldiers into three companies of one hundred each. To each man he gave an empty earthen pitcher. In the pitchers were torches to be lighted later. At the beginning of the midnight watch, i.e., at midnight he ad-vanced to the edge of the enemy's camp with the three hun-dred men whom he commanded. He ordered horns sounded to deceive the enemy. This sound signified the rule of un-canny spirits. Instantly he shattered the pitcher, took in his left hand the torch which he quickly lighted, in his right hand his drawn sword, and then shouted the war cry, "Yah-weh and Gideon," out into the night. Already his followers called their leader the "Grim Warrior." The custom of using the names of illustrious people as a watchword is common also in Arabia. Their spirit and their help are supposed to hover about the warriors in battle.

The other two divisions of one hundred men each who had been told just what to do were stationed at other points outside of the enemy's camp so as to surround it. At Jerubbaal's command all three divisions did exactly what he himself did. The sudden crashing of three hundred pitchers startled the sleeping camp. An uncanny deafening sound reached their ears. Instantly three hundred torches blazed and turned night into day. By this light hundreds of drawn swords were swung threateningly toward them by the death-defying warriors outside of the camp. Not a hand was raised, not a step taken; only an uncanny shrill war cry from three hundred throats was simultaneously uttered, wildly threatening and filled with rage, and increased the uncanny terror.

The camp was awake. All were motionless and stupefied with terror. Then came wild cries of a thousand voices, then confused running hither and thither and into one another. They could not escape from the camp, for it was completely surrounded. Wherever they attempted it, drawn swords faced them. They turned back. Those crowding forward believed the returning soldiers were the invading enemy. A battle of all against all began in their own camp. The enemy without had only to look on. After much slaughter, those that were left finally found a means of escape and fled toward the Jordan. In the meantime Jerubbaal had taken the precaution to send messengers to various places in Ephraim, and called upon the people of Naphali, Ashur, and Manasseh to pursue the enemy. After the main work was accomplished, they might be willing to pluck the last laurels. Thus the enemy was prevented from returning across the Jordan, and its hosts were fully annihilated. The heads of their chieftains, "Raven" and "Wolf," were sent to the victor.

Jerubbaal deserved the victor's prize. The countless spoils
of the enemy's camp belonged to him and his three hundred
daring men. The attitude of those who were called upon to
pursue the enemy, and later looked askance and complained
because they had not been called upon sooner, is one that is
common everywhere where great deeds are accomplished
through the result of the courage of one or of a few persons.[3] "That was nothing unusual: We could have done
that" has always been the watchword of lesser spirits to
extraordinary men. All the clan honored Jerubbaal (except
the leaders of the booty) with the proud title of "Grim Warrior."

His noble decision, his bold venture, his ingenious strate-
gem had gained a success for him, which was very significant for Israel's future. At least the danger that threatened
was temporarily overcome. More than this; the act of a
determined man had given new proof that there was enough
warlike power and national pride in Israel to prove false all
the cares and fears, all the pitiful intimidation of the masses,
and the timorous aloofness of the prominent men in the
tribes. They merely needed some one to rouse them and
make the tribes conscious of what they could do if they
were determined.

Jerubbaal, whom we may hereafter call Gideon, accomplished an heroic feat common only in fairy tales. Little
wonder that it was assigned now to legend and now to the
fairy tale. Many a fairy-tale trait may have been added to
embellish it. The Israelite narrators could not allow such a
splendid story to escape them. It was told and retold hundreds of times throughout the length and breadth of the
country. It is the most natural thing in the world that in
the retelling, certain features were added or changed, but
the story in its characteristic features, about the way it was
told above, contains nothing that could not have been thought
out and carried out by a wise and bold leader in his position.

To prove that this story is not entirely legendary, we know that even Isaiah knew of this victory.

Gideon could not long enjoy the peace gained by the bitter struggle. The desert is inexhaustible. It constantly sends out new hordes whose occupation is foray and plunder, which they called *razzia.* If one group meets with misfortune, another may be more favored, as has often been the case during thousands of years. Indeed after a period of peace, a new advance of the Midianites seems to have been successful. Before Gideon could gather his brave warriors, the swift-mounted hordes were already on their way back to the desert heavily laden with booty. They had already crossed the Jordan without meeting resistance, but this time the hero's sword was whetted by blood vengeance.

Robbing and murdering, these sons of the desert had advanced as far as Mt. Tabor. This isolated mountain peak commands a splendid view and is visible at a great distance on the Galilean landscape north of the plain. Jerubbaal's brothers were on this ancient sacred mountain, perhaps for a feast of sacrifice, perhaps occupied with their cattle or in their fields in this fertile region. They fell by the robbers' weapons. Now blood was shed in Joash's own family, and the younger warrior son was the natural avenger of his brothers. Blood revenge had ancient, severe and barbarous laws, but it was indispensable for the citizen where there was no state and no legal protection. It meant self-help and self-protection for the nomad, the peasant, or shepherd who lived in those primitive conditions. It was the law of the desert and of the farming and pasture lands that were unprotected by any state. It was also an institution for equalizing justice. Blood for blood, man for man also meant that no tribe may weaken and lessen the martial power of another tribe without punishment.

As soon as Gideon had gathered his three hundred trusted warriors, he hastened toward the Jordan. In forced marches he hurried onward. He easily found traces of the robbers riding at full speed, for there is only one main road to the southern steppes, the ancient caravan road still in use. Merchant caravans have traversed it for centuries from Heman and the Hedjahs to Damascus and the Euphrates. Since Medina and Mecca have become holy cities, processions of pilgrims travel it. The Hedjah railroad follows it to-day. To reach this road Gideon hastened across the country east of the Jordan.

If he crossed the Jordan at Adam, then the best road led eastward through the valley of the Jakkob to its mouth. He had all the more reason to choose this route, because there were two tribally related cities, Succoth and Piniel, there in Gilead. There he hoped for a short rest and for food for his exhausted warriors after their forced marches.

Gideon was bitterly disappointed. The princes of Succoth said, "Are the hands of Zebah and Zalmunna now in thine hand that we should give bread unto thine army?" [4] Gideon was having the same experience that Deborah had had. The long trying years and the forays of revenge had crushed the spirits of the faithful Israelite districts and cities. They did not dare side with Gideon and his men before the enemy was conquered. We can understand the bitterness with which he continued his march, swearing bloody vengeance upon them. When he reached the caravan road, his way led southward. Here he was sure he would meet the enemy.

Gideon's common sense had led him correctly. He had not yet gained a victory, and now he wished fully to annihilate the enemy. If defeated camel riders had once reached the Jordan and especially the caravan road, then it would be impossible for Gideon to overtake them. A later tradition assumes this to be the case and tells of many thousands that small remnant. But the bitter rebuff which sounded like were slain, of whom those Gideon now sought were only a scorn and which Gideon received from the two cities shows all too clearly that Gideon had not yet conquered the enemy. But his clear vision counted upon human weaknesses and shortsightedness.

After the enemy hordes, laden with spoils, had reached the road and with it the edge of the desert, and had traveled a considerable distance southward, they thought it unnecessary to be longer on their guard. They were already several days' march from the section they had so despoiled. If an enemy appeared, in a trice they could disappear into the endless desert where neither peasant nor knight from the country about Shechem and Ophrah could find his way. Thus they believed they might safely indulge themselves.

At a place in the road called Jogbehah (the place is still called Agbehat), a little north of the thirty-second parallel of latitude, they rested comfortably. Carefree, setting only a few guards, they enjoyed a feast. Everything that the fields and orchards produce, is a delicacy to the Bedouins who are almost always half starved. The well-filled Canaanite wine skins did their part to increase their feeling of ease and comfort. So they lay unsuspecting, some feasting and drinking, others drowsy from the wine, still others sleeping. Then like a thunderbolt from a clear sky, misfortune came upon them. With the clash of swords and with wild war cries, Gideon's men fell upon the surprised camp. Rushing in all directions, they sought to escape into the nearby desert. The two chieftains, Zebah and Zalmunna, were captured alive.

Again Gideon had proven himself a wise strategist in military matters, and a daring enthusiast. Again the immediate reward was great booty. The Bedouins were glad to escape with their bare lives on their fleet camels. Their tents, all that they had of treasure, both what they had stolen and what they had brought with them, and the living captives (among them were the two chieftains) fell to the victors. There were many golden rings, golden crescents, earrings, necklaces for man and animals, valuable hangings, cloaks, and whatever else of ornaments and amulets.

But before Gideon could rejoice in his victory and return home, he must avenge Israel and his brothers. His first revenge was to the honor of Israel, for honor was not a mere idea or word in olden Israel. Honor meant life, strength, and power. Who desecrates it injures life and takes from it its best elements. Gideon entered the cities with his captive chieftains, a living testimony of his victory.

Before entering Succoth, he had had a young man make a list of the prominent citizens and of the nobility of Succoth. Even at this time it was possible. There were individuals who had long ago learned to write. In Mohammed's time seventeen men in Mecca could write. Scribes have not been and are not always people of high rank or particularly wise men. Only recently, the following took place in central Arabia. Some one asked the Emir, "Have you a scribe?" and the only scribe of the village was produced. He was a boy of twelve or fourteen years of age who looked half-witted. He took pen and paper, knelt before Ibrahim, and wrote to his dictation, with a characterless, childlike hand, by the dim light of a flickering oil lamp. Armed with a list of seventy-seven names, Gideon reached Succoth, and true to his threat, he had the seventy-seven prominent men "threshed" with desert thorns and spines. The under side of the threshing cart was studded with a mass of sharp flint and basalt stone. For threshing it was drawn across the grain to break open the hulls. The thorns of the desert bramble are like sharp nails and are as long as a finger. Only with reluctance can we imagine the tortures of those who slowly met death in this way. In Peniel, a fortified city, and which had perhaps even offered resistance, he had all the citizens killed and the fortress destroyed.

Now came the vengeance for his murdered brothers.

First he wanted the captives to acknowledge their deeds. Gideon did not wish to shed innocent blood. "What about the men that you killed at Mt. Tabor?" They did not deny the deed. Proud and yet free in their fetters, they frankly acknowledged that their swords had shed noble blood. "They were just like you. Each one looked like a king's son." Now he knew they were the offenders. He gave the command to his son Jether, "Strike them down." This was the old custom. Saint Nilus reports that the Saracens also had their captives killed by boys who proved their manhood by the act. The boy shrank from the deed and could not do it. The Bedouin pride of the desert chieftains was roused. They did not beg for their lives but asked for death at the hand of a man. Then Gideon himself killed them.

Now Gideon was to receive his real reward for his new deed of rescue. "Then the men of Israel said unto Gideon, 'Rule thou over us, both thou and thy son, and thy son's son also, for thou hast saved us out of the land of Midian.'" Now suddenly Israel was awakened. Gideon had set out both times with Abiezer. When he returned a victor the second time, Israel came and voluntarily offered him the hereditary rule.

They did not call it a kingdom. The name "king" stood in ill repute because of the many Canaanite city kings. Yet it meant the same. It is not likely that all of Israel came to him, but probably Manasseh, perhaps a part of Ephraim, and very likely the region to which the name Israel had clung since antiquity.

Legend tells us that Gideon refused the offer at first because God alone was ruler in Israel. If he said this (it is not probable) he quickly changed his mind. He took much of the gold of the spoils, and with it he fitted up a princely sanctuary in Ophrah. He also built a royal palace there with a stately harem. He is said to have reached a very old age and to have left seventy sons.

The noble families and the heads of the clans of Manasseh who had now given Gideon a regal and an hereditary power similar to a kingdom, curtailed their own rights by so doing. They voluntarily gave up a part of their own power to one man, but they knew why they did this. Constant annoyance from the eastern nomads, and at an earlier period, the sufferings at the hands of the Canaanite city states had taught them that it was no longer wise to trust to chance if they wished to maintain their existence; that at the moment of danger, there might not always be armed troops ready to face the enemy, even less a capable leader willing to assume the responsibility.

With Deborah, the woman of God, they had been very successful. At this same time a courageous man named Ehud had appeared in Benjamin and had put an end to the despotism that Moab exercised over Israel beyond the Jordan by assassinating Eglon their king. While farther north, east of the Jordan, Jephthah appeared perhaps at the very same time that Gideon did. Jephthah quieted the hostile Ammonites. But who could guarantee that in the future the leader and the necessary troops would be at hand? The story of Samson leads us to believe that the Philistines were gradually becoming restless and were threatening the interior sections.

Thus it was only an act of self-protection, the outgrowth of their needs, when at least one tribe decided to follow the Canaanite example and establish a permanent government. This hereditary tribal government grew out of the office of commander-in-chief of a tribe or district, or of several tribes which, in the hour of danger and while that danger lasts, had occasionally been established in various places. It was the first attempt to establish a monarchy over a limited territory, the tribal kingdom of Manasseh. Its establishment at this place shows that, at least in the tribe most exposed to the enemy, they had learned to consider political necessity. The first modest attempt to found a state gave evidence of the awakening of political understanding.

Jerubbaal Gideon, the fearless and farsighted leader, twice victorious, the uncompromising avenger of Israel's honor and of his own blood (by which he had proved the nobility of a true knight), was the chosen leader of his tribe. Until old, he held court at Ophrah like a real king. In long years of peace he enjoyed the fruits of his early heroism.

All this we know of him. But what do we know of his attitude toward religion? This question is of real interest to us in connection with this man and with his time.

The name Jerubbaal, meaning Baal battles or Baal is strong, was doubtless chosen as his father's confession of Baal worship. Thus, if we will, his father and he also were Baal worshipers. Then it is very strange that his war cry to the heathen was "Yahweh and Gideon." How did it happen that he put himself under Yahweh's protection, and called upon His helping spirits and powers against the enemy rather than upon Baal? Thus at the very beginning, legend has Yahweh appear to him and say, "Surely I will be with thee and thou shalt smite the Midianites as one man." [5]

This shows us how we may understand his father's naming him after Baal. Saul and even David, whose Yahweh worship is beyond question, each named one of their sons after Baal. Saul's son and successor was Ishbaal, erroneously called Ishbosheth in the text of to-day. This name means a man of Baal. David had a son named Baalyada, i.e., Baal has understood. Jonathan had a son Meribbaal, signifying the man of Baal. On the other hand, Gideon's youngest son was called Jotham, i.e., Yahweh is above reproach; Saul's eldest son was named after Yahweh, Jonathan, or Yehonethan, or Yahweh has given; and David's first born was Adonijah, or Adonijahu, i.e., Yahweh is master. Thus Yahweh then was the God whom David and Saul worshiped, but Baal was the god of the country. His

[76]

altars were everywhere, and with the Canaanites, the Israelites celebrated his feasts. They dared not break with him entirely, and so the first born was named for Yahweh, for they really worshiped him, but in a different sense they dedicated a younger son to Baal. In this way they clung to both deities but not in an equal measure.

Such was probably the practice of both Gideon and his father. We have, therefore, no reason to question the war cry for Yahweh or to believe that the legend that tells us that Yahweh appeared to Jerubbaal erroneously names Yahweh for Baal. Yahweh is correct, except for the fact that this Yahweh was no longer the Yahweh of Moses, not even the Yahweh of Deborah.

After the Canaanite Baal had been shaken off for a time by Deborah, he again gained great power. Yahweh was not consciously rejected; in commerce, in agriculture, in the arts and crafts, and in many of the affairs of everyday life, the Israelites were dependent at every step upon the Canaanites. When the Israelite farmer wished to cultivate his field, he had to learn from the former inhabitants, who for centuries had known the peculiarities of the soil, what it needed and what crops were best. He had to know, also, who the particular deities were who blessed the crops, where they dwelt, in which tree or spring or bowlder. He had to know the wishes of the protecting spirit, the Baal of the place, the secret rites for fulfilling these wishes and for blessing the field. Where could he learn this if not from the Baal worshipers?

Thus the Israelite very naturally came in touch with Baal and his worship. He saw what the Canaanites did. He looked on at their noisy feasts. Occasionally he took part in them and learned to like them. He saw them give thanks for the growth of their crops and observe rites to achieve greater gain. Should he stand apart? Could he do it without injury to himself?

To be sure, the God of his fathers was not Baal but Yahweh, and to the man who upheld Israel, Yahweh he must remain. But the Yahweh of Moses was enthroned upon Mt. Sinai. He had come into the land and had afflicted the people. He had come to help Israel especially when it went to war with its mounted hosts. But was he a god of the fields? of the olive tree and the vine? of the flax and the wool? Was he a god of the fruit trees, or of the springs that brought fertility? If so, how could they gain his favor for the prosperity of man and beast and the increase of garden and field?

These were questions to which neither Moses nor Deborah had given an answer, nor could Gideon answer them. Here was a fatal gap in the religion of Israel which sooner or later must be filled to avoid permanent harm.

Indeed Moses had brought the Yahweh of Sinai to his people, and had impressed this Yahweh deeply upon their souls. The Israelites depended very much upon the great leaders. It was an historical catastrophe for Israel that at the very moment when the Yahweh of Sinai and his people were about to enter Canaan, the great master was taken from them. Upon entering Canaan, the Israelites had to adjust their religion to meet the problems that faced the people in the new country. The religion of Moses, the Yahweh of Moses, must help and counsel his people in their new living conditions. Religion could do this only if Yahweh also became the god of the country into which he led his people. To be sure, in the course of time he did become the god of the country, but at this time he was still the god of Sinai. Thus it happened that, beginning with the post-Mosaic time, the Israelite religion yielded repeatedly to a tendency "to limp on both sides," with which words Elijah reproaches it. They wished to have and to keep Yahweh, yet they believed they could not do without Baal. They compromised as best they could by worshiping Yahweh in their religious services and in other ways, but frequently in rites in which the Canaanites served their Baal. Thus in actual practice, it was often difficult to distinguish between the Yahweh and the Baal service. Much that was intended for Yahweh went by the name of Baal. They named their children for Baal as well as for Yahweh. In these names they partially mean Yahweh, partially Baal. This condition, however indefinite, not final, and frequently wavering, was a true and correct expression of the restless, unsettled, and unfinished conditions in this period of hard struggle.

We have a narrative which tells us that one night Gideon, with the help of ten servants, demolished his father's altar to Baal at Ophrah; that he cut down the asherah, the sacred pillar dedicated to Ashtart, and used the wood for a sacrificial fire at the newly erected altar to Yahweh. This is said to have given him the name of Jerubbaal, Baal disputer.

The very interpretation of the name proves that the narration is not history. But it tells us how the place of sacrifice at Ophrah looked in Gideon's time. Beside the altar on which sacrifice was offered to Yahweh, but in such a way as though he were a Baal and frequently in the name of Baal, stood the emblem of Ashtart, the sacred fruit tree, or its artificial representation. Ashtart was the wife of Baal, the female goddess of fertility for man, beast, and the soil. Since a wife of Yahweh or any female counterpart of him is inconceivable, the people made use of the female counterpart of Baal. Probably much was practiced in the names of Yahweh and Ashtart, which a later period had good reason to designate as "ogling" away from Yahweh, for dissolute actions were characteristic of the Ashtart worship even in the religious services.

At a later time after the Israelites had gradually recognized the evil results of this interchange of Baal and Yahweh, these sanctuaries, like the one here described, were doubtless purged by violence. This may even have been the fate of

[79]

the height at Ophrah at some time, but was not accomplished by Gideon until at a much later time when the people began to purify the ritual.

If all this is merely a legend, the information is certainly historical that Gideon had an ephod made of the rich spoils that he gained from the Midianites. This ephod he set up at Ophrah, so that the people might worship at it. To this day we do not exactly know what an ephod was. It is usually supposed to have been an image of a god. Some suppose it was a bag for lots, others, a valuable garment. The essential fact is that it was something used in worship, originally foreign to the service of Yahweh but usual in the Baal worship. The ephod was certainly a concession to Baal worship, or was used in a form of Yahweh worship similar to the Baal service. This fact was sufficient for the later reviser to see in its use a part of the unchaste Baal worship that became a "snare to Israel."

We do not definitely know, but may assume that Gideon's rule extended over Shechem. At any rate, he had close ties with this old and important city. He had a concubine there who belonged to an old noble family of the city and by whom he had a son who was grown at the time of his death. Whether he himself worshiped the Baal at Shechem is not certain but at the same time is not improbable. At any rate, the Israelites are said to have done so after his death. This makes it seem likely that during his lifetime he had sought for and gained influence in Shechem.

Summing up our facts, we find that in the main Gideon's religion was the same as that of his father, Joash, of his tribesmen, and later subjects. The ceremonies contained so large a mixture of elements of Baal worship that they could hardly be called Yahweh worship. Gideon would have considered himself a Yahweh worshiper, but he would have expected that the altar at Ophrah, its asherah, and the ephod (although both were adapted from Baal) be recognized as belonging to Yahweh. From this we can see how much were the two conceptions of worship already interchanged.

After Gideon's death the supposed hereditary power soon crumbled. There was no dearth of heirs in the palatial home at Ophrah, but Abimelech, the son of the Canaanite concubine at Shechem, was an ambitious bastard. Why should he, a Canaanite half-blood, on his mother's side also of noble family, stand back beside the other sons of Gideon? His decision was quickly made. Perhaps in view of his father's approaching death, he had long harbored the thought which he now quickly carried out.

His mother belonged to a noble family of high repute in Shechem. He succeeded in making the family believe that it would fare better if it were ruled by one of its own people than if it obeyed a stranger. Gideon's seventy sons did not concern Shechem. One man was sufficient to rule the city. The nobility of Shechem were pleased with the proposition to have one of their own citizens as the ruler. Abimelech was clever enough to make no point of being half Israelite. The nobility proposed Abimelech's idea to the burghers, the wealthy landowners who were mostly Canaanites. They, too, favored the plan.

The god of Shechem was called the Baal of the Covenant, or covenant god. It seems that since ancient times the relationship of the god to his people was considered a sort of contract or covenant, and that the name had grown out of this relationship. We know that (perhaps since ancient times) Israelite families had been admitted to Shechem. They may have long dwelt in tents outside of the city gates and gradually have gained entrance into the city. Probably the narration preserved in chapter thirty-four in Genesis makes certain references to this. The Israelites were obliged to adjust themselves as best they could to the Canaanite families, who were descendants of Hamor and named after him. Perhaps it was this conception of a covenant that made

[81]

an understanding possible. Since Moses' time, Israel also had been devoted to the idea that Yahweh had made a covenant with it. With this God of the Covenant, the two parties in Shechem had common ground. It is possible that they accepted their mutual, friendly understanding as a covenant and placed it under the protection of this god.

The people of Shechem took seventy shekels from the temple treasury of the God of the Covenant for Abimelech's ambitious plans. With it he hired a band of unscrupulous adventurers and went with them to Ophrah, forced an entrance into his dead father's palace, and had all his brothers (they are said to have been seventy) slaughtered. He knew every secret corner place in the palace, for he had grown up there together with his half-brothers. In spite of this, the youngest one, Jotham, who had hidden, escaped. The escape is a typical feature in such stories and, therefore, may not be a part of the original one, at least in this form. Then Abimelech returned to Shechem and was solemnly made king by the assembled burghers and the garrison at a holy place, the oak with the landmark near the city. Gideon had never been called king, but his son had the title. After he had prepared the way for his reign by murdering all in the palace at Ophrah, we may safely assume that his rule extended over Ophrah itself and over all of Gideon's territory, except where the people directly refused allegiance to him, as was the case in Thebez and Beer.

Abimelech did not long enjoy the possessions gained by murder and violence. He had scarcely ruled three years over Israel when his fortune changed. It is strange that now again as in Gideon's case when control was offered Abimelech, the narrator speaks of "Israel." Again it seems that Abimelech took over his father's government as it was. The people of Shechem became unfaithful to him. They began to injure him by robbing his caravans. This was reported to him.

It is strange that Abimelech who was city king at Shechem did not live there. This, too, indicates his being or wishing to be king of Manasseh. He was much occupied outside of Shechem; probably there were many feuds. A lucrative caravan trade seems to have provided the means for them. The Phœnician ports needed various products of the interior, especially grain, oil, figs, wool, and flax. Whoever had power in the intermediary region could carry on a thriving trade. Of course, a large share of the gains came to the king's residence. If Abimelech permanently remained away from Shechem, the citizens felt this absence in their diminished wealth. Therefore they were dissatisfied and arbitrarily reimbursed themselves. They had touched the weak spot of the new king. If his income ceased, how could he reign, much less carry on war?

Abimelech could not allow this state of affairs to continue. Something must be done. If he hesitated longer than seemed wise, it may have been because of the city's internal quarrels. Perhaps he hoped that the different parties there would mutually bring about peace and make his interference unnecessary. We do not definitely understand conditions because we do not know the details concerning the parties. We recognize at once, however, that there was much confusion in the city, and that the citizens together with a certain Gaal, who with his adherents had come into the city, were glad of an opportunity to find much fault with Abimelech; and that Abimelech's city captain, Zebul, who ruled the city in the king's absence, had an increasingly difficult position.

Finally, Zebul became helpless. Gaal grew so increasingly hostile that Zebul feared he would gradually lose control in the city. He then sent messengers to Abimelech urging him to action. Gaal marched out to meet Abimelech who drove him back into the city. Defeated, Gaal entered the city but was finally driven out by governor Zebul's men.

Even now the city was by no means in Abimelech's hands.

The estrangement was too great, and the insurrection against the new king had apparently taken all too deep roots. This may explain Abimelech's puzzling retreat immediately before the city gates. His governor, Zebul, was not well enough established to support him. Abimelech waited for an opportunity to surprise the people. The next morning he attacked the unsuspecting inhabitants from an ambush in the fields. He killed without mercy all he captured. At the same time he occupied the gates, took the city by storm, and killed all who were within. He destroyed the city itself and scattered salt over it.

Only the fortress which stood apart could hold its own. There, also, was the temple of the God of the Covenant. A thousand men and women had fled to it. After the city fell, they hid in the subterranean chambers of the temple. Abimelech and his followers ascended a neighboring hill. He cut down a bush and carried it on his shoulders and, commanding his followers to do the same, returned to the temple, heaped the wood around the cellar, and set it afire. The fire and the smoke that penetrated all the passages of the cellar killed all who had taken refuge there.

Now Shechem, although a heap of ruins and a field of the dead, was in Abimelech's possession. The many feuds of which we already have heard continued. Thus soon after this, Abimelech was obliged to fight at Thebez a little to the northeast of Shechem. He had already captured the city, but the fortress, a castle tower, remained unconquered. After setting fire to the gate, he hoped to gain the tower by storm. With firebrand in hand he approached the tower gate. Then a woman on the battlement above seized a millstone, threw it down upon his head, and crushed his skull. Women and maidens had charge of the millstones, for they ground the daily supply of meal between two stones which they laid one over the other. The dying king quickly called to his armor bearer, "Draw thy sword and kill me, that men say not of me, a woman slew him." [6] The servant did as he was bidden.

When the woman on the tower crushed Abimelech's skull, she shattered his power also. For generations the disgrace suffered by Abimelech reëchoed in Israel, but Gideon's deeds and his fame shone brightly through the centuries.

Abimelech was really a straggler of the Amarna period. His type is in keeping with the adventurers who flourished at the expense of the Egyptian government as well as of their own city states. He belonged with Abdi Ashirta, Ribaddi, Aziru, and especially with Lapaja. It is possible that he consciously took up their work again. Lapaja had formerly founded a kingdom in the same region. It crumbled when he died, but its memory may easily have been retained in the country about Shechem.

V

SAMUEL AND SAUL

THE first attempt to found a state in Israel had failed miserably, stifled in the blood of Gideon's sons. The little that remained of the state lay trampled underfoot with the crushed head of Abimelech, but the time was not distant when, instead of a state in Israel, a state of Israel must come. The experiment had shown the one thing that was worth the making. As long as Gideon had power, no enemy had ventured to disturb Israel's peace. Should any one now attempt it, the only way to maintain Israel's nationality would be to create a strong government including all of Israel. In Gideon, the elders of Manasseh had pointed out the way. Now the elders of Israel must follow in Manasseh's footsteps.

The only serious disturbances reported in the time when Gideon and Abimelech ruled occurred in the east. The territory of Gilead was so near the extreme border of Israel that the people as a whole concerned themselves little about its welfare. Thus disturbances might happen there without having serious consequences for Canaan as a whole, especially when these border people succeeded in conquering the enemy with their own forces.

The example of the Midianites seems to have stimulated the Ammonites, and perhaps also the Moabites, to similar action! The latter dwelt east of the mouth of the Jordan and the northern half of the Dead Sea. The former were settled to the north and partly to the east of them. Probably at the time of Israel's immigration they occupied the back country east of Gilead and were the link between Transjordania and the desert. They desired to extend their territory westward, and, therefore, persecuted the Israelites of the tribe of Gad and Manasseh who dwelt there. A banished Israelite bastard named Jephthah left the country and became the leader of a group of daring fellows—adventurous freebooters. In their distress, the people of Gilead remembered and recalled Jephthah. He was willing to come and help them only if, as a reward for his help, he should be made chief of Gilead.

The nobles of Gilead agreed, and he came. He conquered the Ammonites, and thus attained the position in Gilead that Gideon had occupied in the house of Joseph as ruler and judge of the district. This principality seems to have been displeasing to its southern neighbors in Moab and to have caused a feud with them. Here again Jephthah was victorious, but he had to pay most dearly for his recovery. In the stress of battle he made an ill-considered vow. His daughter, his only child, who with her maidens danced the dance of victory, was the sacrifice for his vow. A feast of mourning, celebrated every year by the maidens of Gilead in the mountains, tells posterity of Jephthah's fame and of his great sorrow.

Such mourning feasts are so frequently reported that we cannot discuss the mourning for Jephthah's daughter alone. We know that there were mourning feasts for the departed Osiris, for Tamiz, for the Phœnician Canaanite Adonis, for the Aramænan Hadad-Rimmon, for the Phrygian Attis, and for the mystic Hylos. In the case of Jephthah, too, the celebration was probably an old feast of nature in honor of the early dying of spring. From this viewpoint, the already-colorless figure of Jephthah becomes even less tangible than it was before. As to the rest, the description given above covers the principal facts.

At this time, neither Ammon nor Moab were a real danger to Israel. Therefore, conflicts with them did not seriously influence the nation's fate. The blow that set the ball rolling came from a different direction.

We have already heard that, from the days of the Pharaoh Meneptah and, especially, during the reign of Rameses III, the so-called Maritime Peoples oppressed Egypt greatly. They came from different direction by land and by sea; many from the southern and southwestern parts of Asia Minor. Before they attacked the delta, great hordes of them overran western Syria and the coast regions of Palestine. To be sure, Rameses III defeated them and ostensibly destroyed them, but he could not prevent individuals among them from settling in the country. One group of them, the Philistines, we are certain of. In the Egyptian inscriptions they are called Pursati, a name which vocally corresponds to the Hebrew Pelishti, the Israelite name for the Philistines. The Old Testament connects them with the Island of Crete. This association is supported by the type of costume which we find in Cretan monuments. Their armor of felt helmets, cuirasses and large shields, spears and swords suggests that they may have come originally from Asia Minor, having been forced as a whole or in sections into Crete by Rameses III, but from there again found their way to Canaan. The year 1100 found them in the region south of Mount Carmel.

Here they made a number of independent settlements: Gaza, Ashkelon, Ashdod, Gath. These were city states similar to those of the Canaanites, except for the fact that they were all ruled by Seranim, which word probably signifies a type of tyrant. The different communities were in closer touch with one another than were the Canaanite cities, and they seem to have formed a confederacy in which each city in turn served as the capital.

The sea was their natural boundary. Thus every attempt to extend their territory, except toward the north, was at the

expense of Israel, for the desert begins just south of Gaza.
When with ox teams their first hordes entered the country
about 1200, probably from Asia Minor, the Israelites were
having their first struggles to conquer the country. Thus
early the Philistines must have quarreled with the tribe of
Dan and certain clans of Judah for the possession of the
western slopes of the southern mountain region. In the
history of the tribe of Dan and its wanderings northward, we
have a part of these struggles; another part may be gathered
from the story of Samson. At least, so much of the story is
history that for a long time the Israelites and the Philistines
of that section had much to do with each other and occasionally attacked each other. But the time of petty annoyances
ended. What had been successful in Dan might also succeed
in Benjamin and Ephraim, and then in Israel as a whole. No
time seemed more favorable than the collapse of Gideon's
government and the death of his son.

Certainly, Ekron, Ashdod, and the interior of the Philistine country watched eagerly all that was happening in
Israel. Twice after the Philistines had come into the country, a short-lived attempt had been made to unite tribes, or
at least clans. After a short period of success both attempts
failed: the first, in Deborah's time; the second, under Gideon.
Would they make a third attempt? And, if so, would they
succeed better than before? Internal quarrels among the
tribes of Israel (a hereditary weakness) and the Canaanites,
whom they had not yet conquered and who were like a great
thorn in Israel's flesh, made it seem worth while to venture
a counter attempt.

Thus a decade or two after Gideon, about 1080, we suddenly find the Philistines making a great attack upon the
Israelites' country. This time their goal was no longer the
border villages of Judah, but the far more fertile mountain
region of Ephraim and the plain of Jezreel. The gathering
of their armies at Aphek in the Valley of Sharon indicated

[89]

this. From there they hoped to force the ascent to the ridge of the mountain region, to go on toward Shiloh, and to enter the plain. The Israelites met them in battle and were defeated. Shiloh seems to be near the place where the battle was fought, or rather the place from whence they retreated. Thus the enemy must have advanced through the *wadi der ballut* which runs from the plain along the coast toward Shiloh. The battlefield of Eben Eser must have been in or near it.

It is significant that we hear only of Israel or of its elders. The latter made the decisions. No general is named, nor are the tribes that took part in the battle. It seems that the people of Ephraim, who were most threatened, joined with Benjamin and parts of Manasseh to gather as many troops as they possibly could. Apparently they lacked a united leadership. Certainly they lacked a strong man in command. Apparently a good warrior would not have had difficulty in so favorable a position to defend the mountain region against an attack from below.

When the tribe was seriously threatened in battle, the Arabs resorted to an extreme measure to rouse the discouraged warriors to renewed activity. A sort of sacred tent or palanquin was carried on the backs of camels to the battlefield. The sight of this token, supported by the women who accompanied it to incite the warriors to increased martial action, often worked wonders. The King of Persia did the same thing. Xerxes was preceded by an empty chariot drawn by three white steeds. It was the throne of the invisible god of heaven. What the holy tabernacle was in Moses' time, the ark seems to have been now. Thus the Israelites brought the holy ark of Yahweh from Shiloh into the camp of Israel. It cannot have been far to the east of the battlefield, for on the eve of battle the messenger had returned.

The appearance of the ark in the camp of the defeated Israelites was greeted with a cry of joy so loud that the earth seemed to tremble. Now Israel must succeed. The Philistines, into whose camp the noise and its significance penetrated, were seized with cold terror: "God himself has come into their camp!" But they proved themselves true warriors. Danger caused them to summon all their strength. Death or servitude—that was their fate if defeated. With this watchword they rushed forward, and the victory was theirs. Israel's ranks wavered. They had been overconfident. Thirty thousand dead are said to have covered the field. Four thousand had fallen the first time. The ark was captured by the enemy. Its priests, Hophni and Phinehas, were killed.

After the unfortunate battle, a messenger rushed to the temple city of Shiloah where the venerable old priest Eli, the father of the two priests who had been killed, anxiously awaited news. The terrifying report—"Thy sons fallen, the ark lost"—caused the old man's death. With a stroke of apoplexy he fell from his chair. The victors followed closely at the heels of the messenger. The city was captured, the sanctuary demolished. Then the victor occupied the mountain districts and installed governors in the south as far as Gilbeath near the Judean boundary. In the north, too, they seem to have spread as far as the plain of Jezreel and to have gathered tribute from all the country, so that of central Canaan, all that was Israelite, now came into the control of the Philistines. The victors took the ark with them to Ashdod. In the temple of their god Dagon, as a splendid trophy, it was to bear witness of their victory. A great misfortune in the form of a pestilence, perhaps a pestilence connected with a plague of mice, overran the whole country. The soothsayers among the Philistines explained it as caused by Yahweh's injured feelings. Then the ark was returned to Bethshemesh near the Israelite border. Although we know that the narrative was embellished with much of a legendary nature, I cannot agree with some modern scientists who say that the Philistines would never have given up Israel's holy palanquin had they possessed it. Superstition knows no bounds; fear of the revenge of the gods defies all reason.

In Israel itself conditions were grievous. In sections both south and north of the mountain region and even in parts of the interior, the Canaanites still held their cities, while in other sections they were partially or entirely feudal servants of the Israelites. All these people may have rejoiced at first over the Philistine victory! By an alliance with the latter, they might still realize the hope that they had buried after Gideon's time; i.e., to be rid again of Israel. Possibly they soon learned that they fared better under the Israelite rule than under the Philistine yoke, for we hear nothing of their joining forces with the Philistines and have no evidence of their causing Israel difficulty later in its war of liberation.

We do not know how long Israel lived in ignominious servitude, but a generation or more must have elapsed before any effort was made in Israel toward freedom. If this condition continued, then there was reason to fear that the masses would accustom themselves to it. A people unaccustomed to freedom is incapable of making great decisions. In its servitude it soon sees dependence imposed upon it by God. The danger of succumbing to this condition rose threateningly on Israel's political horizon. Unless a man appeared who had power over them, the history of Israel was to end before it had really begun, with the nation only in its early stage of development. They could be helped only by remembering Gideon, or perhaps more, by remembering Deborah. If Israel still had strength enough to rouse itself and shake off its fetters, it could attain actual freedom only if all who were now under the Philistine yoke formed a strong alliance. If the present distress did not unite them, they were hopelessly lost. Perhaps the union itself was not sufficient to free them from their present state. If we study the reason for their collapse by looking below the surface, we perceive that the cause was not merely the military superiority of the Philistines.

Wherever in history we see a political collapse occur, or whenever we ourselves experience one, we do well to remember that the deepest roots of a nation's power rests in its spiritual strength. If these roots are healthy, the outer life of the people will develop along a sane course; if unhealthy, the consequence will unfailingly appear in the decisions and actions of the people. What we know of Gideon's religion leads us to suspect that the Israelite masses from the time of his coming were exposed to the enervating influence of the Canaanite Baal religion, and that this influence increased with time. If, then, a union was to be effected and the united peoples were to assume the responsibility for the continued success, the moral attitude of the tribes must again be brought into a condition suitable for success. In Deborah's time two things had worked together: the unification of the people, and their return to the Yahweh of Moses. Now, too, only the fulfillment of this double requirement could lead to success.

The man who possessed both of these ideas was Samuel. According to trustworthy tradition, Samuel's birthplace was Ramah, perhaps to-day *er-ram* on the southern slope of the central Palestine mountain region and only a few hours' journey to the north of Jerusalem. His family belonged to the tribe of Ephraim. His mother is said to have brought him, as a little child, to the sanctuary of Shiloh, and dedicated him to God. There under the guidance of the priest, Eli, he was initiated into the ritual of the service in the temple. When still very young, he had strange visions. Shocked, he looked on at the unworthy, shameful actions of Eli's sons, who, it seemed to him, desecrated the temple of Yahweh; perhaps they even served in the temple. One night Yahweh appeared to him, the severe, jealous Yahweh of Sinai, not the negligent, weary Yahweh of Ophrah. What

[93]

Samuel heard frightened him so much that he ventured to tell Eli of his vision only when the priest earnestly pressed him to do so. He had seen the judgment that was to come over Eli's house; the evil was not to remain unpunished.

Thus early, Samuel became both a seer and a priest, and he remained both. With the Arabs and with many other peoples, these characters are virtually one: the prophet to whom God reveals Himself, the seer who sees God and His will, and the priest who conducts His services and makes known God's laws, his tora, to the people. All this the seer knows only by revelation from God. As a priest and a seer, Samuel later traveled about the country each year to "speak justice" in Bethel, in Gilgal, and in Mizpah. Then he returned to Ramah, and the rest of the year he spoke justice there. In Ramah he also built an altar for Yahweh. So much we learn from a narrator who expresses himself thus about Samuel's work. We also hear much of the so-called "Judges" from other sources; apparently they were men like Jephthah or Gideon. His building an altar shows Samuel to have been also a priest, and his speaking justice and instructing the people shows him to have been the priest and a man chosen of God, as Deborah was a woman chosen of God. As a priest he slaughtered the sacrificial beast, and as a man of God he blessed it, i.e., he spoke the priest's blessing over the sacrifice. This priestly service made the sacrifice of value. Thus we see that the offices of priest and judge were closely connected.

Doubt has been expressed as to whether Samuel ever was in Shiloh. I do not share this doubt. Even if he did not grow up in Shiloh, the destruction of the house of Eli and of the sanctuary at Shiloh must have made a deep impression upon the young seer. The terrible judgment of the god whom Moses had known as a consuming fire, and of whom he had told his people, left no doubt in Samuel's mind how he should look upon the present and the future of his people.

[94]

From Samuel dates the expression that obedience is better than the best sacrifice. For a long time we doubted whether a man of his time could have expressed so great a thought. Now we have proof that the same thought was uttered in Egypt long before Samuel's day. Thus our doubt recedes, and the possibility that a man of God in olden Israel harbored such thoughts seems more likely. To us Samuel's conception seems to approach more nearly the earnest Yahweh of Moses who judged strictly and punished moral failure severely. We need have no hesitancy in considering Samuel as the one who revived Mosaic thought and traditions.

A late tradition tells us that when Samuel came unexpectedly to Bethlehem to anoint David, the elders of the city, trembling in awe and submission, came to him. This is an exaggerated description of admiring posterity. It does, however, reflect the fact that he made a deep and lasting impression even upon his contemporaries. Posterity may make a pious man into a saint and paint a halo about his head, but it seldom makes the mistake of giving a halo to one known to be unworthy. If Samuel traveled about the country, pursuing his priestly office, sacrificing, preaching Yahweh, teaching, blessing, ministering to the people, as is the duty of the true priest, if the people came to him to ask for counsel in their affairs and to know God's will, he was surely a highly respected man, whose word was authority far and wide, at least in all of Ephraim and Benjamin and, probably, beyond their borders. Had it not been so, and even if, at this time, he had not been an illustrious and far-famed personality, would the elders have listened to him, and would his time and posterity have looked upon him as the man who should crown Saul?

The people's distress was so great that it stirred the heart of every one interested in Israel's welfare. The question as to what was to become of Israel had to grow more disturbing in each decade lest action come too late. If Samuel was fifteen years old when he had that vision, twenty when Shiloh was destroyed, at the time of Israel's distress, he must have been between fifty-five and sixty. We meet him again only as a man of mature years, if not as an aged man. Surely he had not been idle during the intervening years. In his wanderings and his services as priest and seer, in teaching and preaching to all, in ministering to individuals, he may always have emphasized this one thing: "Forget not the distress of thy people! forget not the state it has fallen into, and consider how to turn it aside!" In the days before Germany's humiliation in 1813, from hundreds of pulpits, in hundreds of workshops, and in thousands of discussions and addresses, without agitation and without political tendency, the one theme was: How can our nation attain inner resurrection from its collapse? As it must be and should be everywhere where a people hopes to rise from downfall, here in Israel it also came to pass.

Samuel surely was not the only one who keenly felt Israel's distress; supposing he were the only one, he was not the man to remain so.

The government of Israel was fundamentally the same as it had been at the time the Israelites entered Canaan. The Canaanites had long developed what ancient Greece called city states; the noble families of the city, through their representatives who were called city elders or city councilors, had charge of the government of the community. Wherever there was a city king (as was almost invariably the case) in the Amarna period and even later, although gradually the city government under the oligarchic monarch seems to have predominated, the king had to make his peace with the nobility, and, because of this, his position was frequently a difficult one. We need only remind the reader of Abimelech in Shechem. The Israelites were still in possession of the lesser number of the more important cities. Wherever this was the case, they probably kept the arrangement of govern-

ing the city by nobility or elders, but abolished the city kingdom, as the examples of Jabesh in Gilead and, probably, also
of Succoth and Peniel in the Gideon story show. When the
Israelites entered the cities and occupied them along with
the older inhabitants, as they did at Shechem before it was
destroyed by Abimelech and, probably, in many other cities,
they doubtless succeeded by means of the prominence of their
families in gaining influence and representation in the gov-
ernments. At that time, certainly, a large part of Israel
lived outside of the cities on their farms or with their flocks,
like the man in the mountains of Ephraim whom the Danites
in their wanderings northward attacked and robbed. These
are the people of whom, at a much later period when the army
was disbanded, it still was said, "Every man went to his
tent." They, too, were represented by noble chiefs and
elders. The local federations established in Canaan were
not so authoritative as were the clan federations retained
from olden times, for the later were preserved and were
effective together with the newer forms. Thus it happened
that for a long time in Israel and, certainly at this time, the
elders of a district or of the nation were mentioned together
with the elders of the cities.

From this we can imagine who the people were who were
willing to save Israel when the danger of extinction was
greatest. Surely, there were men among the city nobles and
among the elders of the clans and families who thought as
Samuel did. If this were not the case, surely Samuel did not
allow the years and decades of his activity to go by without
working among the influential men whose voices were heard
among the people, that they might know how much was at
stake for the nation. Surely, when they felt the danger, they
must have been willing to act when opportunity presented
itself.

Just here Samuel must have begun his work. We know
that where there is mention of measures to be taken to help

Israel out of her present distress by making new laws, the elders of Israel are represented as playing a prominent part. All the elders of Israel gathered and came to Samuel with the request: "Give us a king." This account, doubtless, includes a part of what actually happened. A kingdom, not merely consisting of a tribe but of all Israel, the State of Israel, not merely a city state, was their goal. If we would answer the question how Saul became king, we must begin at this point. In him we have mentioned the second name without which this period cannot be understood. From our youth we have been familiar with the tale that the son of a distinguished man in Benjamin, therefore one of its noblemen, named Saul, set out with his servants to seek his father's lost asses. While doing so he made the acquaintance of the seer, Samuel. Samuel was pleased with the stately, unusually fine-looking young man who towered a head taller than all other people. He kept Saul with him a day, and when they parted, he pronounced the words of the Seer, "Yahweh has anointed thee to be a captain over his inheritance, and thou shalt save the people out of the hand of the Philistines." With these words he anointed him with the sacred oil, and Saul became the anointed of God.

We have a second version from which we have already quoted a sentence. The elders came to Samuel asking for a king. In this request Samuel saw treason to Yahweh, the sole king of Israel and a turning to heathen customs. The elders wanted to be like all the heathen round about them. Samuel showed them the consequences: the King would take their sons and daughters for his service, their fields and orchards for his officials, and make them themselves his servants. Yet they insisted upon their wish, and he granted it. The choice was made by lot, and Saul became King.

Much comment is unnecessary. We can clearly see that neither of these versions is a true chronicle; both, however, contribute something to an understanding of the facts. The first narration is a beautiful idyl which pleased every Israelite who heard it, but kingdoms are not distributed in this idyllic fashion. Then, too, Saul, the father of a grown son, was not the youth the legends make him. It is probably true that Samuel played an important part and that he anointed Saul, and it is probable also that this came as a complete surprise to Saul. The second version is erroneous in portraying Samuel as advising against a king or, indeed, as being roused to anger by their desire for one. A later generation having unsatisfactory experiences with the monarch may have thought thus. We must remember the unfortunate decay that was so soon to be the fate of the kingdom, especially the northern partial state of Israel. With this in mind, the well-intentioned patriots seriously asked the question: Was the introduction of the monarchial government a failure, after all? Would the country not have fared better with its old freedom and its ideal kingdom of Yahweh? This narration is the result of such considerations. The narrator does not conceal his opinion about republics and monarchies, as we call them to-day. He imagines Samuel thought as he thinks, but this is not the case.

In spite of this, the narration contains important truths. It teaches us that the nobility, who were the leaders of the people, joined with Samuel to bring about a new form of government, the state of Israel. A whole train of circumstances has led us to recognize that this was very possible. Here we have it verified. The narration also shows us that Samuel was held in great esteem; his word, his counsel, and his decision were decisive for the fate of the nation. He neither acted without other men, nor followed sudden and unconsidered impulses, as the idyl states in an account as impressive to the hearer as it seems improbable to the historian. He acted, jointly with the elders, after careful consideration. This, doubtless, was the course of events.

If Samuel agreed with the representatives of the nation

[99]

that there was no other outward way to restore the nation to power and free it from the Philistine yoke than to return to the tradition of Gideon and even to go beyond it by placing the government of the tribes permanently in a strong hand, he still lacked the strong man. To find him was a task in itself, and when found, the man must be given an opportunity to prove himself the one chosen of God. All this came about.

Jephthah had conquered the Ammonites, the robberlike semi-Bedouins of the east. As long as Jephthah ruled, the Ammonites did not dare make any warlike movements. After his death, the government may have collapsed and the enemy again begun to assert itself. After the fall of Gideon's kingdom and, especially, after the decisive Philistine victory, the Ammonites had a splendid opportunity to profit by the favorable conditions. Thus we now find them united under King Nahash, i.e., serpent, and very actively extending their territory into the eastern part of the country at Israel's expense. It may be accident that we hear of only one city that suffered violence at their hands. It probably was not the only one. The cities on the Jakkob, such as Succoth and Peniel which we have already assumed to be Israelite cities, may have suffered the same fate; perhaps, also Mahanaim in the upper wadi of Jabesh, the northern valley parallel to the Jakkob valley.

The city of Jabesh must have been in this same wadi of Jabesh. Nahash attacked it. He haughtily refused settlement offered by the people, but he did agree that Jabesh should first seek help in Israel. If it did not come in seven days, the city would surrender. The story of this agreement seems possible. Israel's hopeless condition and the civil strife made the arrival of auxiliary troops seem out of the question. But Nahash wished to prevent, in his own ranks, bloodshed so inevitable in any attack. Contrary to all expectations, assistance came. The messengers crossed the Jordan. In

Gibeah, where Saul dwelt, there was great mourning. Returning from the field with his cattle, Saul heard it and its origin. Moved by the spirit of Yahweh, he seized two oxen, quartered them, and sent the messengers with them throughout the country bearing the message: "He who does not follow Saul, his cattle shall suffer this fate." This call aroused the people. They arose, and the storm broke. By way of Bezek, Saul crossed the Jordan. Very early in the morning he attacked the Ammonite camp and destroyed it. In the glamor of victory the knightly hero returned. At Gilgal, a place of sacrifice near Shiloh, the grateful people, at Samuel's suggestion, crowned him.[1]

Now Saul was king. How it happened the description above tells us. Samuel, the seer, was the leading spirit, and with him the elders of Israel joined in the desire for a kingly leader. The seer's eye fell on the tall, handsome, vigorous nobleman of Gibeah in Benjamin. Physical advantages were a sign of divine favor. It is possible that Samuel had observed him for some time and had been pleased with him. Ramah and Gibeah are so near each other that if the people wished, they could see each other daily. When messengers came from Jabesh, they certainly did not pass the great seer by. He called their attention to Gibeah and the stately nobleman there. If Saul stood the test, Samuel knew what was Yahweh's will. Saul stood the test and returned victorious. The crown was his. Then Samuel must have anointed him before all the people and must have spoken the words that we have already heard.

Now the people had a king. He knew for what purpose they needed him and the task that awaited him. Every one talked of it. Not in vain did Samuel (according to the legend) whisper to him as he anointed him to do what his hand found to do; God would be with him. The words were not spoken at that time, but they admirably expressed the reason for the choice of a king and of the anointing. Freedom from the Philistine yoke, that and nothing else, must necessarily be the watchword of the new ruler. He must act quickly. Long delay and elaborate plans might kill the project in the germ. Certainly, the departure for Jabesh, the sudden raising of the siege of the city, the victorious return, the choice of the king, and the first attack of the Philistines, all followed in rapid succession. All this can have been the work of but a few days. We cannot otherwise explain why the Philistines did not interfere. If from the very day when they saw Israel taking serious measures they did not interfere and violently check the movement, they gave themselves the death blow. Events must have followed in such rapid succession that the governors in the country, still bewildered, would be considering what to do when the second and third blow followed. Only by the fact that one event crowded upon another can we explain the passive attitude of the enemy and Israel's success. The present narrative blurs the train of events by the use of diverting interpolations, such as Samuel's farewell speech. Immediately after his return from Jabesh, Saul and his grown son, Jonathan, began the struggle for freedom. A part of the collected troops were not even dismissed. Jonathan gave the signal for a general insurrection by murdering the hostile governor in Gibeah, and, meanwhile, Saul again sounded the call to arms. The battle cry, "Our own freedom and the downfall of the Philistines!" and the fresh military laurels of the new king were far more effective than his first call to arms for Jabesh. The Philistines, too, gathered their hosts. They are reported to have had fine cavalry. The people were already fleeing into caves and cliffs as in Gideon's time. While the two hostile armies were facing each other for some time, a bold stroke on Jonathan's part brought success. Climbing recklessly, he and his armor bearer crossed the canyon of Michmash, surprised the enemy, and brought disastrous panic into the enemy's camp. Then Saul began the battle which soon became the pursuit of the disbanded enemy. He gained a great victory. It even seems that the Philistines, at least most of them, were pushed back beyond Aijalon to the coast plain. They may have rallied there again, for they were not destroyed.

We can state only approximately how large Saul's territory was. It certainly included the entire mountain region of Ephraim, the tribe of Benjamin, also the tribal territory of Manasseh, as well as the greater part of Asser and Zebulon. How far Saul's territory reached over into Galilee and Judah in the beginning, our sources do not state. Since Samuel's sons are supposed to have dwelt in Beersheba, it is probable that this sanctuary was included. In time Saul probably also claimed both Galilee and Judah, even if, as David's story shows us, only with partial success. By his victory at Jabesh, the eastern part of Israel, as far as it was free to do so, unconditionally fell to Saul, while the war with Amalek suggests possession of Judah.

King Saul was like a brilliant meteor vanishing as rapidly as it came. Attracting the attention of all, making all hearts beat proudly with joy, and arousing great hopes, it appeared on Israel's horizon. Hardly risen, not yet having reached the zenith, the meteor turned quickly, only to sink and to fall slowly lower and lower. The brilliant hero, like a shining Siegfried, had killed the dragon, Ammon, and then in a swift course of victory, cheered by the people, with laurels crowning his brow, wearing the sparkling regal crown, having driven the country's enemy to the boundary, was suddenly halted and held as if spellbound by an invisible hand. Saul was like a steed that is unexpectedly checked in the midst of the joyful course, that stops, leaves the road, shies, and is turned from its course. The tall hero, whose noble appearance had been the delight of all who saw him, was bowed down. His clear, frank countenance was darkened, his sparkling eyes dimmed, clouded the brow that had formerly

[103]

been held so high, that had reflected confidence, good fortune, and success. Furrows of grief and care marred his noble visage. Saul was the image of a man suddenly broken, an oak that was shattered in a night by lightning, or uprooted by a hurricane.

We do not definitely know what happened, but from many hints and from the whole course of events, we can attempt to surmise it.

He succeeded in one more deed, the last one definitely attested. Already fate threateningly cast its dark shadows ahead. He could not rejoice in his success. Then with gigantic strides, he approached the abyss.

In Moses' time the desert tribe of Amalek had pitched their tents in the region about Mt. Sinai and had contested Moses' right to the oases there. Moses fought against them. Then they seem to have controlled the steppes between the Sinai Peninsula and Palestine. The feud was of long duration. Meanwhile, they succeeded in establishing a kingdom on the southern border of Judah. Its mere existence was a threat for Israel. The robber-like nature of these Bedouin states made trouble a certainty. Indeed, it seems that the struggle with these ancient and ever-hostile opponents was a struggle for life or death, a struggle which the Israelites regarded as a holy war. Certainly Samuel considered it such. Already there must have been much bloodshed. In such cases blood revenge, the wreckless slaughter of all enemies who fell into their hands, was the traditionary and sanctified custom. This custom Israel had followed ever and anon; this, the Moabites followed now. The custom was certainly an unworthy one. But when we of to-day, considering such matters, are overcome with sympathy and give expression to our feeling of revulsion, we may forget, all too quickly, that in our own recent wars there have been times and places when without much hesitancy the word has been: "We grant no pardon."

Saul made the attack and drove back the enemy to the Egyptian border. He captured many soldiers, much cattle, and even King Agag. The captives, according to an agreement with Samuel, seem to have been killed. The cattle and the captured king, Saul spared. Why destroy the valuable booty? Why should he, though victor to-day, draw the bow all too taut? Amalek still existed even though Agag was captured. And who can say whether it is wise, in facing the morrow, to burn the bridges of to-day?

We of to-day can understand this reasoning. It does honor to Saul's heart and, in this case, perhaps, to his sound reasoning, yet of this we cannot be sure. Samuel thought differently. It seems as if a second Moses stood before us. Michel Angelo would have represented Samuel thus if he had portrayed him. As Moses appeared with eyes flashing in righteous indignation, and broke his tablets in the idolatrous camp, so the seer now cast to the ground the crown from the head of the king whom he himself had crowned, saying, "Yahweh hath rejected thee!" Then the man of God seized a sword, and with his own hand, struck the captive king dead.

"As thy sword hath made women childless, so shall thy mother be childless among women."

With this Samuel departed: "And Samuel came no more to see Saul until the day of his death." [2]

An abyss opens before us, as deep and as tragic as few in history. Two men, who had worked hand in hand for the welfare of the people and whose highest aim was the prosperity of the people, saw a rift open between them over which no bridge led, a rift which was to separate them for all time. They were men so different that they repelled each other; they had different points of view.

This incident gives us a glimpse of the many differences which later separated the kings of Israel and Judah from the men of God: Elijah, Isaiah, Jeremiah. Indeed this is

[105]

only the prelude to many struggles. Modern historians have even interpreted the clash between Samuel and Saul as the first example of the gigantic conflict between spiritual and worldly power, a conflict which extends through all history and which reached its climax in the struggle between the emperors and the popes in the Middle Ages. The rôle of the tyrannical and quarrelsome priest is ascribed to Samuel. The present frequently unintelligible texts suggest this more than do the historical facts. As far as we can see, it was not a question of power with Samuel and Saul. Not as opponents, in a struggle for power or control over the people, did Samuel face Saul, but as opponents in a struggle for God. It was their philosophy, their conception of God and things divine, that separated them.

Primarily the question was not one of blood revenge; whether Agag and his flocks lived or died was not the deciding and the final question, but one of many questions. Saul championed the conception that is pleasing to us from the human standpoint: why shed more blood and cause more misery than is absolutely necessary for self-protection? Samuel championed the old severity that would hear nothing of modern weakening of the ancient holy laws. The difference was not one of persons or single instances, but of principle. The day when Samuel killed Agag and returned home was certainly not the first day upon which the two men had had differences. It was only the day when the break became public and irreparable. The difference had long existed, but now they both saw clearly, Samuel first, that they could no longer work together. We ask what occurred?

In youth Samuel had received deep and lasting impressions. In ardent prayer his mother had besought Yahweh for her son. In fervent thanksgiving, she had praised Yahweh for hearing her prayer, and had dedicated her son to his service. Samuel was a St. Augustine, the son of many prayers and tears. They influenced his whole life. After

[106]

such impressions he went to Shiloh. The venerable form of the aged Eli could not deceive him into believing that in Shiloh they served Yahweh as he did in his heart, nor did they revere the Yahweh of Samuel's heart. The saying is ascribed to the aged Samuel that sorcery, magic, resistance, and teraphim were evil and unchaste. It is quite possible that he said this. At any rate, we see how immediate posterity regarded him: it justly assumes he might have said this. What is ascribed to him here corresponds with the experiences that he had daily in Shiloh. The base dealings of Eli's sons greatly impressed him. How could they reconcile their acts with the stern Yahweh of Moses? Samuel saw at Ophrah, and probably at many another sanctuary as well as in the homes, the ephod, teraphim, images of God and all sorts of unwholesome ritual. All this may have been called magic, evil desire, or by some other name; to Samuel it was far more like what he knew of Baal and Ashtart than of the old Yahweh.

Then came the catastrophe. Israel's armies were conquered, the ark captured, its priests killed, their sanctuary destroyed, and the whole region in the enemy's power. Was that not clearly Yahweh's hand, a judgment upon his people? But Yahweh's judgments do not only destroy; they also heal. Should that not be the case now? From this time on, Samuel's life, his gift as seer, his office as priest, his wandering throughout the country, all served this one purpose: to bring about resurrection, freedom, and salvation through inner uplift. Outward prosperity can be a result only of this inner uplift.

In the seventh chapter of I Samuel we have a narration that expresses this thought. The Philistines had long controlled the country. The people longed to be freed from the hard yoke. Samuel gathered all the people at Mizpah, and explained to them that only the return to Yahweh and the removal of the Baals and Ashtartes could restore Yahweh's favor and thus bring about their freedom. The narration in its present form dates from a later time and, doubtless, contains unhistorical features, but according to all we have heard, the part I have recorded bears marks of truth. Samuel, at any rate, met with the approval of his fellow countrymen and thus set about to find a king.

If this was the man who sought a king for Israel, then it was clear to him what he expected of Saul. Saul did not fulfill his expectations. Samuel had grown up in Shiloah with the holy ark. When it returned from captivity, Saul left it unnoticed at Kirjath Jearim. To Samuel it was most important; to Saul it meant nothing. Instead of rebuilding Shiloah or having the ark taken to Gibeah where he was, he favored the descendants of the priests of Shiloah, whose doings Samuel had formerly witnessed.

Phinehas' son, Ahitub, and after him his grandson, Ahiah-Abimelech, went to Nob and there set up a new priesthood. In place of the lost ark, they had an ephod such as Gideon had formerly had at Ophrah. They revived Gideon's form of worship, and Saul favored them. Samuel certainly had not expected this. Thus early a chasm opened between them. Samuel remembered the Yahweh of Moses. Saul followed the Yahweh of Gideon. Saul, also, named one of his sons after Baal. There may have been a number of misunderstandings. Finally when Saul attempted to lessen the severity of the Yahweh law in regard to blood ban, the seer realized that they had different spirits. The break had long been inevitable.

Saul was dissatisfied, and so were Samuel and his supporters. Saul's brilliant victory over the Philistines, which, however, was in a large measure Jonathan's victory, was not followed by a second one, although the Philistines were by no means conquered. All his life Saul had difficulties with them. When he died, both Israelites and Philistines occupied about the same position they had held when he began his reign. Conditions were rather worse than better for the Israelites. To realize this and not to be able to remedy matters was a bitter lot and a cause of great depression, even before another man had plucked the laurels of his early success.

Every kingdom needs a worthy and a secure capital where the threads of the government and the executive power of the state unite. Every attack of the enemy is naturally directed against it. With the eye of a genius, David recognized this fact and acted accordingly. Saul was established on the peasant estate inherited from his father and grandfather at Gibeah. Its position was not unfavorable, and he seems to have fortified it somewhat. It remained a modest town, as it had neither historical nor natural advantages. If Jerusalem was not available for Saul, why did he not restore to its power the renowned old city of Shechem which the Israelites had already rebuilt and inhabited? If he wished to remain on his native southern slope of the mountains, why did he not choose the commanding view of the Nebi Samwil which many people suppose to be Mizpah? Certainly, Samuel and others must have put these questions to Saul, but he had neither the energy nor the power of decision necessary and, yet, he suffered under his indecision.

Thus even before the break with Samuel, Saul's mind was troubled by care and depression. That the man of God, to whom he owed his kingdom, deserted him and renounced him in anger was not only a hard blow to his emotions and temperament, but it had a disastrous effect upon his people. What did his people think? What had become of the respect of the elders, without which no king is king?

All this was only the beginning, at least only the first act of the tragedy of the life of this first king of Israel. The severe blow which completely destroyed his equilibrium was still to come. It suffices to mention David's name. Before his very eyes, Saul's youthful armor bearer, his greatest

Philistine warrior, gained the heart of his people, the love of his daughter, and the friendship of his son. He himself failed in everything; all gifts were showered upon David. It could not be otherwise. David would rob him of his throne, also. He hurled his spear at him. He sent his bailiffs after David into his house. He himself set out in pursuit of him as of a hunted stag. He exhausted his best strength in his pursuit, and did not realize that all the energy that he thus lost to himself and his people was increased strength for the Philistines. Suddenly the enemy appeared within his borders, and he had no power to stop them. A battle was fought. Among the dead on the battlefield lay Saul. Defeated and deserted by his warriors, he had sought death by his own sword.

Thus the first king, the founder of the first national state in Israel, died. He had begun his reign as a knightly hero in the splendor of manly strength, good fortune, and victory; he died, harassed, embittered, deranged, giving himself the death blow, avoided and forsaken by every one—by his trusted seer and counselor, by his greatest warrior, and, finally, by the last of his faithful followers. What had brought him to this? Was it jealousy of David? Was it the feeling of his own inability? Was it the anger of the man of God?

Certainly, each one of these factors gnawed deeply at his soul and helped slowly to sap his strength. With the loss of the seer, he lost the favor of God and the confidence of the people and the nobility. His jealousy of David, whether reasonable or purely imaginary, did not allow him a moment of joy from the very hour that it seized him. The feeling of incapability, also, may have come over him strongly when, after the first Philistine victory, he had no success. This feeling may have been strongest and, with good reason, when he thought of David. Later in David's reign, people believed this as they compared the two men. The struggles with the Philistines occupied Saul all his life. David conquered them quickly. Apparently, Saul was more of an impulsive fighter, more of a knight than a general. During his whole lifetime, he did not succeed in establishing a capital worthy of the name! David chose a capital at once, for David was a king. Saul, even though he was crowned, was only a superior officer of high rank. Samuel, probably, was not the only one who realized that the choice, fortunate as it had seemed, in reality was a failure.

All this made Saul what he finally was. The more he realized it, the more it disturbed him. But who will say that for another man this must necessarily have been the case? Could a strong man not have risen above the break with Samuel? Could not a deliberate man with poise, who suspected his armor bearer, have found means of doing away with either the suspicion or the man? Could not a discerning man, even if he were incapable in some things, have put his strength and his gifts into the service of that which lay in the range of his capabilities and so have been valuable to his people? All this did not seem possible to Saul. From the beginning he seemed mentally incapable of that fortunate mixture of the various powers and capabilities which we call a normal disposition and which we consider the foundation of complete mental sanity.

A proverb of that time testifies that Saul had an excitable nature, inclined toward the ecstatic. That he was inclined to violent outbursts of passion and rage is well attested. Saul was temperamental. Success elevated him; failure discouraged him. He was choleric. His anger and his bitterness knew no bounds and led to orgies of wild, unrestrained rage. Saul was phlegmatic; frequently he was incapable of carrying out pressing and necessary decisions or deeds. At times he was melancholy; his depression often caused those about him to despair and to consider means of cheering him. The healthy, sanguine principle, which every one needs to be hopeful and to find joy in activity, seems at an early age to have changed into unhealthy melancholy which occasionally expressed itself in uncanny outbursts of choleric rage. These surely are symptoms of a diseased condition. It is possible that they might not have appeared had he had a different life. Without the crown, following the plow at Gibeah, Saul might have been able to avoid this fate.

In spite of all this, posterity has not forgotten what he did for Israel. The citizens of Jabesh remained faithful to their noble deliverer even in his misfortune. When the victors desecrated his dead body, the Jabeshites carried it away and gave it honorable burial. David sang a touching dirge for the creator of the State of Israel and for his son Jonathan. The song of Bileam, which David early composed in the name of all Israel, honored the victor of Agag and Amalek without naming Saul, but with clear reference to him.

Samuel's fame, too, has not faded. Legend, later, in grateful recognition of what he really was, ascribed even more to him than he actually did and also made him a permanent ruler in Israel. Whenever the devout, the especially favored of God, are mentioned, there among the first and close to Moses appears the name, Samuel.

VI

DAVID

THE plan associated with Saul's kingdom was very definite. All Israel was to be united under the scepter of the people's chosen leader, and under him they were to wage wars. The union was not accomplished in Saul's reign. Judah and perhaps several of the Galilæan tribes were temporarily but never completely subject to him. Saul never was in undisputed possession of his country, and, in reality, instead of the intended national state including all Israel, a state consisting of some tribes within Israel was again the result. At Saul's death this state, too, was of uncertain strength, and for the most part, matters stood as at the beginning of his reign.

That Israel did not again become a vassal of the Philistines and, indeed, a permanent one, was due solely to David. In him, Israel was given one of its greatest men, in fact, its greatest ruler. David was the only king of Israel of truly great proportions, a general as well as a statesman, one of the real geniuses of history. Although posterity has made of him almost a saint and retouched his image greatly, through it all we can see his real form; a real man of flesh and blood, shining in the splendor of his fame, genius, and bigness of soul, but casting dark shadows as is usual with men endowed with will power, vitality, and energy, and almost inevitably so when they are seated upon thrones.

At a time when Samuel had renounced Saul and the king's mind had begun to be deranged, he made the acquaintance of a young man from Bethlehem in Judah, David, Jesse's

[113]

son. The men of Saul's court, alarmed at their master's condition, sought, so we hear, for a man who was able to banish the king's melancholy. Even in ancient times, music was considered a means for calming the soul. It rouses certain spiritual powers, and gives inspiration as it did in Elisha's case, but it also calms the excited feelings and relieves the strain of inspiration. Because David was a skilled lute player and also an accomplished poet and minstrel, he was invited to the court and became the king's armor bearer. Whenever Saul was overcome by a fit of melancholy, David's music dispelled it.

This story corresponds with the facts in that David must have been a talented singer and poet. As such he surely could be a desirable companion and help to the sick king in his hours of melancholy. In Israel as in Greece, minstrel and poet were often combined. Almost every poet was a composer as well. Even in Italy in the nineteenth century there were whole guilds of minstrels, of whom some were called "finders" of new songs or trovatori, while others were merely singers. In ancient times we find wandering minstrels, frequently with their own songs, and we still find them among a great many peoples, even in Germany here and there. I do not mean the modern imitators found in large cities, but singers, who in the old, entirely spontaneous manner, play and sing to the accompaniment of the lute or zither, and offer, not only the songs of others, but also their own productions, often several new ones each year. In present-day Palestine almost every wideawake Fellach boy, who cares for a horse or a mule, in a few good or bad, improvised verses, sings the praises of some incident of the road. The spontaneous poem is far more natural to the Oriental than to the deliberate Occidental.

That David belonged to this class, because he was an artist of this kind, is certain, according to tradition. He composed a dirge after the death of both Saul and Jonathan, a lament after the death of Abner. When the ark of the covenant was taken to Jerusalem, he led the festive procession with music and songs of joy, which probably means with festive hymns. According to the testimony of the prophet Amos, he composed all sorts of songs "to the sound of the harp." [1] If he was poet and bard, then we may cling to the belief that when once a member of the royal court, he used his art and talent to cheer his master in illness.

Thus far we can agree with tradition. But it is another question as to whether this gift was the real cause of his acquaintance with Saul, and whether, because of it, Saul called him to his court. Here another record seems to deserve the preference, but not the record of Samuel's visit to Bethlehem, when he had Jesse's older sons presented to him and finally anointed the youngest, whom no one considered because he was still hardly more than a boy. Neither this narrator nor any later one seems to know anything about a public anointing, which was reported to have taken place in the midst of his brothers. Tradition does recount David's military successes in the battle with the Philistines.

The struggle with the Philistines went on. Although they were no longer the masters of the country as before Saul's time, they continually disturbed the western borderland south of Mount Carmel. Early in these struggles David had won laurels and, probably, had succeeded also in killing a much-feared Philistine warrior. Saul's attention was attracted to the splendid feats of arms of the young man from Bethlehem and noticed, also, his physical superiority and charming personality. He brought David to his court. David even became the king's preferred leader of troops in the war with the Philistines. His irresistible personality then won, in succession, the heart of the people, the friendship of the king's son who exchanged garments with him as did Glaucis with Diomedes, the favor of the ever-jealous courtiers, and lastly, even the love of the king's daughter.

[115]

In this setting, the minstrel David fits admirably. Here was the Round Table in Saul's palace with the king presiding; about him his paladins, the victorious warriors; Abner, his general-in-chief; and surpassing him more and more, the youthful hero, David; and the other members of Saul's select circle. Here were also, Jonathan, the noble prince and David's confidant, and in the adjoining room the women who with becoming reticence merely watched the men's faces and listened to their speeches. Stories added zest to the meal. The cup circulated, cheeks glowed, one man made a hearty speech, and another spoke a good word. Then the handsome officer from Bethlehem struck a chord and sang of triumph over the defeated Philistines, or in praise of Saul's freeing of Jabesh and gaining the king's crown, or of Jonathan's bold stroke in bringing confusion into the enemy's camp and so gaining a great day for his people. The men's eyes gleamed; much as they would like, they could not be angry with the young hero, even though he threatened to overshadow them. The hearts of the women, and more than all others, that of the charming princess, beat faster. His blond hair, his beautiful eyes, his comely person, and the fame of his deeds had long enthralled her. And now when he sang the fame of her father's and of her brother's deeds, she could no longer withstand the knightly singer; she gave her heart to him.

Many others, at this time or soon afterwards, felt the same toward David. More and more he was exalted even above the king, and when he returned from the war with the Philistines, the women received him with the cry:—

> Saul hath slain his thousands,
> And David his ten thousands.

For whosoever hath, to him shall be given, that he shall have in abundance, and so it was that posterity finally heaped the glory of the long Philistine struggle almost exclusively upon David's head. Probably David had slain some mighty Philistine warrior, thus occasioning his inclusion in the intimate circle of the paladins. Much later, it seems, one of David's own warriors, his country-man Elhanan of Bethlehem, killed the most-celebrated and most-feared Philistine warrior, Goliath of Gath. In Egypt the king was customarily represented to his warriors and subjects as a mighty giant. In the inscriptions of the ancients, the achievements of the army and warriors were usually ascribed to the king. Thus in grateful Israel, legend later had David slay the giant Goliath. In this way was created one of the most charming stories of the Old Testament. An innocent shepherd boy came unsuspectingly into camp to visit his brothers. There he heard that an insolent giant was deriding the battle ranks of Jahweh. No one dared accept the challenge. So he himself entered the lists for the warriors. He took five stones from the stream, put them in his shepherd's pouch, and advanced toward the giant. He slew the giant and, when this deed was reported to the king, this boy turned out to be David of Bethlehem.

Whenever we read the story of the shepherd boy, David, and the giant of Gath, the inimitable charm of the story makes us rejoice anew with the innumerable sons of Israel who long ago heard the story and repeated it to their children and children's children. Our hearts go out to the plucky youth who later achieved the well-earned crown, and in spirit we watch him grow to manhood, win a hero's fame, and at last become king. But the fact that one other than David slew the real Goliath of Gath is too well attested to be doubted.

How all this reacted upon Saul we already know. Doubtless the process of change covered years. We see only certain single features of the case from which we may divine the gradual advance. Saul's mind, tortured by melancholy, became very suspicious, and suspicion brought on the mania for persecution. His trusted general—of this he became more and more convinced—whose false charm no one could withstand, neither his son nor his daughter, neither his people nor his court, was at heart the king's worst enemy. Encouraged by good fortune and military glory, sustained by knightly favor, popularity with the people, the friendship of princes, and woman's love, David's one aim apparently was to put him, the king, prematurely aside, and to seat himself upon the throne in the king's place. Suspicion and the mania for persecution were transformed into blazing hatred, and this disastrous fire henceforth fed on the very life of the unfortunate man. Soon Saul knew no other thought than protection against his pursuer, and revenge upon and destruction of the presumptuous ingrate. Thus he deprived himself of his best warrior against the Philistines. His own work in war and peace had to suffer greatly, for thereby he broke down the protection of his people against the enemy. Finally and almost unavoidably the end came, as we already know it.

There is no dearth of information testifying to all this. Probably every one knows the many thrilling stories of Saul's cunning attempts to bring about David's downfall, how unexpectedly he hurled a spear at David, how he sent detectives into David's house to capture him but was thwarted by the cunning of David's wife, how Jonathan helped his friend to escape, and how finally there was nothing left to David but to flee from the king's wrath to his native Judah. There he led the life of an adventurer, lived with a group of people who, like him, had no home and no protector, but who for the most part had an evil conscience and lived by their swords alone. They provided for themselves partly by military service, and partly by accepting gifts from the willing or unwilling herd-owners of the southern steppes in return for protection against other raiders like themselves. Such has been the custom for centuries, and such it remains to this day.

Saul set out to hunt him down ·as the vulture the partridge in the mountains." From place to place, David was pursued by the mad king and his men, until he seems to have had no choice but to cross the border and seek protection of Achish, king of the Philistines. His followers seem to have increased gradually in numbers until there were several hundred of them, for now we hear of four hundred and again of six hundred bold men. Among them were many of his own near kinsfolk, such as his brave stepnephews, Joab, Abishai, and Asahel. There were enough dissatisfied people in Israel even then and such as had been driven from hearth and home by their creditors. They may have hoped for better things with David. At the priests' city, Nob, not far from Jerusalem, the priest of the ephod provided him with bread and a sword, supposedly that of the the giant he had slain, and also prophesied his success. David reached the mountain fastnesses of Adullam on the western slope of the Judean Mountains. From there he moved with his followers to Kezila, to-day Keilah, not far south of Adullam, ostensibly to protect the place from an attack of the Philistines. He might have seized an opportunity here to ingratiate himself among his own people, but he could not remain, for Saul had discovered his abiding place and threatened to take him captive. Previously Saul had taken bloody revenge on the priests of Nob, eighty-five of them, it is alleged, and on the whole city of Nob.

David fled farther east. There the steep slopes of the Judean Mountains toward the Dead Sea gradually merge into steppes and into inaccessible desert lands. Here close to his native land in a section little known to Saul, he felt himself safest against Saul's superior power. He felt confident of his tribesmen from Judah, and he knew every secret nook of the country. This was the region about Ziph

Carmel and Maon, places whose names still exist, and in the region a little south of Hebron in which a long time before this the desert tribes, Caleb and Jerahmeel, had settled and were merged with the people of Judah at an earlier period.

The section is well adapted to raising sheep and goats, and even at this time was inhabited by scattered well-to-do owners of flocks and herds. David came to them in the manner described above, as their "protector." Some of them favored him. Among them, in Jezreel, which belongs to this region, was a man who gave his daughter, Ahinoam, in marriage to David. A second rich man, Nabal at Carmel, paid dearly for his resistance. After Nabal's death, David married his widow, the beautiful Abigail. Thus a second time David gained a foothold in the midst of his own tribe. Two rich families of Judah were now related to him by marriage. To understand the far-reaching importance of this fact we must know what family and clan relationship have meant to the Orient since antiquity. Bethlehem in the northeastern part of Judah was related to him by ties of birth. Now he had also Jezreel and Carmel in the southeastern part. Kegila in the northwestern part he had also gained for himself by valiant services.

In spite of this he did not long feel secure here. The people of Ziph are supposed to have betrayed him to Saul and offered to disclose his hiding-place. Saul set out in great haste. David is alleged to have succeeded twice, once at the oasis Engedi on the Dead Sea and again on the steppe of Ziph—in getting the king in his power. Once Saul was at his mercy in a cave, at another time David crept after him into his barricade of wagons. In the one place, he secretly took the king's spear and water-cruse; in the other, he secretly cut off a piece of the king's mantle, but magnanimously spared the anointed of Yahweh. But he dared remain no longer and, therefore, made an agreement with the Philistines. With them he was safe from Saul but must become a vassal of the Philistine king. He could expect nothing else.

The reader may imagine what rich material this offered to the bards and narrators of Israel. The most illustrious king of the nation who had raised Israel on high, higher than it ever had been and higher than it ever would be again, was the hero of all these adventures; from shepherd boy to the king's confidant, and from king's son-in-law to a pursued outlaw, and again from outlaw to king. This indeed was a life without parallel. After David's ascent to the throne, whenever Israel's greatness and its heroes were mentioned, either at court or in the palaces of great men, or in the cities and villages, or by the shepherds' camp fires, there David's rise from hut to throne, and above all his adventurous deeds, were unfailingly recounted. And after the king's death, more than ever his praises were sung, first throughout Judah and, soon, among the other tribes. The division in the realm did not check this. Just as the deeds and adventures of Charlemagne were heralded alike in Paris and in the baronial castles of France as well as in the cities and castles of Germany, so not only at the court and in the cities of Judah, but also in the northern state, the people did not cease to sing and tell of David's great deeds.

But the greater and richer, and at the same time the more popular the subject matter, the more manifold were the possibilities of change. One person emphasized this characteristic; another, that. One preferred one phase of David's life; another, a different one. Here a special characteristic or an episode was stamped upon the memory of some in one light; upon the memory of others, in a different light. Thus we do not lack for information, but have rather a superfluity. It is not always possible to sift it. To begin with, we may assume that the tender devotion to the greatness of the hero and the reverence shown him by his contemporaries and posterity were as important to those who worked over the material, as the idea of teaching posterity historical facts. If we seek facts, then, we may accept the main features of the above sketch as confirmed. We cannot, however, overlook the fact that many romantic minor points, such as David's surprising and magnanimously sparing Saul, must be read from the viewpoint of the sympathetic narrator, rather than from that of the critical historian.

When we consider this fact, we understand another one. If the charm of the stories of David's adventures and experiences at the time of his persecution by Saul lies chiefly in the subsequent impression of unbounded admiration that the bards and narrators of his own time and especially those of a later time felt, then it is evident that from these men we cannot expect any strictly objective reports. An admirer is not a critic; least of all, an admirer who is a narrator or bard in the palaces of the great, or in the villages and camps where the people wish to hear the praises of a great king, but not to learn history.

If we wish an answer to the question as to whether David was wholly or partly guilty of what Saul accused him, we must not be influenced by the final verdict of the narrators. That Saul was a sick man, neither they nor we can doubt, but if they deduce from Saul's unfortunate mental condition that David was entirely innocent and that all of Soul's reproaches were the outgrowth of an abnormal imagination, then, at least, there is no reason for accepting this belief without examining it.

We are not justified, however, in believing David capable of planning to seat himself upon the throne by ignoring Jonathan's claim or killing him. We can hardly believe David capable of such treachery to Jonathan, in spite of the injustice done to Uriah, of which we shall speak later. But it is quite another question, whether there are not some indications that possibly David, together with Jonathan, sought ways and means of taking the power out of the sick king's hands and of placing, either themselves, the two friends, or one or the other of them in the king's place. The removal of Saul did not necessarily signify killing him. King Uzziah lived for years without actually ruling. Still less need it mean doing away with Jonathan, especially by force, although tradition very frequently and very clearly has Jonathan voluntarily take a position below David. It is not impossible that Jonathan himself recognized David's superior qualities and made decisions accordingly.

At any rate, we may ask how Saul came to believe not only that David had joined forces with Jonathan for Saul's removal from the throne, but that his own son was the instigator of the plan. To be sure, Saul's suspicion of David made him regard him as an enemy. It would not be surprising if Saul interpreted the bond of friendship between the two as directed against him. Even if he wronged them both, his condition explains his suspicion. But it is difficult to understand even in a sick man a suspicion against his own son as the originator of such a plan. As far as we can see, Jonathan withdrew completely after that first warlike deed. After David's appearance, he had played no independent part. Saul, therefore, however suspicious he was, had no reason for such thoughts against Jonathan. We may apply certain standards of logical sequence to inherent probabilities even to a sick man. We must conclude that this apparently improbable report had come to Saul's ears. I consider it possible that there was some truth in the report.

If before this time, David had thrice seized opportunities for gaining advantages for himself in various part of Judah and if at the very last he used the spoils from the Amalekites to gain favor with the Judean elders in the south, then we may hardly assume that he acted without some definite purpose. His intention must have been to become ruler in

Judah after Saul. There is no doubt in my mind that, after this time, he cast his eyes on the kingship over Judah. But it is conceivable that these thoughts were first awakened during his enforced stay among his close kinsmen.

If from this viewpoint we look back upon the historical bond of friendship with Jonathan, which seems to me unquestioned, and also into the manner of his flight into Judah, then his efforts to gain control of Judah, of which we have just spoken, appear in a new light. That David set out to carry out royal commands, accompanied by warriors but without bread which he later procured from the priests of Nob, if you stop to think of it, presupposes a more than probable confidence in him on the part of the priests. Even a strictly secret commission, if it were a king's commission and if, therefore, their departure took place with the king's knowledge, would not have hindered the soldiers from taking bread enough to last for a few days. It must have been even more noticeable to the priest that a distinguished warrior of the king, and as such he respectfully greeted David, should come to him on such an important matter with men but without arms. And yet the commission that David was to carry out was of such importance that he, as he had frequently done in the past, asked the priest for the oracle of Yahweh for himself and his mission.

What could have been the former occasion upon which Abimelech had given David the oracle and blessing of Yahweh? Surely, his numerous campaigns against the Philistines. Because of them David may have been a well-known figure here in Nob at the Yahweh oracle of the descendants of Eli. All the more strange must David's speech and behavior have seemed to Abimelech. He was setting out on an alleged, peaceful mission with the king's men, perhaps to settle legal matters somewhere, but without a weapon, and yet later he demanded one. Why did he need one now, if he did not need it at his departure? Why did he request an oracle when his mission was the question of a lawsuit concerning an inheritance, or something similar?

Truly the priest must have been stricken with blindness if he could not see through all this, and David himself could not have been the wise and farseeing man whom we formerly knew, if in all seriousness he tried to hoodwink the priest with this story. To be sure, he may have said this for his life was in danger; he was in a position where only cunning and craftiness could save him. His bond, however, with Jonathan and his striving to gain influence in Judah, together with the gathering of a group of several hundred determined men, could be understood only psychologically and historically by the conclusion that already at Saul's court, David, together with Jonathan and the priests of Nob, and probably with many others, had secretly considered certain far-reaching plans as to the meaning of which Saul's suspicion seems to have been correct.

An objective presentation of the events of a far-distant time cannot assume the task of measuring those events with the standards of our own time. Yet the reader may try to enter into the feelings of David and Jonathan. It is possible that at the point where our narration now stands, perhaps ten years had elapsed since the unfortunate break between Samuel and Saul. The break was accompanied by a deep rift in the king's soul. His melancholy became noticeable and soon took such a threatening form that his people looked about for a means to calm him. David came to court. Even if he were not summoned for this purpose alone, his coming served it for a time. The higher his fame and favor rose in the course of the years, the more discontent and malice ate into Saul's soul. The affairs of state were at a standstill; his interest in the war with the Philistines and the protection of the borders waned. Already there may have been occasional attacks on David and pointed

speeches of jealousy and hatred that showed what heavy
darkness had settled upon the king's soul.

What wonder that David and Jonathan had taken counsel
together and with others as to what could be done. There
may have been thoughts of self-protection for David, perhaps also for Jonathan. Who could tell what form the
king's suspicion might yet assume? The state must have
protection also, for its future was at stake. To Saul such
thoughts, if they reached his ears, seemed high treason.
They could only strengthen his suspicion and increase to
the utmost the darkening of his mind. David, also, was
driven on by the course of events.

We do not know positively what the intentions of David
and Jonathan were beyond deposing Saul. Perhaps they
thought of Jonathan as his successor and of David as general; perhaps of Jonathan as king of Israel, and of David
as king of Judah. It seems clear to me that during David's
sojourn in Judah, his thoughts turned toward a deliberate
struggle for the throne of Judah. Who can blame him?
Conceptions such as treason to one's country and high
treason are to this day so disputed and many acts are so
differently regarded by individuals that we can reach no
unity of opinion regarding them. This was no different
in the past. Who would call General York, who withdrew
his vassal fidelity to Napoleon I at Tauroggen, a traitor?
Who would pronounce guilty of high treason the ministers
of Ludwig II of Bavaria because they dethroned him?
That the king of Israel occupied a favored position because
he was the anointed of God, did not prevent the removal
of the sick King, Uzziah, and not a word of reproach
appeared in the written account.

David gave the Philistines an unheard of triumph by
entering their services. One can express this in no other
way than by saying that he went over to the enemy of his
country with all his troops and the women and children.

We may ask, if he could no longer remain in Judah, why
he did not seek some other solution of his problem. Could
he not have chosen as a dwelling place Moab in the East
or Amalek in the South, and so have avoided this extreme
measure? We, however, know far too little of conditions
in those regions to be able to say whether Moab and Amalek
were at all inclined or able to receive David and to provide
his followers with a refuge and sustenance. The Philistines
could give both, and perhaps David chose this course from
sheer necessity. It is obvious that he was received with
open arms. Many Philistines were greatly relieved by
David's coming over to their side and said, "Our most
feared opponent from now on is on our side." It is also
obvious that David's going over to them necessitated his
entering the service of Achish as his vassal, and of doing
his bidding.

From the beginning David's clear vision saw that this
act, immediately and later even more, would bring about
the most tormenting entanglements. Could the Philistines
trust him, knowing his past? Was not the whole affair
a well-played comedy? It seems that such ideas were
expressed from the first at the court and in the presence
of the king at Gath. For this reason the king may first
have considered stationing David and his followers in the
capital. There they could be watched and their actions
checked. In this case David could only hold his own if
he daily gave proof of his dependability. This meant raids
and forays into Israel, especially into Judah, the nearest
neighbor. A sad prospect from the very beginning!

This first danger was fortunately avoided. David's
sagacity and perhaps special considerations, unknown to us,
on the part of Achish himself, resulted in David's receiving
the town of Ziklag, probably Zu-he-like of to-day, rather
distant from Gath and southeast of Gaza. David seems to
have bought it as personal property. For payment of the

debt, rich possibilities were offered in the leader's share of the spoils. From here, too, Gath expected constant proofs of his good faith, and David showed himself a master of prudence and cunning, not exactly particular about means and always keeping his goal clearly before his mind's eye.

Ziklag is situated in the most southern part, just where the steppes and the fertile lands merge. In the steppes of Negeb, i.e., of the southland, the people of Judah had long been settled; with them, the people of Caleb and Jerahmeel and also the Kenites. All had gradually been absorbed by Judah. The commission which Achish gave to David was to injure Judah by repeated raids. Here in the southland dwelt also the Amalekites, of whom we have already heard, and related nomadic tribes. Saul had defeated but not destroyed them. And they seem to have remained troublesome to the Judeans. A desert tribe of the Asshurites was also probably mentioned. David's cunning, apparently, enabled him to completely dupe Achish and his people for a whole year. He invaded the other desert tribes. In his raids, he slew without mercy men and women, in order to remove living witnesses against him, and delivered the spoils to Achish as spoils from Judah. Achish could be well satisfied with him, but in reality, instead of injuring his native land, he had not only done it good service, but had also gained for himself a good reputation there.

The clever stratagem was so hazardous and so daring, and at the same time so cunning and so cruel, that one is tempted to consider it an invention of later legend to glorify David. We must not, however, measure David by the standard of later times. The people of his time thought and acted thus. Even to-day a man like Ibn Sa'd would be capable of acting thus in case of need. We must remember that if legend ascribed this to David as a glory and if the narrator in this way secured for himself favor and success, this could be only because the people believed David capable of such a feat and rejoiced in the splendid duping of the Philistines. Then, perhaps, we also may believe this of David, for it belonged to the time and its ways. David was the child of his time and of the country in which he lived.

Certain consequences were, of course, inevitable. Without David, Saul was not an important enemy. The Philistines knew this from actual experience. Thus a year after David had gone over to the Philistines, they took advantage of the situation and made a vigorous attack upon Israel. They called out the army, and again, as in Eli's time, attempted to advance from Aphel in Sharon toward the mountains and the plain of Jezreel. —As vassal, David was briefly reminded by Achish of his duty, and without objection set out with the army. Only when matters became truly serious did the other Philistine princes apparently urge Achish to send David back. They did not trust him after all. "For wherewith should this fellow reconcile himself to his lord, should it not be with the heads of these men?" [2]

Possibly by some clever means David knew how to awaken such thoughts. But who could vouch for the desired result? It came, however; that was his fabulous fortune. Had David failed at this time, he would have found himself in a very precarious position. No one can say what he would have done if fortune had not favored him. Would he have fought in cold blood with the Philistines against Judah? Because of David's sagacity, I cannot imagine his doing so. For, in case of victory, he must have had at best the doubtful prospect of becoming city governor for the enemy in Gibeah or elsewhere in Israel. Or would he, as those Philistine leaders feared, have gone over at the critical moment to Israel with his troops? But to what advantage if Saul's enmity continued against him?

I rather surmise that David could not have answered these questions even to himself. His position was such that he drifted wherever Yahweh and fate impelled him. Little else was left to him. At the very entrance of the Philistine territory, a man of David's clear mind must have realized that matters might and probably would turn out as they actually did. If he could have expected advantage for himself from a new attack of the Philistines upon Israel, then one might imagine that he desired the war. But could a vassal kingdom under Achish attract him? He could expect nothing more, and even this with no certainty. If I see clearly, there remained nothing for him but a deed of desperation, a tremendous va-banque game. He risked all on the one card. If he won, he would be saved; if he lost, then he would be ruined. He was like the gambler who with his pistol in his pocket approached the gambling table, determined on either fortune or a bullet.

The battle began without David. Saul's fate was sealed on Gilboa at the southern edge of the plain. David heard it in Ziklag whence he had returned. With Saul fell also his three sons, Jonathan, Abinadab, and Malchishua. The country was again in the hands of the Philistines, and Saul's surviving son, Ishbaal (Ishbosheth), was limited to the East as a sort of vassal king of the Philistines. Benjamin was unwilling to give up the leadership in Israel.

But what was to become of Judah? From the beginning Saul's rule had been less well established here than in the mountains of Ephraim, for Judah had thus far had a separate government similar to the one which even in Saul's time existed in the Galilean tribes. After David had taken refuge in Judah, the bond with Saul had grown even weaker than formerly. After David's departure, and above all after Saul's death, there was, in reality, no ruler in Judah. Haste, therefore, was imperative. If the succession to Saul's throne were not soon settled, there would be grave danger that the Philistines would seize the territory so near them.

Together with David as a claimant to the throne was Ishbaal, supported by Saul's surviving general, Abner. For

David, all depended upon quick action. On his return to Ziklag he had found an unsought opportunity to carry away rich spoils from the Amalekites. These he used to gain the cities of southern Judah. He seems to have formerly had the good will of the other Judeans, at least so much so that he expected no serious resistance. He chose the shortest means possible—he simply came with all his followers, together with the women and children, and firmly established himself in Hebron and the neighborhood. Once there, who would venture, even though he were unwelcome to individuals, to drive him thence? "And the men of Judah came, and there they anointed David king over the house of Judah." In reality they had reason to welcome his coming, and the majority realized this. Recently he had been their strong protector against the robber Bedouins, and they hoped for much from him. He promised them a strong Judah of great influence in Israel. What Benjamin had become through Saul, now Judah might become through David.

Now David was king of Judah, but there was also a king in the land east of the Jordan, and the Philistines ruled in the mountains of Ephraim. The national state, toward which Saul had moved and which, according to the original intention, was to include all Israel was now broken into three parts. Thus David had only a tribal state. From the union of tribes partially achieved under Saul, Israel had dropped back again to the single tribe, as under Gideon. David's reign here is said to have lasted seven and a half years. He chose Hebron as his capital. By so doing he proved that the step, seemingly backward from Saul's, was really a step in advance of him—not, of course, in extent of territory, but in the spirit of the government. If he had acted in Saul's way, he would have ruled at Bethlehem. His clan lived there, but difficulties with the Philistines and the Canaanites, who still controlled Jerusalem and its vicinity, were to be feared much sooner in Bethlehem than in Hebron which was less accessible from the west. Perhaps his choice was due also to troubles with the tribe of Benjamin, which still clung to Saul's memory. In addition, Hebron was in the midst of clans of south Judah, which had recently been particularly favorable to him, partly because of kinship and partly because of rich gifts. Of Bethlehem he was sure, but he must bind Hebron to him permanently by strong ties. Again Hebron was a very ancient settlement with an old and famous sanctuary. Abraham's field and, later, his grave have been pointed out there. Thus for location and importance it was much better suited to be the center of the Kingdom of Judah than was Bethlehem.

The choice of the proper capital was of special importance, because David had already begun to look beyond Judah's borders. Immediately after ascending the throne, he sent a commission from Hebron by way of Judah to Jabesh of Gilead, announcing that, since Saul was dead, he wished his sovereignty recognized in the country east of the Jordan. Doubtless, he wished this done before Ishbaal appeared. But here he miscalculated. It was, therefore, all the more important for him to avoid a clash with Ishbaal and the people of Benjamin. Should it come, as was probable, he would need the support of all of Judah, including its southern part, not only that of his own clan.

The clash came. Ishbaal, although little more than his own tribe of Benjamin were loyal to him, or rather to Abner who thought and acted for the "shadow king," considered himself king over all Israel, and announced himself thus. He could look upon David only as an insurgent against the house of Saul. Thus the attack seems to have started on Ishbaal's side. A battle took place between very modest armies; three hundred and sixty dead on the side of Benjamin meant for Ishbaal a disastrous defeat, and with it, Abner's vassal fidelity began to waver. Soon he had betrayed his master, and David was in a position to accept or reject the terms offered him. Before a decision was reached, however, Abner was treacherously murdered by David's general, Joab, who would not tolerate a rival. David condemned the act most severely and gave expression to his feelings in a song of lamentation, but in spite of this, even to this day, he is considered guilty of Abner's murder. Neither could he prevent Ishbaal's murder from being ascribed to him, when soon afterward several officers from Benjamin broke into the palace of Nahanaim and murdered the king whose "hands" had long become "feeble."

In both cases I consider the reproach unjustified. David, indeed, was no saint. He may have known that Abner intended to betray his master or even to do away with him. He heard of it, but let matters take their course. He had no need of interest either in Abner's or in Ishbaal's premature death, at least, not in Ishbaal's, if his patience could last until the fruit, so nearly ripe, should inevitably fall into his lap. From the beginning Ishbaal had lacked firmness and after Abner's death doubly so. David's sagacity would not permit him to arouse public opinion unnecessarily by forcibly removing Ishbaal. Only one who considers David capable of great folly will ascribe such an act to him.

That David by nature was not impatient in waiting until conditions were ripe is shown by his behavior after the victory of Gibeon. It is possible that worry over a counter stroke from the Philistines kept him from further pursuit of them by an attack on Benjamin. But it is more probable that he avoided obtaining the crown by spilling blood, for the crown must of necessity come to him later. He feared a host of cases of blood revenge. The same principle that guided him here probably did also in the cases of Abner and Ishbaal. Not constraint and violence, but rather the free choice of the tribes alone could bless his future as king of all Israel.

David was right in his expectations. All the tribes of

Israel, we read, sent their representatives to him at Hebron and solemnly offered him Saul's crown. They even called him their own "flesh and blood," so much was Judah already considered a part of all Israel. He made an agreement with the delegates in which the rights and duties of the king and the people were determined: an interesting proof of how little the Kingdom of Israel as such resembled so-called Oriental despotic rule.

This act of fealty at the very outset seems to be more than had ever been offered to Saul. Judah had at first stood aloof from Saul, and only because it was most subjected to the attacks of the Philistines had it gradually come under Saul's rule for protection. Now Judah considered itself actually a part of Israel. Galilee seems, in the main, to have kept apart. Now "all the tribes of Israel" came forward. The national kingdom, the national state became a reality, for all who considered themselves a part of Israel voluntarily came under David's scepter. Even at this time David's reputation was so good that, for the sake of union under him, all disagreement and dissension among the tribes disappeared. Of course, one could not expect a unanimous agreement in this general movement at Hebron without detailed discussion and much preparation.

A great deed thus had been accomplished, such as never before had been seen in Israel. David had not disappointed Israel's expectations, but had exceeded them.

It was to be expected that before David could really begin to reign in Israel, indeed even before he could rejoice at all in his accomplished goal, a different arrangement must be made with the Philistines. They could hold loose reins as long as two kings in Israel checkmated each other. With the elimination of the weaker one, and, above all, with the choice of David for the united kingdom, the policy of laissez-faire ceased of its own accord. Now the Philistines must act before it was too late. In reality, it had long been too late. Not in vain had David under Saul been a terror to the Philistines. Now, apparently, a few vigorous attacks sufficed to make them unwilling to return. It seems that the glamour of David's name and the fact that all Israel stood together under his banner, brought about the victory over these old warriors and obdurate opponents of Israel. David defeated them from "Gibeon to Gezer," i.e., they were driven out of Israel. Later he seems to have invaded their land in an attempt to capture their capital, Gath. The Philistines were thoroughly subdued for a long time.

That David was a splendid soldier and general, he had long ago shown and had again proven. He now had an opportunity to show his ability as a statesman. Probably he had not been entirely idle in Hebron, but we know of only the one act that has come down to us from that period —his choice of Hebron. Now, after the soldier in him had done what was necessary for the time being, the king in him began to stir his wings mightily. His first act showed that they were the wings of a royal eagle, for again, as in Judah, his immediate care was the choice of a capital.

The significance of his choice lay, to begin with, in what Jerusalem, upon which his eyes immediately fell, was not. David could have remained in Hebron, and even then he would have had the seat of his government in a famous old city of no small importance. His tribe and his kinsmen would then be in his immediate vicinity. He could do as once in Gibeah Saul had done, who, resting on his spear, assembled about himself the princes of Judah and reminded them that he had bestowed upon them fields and vineyards, and had made them captains of thousands and captains of hundreds. In this case, however, David would have been obliged to attempt to govern his state from the extreme southern border of his territory. Above all, he would have been checked at every turn by demands and claims from his own tribe and, also, by the jealousy of the other tribes.

It was absolutely necessary for him to gain the favor of Benjamin and Ephraim, Manasseh, Saul's tribe, and the old main tribes of the central section of the country where Gideon was by no means forgotten, and all this without losing the favor of Judah. David was, therefore, very clever when he chose a capital belonging to none of the tribes and thus, as far as Israel was concerned, with no historical significance—a fresh sheet of paper. The territory was absolutely neutral, with obligations and responsibilities to no one, and thus admirably suited for a fresh beginning. Here he might create his own future. The city and city-territory were the possession of the little people, the Jebusites, who seem to have stood aloof and to have had little connection with the Canaanites outside their borders.

Furthermore, Jerusalem was not favorably located for a center of traffic and trade. The principal roads, facilitating communication, were: the one along the shore of the Mediterranean; the other along the edge of the desert in the east. Only the traffic from the section south of the eastern Jordan toward the coast and that from north to south passed through Jerusalem. Jerusalem had, however, the advantage of having been a very ancient, strongly fortified settlement with an equally ancient sanctuary. During the Amarna period the city king, Abdi-Chipa, had ruled there. The city had its name, Ursalim, from an old god Salem, in whom we may probably recognize the highest god or El-eljon of that king and priest, Melchizedek, in the story of Abraham. His holy rock on Mount Zion, over which later Solomon erected the temple altar, had probably already been the sanctuary of the El-eljon. Thus Jerusalem had known a great history: it had been an ancient fortress, an ancient royal residence, and an ancient place of worship. Such a place could lend splendor to the new king. Aside from this, Jerusalem, as long as it was in foreign hands, was a constant menace to the unity of the state. The state could be expected to endure only when the wedge between Judah and Benjamin-Ephraim should be permanently removed.

Jerusalem had thus far successfully withstood all the attacks of the tribes of Israel and, probably also, of the neighboring Canaanites. It felt so sure of its firm position and good fortification that it could mockingly retort to David that the blind and the lame sufficed to protect the city. David with his men led by the reckless Joab made possible the impossible. The city was taken by storm. David then took possession of the fortress and remodeled it for himself. It was then called the city of David.

The government and national life now had a center, and David, a fitting royal residence. David, however, would not have been David had he stopped halfway. He would then have only partially and not entirely overtowered Saul in his achievements. Because of his having been anointed with the sacred oil, the king of Israel was above the limitations of ordinary humanity. Like the seer and the priest, he was placed at God's side. He was filled with divine power and blessing. He was so near to God that he was called God's son, indeed in exalted language, he might occasionally even be called God Himself. Thus it was with other peoples as well as with Israel. From this belief it was obvious that where the king was, there must his God be also. Saul had not recognized this, which fact shows anew that he only half felt himself to be king. David had a different conception; he was king in every fiber of his being, and he saw things with the eyes of a king. At this time there was everywhere this unquestioned, uncontested idea; the king was associated with the god, the dwelling-place of the king was the dwelling-place of the god—his sanctuary. For this reason there were the great temples of the gods in the capitals, Babylon and Nineveh; the gigantic halls and magnificent temples of the gods of the state in Memphis and Thebes. In Broussa, too, the capital of the caliphs was the sanctuary of the Ottoman Turks; and in Moscow, the national cathedral stood beside the great palace of the czars.

Saul had left, unnoticed and resting in an out of the way place in the country, the ark of the covenant—the abode of the Lord of Hosts who "dwelleth between the cherubim"—and had not even sought a substitute for use in his capital. David changed entirely this condition, so unheard of and so contrary to the feeling of the Israelites. As soon as he had a capital, his first care was to bring the God of Israel into it. Only as the City of God, as the center of the worship of God and as the center of national life, was Jerusalem to David what it must be as a capital.

In Egypt and in Babylon, the god's ascension of the throne was celebrated on a great feast day, together with the king's ascension of the throne; for to the people the king was closely associated with the god. In a festive procession the image of the Babylonian god was brought from the sanctuary, carried about, and then returned to its place. Thus each year he ascended the throne anew, and with him the king, his earthly representative. In Israel, also, a similar procedure seems to have prevailed, perhaps dating from the Canaanitish worship of Adonis. Perhaps the old autumnal feast of thanksgiving, celebrating the end of the harvest and the beginning of the new harvest-year, was used for this purpose.

At any rate, David, with great pomp, approached the place where the holy ark of the covenant had been left. In festive procession, with singing of hymns, playing of zithers, harps, and drums, and ringing of bells, the procession, passing toward the holy sanctuary, moved from Kirjath-Jearim to the capital. The king himself in priestly robes preceded the group of dancers, "leaping and dancing." In the capacity of priest, he, himself, performed the sacrifice and gave the people the priests' blessing. Such a thing had not been known under Saul. The priestly robe only partially covered David's body. Michal, Saul's daughter, looked askance at such actions: the king "as one of the vain fellows uncovereth himself." David's answer coincides with present-day Oriental feeling. What mattered it to him what men considered decorum when the question involved was the worthy service of Yahweh. Such display belonged to the religious feeling of the time, as part of reverent service to God.

Decorous Arabian women dress their hair with special care and often cover it. The veil is also a matter of decorum. A certain sanctity is associated with the hair. The moral woman would prefer to be seen naked than with uncovered head. But if a question is of the honor of God and the protection of the holy paladin, then she dances a wild dance in emotional fervor and with her hair loosened in order to stimulate the warriors to defend their god. In Mecca, too, where the heads of the leading families accompany the festive procession, the women with loosened hair, beating tambourines and uttering shrill cries, walk among the men. In battle to rouse the fury of the combatants, women might mingle unclad among them. The Oriental is capable of sacrificing for the highest purposes—especially for religion —everything, even the standards of moral decency.

David now placed the sacred ark of the covenant in a tent, which he is said to have set up for it. The ark now had an abiding place, and religious worship, a center.

How did David worship Yahweh before the ark of the covenant was in Jerusalem? With what ceremonies had he served him in Hebron? I believe this question has never really been considered. It should, however, be asked. As long as he had been on the march, he seems to have used the ephod that Abiathar had rescued from Nob. This was the same custom of Canaanitish pattern, although in the name of Yahweh, which Gideon and Saul had followed. Here David had already made use of the word of the prophet and had been given an oracle by the prophet, Gad. Probably from the time of David's stay in Hebron, and certainly after he took possession of the ark of the covenant, the ephod noticeably lost importance, and in its place appeared the old ark of the covenant. With the withdrawal of the ephod, its official guardian, Abiathar, also passed into the background. He, however, did not disappear, but became the priest of the ark of the covenant. Before him, however, another was mentioned, Zadok, who later was destined to supplant Abiathar. The connection here is close and almost unmistakable. The situation becomes clearer when we remember that at David's death, Abiathar's political enemy, Zadok, was favored by the prophet Nathan, whom we know as the zealous opponent of Canaanitish ceremonies, and, therefore, of the ephod, and as an advocate of the old Mosaic tent-worship.

From this we may conclude that probably even in Hebron, David as well as Nathan was under the influence of representatives of the still-unchanged desert traditions of the Judean shepherds and of the inhabitants of the steppes. Here in Judah they knew neither a temple like that in Shiloh, nor the ephod. The dwelling place of Yahweh was a tent or a tent-like habitation, such as the Arabians call *bait* or *kobba,* and which they carry about on a camel in war and peace. In earlier times as long as they considered the god visible, an image or some fetish of the god, perhaps a holy stone, may have lain in the tent. If they made no image of the god, his presence there was invisible but effective.

Thus David may have served Yahweh in Hebron, and thus he continued to do for a time in Jerusalem. The tent was called the tent of Yahweh, was in Zadok's charge, and was specially favored by Nathan. Here was kept the holy oil. Here stood the altar, the horns of which were laid hold of by those seeking protection. Thus it was at least in David's later time, probably always so. When the ark of

Yahweh came to Jerusalem, David also pitched a tent for it, evidently a new and special one, that became its habitation in place of the former temple of Shiloh. Presumably the other one had first stood on Mount Zion, but now had to give way and was removed to Gihon. The main sanctuary became that on Mount Zion; the other lost prominence, but always retained its altar for occasional sacrifice. The ephod seems to have disappeared. Its protector, Abiathar, was transferred to the service of the ark of Yahweh as second priest with Zadok.

The whole new arrangement had the great advantage that the old desert tradition surviving still in Judah seems to have been as satisfactory there as the traditions and customs of Ephraim. There is no doubt that the ark, whatever may have been its last resting place, had long had its habitation and, therefore, its adherents and friends in Ephraim. David's new arrangement was a further proof, also, of his political genius. It created a bond of unity between the two parts of Israel, long estranged and ever at variance. It united the north and the south and Ephraim and Judah on a religious as well as on a political basis.

The matter of greatest importance, of course, was religious activity. David who had begun in the ways of Gideon and Saul and, like them, had named a son after Baal, resolutely broke away from that tradition. He returned to the Mosaic tradition still surviving in Judah and among the Levite clans of the south. This was the same tradition which had existed in the days when Shiloh flourished, and the tradition which David had taken over from Samuel. From this point on, David's connection with Samuel, mentioned only in the legendary tale of the anointing, becomes probable. Perhaps it does contain a certain historic nucleus. Samuel had a second time searched for the right man for the throne and had thought to have found him in David. The fact that David took part in a religious procession of

the kind previously described, whose forms were of Canaanite origin, can hardly be considered as a weighty contradiction to his procedure. The kingdom itself was a heathen
organization. For the celebration of the ascension of the
throne they could hardly do otherwise than follow foreign
examples. We may also assume that this festivity very
early took on a religious character.

David's kingdom was now established. With wise insight
and untiring energy, he had created it for himself. All this,
however, was only preparatory, even though significant historically. His real work was to follow. David had prepared
the way for action. The eagle, now, had his eyrie and could
try his wings. He spread them for a gigantic flight.

It is easy to realize what was David's goal. Saul had
never really succeeded in creating the national State of
Israel, for he never got farther than the tribal state. Now
everything belonging to Israel was united under David's
scepter but great activity was necessary to maintain the
vitality of this united Israel which David had called to life
A family cannot exist if neighbors interfere; a garden cannot thrive if stones are thrown into it from without. In
such a light we must look upon Israel. In truth, there were
present the well-known "political necessities." A settlement
with the neighboring peoples was inevitable. The Philistines
on the west had already been overcome, and a pleasant relationship now began with the Phœnician cities who were
dependent upon Israel as the best purchaser of their products,
as well as the purveyor of cedar-wood and products of the
industrial arts. The Amalekites in the south, apparently,
dared cause no trouble. One after another, the Edomites,
Moabites, Ammonites, and the Syrian states in the north
were overcome in battle by David, with the result that
Israel ruled uncontested over Syria from the Mediterranean
Sea, indeed from the Red Sea to the eastern desert, and
from the southern steppes as far as the Orontes and on

toward the Euphrates. All their neighbors except the Phœnicians were forced to pay them tribute; all the territories were either provinces or, at least, dominions under Israel. Out of the State of Israel had developed the Great State of Central and Southern Syria, extending far beyond the peoples of Israelite blood—a state which had the right to be rated as a commanding factor in the political life of the Near East.

The greatest genius has human limitations and is bound by them. Even a genius is dependent upon the favor of circumstances. It was David's special good fortune that neither Egypt nor Assyria at that time was in a position to look after its hereditary interests and claims in Syria. Thus on all sides he had to deal only with less or moderately powerful opponents. The really great powers took no part, for they were unable to restrain his activity. He, himself, was wise enough to limit himself to the essential and possible. David achieved what was most essential for Israel's prosperity—freedom of action in every direction. He did not attempt more. No one can tell whether his genius would have been capable of successfully carrying through a conflict with the Egyptians of that time. His army was never conquered. Why should he be troubled by the war steeds and chariots of others! Superior tactics with well-trained and courageous troops can gain the mastery over great masses and over advanced technique. But to David's greatness belongs also the fact that he seems not to have thought of attempting the adventure.

Provocation came, as it seems, from Ammon on the east. Ammon may have been humiliated by Saul but by no means subjugated, and is said to have acted unbecomingly toward David. We have long known how to look upon unjust, or unseemly "causes" and war-guilt actions of this sort. A strained relationship had long existed and threatened explosion. David's very existence, according to Ishbaal, was a threat against the Ammonites. If they stood alone, David needed to concern himself little about them. Danger threatened David only when the Aramean states in the north and northeast joined forces with the Ammonites. In spite of this, however, the powerful and wise leader, Joab, succeeded in overcoming them both. The remnants of the once powerful old Hittite and Ammonite states collapsed entirely under his blows. Naturally, under these circumstances the Moabites could not offer resistance, and the Edomites could no longer contest David's rights to Stony Araby (*Arabia Petræa*) and access to the ports of the Red Sea.

The great man had now reached a height that no one before him or after him ever attained in Israel. David could look back upon an unsurpassed career. Resplendent with glory as the victor in all battles, crowned with laurel as the unparallel benefactor of his realm, surrounded by the splendor of prosperity in the newly gained capital and the recently erected royal palace, and exhilarated by the proud joy and admiring love of his people, David, in the quiet of peace he had gained only after heated struggles, could now devote himself to the tasks which the public welfare imposes upon every ruler and, doubly, upon the warrior-ruler. Aside, however, from the plan, soon abandoned, of building a temple for the ark, we hear nothing of this activity. David seems to have had less interest in the duties of peace than in his own pleasure. Splendid feasts, comfortable, indeed voluptuous living seemed to him the reward for the cares and dangers so long endured by the army and the ruler.

Inactivity and voluptuous living have never been the wells of true happiness. They now mastered him who formerly had mastered so many. The man who had been the terror of all his enemies was unable to conquer an enemy within himself, passion. Whoever cannot do this is also unable to keep his own house in order. Thus before the eve of life came on, there began for David that terrible tragedy which violently disturbed the very roots of his being and, indeed, poisoned the rest of life for him. Frequently, it is the friendly fate of a storm-tossed life to close quietly with a pleasant evening. David's fate was that deep, twilight shadows should darken the evening of his life, and that evil and storm should not relinquish their hold upon him, even in his very last hours.

When we read of his later life, we seem to have before us a piece from the tragic muse of Sophocles. But quite different! There, unconscious guilt, engendering unconscious guilt, worked out in evil and destruction. Here, the conscious guilt of the father, bringing conscious guilt upon his sons, worked out in judgment upon the king and the people. Hellas knew fate, but fate was unknown in Israel. Here all was guilt and atonement.

To relate more than the main features of events is unnecessary. Every one of us has known them from his youth. The army was in the field. The king was enjoying himself at home in the luxurious royal residence. One evening after he had had a good meal and had rested, he wandered aimlessly about on the flat roof of the palace. About the palace were built the homes of his warriors. In the open court of one of them, he saw a beautiful woman bathing. He desired her. He sent for her and she came. It was Bathsheba, the wife of Uriah, one of his warriors in the field. We are in the habit of putting all the blame upon David, but it is the old story of the warriors' wives at home. If the husband had been at home, Bathsheba would probably have bathed at another time or place. All her life, Bathsheba had known the art of luring men. The meeting was not without consequences. To cover up the matter, David had the officer home on a furlough. He refused to be a party to the matter. He must, therefore, die. A letter from the king to Joab caused Uriah to be placed in the front ranks before the enemy's arrows which killed him. David could now marry the young warrior's widow.

The matter became known. A murmur, indeed, a cry of indignation was heard throughout the nation. The King of Israel was no Oriental despot. We would say to-day that he had taken the oath of the constitution. At that time they said he had made a compact with them, i.e., agreed to a contract setting forth the rights of the people. Certainly, such sultanic actions violated this contract. In the parable of the poor man's sheep which the rich man took from him, the prophet, Nathan, in the name of Yahweh, gave clear expression to the public conscience. "Thou art the man." The king bowed his head, and the death of his first-born child was considered the price of atonement. In truth, however, this unwilling sacrifice of the first-born was only the first installment.

Years passed. Immense sums of tribute money and "reparations" in great quantity coming to Jerusalem became a curse to the new generation, unaccustomed to war. The king's example found followers. The petted youth in the capital and at the court also sought pleasure wherever opportunity offered. The crown prince, Ammon, so far forgot himself as to do violence to his half-sister, the princess Tamar, and then basely cast her off and public stigmatized her. Her own brother, Absalom, avenged her by having Ammon stabbed at a drinking bout. Absalom then fled from the country. After three years, Joab, by cunning, managed to bring about his return home, but he was still banished from the court. Two more years passed. The public slight vexed Absalom, for he felt he was innocent. Finally the king yielded and agreed to his pardon.

Meanwhile the king had grown older. He seems never to have concerned himself much with the affairs of state. The administration of justice gave cause for complaint. Absalom now played the part of crown prince, with a bodyguard, chariot, and steeds. Bathsheba's watchful eyes saw this with anxiety. Ammon's death and Absalom's banishment and disfavor, matters in which she was certainly not entirely innocent, had awakened hopes within her for her own son, Solomon. Probably Absalom's suspicious behavior had provided her with the occasion for obtaining a promise from the king for Solomon's succession to the throne. Absalom belonged to the type of heirs who grow weary with waiting. Perhaps because he knew of the other claimant, he ingratiated himself with those· seeking justice at the city gate. With friendly speech, affable manner, and the promise of better justice, "he stole from the king the hearts of the men of Israel."

Four years he continued this practice; the way was prepared. Except for David's evident weakness in government, his best ally in the far-reaching conspiracy was the old dissension between Judah and Benjamin. Absalom raised the flag of mutiny in Hebron, and everywhere his summons found an echo. And so the king, as he grew older, had the bitter lot of being deserted by almost the whole nation that had so often applauded him. He fled from Jerusalem toward the Jordan. Absalom entered Jerusalem. David's crafty wisdom, of so great a service to him in former times of dire need, did not desert him now. To this alone he owed his escape. He left the cleverest man of his associates behind him in the city. This man was to pretend that he had deserted David, to ingratiate himself into Absalom's confidence, and to give him false counsel in war. Absalom fell into the trap, and, following Hushai's advice, instead of acting at once, allowed David to escape over the Jordan where eastern tribes who had remained faithful supported him and helped him gain time. In the ensuing battle, the old military skill of David and Joab won a victory. Absalom died, and the insurrection was suppressed.

David, again a victor, returned to the capital and to the

royal palace. The break between north and south was in-differently patched up, but had a brief echo in the further insurrection of a certain Sheba. David, already an aging man, was so shocked by all these recent experiences and, most of all, by the death of Absalom, to whom, in spite of every-thing, he had clung with paternal pride, that he was changed into an old, old man. He came home completely broken.

We might suppose that the drama of guilt and atonement had now come to an end. Bathsheba's little son dead, Tamar ravished, Ammon dead, Absalom dead, the king, barefoot, weeping, and with his head covered, fleeing from the palace and place of his splendor—had not all this been punishment enough? But only the grave was to afford him peace.

Absalom's death gave to David's son, Adonijah, accord-ing to age, hope of succession to the crown. Now he played the crown prince as Absalom had done before him. The aged king, from whom the warmth of life was last ebbing, was no longer able to prevent this. He had always been a weak father. Bathsheba was still alert, lest her hopes for Solomon should be shattered a second time. She found pow-erful patrons for her favorite son in the prophet, Nathan, and the priest, Zadok. Adonijah was favored by the old warrior, Joab, and the old priest, Abiathar. The ambitious woman succeeded in reminding the dying king of his former promise, if he had made one; if not, in persuading him that he had made one and must act accordingly. An indiscreet, perhaps, also an incriminating feast celebrated by Adonijah with his political friends alone on the Snake Stone in the Kidron valley, gave Nathan and Bathsheba a just or unjust reason to torment the weary, old man to his very death with the thought that Adonijah was playing Absalom's part, and that Bathsheba and Solomon might, on the morrow, be the victims of his murderous steel; the king, perhaps, that very day. In mortal fear, David commanded that Solomon at once be proclaimed king. Fright and anxiety brought death to the old man. Solomon was king, Adonijah and Joab suffered the fate that they were supposed to have prepared and perhaps really had prepared for Bathsheba and Solomon. The Orient does not have many scruples in such cases.

Looking back, we are glad that the hero, after so much persecution in his later years, finally found rest in his castle. May the spade that seeks his grave not disturb it. What David had once said of Abner, that in him a great general in Israel had passed away,[3] may be said of David himself with greater justification. From the time of his death, and the farther removed that became in time, the more were wiped away from the memory of his grateful people all the shadows that had dimmed his image. Only the bright colors remained. There are so many of them that we surely may forget the shadows.

The splendor that radiated from David as the brave soldier, the never-conquered general, the incomparable king, as well as the founder of the City of God, after centuries was still shining. How strongly David reacted upon his people is proven by the many tales, anecdotes, and legends about him that were spread abroad in cities and villages. Even stronger evidence appears in the fact that by posterity he was considered the religious hero of his people whose second coming, as a second David of Israel, was to bring to the world a time of joy and blessing.

His sagacity amounted almost to wily cunning, but this is not a fault to the Oriental; his foresight, which enabled him clearly and firmly to hold in view the distant goal; his self-control in political matters, i.e., his desire to harvest only ripe fruits; all these qualities are unquestioned. His fascinating, lovable personality, that in his youth had charmed every one, did not change in later years.

His humanity was not entirely stifled by political demands

nor by good fortune and the splendor of court life. Repeatedly it came to the surface, but was most apparent in parental love, which was so strong that it became a fault. Love of friends, fidelity, and reverence, qualities cherished by David, prove his humanity. It is more difficult, perhaps, to believe in his magnanimity, because diplomacy and clever calculation often seem to have overbalanced his human side, and the narrators have perhaps laid undue stress upon these qualities. In certain cases, however, they seem to be unquestioned. The fact that David shed much blood and occasionally was harshly cruel is in accord with the old and new Orient. The fact that he practiced diplomacy by misrepresentation and cunning is in accord not only with the Orient.

His conception of God and his religious observance may have undergone changes, the greatest being, perhaps, the taking of the ark to Jerusalem. Honest piety seems always to have been a fundamental characteristic of his spiritual being. To render homage to Yahweh was not mere political wisdom for him, but a real need. It is true that the passion of unrestrained impulses, together with the temptations that possessions, power, and high position always include, made of him a wrong-doer. In honest humility, however, he accepted the reprimand given in Yahweh's name, and in the tragic course of his later life, atoned more than doubly for his guilt. His thoughts and deeds, like those of his contemporaries, were not free from fear of the uncanny and gruesome from which one must secure protection by special measures. But even here his personal welfare concerned him less than the welfare of the state.

The bard and poet in David we have no right to blot out from history. Even if no direct evidence had come down to us, we feel he must have had a share in the hymn composition of Israel, which surely went back as far as his time. The finest monument to his mental powers David erected in the dirge for Saul and Jonathan:

DAVID

How are the mighty fallen
In the midst of the battle!
How are the mighty fallen,
And the weapons of war perished.[4]

And the finest monument to what he wished to achieve as a
ruler, even though he did not always attain it, is contained
in a contemporary song that appears as David's swan song:

One that ruleth over men righteously,
That ruleth in the fear of God,
He shall be as the light of the morning, when the sun riseth,
A morning without clouds;
When the tender grass springeth out of the earth,
Through clear shining after rain.

VII

ELIJAH AND THE RELIGIOUS ENTHUSIASTS

DAVID's older sons saw their father's hard struggle in climbing the steep ascent to power, but Solomon was born after his father had attained the height where neither care nor dangers molested him. Not every one thrives under a rich heritage, and Solomon succumbed to its dangers. David did not train his children well. In his youth Solomon was surrounded by the heavy atmosphere of voluptuous court life. In the midst of this effeminate court and harem and, later, of the intrigues to secure succession to the crown, how could he as a boy and later as a youth gain a sense of duty and of the seriousness of life? He saw only the uncontrolled life of the king and of the royal family and the pleasant side of regal power. If the father showed only a few sultan-like inclinations, the son appeared as a real sultan, although by no means one of the worst type. From the human standpoint, we cannot entirely blame Solomon for this.

Solomon was an enlightened despot who certainly deserved the fame for wisdom and justice which posterity has attributed to him. He, also, deserved credit for the way in which he ruled his people. David, as we have heard, paid little attention to judicial matters and probably little also to matters of state; Solomon remedied this fact. In the many idle hours of a long period of peace, his interest was not only in feasting and in harem life, but also in gathering about himself a Round Table of wise men and writers of proverbs, so that he might enjoy clever and witty speech. This policy was to his credit and a gain for the intellectual life of the nation. We have definite evidence that Egyptian aphoristic writing was early introduced into Israel. Solomon's strength, however, lay elsewhere.

When we read descriptions of the household at Solomon's court, we learn of his real interest. Thirty kor of fine flour (each kor equals 364 liters) and sixty kor of bran meal were brought daily to his table and to that of his large household; also ten fatted and twenty pasture-fed beef, one hundred sheep, "aside from stags, gazelles, and fattened geese." David had had the sinews of the horses he captured cut, because he carried on warfare in the old way and scorned the new. Solomon kept 12,000 horses and 1400 (according to another account 4000) war chariots. He controlled fabulous wealth. Six hundred and sixty-six talents of gold came in as his yearly income, and, in addition, the treasures and the valuable commercial products that his ships and caravans brought from Arabia and other distant lands, even from Ophir on the Indian Ocean and from Tarsus or Tartessus on the Quadalquivir. He had five hundred and fifty governors who pressed his subjects, both Canaanites and Israelites, to hard service. Yet in the end he was in debt to the king of Tyre one hundred and twenty talents of gold.

Even if a few of these figures be exaggerated, the picture as a whole is correct. He built splendid edifices and was a great merchant for whom his subjects were rather the means of satisfying his own manifold desires than subjects to whom as such the ruler had serious obligations. The report that circulated several generations later about him, that in his day silver was lying about like pebbles and that cedars were as plentiful as mulberry trees, may be a part of the nursery tales that elevated Solomon to a fairy prince. He was really considered such by all the people of a later period and even by people in distant lands. This story had a very serious

side, for Canaan was not a rich country. Solomon could
accomplish great things only by heavily burdening the citizens. The great commercial gain from foreign goods could
enrich only a small minority. The vast sums that Solomon
needed could be gained only by great pressure upon the population by means of statute labor and heavy taxation. In such
cases the masses are always impoverished and forced to sell
themselves to the rich to whom they are in debt, and finally
national riches pass into the hands of a few prominent men.
The petty farmers, tenants, and cattle raisers in the country,
and the mechanics and lesser burghers in the cities suffered
most. They necessarily became dissatisfied. Uprisings in
Solomon's time and the great revolt after his death show
this. For decades the people grumbled. When Solomon
drove through the city in his carriage of state, they may
have pointed their fingers at him saying, "See the man whose
father, the shepherd of Bethlehem, was one of us. See how
puffed up he is!" Finally their pent up wrath burst forth.

Nothing characterizes the situation better than the fact
that one of Solomon's taskmasters, Jeroboam by name, who
had charge over all the statute labor of the house of Joseph,
became the leader of the dissatisfied people and led the revolt.
At this time Solomon succeeded in suppressing it, and
Jeroboam fled across the border. Hardly had the king died
when Jeroboam returned. A new and strong insurrection
broke out against Solomon's son, Rehoboam. This time the
revolutionists were victorious and divided the kingdom.
This was the result of the unwise policy of the wise Solomon.
The proletarian revolt, started by dissatisfied laborers, took
on the proportions of a national uprising. It is significant
that Adoniram, Rehoboam's taskmaster and commissioner
of labor who conducted the proceedings, was killed by the
enraged masses. In spite of all this, we must remember that
Solomon did his part to maintain Israel's excellence in war,
to better the government, and to increase its commerce.

Wherever we may seek Ophir—whether in Africa on the Somah or on some other coast, whether in Eastern Arabia or just opposite, in India—by his trade with Ophir, Solomon opened up distant territory for his country from which the astonished inhabitants of Palestine gained not only rich treasures and valuable articles of trade, but also many mental benefits, such as knowledge of foreign peoples and countries, of foreign customs and legends. The same is true of the expeditions that his ships made beyond the pillars of Hercules to Spain. This achievement made Israel a peer of the maritime Phœnicians, and greatly increased its western horizon. The same is true of Solomon's commercial relations to Kue, in Cilicia in Asia Minor from whence he imported horses. (The horse came from the Caucasian steppes to the Mediterranean countries by way of Asia Minor.)

Besides regulating statute labor and taxes, Solomon's new governmental plans, probably, served the same purpose as his military building, i.e., security in case of war. What David sought to attain by a great national census and by making lists of the inhabitants, Solomon continued by dividing the country into provinces. He divided it into twelve governmental districts. At the head of each of these he placed a governor whose first duty it was to gather the tribute and remit it to the palace. His other task certainly was to regulate statute labor in times of peace, and organize the call to arms in times of war. The boundaries of the twelve provinces were made to retain as nearly as possible their historical relations. Historical unity was the basis of the division into districts which followed in the main the old tribal borders; almost all the hereditary tribal names were retained. Former Canaanite city territory kept the Canaanite names in addition to the Hebrew ones.

Solomon gained his greatest fame by his splendid buildings, especially the temple. The Jebusites had already had a sanctuary on the hill north of David's castle. To this day the Holy Rock over which the so-called Rock Cathedral is built gives evidence of it. Approaching from the south the visitor first came to the House of the Forest of Lebanon, an immense building resting upon three rows, each containing fifteen pillars. The upper story was the arsenal; adjoining it was the throne room with its splendid ivory throne. A hall in front of the throne room may have been an ante-chamber for those desiring audience of the King. These buildings were all in the "large" court. The king's palace and, with it, the women's harem quarters were in the central court. Only after the visitor had entered the inner court, or the forecourt proper of the temple, did he reach the temple itself. Here was a forecourt, and behind it, one large and one small room, called the Holy Place and the Holy of Holies. The latter was completely dark and contained only the seat of the presence of Yahweh, a movable throne chariot with cherubim carved in olive wood under which the Ark of Yahweh stood. The altar and ten sacred candlesticks were in the Holy Place.

In the forecourt there were many objects suggesting foreign influences; the so-called bronze sea, symbol of the heavenly oceans, a large water-container resting upon twelve oxen; a number of strange movable kettle wagons; and brazen pillars flanking the entrance. Because Tyrean architects had worked on the temple and a Tyrean brass worker had cast the brazen figures, and because the two pillars were Phœnician, we may assume that Solomon's temple in its essentials was like a large Phœnician temple. Phœnician architecture, however, was not original but was much influenced by Egypt, Assyria, and the Hittites. We must not conclude from this that the Yahweh worship in the temple was in the name or to the image of Baal. At least I find no convincing evidence for this.

The question is not of vital importance because Solomon's form of worship actually differed little from that in a Baal sanctuary except that, as far as we know, Israel at this time was spared the coarse orgies and abuses of the Baal religion. The fact remains that prophetic circles opposed Solomon more and more. Their leader was Ahiah of Siloh who apparently was a spiritual successor of men like Samuel, Gad, and Nathan. Ahiah is said to have encouraged Jeroboam to revolt.

To appreciate this fully, we must remember how strongly Nathan had opposed David's project to build a temple. Should what then seemed contrary to God's will now seem pleasing to Him? A substantial building in place of the old desert tabernacle meant breaking away from the Mosaic tradition; Yahweh dwelt on Mt. Sinai and not in a house in Canaan. A richly equipped sanctuary, especially one with heathen symbols like the kettle wagon, the bronze sea and the pillars, seemed a return to Canaanite ways. But Solomon believed he was serving Yahweh. In reality, his opponents were right when they considered the temple at Jerusalem the seat of Baal rather than that of the Yahweh of Sinai. It seems all the more strange that soon this very temple should become the special symbol of Yahweh's presence, indeed the real palladium of Israel—a new proof of the adaptability of religious conceptions and values. At this time, however, Baal appeared to triumph.

This was the natural course of events. When David's kingdom was broken asunder after Solomon's death, the best thing that Jeroboam and his followers could do was to free themselves entirely from Jerusalem and to establish a god of the kingdom to replace the god of the temple. Now the bull, the symbol of Baal, was made the image of God for the people and introduced into the official worship. Yet he was still called Yahweh. In reality, Yahweh had become a kind of Baal, one of the many Baals that existed. I consider Jeroboam's aversion to Jerusalem and his great desire to oppose Jerusalem and its form of worship, the best proof that Solomon had not called his god Baal and worshiped him in the form of a bull, as some scientists believe.

Until Omri's time, Jeroboam's successors followed his example. After all, this was a natural process. We might expect that the Israelites had long had neither the desire nor the strength to seriously withstand the lure to turn toward the crude Baal worship in its original form. He who counts upon the lower instincts of man is usually right. There are few periods of the world's history in which this truth is more clearly demonstrated than at the present time in the great political upheaval in Germany and in other countries. The Israelites of Ahab's time prove that this truth is very old.

Canaanite Baal worship, as it existed in Tyre in the worship of the city god Melkart, was not merely Baal worship with an image either of a person or a bull to whom sacrifice was brought, but consisted of all sorts of orgies connected with it since antiquity. Whether this worship was native to Canaanite and related peoples, or whether it was brought to them from without, we cannot definitely determine. It went far beyond the mere ecstatic, which was widespread, and has been proven to have existed in other countries also. Similar manifestations were known among the Phrygians by whom they were introduced to the Thracians.

The description of the Baal prophets, with whom Elijah was at Mt. Carmel, is clear. The narrator states that priests dressed a bullock for sacrifice and danced about the altar which they had erected, crying from morning until evening, "O Baal hear us." No reply came, and they called louder, "and they cut themselves after their manner with knives and lances till blood gushed out upon them. When the midday was past, they prophesied until the time of the offering of the evening oblation." This description reminds us of the ever-increasing speed and wildness of the motions of the present-day dervishes as they gradually become intoxicated, raging and tottering and whirling in the dance, until finally they reach an ecstasy and, in it, a union with the deity. It is similar to the behavior of the insane. After the great excitement, the dervishes collapse exhausted, foaming at the mouth, almost senseless. It was probably much the same with these priests. Heliodor testifies that Tyre was especially famous for this strange demeanor. In his report of Tyrean seafarers (he must have meant the priests) who worship Heracles, i.e., the Melkart, "they jumped sometimes in rapidly succeeding bounds, sometimes scurrying over the ground and whirling their whole body as though possessed." The description goes far beyond the actions of the ecstatics when it speaks of bloodshed and self-inflicted wounds.

This suggests the Korybanic frenzy of the Phrygian Cybele priests, the forerunners of the dervishes of Manissa (formerly Magnesia) who in their holy rage cut their arms with knives till they bleed. Apuleus gives the following testimony of the customs of later antiquity:

Then with arms bared to the shoulder, they swung real swords and knives and jumped up shouting, while the notes of the flute spurred them on to mad dancing . . . they wrenched their necks with rapid turning, their loosened hair fluttered about them in circles. They occasionally bit into their own flesh. Finally they cut their arms with a two edged knife that they had . . . lastly they seized a scourge . . . chastised themselves with the knotted lash, marvelously immune against pain through determination. We could see the ground become wet with filth of the effeminate blood caused by sword strokes and scourge lashes.

Baal service did not limit itself to this. Ashtart, Baal's companion, was the goddess of fertility. To her honor and Baal's, all manner of dissolute customs were introduced into the worship, at first magically, to fertilize the fields. Non-biblical antiquity gives examples of these practices in the worship of Adonis, which was similar to the worship of Baal, and in the worship of Ashtart and of Atargatis of northern Syria. But the Old Testament itself explains it sufficiently. When Jehu crushed the House of Ahab and Baal worship, he shouted a remark to Joram, Jezebel's son, about Jezebel (Jezebel was the soul of this worship) about "the whoredom of his mother." Undoubtedly he referred to those abuses of the Baal worship. In this connection repeated reference is made to the so-called Kedish women or harlots who sacrificed their chastity in the service of the god to increase the temple treasury. Such a scene is described in a later text. Even if this event itself did not occur, its narrator tells us what was the custom in the worship of the Baal Peor. Because of this trait of the Baal worship, Israel's prophets and the narrators introduced a peculiar figure of speech, whenever they spoke of the Baal worship: like Jehu they call it "whoredom," and speaking of its adherent they say, "He whores after Baal"; so great was their aversion to this supposed worship of God and so closely in their minds were Baal worship and unchastity connected.

We can readily see that there was a great danger for Israel in this. What was taking place in Phœnicia on the Israelite border, and among the Canaanites still scattered within their own country, was nothing other than nature religion on a particularly low plane and in a form that mocked human dignity. As we have long known, the strongest among the people were obliged to summon their full powers to check the increase of the Baal religion in Israel. Even Deborah, Samuel, Nathan, Ahiah, and many of the discerning Israelites who struggled against the invasion of the Baal spirit and champions of the Mosaic Yahweh, could not prevent the Canaanite spirit from constantly encroaching upon Israel's religion to conquer Israel's soul. In Jeroboam's rule the union of Yahwehism and Canaanism was, so to speak, systematized and elevated to the state religion. Ahab, Omri's son, found this condition when he became king.

In many respects, Ahab seems to have been a satisfactory ruler. His father Omri had already rendered valuable services in restoring order and a firm government, after the great confusion and the struggles for the succession to the crown which had brought the country to the edge of ruin soon after its separation from Judah. Following David's example, he had established a worthy and strategically valuable center for his country by founding the city of Samaria. Ahab continued his policy. Both he and his father before him understood that the increasing strength of the Syrian power in the north must be counteracted. Damascus was inclined to play special politics even in Solomon's day. The disruption of the Israelite state after Solomon's death gave the king of Damascus ample opportunity to carry out this desire. Damascus had already become a serious menace to Israel. Only in the west among the Phœnician coast cities could Israel find an ally against Damascus. An alliance with them was in keeping with Solomon's tradition, perhaps even with David's, for they had fostered friendship with Tyre. Above all, it would bring a much-desired increase of power through lucrative commercial relations with the coast and overseas, by covering a part of the northern boundary and by securing access to the Mediterranean for Israel only.

This alliance was looked upon askance by many in Israel. Because of the evil attendant phenomena that soon appeared as the first and main results of the alliance, we understand their objections. Yet these phenomena were not necessary under the conditions in which Omri and Ahab found the country. This alliance with Phœnicia was an act to further political advancement for Israel. In other respects, Ahab appears in a favorable light. Although tradition, as we have it to-day, is influenced against him because of his religious attitude, we have evidence that he rendered valuable services in the war with Syria and especially in his heroic endurance in the last battle where he proved himself a wise, successful, and heroic ruler. In the thick of the battle, when an enemy's arrow had given him his death blow, he forced himself to an upright position until the battle was ended in order to spare his troops the discouraging sight of their dying king. Holding himself erect with his last strength, standing in his chariot, into which his life blood was flowing, the king was that evening driven home dying.

But the respect and even the love that was bestowed both upon the living and the dead king during his lifetime and still more after his death, to many people, did not counterbalance the attitude he took toward religious questions. Personally Ahab had the same attitude as many others; he may have revered Baal, but his real god was Yahweh. He built a temple for Yahweh in Samaria and named his children Ahaziah, Joram, and Athaliah after Yahweh. Yet the result of the alliance with Tyre was that Ahab married Jezebel, the daughter of the Tyrean King Ithobaal. This of itself was nothing unheard of. Solomon, too, had foreign women in his harem. If they were women of high rank, they were permitted to serve their native gods. Later opinion blamed Solomon and probably Ahab, also. Doubtless even among the contemporaries of both Solomon and Ahab there even were people who feared serious consequences. They were justified. Yet there is the question whether Ahab or even Solomon could have acted differently, and also whether the consequences were inevitable.

In Ahab's case they came to pass. The princess of Tyre had an ambitious and quarrelsome disposition. Ahab was a plain straightforward man of sterling worth who could not cope with the hot-blooded foreign serpent. For centuries, dissolute, voluptuous and profligate living had been common in the Phœnician commercial centers. All the arts of suave trickery that are usual in a decadent civilization were long practiced in Tyre. The plain man of Israel, even if he was a king, was not able to cope with them. Thus Ahab became the prey to Jezebel's influence (he was a better-trained husband and head of a household than he was king and supreme judge). He became a tool in the hands of a demoniac wife.

The plan and the object of the princess' ambition was to bestow upon backward Israel, pursuing its way in harmless rusticity, the blessings of an advanced religion and civilization. Only Baal, only the Dionysian civilization, only the free uncontrolled activity of human nature and its natural impulses were worthy of man. It was the gospel of the freedom of unfettered, unrestricted living of one's own life. How often we have heard this even in our own day! How many thousands have been deluded by it! Jezebel of Tyre is the progenitor of this particular gospel for bringing happiness to humanity. Tolerated by Ahab, she set about to crowd Yahweh out of Israel and to substitute the Tyrean Baal in his stead. Besides the Yahweh temple in Samaria, she had a second temple erected for Baal with an asherah in Samaria. The temple seems to have covered a large area. A great many priests and prophets of Baal spread the new religion. According to reliable report, they even went so far as to persecute the Yahweh worshipers, and Ahab did not interfere. Then the measure was full and the reaction inevitable.

We ask what particular thing happened. Baal had always been in Israel. What could Jezebel bring that was new to Israel? The question is justified, but the answer is in what has already been said. As far as we know, Elijah, too, worshiped in Jeroboam's way, and Jehu also, after he had abolished Baal, but neither they nor Jeroboam or his successors thought of opposing Yahweh. They wished to be conscious Yahweh worshipers even though they worshiped him with the forms of service which in practice frequently approached close to Baal worship. Yet if an attempt was made to replace Yahweh by Baal or to rob Israel of its Yahweh, then not only the pride of the Israelites but, even more, the conscience of the Yahweh worshipers was roused. Only now did many people in Israel become conscious of what the Yahweh of Sinai meant to them. Many forgotten memories of him were thoroughly roused, although many Israelites had previously been weak or indifferent.

Another important consideration was that the Israelites in general and, perhaps, the Canaanites of the interior had not fully realized the consequences of the Baal and, especially, of the Ashtart worship. It is significant that special stress is laid upon the fact that Ahab and Jezebel erected the Ashtart symbols. This causes us to conclude that these symbols and all the particularly offensive phenomena of the Ashtart worship was native to Melkart in Tyre, but not so common in Israel or in the inland country. If it was at all practiced there, it was only occasionally. It is true they served Baal, but only half heartedly or at least in such a way that they did not fully realize its possible consequences. Suddenly all changed. That is why Jezebel's innovation was so shocking to those who were faithful to Yahweh and who would not submit either to violence or to gentle pressure from the authorities.

Their leader was Elijah of Tishbe in Gilead. At this time he was the most powerful among those who opposed Baal. He was more than a head taller than the others of his time. Indeed, he stood alone, a giant of superhuman stature, but he was not the only one of his kind.

Men like Samuel, Nathan, and Ahiah had, as we know, taken up this struggle before him. In them and all who were like minded, the memory of the great Moses lived on, and with it the spirit of the Yahweh of Mt. Sinai. In the south, in Judah, and in parts of the southern and eastern steppes, as far as they were inhabited by Yahweh worshipers, there was little or no interest in Baal. There, fostered by the Levites, of whom many had remained in the south, the tradition of Moses' time was more alive than in the cities and northern agricultural regions.

Suddenly new characters appeared, called upon the scene like Elijah, but probably earlier than he, on account of Baal. These men now became doubly conscious of their task because of Jezebel's actions. When Jehu, the revolutionist, arose against the house of Ahab, when the time was ripe for Jehu to appear before the masses, we hear that he called a certain Jonadab, son of Rechab, to ride in his chariot. Elijah, the prophet, and Jonadab, son of Rechab, were the men upon whom Jehu depended and under whose protection he began his work. The Rechabites, as well as the prophets, had definite plans.

What did they want? As do many brotherhoods in the Orient to-day, so they formed a sect, a sort of order in Israel that must have been established because of the increasing decline of nomadic life and of the simple life of former times. They believed all the evils of the time, primarily the religious one but, also, the moral and social ones, were the result of the change to agriculture and the Dionysian civilization in the fertile lands. Rousseau's return to nature, the return to the simple life of their fathers, was to them the means of salvation and also the return to the faith of their fathers. They themselves were descendants of an old nomadic clan, thus nomadic life was their ideal. With clear vision they realized that the sexual orgies of the Baal worship with its Dionysian drunken celebrations was a caricature of true religion. All the evils that followed in its wake would not exist if they had not exchanged the field, the vineyard, and the house for the tent and the steppe. Therefore they declined to live in houses and in cities and to cultivate the soil. They remained what they fathers had been, steppe dwellers living in tents. As later Mohammed taught his followers, so they now protested against all the features of modern civilization which are symbolized by wine and alcohol. They did not stay the tide of history, but they did pay honorable tribute, most valuable for their time, of honest desire and noble abstinence in the service of mankind.

The Nazarites, or consecrated ones, also made an attempt to correct the wrongs of the time. They were a voluntary organization, consecrated to the service of God. Voluntarily they made a vow (sometimes in their youth, even, they were consecrated by their parents) which bound them closer than other men to Yahweh. They, too, probably originated in the cattle-raising clans in the south. They did not protest against houses, but refrained from the use of wine. The outer sign of their belief was their long flowing locks. By this disheveled appearance, which is still maintained by whole tribes on the Arabian desert, in their way they expressed objection to the influences of civilization. Their long hair expressed even more. It seems that the custom followed by these men, who thus were especially consecrated to God, dates back to the holy wars of Israel's heroic times. They were the ecstatic warriors (savages) who did great deeds for Yahweh. Samson was an example of them. They believed that shaggy hair was the seat of the divine fluid that gave them marvelous strength in battle. Thus they had formerly been warriors; at this time and probably after Samuel's time, they may have ministered at the sanctuaries.

Amos knew them in his time. Elijah's appearance and manner were similar to theirs; at least, he certainly felt that they were his confederates. He had still another group of important allies. As early as Saul's day, we hear of a group of strange men who, unusual as their actions were, unmistakably belonged to the large class of religious men in Israel, to those particularly under the influence of the deity. They called themselves the Nabi people, or Nebiim. We often translate the word by "prophets." Later it did have the meaning that to-day we connect with prophets. But if we attempt to give its meaning at that time, we should speak rather of men, uncannily excited, ecstatic, almost raving.

After Samuel had poured the anointing oil on Saul's head, we are told Saul met a group of the Nebiim coming from a sacrificial place "preceded by harp, drum, flute, and zither; they themselves were in a state of ecstasy." Then the spirit of God came over him, also, so that he behaved like one of them. They were enthusiastic, excited people who carried all before them in wild frenzy. At first we might have believed that it was a mere worldly phenomenon, a procession of strange figures at a local celebration carrying on a strange mummery. But they were coming from the high place of sacrifice when the spirit of God came over Saul and made him like them; thus, evidently, they were religious enthusiasts. But what was the nature of the God they served and of this spirit controlling them and driving them to such outbursts of stormy excitement?

If the reader has read the foregoing pages attentively, he will at once realize how similar was the behavior of these people to that of the prophets of Baal on Mt. Carmel and to those that corresponded to them among the Phrygian and Thracian Korybantes. They did not go to the extreme of bloody excesses, but they had the same ecstatic nature, being possessed of a god only in a milder form. The enthusiasts appeared in the name of Baal on Mt. Carmel. It is probable that this ecstatic phenomenon in Palestine had its origin in the Baal worship. This, naturally, recalls the fact that, as the fertility god of the fields and vineyards, Baal corresponds in many ways to the Greek Dionysus or the Thracian Bacchus. In Greece and Thrace their worshipers were also ecstatic men. Nor can we overlook the fact that, long before Saul and Samuel's time (1100 B.C.), a similar phenomenon appeared on the Canaanite coast. Thus they seem to belong to Canaan and its religion.

To many people in older Israel, the dividing line between Baal and Yahweh was indefinite. Thus in addition to many other things, this strange ecstatic behavior seems to have been taken over from the Baal worship. The real men of God in older Israel were the seers; Moses and Samuel. To them Yahweh revealed himself in visions, or in dreams, or by the inner voice. Now those men who felt that Yahweh had revealed himself to them in such ecstasy as the Baal worshipers had confessed him. Thus the seers in Israel became Nebiim, and the Nebiim were now called prophets.

The characteristic of the Nebiim seems to be that the "spirit" hovered over them as a power that perceptibly entered into their beings, exciting them to the utmost. In both cases it was a power that penetrated ino the inmost depths of their beings. They were filled with the divine spirit, but not all in the same way. The Eternal has no definite mold in Israel or elsewhere. Even among the contemporaries of David and Solomon, men like Nathan, Gad, and Ahiah were called "prophets," probably by their contemporaries and later chroniclers.

We frequently assume that the religious enthusiasts of Samuel's and Saul's time served Yahweh's cause politically and that, together with Samuel, they planned and carried out the uprising against the Philistines. In that case we might compare them with the dervishes who preached holy war in Islam. If this assumption were true, then Samuel would have used them for a purpose and would have made every effort to brush away gradually the naturalistic and the Baal-like in their behavior in order to grain them entirely for Yahweh and gradually adjust them to the Mosaic Yahweh. Whether we suppose conditions thus or otherwise, the fact remains that, after several generations, these wild dervishes formed common ties and devoted themselves exclusively to the service of Yahweh; they lived a community life with their families and, in a relatively quiet way, they instructed the people; they pronounced oracles, and advised the people in religious matters, probably, also, in the sacred Israelite traditions, i.e., those not in the priests' hands. They called themselves prophets' sons, and gathered about a "father" who was their leader and master. These religious enthusiasts, who had formerly been under Baal's influence, now became the centers of the reaction against him and his prophets in Israel. Despite all the obstacles and many dangers, the idea of the Mosaic Yahweh had worked like yeast which permeated Israel like a strong leaven in its soul.

This was Elijah's background. Here this second Moses began his work. Wherever he set foot, the earth rumbled under his tread; wherever his hand rested, there sparks seemed to fly. Fear and trembling were round about him. He was so completely the exponent of the angry and raging God of Sinai that he seemed his personal counterpart. Because Ahab and Jezebel disgraced Yahweh, with flaming rage he announced that a drought would come over the land. In his holy zeal, he made fire to fall from heaven. He cursed the king and his house. He scorned the Baal priests. He approached the king as if he, not Ahab, were the king of the country. He forced the king's dignitaries to fall upon their knees at his feet. From the very jaws of death itself he even snatched its sacrifice. Legend took possession of him. How could we expect it to be otherwise with a man of his type? Things that by their very nature were impossible were included in the narrative; causes such as actuate the whole world were interwoven with the narrative. In spite of all this, not only is Elijah himself historical, but the essential part of what is told of him is also historical.

Josephus tells us that there was a drought in the country when Ithobaal, Jezebel's father, was king of the Phœnicians. He states that it was ended by the king's making a pilgrimage. The pilgrimage may have been to Mt. Carmel, the nearest and most sacred mountain on which from ancient

[169]

times probably both the Phœnicians and Israelites had sacrificial altars. The projection of the mountain range toward the sea may always have been their common possession. There are other cases in his story in which great common suffering has for a time silenced differences, whether national, party, or religious. Both the Orient and the Occident have examples to prove this. When the Nile failed to rise in 1808, the Musulman, the Christian, and the Jew forgot their differences and met in a mosque of Old Cairo for a common prayer of intercession. Since Ithobaal and Ahab were friends and relatives, both may have sent their priests to Mt. Carmel, and Elijah may have gone also. If the altar of Yahweh was in ruins, his worship neglected, Elijah surely improved the opportunity to rebuild the altar.

Even the legend clearly shows what Elijah's object was. His very name was a plan of action. "Yahweh is God." It is possible that this name was given him by his followers in the course of his work; it is also possible that he chose it himself when he began his career to indicate his position. The seers and prophets of old taught him that only the Yahweh of Moses and not Baal belonged to Israel. The Rechabites agreed with Elijah that all the misfortune of the time resulted from deserting Yahweh. They stated their protests with moderation. Elijah regarded no form; he concerned himself with facts. In him Moses was resurrected; he had the same fiery nature, wild and explosive manner, that neither considered nor questioned, but pushed forward, raged onward, and broke forth wherever and whenever he met resistance. Consuming hatred against Baal, who desecrated and destroyed Yahweh's sanctuaries, burned within him. Elijah knew no compromise. Yahweh or Baal was his watchword. He scorned the mingling of Yahweh and Baal, the usual association of the two. He called it "walking lame on both sides." That was the spirit of Moses. That

[170]

was the harsh and conscious one-sidedness and exclusiveness
that was pleasing to the Yahweh of Moses. In him the un-
approachable, the terrible, which we already know as a characteristic of the Yahweh of Moses, were revived. Even if
Elijah did not, as the legend tells us, kill the priest of Baal
at Kishon, this gruesome trait of unsparing revenge is as
much in keeping with his character as the slaughter of Agag
is with that of Samuel.

It is quite natural that legend has him go to Mt. Horeb,
the desert mountain of God, where Moses once faced Yahweh. He, as second Moses, would pour out his heart to
Yahweh there. We do not absolutely know that he really
made the journey to Sinai (Mt. Horeb is meant), for if he
triumphed at Mt. Carmel, he could hardly lament in the
desert and at Mt. Sinai and implore God to take his soul
from him because he had labored in vain. Even if he did
not go, the narrative shows that immediate posterity, as
well as the narrator of his history, could imagine Elijah
only as following in the footsteps of Moses. What Moses
had been to their ancestors, Elijah was to his time. Indeed
after Moses, Elijah was the greatest man in Israel's religious
life. Even his time knew, and he himself doubtless felt that
the purpose of his struggle against Baal was to resurrect
for his people the Yahweh of Sinai, the God of Moses.

As Moses once knew, so Elijah knew also that the very
future of the nation was at stake. If the Baal worship,
demoralizing and crushing human dignity, should gain the
upper hand, it meant the death of the nation; without its own
peculiar religion, Israel would be only a part of the great
Canaanite and Amorite tribe. If Yahweh perished, then
Israel also would perish and be submerged in Canaan and
the Amurru. In this possibility was the spur of his uncanny,
fiery personality, of the frightful determination and inexorable nature apparent in his demands. The honor and the

significance of Yahweh was at stake, for only under him and for his sake could Israel live. If Israel were not willing to do this, it were better shattered.

It was Elijah who introduced into Israel's prophecy the terrible seriousness of the demands, the categorical imperative with which we are familiar in his successors, the classic scribe prophets. They all started with his conception but went a step farther in the same direction, for world politics had changed in the meantime. He demanded and insisted upon his demands, even if they should cause the fall of the dynasty; the later prophets insisted upon their demands, even if the nation itself fell as a result. The difference was only a political one. The principles and demands were fundamentally the same: *Deum habere necesse est, vivere non necesse*. Pure religion, genuine worship of God, was worth more than the life of the king and the dynasty, indeed of the nation itself.

It was significant that Elijah came from across the Jordan where desert and fertile lands meet. As in Judah, so here, the people had better preserved the memory of Moses' time and the Yahweh of the desert than yonder in the fertile lands. Therefore, Elijah seems to have especially emphasized his nomadic traits. They, like his name, were a confession, a watchword. He had the outward appearance of a true desert dweller. He did not live among men but in the steppes. When he had a message, he suddenly appeared and then vanished immediately. No one knew whence he came nor whither he went. Therefore the legend tells that the spirit of Yahweh carried him as he willed, now here, now there. His dress was a hairy mantle of sheep or goat skin fastened about his body by cords or thongs of leather, and he probably had shaggy, unkempt hair. No one knew what his food was. They knew only that he lived and that his God cared for him; God fed the ravens, so also he cared for Elijah. For one reviving the ideals of Moses, nothing was

more suitable than that he should personify the nomadic
ideal.

For the first time since the prophet Nathan, and in the
prophet Elijah, we see clearly that Israel's religion was
entirely a religion of volition; that Yahweh himself was
an all holy and jealous will. Naboth of Jezreel, a
citizen in Israel, possessed a plot of ground. The king,
who had a country seat near by, cast an eye upon
this land which Naboth loved because it was the heritage
of his fathers. He refused to sell it to the king. Then
Jezebel found a means of comforting the helpless, discouraged king. She suggested that he appoint a day of
penance and of fasting, when the people should acknowledge their sins. Whoever refused to acknowledge his
sin should be called upon to do so by others. Jezebel
incited false witnesses who accused Naboth on this occasion
of a crime punishable by death. He and his family were
stoned; now Ahab could take possession of the unclaimed
inheritance. Then suddenly Elijah appeared: "Thou hast
committed murder and wouldst claim the heritage also. There
where the dogs licked Naboth's blood, they shall lick thy
blood."

As Nathan had once appeared before David, so Elijah now
appeared before his king as the warden of justice and
morality. What Ahab had done reminds us forcibly of
David's despotic spell and of Solomon's sultan-like inclinations. Meanwhile these despotic conceptions of a kingdom
had gained a foothold in the north of Israel. Jezebel's influence was hardly necessary in finding people who were
willing to be tools for this criminal deed. Yet just as in
David's day, there were many people who blushed with
shame because of the king's vile deed. The proof of this is
that the deed was long remembered.

Again Elijah was the spokesman. Moses had announced
Yahweh to be the only God, and thus the God of right and

justice. Whoever tampered with justice, even though he wore the crown of Israel, should be delivered to the judgment of the holy one. Elijah proceeded against Ahab and his house with the same inexorable severity that he had exhibited toward Baal. According to legend, he was commissioned to anoint Jehu king in Ahab's stead. In fact it was Elisha who anointed him, but according to all that had happened, it is possible that Elijah had expressed the thought and passed it on to Elisha.

Elijah points beyond himself. When, depressed and crushed, he stood on Mt. Horeb, a whirlwind first appeared to him, that reft the cliffs asunder; then came an earthquake, and a consuming fire. Yahweh was in none of them. Then came a still small voice. Yahweh was in this. This is a contrast to the heavy judgment that Elijah announced immediately afterwards, but we must not forcibly rob the words of their immediate meaning. A new conception was appearing, if not in Elijah himself, certainly in those soon after him who recorded his story, as we have it in the Bible to-day. The new thought tried to tell more correctly the experience gained in intercourse with God, namely, that God is more than the terrible and angry Jahweh. All progress in the understanding of God depends upon ever increasing experience.

VIII

GREAT NARRATORS

FROM ancient Greece as well as from the German and Romanic countries of the Middle Ages we know well the wandering minstrel. We had occasion earlier to recall that on festive occasions at the courts of the princes and in the castles of the knights the minstrel was a welcome figure. His song was intended primarily to praise deeds of princes or knights, or those of their ancestors; it might praise also various types of heroes, knighthood itself, or woman's beauty. The song was a part of the splendor of a knight's or prince's feast. Even to-day among many peoples, who know little of writing, the bard or narrator is a familiar figure. This is true in the Orient to-day, and we have every reason to suppose it was also true in ancient Israel.

We cannot prove that there was a class of bards and narrators in Israel or that one tribe sent poets to other tribes among whom they recited poems as the Arabs are reported to do. We are familiar, however, with the custom of celebrating great events, especially military ones, in a song of praise. Miriam, Deborah, the daughter of Jephtah, and the women in Saul's time appear as singers. Probably the well-known songs of blessing attributed to Jacob and to Moses in Genesis and Deuteronomy originated in this way. They are a collection of songs of praise and of scorn concerning certain tribes. We know also the names of and a few extracts from certain books in which were glorified the deeds of the "Good"—the brave knights of ancient times—and the "Wars of Yahweh." To judge by the parts that are preserved, both books were collections of songs. We are justified in concluding then that these latter songs and many of those previously named were not sung only once but repeatedly at the feasts at the king's court and in the knights' castles after Saul's time and even earlier, as far back as they had existed.

We do not know of a particular class of narrators, or that single individuals or groups of them wandered from place to place reciting their stories. The narrator of the Passover story testifies to the fact that the head of the family was accustomed to tell the assembled household at the feast of the Passover the reason for the feast: the Pharaoh of Egypt had oppressed Israel, and because the Pharaoh of Egypt had refused to allow their fathers to depart, God punished him and the Egyptians severely; Israel departed, and the Egyptians pursuing were drowned in the Sea of Reeds. We may safely assume that the feast of the Passover was not the only one at which this custom was carried out. The other feasts offered opportunities also for telling the household why the feast was celebrated. We may conclude that narrations of this kind did not limit themselves to the household. In reality, the Passover was the only strictly household feast. The others were celebrated at the sanctuary, and the instruction must then have been given by the priest to the people gathered at the sanctuary.

In the twenty-sixth chapter of the fifth book of Moses, we find the injunction to the Israelite peasant to go to the holy place with that part of his firstlings that he was required to render to the sanctuary. He must set his basket before the altar and relate that his tribal ancestor Jacob had immigrated from Aram, had then removed to Egypt, and later, his descendants had been led away by the strong hand of Yahweh and been brought into the land of Canaan. The usual time for bringing fruits of the soil was the great harvest feast in the fall. Here, too, although in the form of a ritual prayer, we have a narrative of the early history of the people. The common people could recite this story only after many previous repetitions. Thus we again reach the conclusion that at least at the celebrations of religious feasts we must assume the teaching of the history of the people. The natural narrators in this case were the priests. They certainly determined at some early time upon the legends of the feasts as well as upon the legends for their own sanctuaries, and passed them on to the believers.

Thus not only originated the stories of the exodus from Egypt and the deliverance of Israel from the house of bondage, with the supposed immigration of Jacob and Joseph and the story of their fate in Egypt and in Canaan, but also stories of the origin of many of the sanctuaries. When, in Bethel, Jacob saw the heavens open and the angels of God ascending and descending upon a ladder, and he anointed the stone upon which he had lain and seen this, and vowed to erect a sanctuary there, it is perfectly clear to us that this was to be reported as the early history of the sanctuary of Bethel. In other words, the story of Jacob's dream about the ladder of heaven is a part of the sanctuary legend of Bethel. The priests of Bethel were doubtless the ones who created the story and passed it on from generation to generation of the faithful who visited the sanctuary. The same is true of the sanctuary of Dan, about which is retained the story of the wanderings of the Danites who robbed a landlord on Mt. Ephraim of an image of god and its priest. They then set up the image at Dan.

From this we see that a great many of the old narratives current in Israel originated in the sanctuary and among its priesthood. Thus in many cases in Israel, the priest may have taken the place of the narrator. Besides the material named and analogous material, there was a great mass of legendary material that certainly did not originate at the sanctuaries, and did not survive merely because repeated by the priests. The stories of David's adventures in his flight

from Saul and, even earlier, of his battles with the Philistines, of his coming to Saul's court, and of his life there;
those deeds of Saul and Jonathan, and farther back, of
Gideon and Abimelech, or of Jephtah and Samson, and of
many others, probably, did not enter the sanctuary and were
not taken over by the priesthood there. From the very beginning they were fashioned and repeated by narrators of
non-priestly rank. The question whether they were in a
class by themselves or not is not significant in this connection. They may have consisted of ordinary heads of families, or of citizens, or of peasants, who had a liking and a
gift for narration and who regaled the village and city people
with their tales. The bards and the poets, because of their
greater technical skill, may have frequented the courts and
the manor houses; the narrators, the homes of the citizens
and peasants.

In the very nature of the case, the most varied materials
were combined in these tales: the legend in which the people
interwove persons and events of the past; the fairy-tale in
which they combined imaginary with actual events, such as
great deeds of war and peace. The narrator did not always
separate his elements; his object was not historical research.
One thing, however, was common to all narratives. They
were repeated orally at first and, in many cases, for a long
time. We know the surprising memory of primitive or un-
lettered peoples. Even to-day certain Moslems are said to
know the whole Koran by heart. In ancient times, there
were people who knew the whole *Iliad* by heart. Popular
singers are said to have memorized as many as 15,000 verses.
Markov published more than 10,000 verses from an oral
recitation of one woman. In this way, much material may
have been passed unchanged through many generations.

Metrical speech has in itself a great protection against
voluntary changes. Rhythm and meter make an unyielding
structure in which variations are extremely noticeable.

Neither a good memory nor verse structure, however, constitute an absolute hindrance to change. Among several people of good memory, succeeding each other, there always may be a few of a weaker memory, with whom the uninterrupted transmission of the material is disturbed and foreign ingredients inserted. Even in verse, the change may take place in so complete a way that the verse still retains the old form. The declaimer may become so imbued with the rhythm and the meter that he finds no difficulty in imitating the form.

If there is no absolute surety of the transmission of the verse unchanged to later generations, then there is much less certainty in the prose narrative. According to the present condition of our historical texts in the Old Testament, we must assume that actual narration, oral speech in prose, was far more common in Old Israel than narration in verse, i.e., song. To be sure, it is possible that many present-day prose narratives that were formerly in verse form were later repeated in prose after the poetic one had been lost. In this case, the narrator took the material from the hand of the poet. In parts of Genesis, e.g., parts of the story of Joseph; and in the Book of Judges, parts of the story of Samson, read like a poem transposed into prose. On the whole, this method seems rather the exception, and the attempt of Sievers to prove that whole books, such as Genesis and Samuel, were written in verse was unsuccessful. We hold to the opinion that besides many retained and numerous lost songs of a narrative character—they are of primary interest to us here—a large and probably the largest number of the orally transmitted tales of early times came from the mouth of narrators who, in prose speech, declaimed to their hearers in a simple style of narration what they had learned concerning the present, of the immediate or the distant past, and of most ancient times.

Here are eliminated many of the great hindrances that do

not make changes impossible but, to a large measure, prevent them. The story of David, of Saul, or of Deborah may serve as examples. The account of the unprecedented good fortune of David in connection with Saul and of his generosity toward the king early took two quite different forms. The one form related that the king was asleep within his barricade of wagons when David crept up to him and took his spear and water cruse from him without injuring the anointed of Yahweh. Others told that, as David was seeking refuge in a cave, he surprised the king who had withdrawn thither to satisfy his bodily needs. David cut off the tip of his mantle, but otherwise did him no harm. This same thought found expression in two distinct tales, and in time both versions were accredited. The manner in which Saul was chosen king, as formerly described, was that, when he was seeking the asses, Samuel found him and anointed him, or that at the request of the elders, he was selected by lot. Here, one version was preferred; there, the other. Finally the two versions grew together, and narrators arranged the form the best they could. When Jacob was made to wrestle at the Jakkob with an El, we have the story of a pre-Israelite knight and an ancient local El who ruled over the stream. This is the story told by the priest of the El sanctuary at Peniel. Afterwards Jacob became the tribal ancestor of his own people in Israel. There the story explained that the ancestor had to gain his new name by an intense struggle in prayer, the content of which is expressed in very pious words: "I will not let thee go except thou bless me." Thus to the people of Israel, every struggle with Yahweh must bring a blessing to the devout.

The recasting of the material is clearer perhaps in the narrative of Deborah. We have already heard that the song of Deborah, which is an important contemporary source describing the course of events, has remained quite unchanged in content. It is historically true except for one slight change already stated. In the recital of the prose narrator, the facts gradually became so distorted that Sisera was no longer leader, but merely a sub-commander of the troop under Jabin, King of Hagor. At first, Sisera certainly must have been the principal character. A later time, farther removed from the actual events, surely heard of Israel's struggles with a King Jabin of Hagor, knew of no details, assumed that the events were connected with the struggles with Sisera in the north, and made the combination in the manner shown. Here certainly was no conscious recasting, but unconscious interweaving of the tales of several narrators.

The examples may show that the material, when orally repeated, suffered alterations, had new factors added, was recast, and in the final version, perhaps, was thoroughly worked over. Each period and each new group of people looked upon the transmitted material in a different way, and unconsciously added certain characteristic details which, from their viewpoint, seemed reasonable. The same character may in time appear quite different from the original one. All this is possible only in oral transmission, or is, at any rate, peculiar to it. If narrators wished to prevent change, the material had to be written, for the written material was fairly, if not absolutely, sure of retaining its special characteristics. The object of the writing was not, however, to prevent changes; prevention of change was only a consequence of the writing. Narrators may have begun to put in writing a text that had hitherto been transmitted orally, simply because the people had begun to read and to write. Presumably, the narrators frequently wrote for their own convenience, just as the magic lantern performers in the Orient to-day have with them their rôles in writing that they may be sure of possessing them permanently and passing them on to their children. Gradually the narrators gave their copies to others to read; thus the narratives became litera-

ture. We must imagine that our historical literature originated in this way, at least in so far as it was the precipitate
of oral narration. That there. is also a literature that was
put directly upon paper we shall see later.

If we examine the historical writing of Israel from this
point of view, we find that chronologically the latter type
appears most prominently, and we have the following condition. For a long time the learned world was dominated
by the belief that in Israel, in Moses' time and for a long
time after him, the art of writing was unknown. After the
Amarna discovery and related ones taught us that even one
or two centuries before this time cuneiform writing had been
used in Canaan, this opinion was strongly shaken. It was
thought, however, that cuneiform writing could not possibly
have been used in Israel, and that, therefore, this discovery
affected Israel but little. Since the excavations in Old
Samaria, in which were found clay fragments with peculiar
inscriptions (ostraka) in old Hebrew writing, the author of
these pages has constantly pointed to the probability which
grew out of the nature of these fragments (without however finding much hearing) that the old western Semite and
old Hebrew alphabetical writing are used from 1200 B.C.
This assumption found a splendid ratification in the deciphering and interpretation of certain inscriptions on the peninsula
of Sinai and, above all, in the newly discovered inscriptions
from Byblos, in which this writing appears as early as the
time of Rameses II.

Without any hesitation we may assume that Moses or
some of his associates were familiar with the old Hebrew
alphabetical writing, and that they were in a position, if they
so desired, to have a competent scribe record in writing certain laws or whatever else they considered worthy of noting,
perhaps a song of victory like Miriam's, or the account of a
battle like that with Amalek. The same is true of the early
post-Mosaic period, i.e., the time of Joshua and of Judges.

If Gideon and Abimelech founded a government in Ophrah and Shechem, apparently modeled after the city dynasty in the city states of the country, we may assume at once that they had archives for depositing important documents of state, as did many petty kings of the fifteenth and fourteenth century B.C. It is also likely that they had a lively correspondence with nearby and more distant cities. If it should be possible to resume the excavations halted by the World War in the old city of Shechem, scarcely anyone to-day would be surprised if some documents of Gideon's and Abimelech's time should come to light. What material is preserved to our day is probably not like the clay tablets from Amarna or of Tanach in cuneiform characters and in the Babylonian tongue, but in the old Hebrew language and writing like the newly found inscription of Byblos.

Besides these products of official political literature, a few heroic songs like Miriam's and Deborah's may already have been put into writing, as well as a few heroic tales such as that of Gideon. I do not have much faith in this assumption, not because the songs and tales could not have been written, but because there were too few people who read them. In the case of political documents and laws, it is not a question of how many people read them, but only that those people whom they concern may read them. With other material the need of writing arose only after many had learned to read.

Who were the scribes at this time and later? I believe they were the priests, or at least some of them. In every other country the priests possessed special knowledge. As the guardians of the sacred laws, with instructions as to the forms of worship, the early priests had occasion to record certain wise sayings—the torot. The archives of the dynasties and of the kings of Israel from the very beginning can hardly have been deposited elsewhere than in the sanctuaries and under the protection of the god. A late report, which

can scarcely be mere invention, tells us that the Rechabites
had their own clan of writers. If we connect this strange
statement with the fact that in the very same location the
Rechabites were very closely associated with the Kenites,
also that the Kenites doubtless lived in the southern steppes
of Judah, then we can make additional deductions. The
Levites seem to have had their early dwelling in the southern
steppes. They seem to have migrated from Kadesh-Barnea
and settled in the south of Judah. From here they spread
out over the country. There is thus a certain connection.
Rechabites, Kenites, Judeans, Levites, and the clans of
scribes of that region were associated. In keeping with this
is the fact that the "city of writers" belongs to this very
region, for Kirjath Sepher, the former name for Debir, signifies the "book city" or, with slight variation, the "scribe
city." Thus we find scribe city and scribe clans just where
we expect, in the old home of the Levites. The conclusion
is that the Levites and the priests in Old Israel, as well as
elsewhere, must have been the oldest, most favored posses-
sors of the art of writing.

What the priestly scribes of the older kings recorded of
political documents is, for the most part, lost. Only a few
fragments have been preserved here and there, such as lists
of officials, annalistic lists of events, and similar material.
They are state documents of the greatest value for the study
of history, but of lesser value from a literary standpoint.
It is certain that what we have is only a poor remnant of
what once existed. Much of the material, such as the enumeration of warriors and their chief heroic deeds, gives the
impression of mere excerpts from longer descriptions. Perhaps they were cues or hints for the bards who sang the
heroic songs. There must have been numerous detailed war
narratives, but lamentable as is their loss for us, the greatness
of Israel's narrative literature does not depend upon such
documents. If Israel had only these documents, it would rise

very little above the dry, bombastic Assyrian, Babylonian, and Egyptian enumerations of battles and conquests, and proclamations in ever new terms of the fame of their kings. If such were the case, the bards and the narrators would have related their songs and oral sagas in the manner described above, and as time went on, would have portrayed ever more falsely the heroes of antiquity. Dry annals and chronicles would have brought written information of the kings and their deeds to posterity. They would not have attained the great narrative style so valuable to posterity.

Because this was the case, Israel was able to create a narrative literature, if not voluminous, yet so very significant that in all antiquity only the Greeks could equal it. The method is due to two circumstances. One may be the special talent of the people. The strong bent toward religious introspection which marked the prophetic religion and which raised it far above the other Semitic cults, seems to be the advantage of the peculiar mental trait of the Israelites as compared with that of the Semitic peoples in general. Israelites seem to have had a strong inclination and gift for reflecting upon and observing the inner life of man. Here we have what is indeed providential in the history of Israel. The characteristic that made philosophers of the Greeks, in Israel turned more to the practical and made of the people geniuses in religion. But wherever reflection sought expression outside the immediate field of religion or the general conceptions of life, there both in the Greeks and in the Israelites we find a great striving to penetrate to the heart of the events of life and of the history of the nation. The mere enumeration of events no longer sufficed. The Israelites wished to understand the events and the reason for their occurrence. If they could not understand events from the framework of great political factors, they could search out the inner psychological destiny of characters as spiritual forces.

To this one factor another is added, without which the first would not be effective. Every natural inclination and talent would be ineffectual, if external circumstances did not give it an opportunity to develop. We had an opportunity earlier to observe that the distintegration of the united State of Israel after Solomon's death, besides being due to the old contrast between North and South, was due primarily to Solomon's attempt to change Israel from a state with a liberal constitution to an Oriental despotism. Strong evidences that there had been a time when they had lived without a king were constantly appearing. The remembrance of this never fully died out in Israel. Even before Solomon's time, the pride of the free citizen was greatly roused against David when he committed a wrong and, again soon after Solomon's time, against Ahab. A sense of freedom and manly pride even before king's thrones was characteristic of true Israelite political thought throughout the best periods of the monarchy. Without this independence the attitude toward their kings of men like Amos, Isaiah, and Jeremiah would have been impossible. It certainly is not accidental that the greatest development of ancient literature appeared in Athens with its liberal constitution. In a similar atmosphere of freedom in Israel, too, a unique development of literature flourished. Official documents might enumerate facts and link them together. The free working over of material was a mental achievement that could be accomplished only by the people themselves. Only a free man in a free country could venture to face things and persons with an independent judgment. Only a free man dared presume to make those in authority and even the king the object of a mental investigation and analysis which naturally culminated in a verdict concerning their doings.

We may, therefore, expect the truly artistic narrative and the truthful writing of history in the time of Israel's kings.

A man whose name we do not know, but whom we recognize as a great artist as well as a man of high moral and religious character, undertook to describe for posterity the pre-regal heroic period from the time of Israel's entrance into Canaan; we are not sure whether he wrote a complete account or included only the most important and best-liked parts. He wrote this perhaps in Saul's time or, at the latest, in David's time. We have only fragments of this work preserved, but they suffice to give us a vivid picture of a unique personage for his time. This was the first attempt to go beyond the single song or the single narrative intended for the moment. It was a gathering together of events from a unified and lofty standpoint; a narrative intended for posterity. I am speaking of the narratives concerning Gideon, Abimelech, and the Danites in Judges, chapters eight, nine, seventeen, and eighteen. Even if we cannot offer definite proof that all three were written by the same narrator, probability is very strong. Were it otherwise, then we should have to imagine two or three men almost contemporaneous or alike in personality. We can hardly imagine this to be the case, unless they were closely related members of the same "school" or children of the same spirit. That in the eighth chapter of Judges only Gideon is mentioned, and in the ninth chapter only Jerubbaal, need not lead us to suppose that the accounts were not written by the same person, for apparently the character was sometimes called Gideon and sometimes Jerubbaal.

The story of Gideon in the eighth chapter takes for granted a previous lengthy description of the invasion of the enemy and their misdeeds that demanded Gideon's interference. Perhaps former misfortunes and the deeds of certain Israelite warriors were recorded in this document. We may even suspect that parts of the first chapter of the Book of Judges belong to it, but its present condition does not give us a clear view. At any rate, what we have in the eighth chapter as a part of the real source gives evidence of a great gift of clear and fascinating description, a dramatic art of presentation, and a fineness of observation by means of which we recognize a truly master hand. Notice how Gideon himself is represented as a true knight, fearless and blameless, who shed blood only because he was forced to do so by the sacred duty of blood revenge. The proud sons of the desert were free even in fetters. They did not ask to have their lives spared; they were willing to die, but only at the hand of a man and a chieftain. Gideon's son could not fulfill the gruesome task, "for he was yet a youth." [1] Here is a complete description in a few words, a picture of the moment, but illustrating the souls of three typical figures, of Gideon, of the chieftain, and of the half-grown boy on the field of battle. This is true art of inimitable charm. We need not particularly emphasize its ethical depth, for here we have a matter of victory and revenge. To discuss ethics would be presumptuous.

In chapter nine, the story of Abimelech fits admirably. Unfortunately this story also seems to be only a fragment. Connection with the Gideon story is lacking. Originally the chief facts concerning the relationship of Gideon and his state to Shechem must have been included, as were also the essential facts of the internal conditions at Shechem, of the relations with the people of Hamor, and of the latter's relations with Israel, as well as with Gaal and Sebul. All these questions that trouble us to-day are not due to the narrator but to unfortunate circumstances beyond his control. In places, as in chapter eight, for example, where we have the narrative unabridged, we are always surprised at the art of presentation and the gift of complete absorption in the subject. Just as the ethical interpretation of the material was included in the material itself in the former account, so, too, in the latter account the narrator justly considered interpretation proper. At the time of his writing, the party struggles described by the narrator were so near at hand that his judgment of right and wrong in Abimelech's conduct often wavers. The narrator took a stand on the highest lookout tower, holding the idea that Yahweh stands above earthly parties. Measured by God's judgment, Abimelech and Shechem were guilty of crime and ingratitude. The way in which this came about is significant. Theocratic pragmatism gives place here to a simple presentation of the casual connection of the events, a connection that was not eliminated as formerly by the miraculous interference of a supreme power. The religious viewpoint of the narrator is satisfied to have proven, in the fate of the criminal, Abimelech, and of the Shechemites, traces of a moral scheme in the universe, which does not allow evil to remain unpunished. It is the standpoint of the religious conception of the universe that the Greeks had about the time of Herodotus and contemporary tragedians. Edward Meyer emphasizes correctly that the narrator was not the Eloist, as some of the newer scientists have repeatedly suggested. Human beings, all in all, act from material and personal motives rather than from religious ones, but in the interlacing of circumstances in the chance events with which fate interferes, the narrator recognized the rules of a superhuman power that punished the guilty one for the crime he had committed. The Eloist thought very differently.

The great artist and high-minded thinker who speaks to us here had disciples. Not long after his time, a man appeared in Judah, the beginning of whose work may have been under David; the end, soon after the great king's death. This man belonged to the king's immediate surroundings. He knew the facts of the later part of David's reign from personal observation. We have already heard how the life of the extraordinary man, David, stimulated all narrators to report orally his experiences and adventures. This man attempted to do more than merely to entertain the masses and to gather a group of pleased auditors about him for an hour. He did not deal with David, the hero, nor with David, the hunted fugitive. The emotional narrators might choose the latter for their subject; for the former, there were official archives. The narrator occupied himself with King David, who was aging now and growing morally weak, and with the portrayal of his later years. Here was a special material, here a problem to present, for one who was not merely the narrator but also the thinker who looked deeply into the soul. Here, too, was a theme calculated seriously to mar the image of the great man and to confound the judgment of posterity. In this way posterity should have a report of David's later years from one who had lived near him.

A man relatively close to the great machinery of state could by no means completely overlook political factors. Our narrator, however, does not call attention to these. He gives us the family and personal history of the man. What he relates of the history of the state is entirely from a personal and individual standpoint. Jonathan's revolt appears as the bold villainy of an ambitious prince. That the weaknesses in the government and, especially, the deep, never conquered dislike of Israel for Judah stood back of all this as a driving force, we read only between the lines. With this limitation he gives us something truly great, not only for his time but for all antiquity.

The introduction presents David's affair with Bathsheba and the killing of her husband, Uriah. Apparently David is then in the full possession of all of his powers, but morally beginning to age. Sultan-like inclinations are awakening in him. The body of the drama represents atonement; David's guilt and atonement, and Absalom's uprising. David's life is nearing its end, but Absalom is impatient. The postlude is of the time when David already had one foot in the grave. Here, too, is the quarrel about the succession. In the drama all three parts are closely knit

together. The material of the introduction is closely connected with the war against Ammon; therefore, the narrator, little as he interested himself in politics, was obliged
to make some reference to this. The part that Uriah and
Joab played in the affair with Bathsheba necessarily brought
the narrator into the camp at Rabbath Ammon and, thus
from one of these official or semi-official descriptions of
David's wars, we hear what is most essential for an understanding of the Bathsheba story. In the description, however, the story of the Ammonite campaign received but
slight rounding off. Aside from this insertion, the essential
parts of the three divisions of the work, I believe, were
written by the same man. Throughout we have the same
atmosphere, the same technique, and the best presentation
of history combined with the art of brilliant short narration.

The narrator himself seems to have been present, at least
from the time of the Bathsheba affair, and to have been
very near the king. He must have written the prelude early;
later, the insurrection. Or he took notes on all the important events at an early period and based his later writing
upon these notes. Where he reports intimate conversations
and proceedings of which he could not possibly have been
a witness, he may have found means to learn the details as
did Thucydides at a later time. Looking about among the
men of David's immediate surroundings, we have little
choice among those known to us. Thus Duhn's thought
that David's biographer might be the trusted priest, Abiathar, deposed by Solomon, is worth considering. But how
do we know whether chance has preserved the name of all
who might be capable? We must be satisfied to possess his
work.

In order to appreciate fully the superiority of this man,
whom together with Thucydides and Xenophon we may consider among the best historians of antiquity, we must read
the stories, especially those of Bathsheba and Absalom, with

an eye to the technique of narration and the spirit that illuminates it. The plot is thickened by David's becoming a despot and an adulterer. In them his own guilt causes a complication that must somehow be resolved. At first, suspense in the reader is aroused by clever enumeration, emphasis, and suppression of individual characteristics, the clear portrayal of woman's slyness, David's artfulness, and Uriah's superiority. The tension reaches its climax with Joab's interference, Uriah's death, and the marriage. This ends the conflict. It it resolved for the time being by David's bowing before the will of Yahweh and by the child's death. But this is only the first act.

The second act apparently begins quite differently. There is much confusion at court. Ammon is a prince with loose morals and little conscience. Absalom has avenged his sister and thinks he has reason for dissatisfaction. This seems to bring about the complication. Absalom is a spoiled son and an ambitious prince for whom the father's rule has lasted too long. He deposes the king, but the latter succeeds in regaining the throne. Here the complication is temporarily resolved by Absalom's death. These events comprise one act. The third one follows. The ghosts of revenge and strife follow David to his very death, and only the grave gives him peace. Death alone finally relieves the strain. To the very end care in construction is maintained. As an example, read the touching scene of David's departure from the capital, or that of his measures to outwit Absalom, or of the scheme that Bathsheba and Nathan carried out with the dying king.

We have here apparently a very simple narration of fact. We are to hear what happened. The writer disappears behind his matter. As little as did Thucydides, so little does he express an opinion or a conviction. He does not accuse the guilty but merely states what they did. The grouping and emphasis of certain points show the sovereign mastery with which he gives and wishes to give the reader far more than bare facts. If we glance over the whole as he saw it or saw it develop, then we perceive with him a great drama in three acts. David is the main character, the tragic hero; all the rest are subordinates. What Ammon and Absalom did were great wrongs signifying guilt and creating complications of a secondary nature, results of the first complication, and only seemingly independent acts. Everything was the result of David's guilt, and could come to an end only when his guilt was atoned for.

To portray all this, the highest art of character drawing and knowledge of human nature were necessary. To the narrator more important than events was the man himself standing behind them and the problem that every human being offers to one seeking the soul and desiring to read it. The principal character was, of course, David. The narrator portrayed him in such a way that the reader felt that the problem was solved—that David's experience was in complete harmony with his deeds and thoughts. He was severely punished to the very end, but finally he fully atoned for his guilt. With this accomplished, his splendid characteristics and his bitter lot had expiated everything. The respect which posterity paid him was well earned. On the one hand, we find in David hot blood and a despotic mood in passion, fondness for luxurious living at court, a bad example to his family, a character not above reproach, and therefore, a weak father; on the other hand, true piety, willing submission to God's decrees under hard blows, a father, faithful to death, a magnanimous friend and foe, always fascinatingly charming, farsighted, wise, circumspect even in the most difficult positions. Thus he is characterized here, and the reader feels that his life must have been as it was depicted. The king's passion was finally checked by piety; his despotism and weaknesses, softened by generosity and true patriotism.

The same is true of the lesser figures. Absalom was a prey to gnawing ambition that he could not restrain even before his father. In truth, he may by no means have been the only one who caused the insurrection. He may have been in part the tool of others and in part the result of his training and of court life. Absalom deserved his fate, but he also deserved the honest sorrow of a father who knew himself and his son's environment. The delineation of the warrior, Joab, is especially fine. Devoted to David from former days, he never forsook him, in joy or in sorrow, but in time he became almost an evil genius to David and more and more uncanny in his relationship to him. His aggressive spirit alarmed David, his unatoned blood guilt frightened him. Weighed down with the blood of Abner, whom he had treacherously stabbed, he maliciously killed Absalom and Amasa. In Uriah's case he also became a willing tool of injustice. As a result he dared appear threateningly before David himself. Here again as in Absalom's case, honest concern in the matter led him. Grim Hagen was a faithful servant of his master. Even if he deserved his ignominious death, yet he is sure of the reader's sympathy.

We see that the great artist was also a deep thinker for whom all that happened had a serious meaning. Since these happenings and their significance are interpreted as having had their source in Yahweh, we see that he was also a man of a deeply religious turn of mind. Even more, when we remember the impartiality with which he faced all the participants, the ruthless frankness with which he unveiled the king's crimes and personal weaknesses, the generosity with which he also portrayed so much good and so much human greatness, the unconditional objectivity with which he so reported of Solomon, Adoniah, and Nathan, that to this day we do not know whom to consider guilty, we must respect his bigness of soul and pure love of truth, which overtower all his other fine qualities.

From this time on the stream of narrators is unfailing. Among them were narrators of a high order. It is impossible to consider them all here, but the best among them, the so-called Yahwist, shall occupy our attention for a short time.

Our presentation of this subject began with the bards and narrators who early spread various information concerning the deeds of national heroes, or of certain bold warriors, or of what they believed of the immediate or distant past of old Israel. At first, they spoke chiefly about their own people. The more their horizon was extended and their contacts broadened, the more they related events of the outer world. As we have heard, at first all was oral singing and recitation. The time came when the oral narrative was superseded in a large measure by writing in the books of legends. Masters of historical writing, like those just described, had not worked in vain for the narrators of legends. These narrators learned from them also to make writing of service in their work.

Thus the books of sagas originated. Legends were still being formed whenever opportunity offered. Such exceptional figures as Elijah and Elisha occupied the public mind especially. Whole cycles of legends sprang up, glorifying marvelous deeds, especially those of Elisha, and showed these men to be miraculous beings. Mere popular tradition could not long retain them for itself. And when the scribe busied himself with the stories, the demand for them among those who could read was very great. Their survival in written form was fortunate, for among these tales we find true works of art, gems of narration. The material for the old legends had been a long time in preparation. Very little was added to them. The need now arose to be able to pass on in writing these old legends, so long repeated orally. There may have been an earlier attempt with certain parts of the older material. In Elisha's time the work was taken up anew and in a unique manner.

We may consider it especially fortunate that the work was undertaken by a man who apparently was greatly influenced by that great historical writer of whom we have heard as a writer of David's life. It was this writer's ambition to present the old legends of antiquity to posterity in a garb that would seem worthy of the work of his great predecessor. We call this man the Yahwist, because his work used the name Yahweh for the deity in the primeval history up to Moses' time, as though Yahweh had been the god of the devout ever since gray antiquity. It would be pleasant to think, and there is much evidence of this, that our Yahwist had a closer relation than a mental one to the recorder of the story of David, that he might indeed have been his son or grandson or some near relative. He may indeed have lived in Judah and Jerusalem and, like the former writer, not far from the king and the temple. Modern scientists have been misled to believe that the former writer should be looked upon as the Yahwist. This idea, like many another erroneous one, entered into textbooks. Mere consideration of the fact, that to write history and to write legends are two distinct things, should have guarded against this mistake that even a layman should not make. The error is not lessened when certain scientists declare that the Yahwist was not an individual but a whole school. We shall hear later what this widespread error signified. Aside from all else, how can a writer of history be the disciple of a writer of legends except in a certain technique? But above all, how could the father or grandfather be a pupil of his son or grandson?

To become acquainted with this truly great man, one of the greatest in Israel and one of the greatest masters of all

[196]

times, we must remember that he faced a double, indeed, a threefold task. Thus his work and his personality cannot be reduced to a simple formula. Every genius breaks through the regular scheme of things; so also does this one.

The Yahwist had before him legendary material, a part of which had had a long history and which had circulated in a form that had been much revised. To gather this material and to sift it was his task. When a man who is not a hack-writer or a recorder, but whose brow the muse has kissed, works over such material as the creation of the world and the succeeding events to Israel's entrance into Canaan, he cannot be a compiler in the ordinary sense. He must be both a poet and a narrator. In the hands of a genius such material necessarily takes on the writer's special characteristics. Thus, also, the *Iliad* is a collection and working over of already existing heroic songs, but under the influence of the will of a great artist's mind, it became a great work of art. Thus Gustav Schwab retold the legends of the ancients, and being a poet he molded them into a form which gave them new life. So also in the hands of a great narrator and poet the material of the Yahwist became a work of art of his own hands.

Even more. Thus far the Yahwist without going far beyond him has much in common with the historian of the last of David's life; like the historian, the Yahwist was not satisfied merely with being a narrator but became also a thinker and greatly surpassed his predecessor. There had been progress in the decades between David and Elijah. The rational thinker had appeared. The question of the why in the world of phenomena had come. Doubtless here is a vast revelation of the human mind which might have led to philosophy in a people with a less practical bent. In Israel it did not go beyond these modest beginnings of philosophy. The Yahwist thus surpassed his predecessors. Even to the Yahwist man had become a problem, but only in so far as to cause him to reflect on his soul life, his character, and to read his fate from these things. Guilt and atonement are the divine power applied to the fortunes of the king and his family. To our Yahwist, not the individual but the world and moving forces of the world became the problem. He would know the reason for death and the army of illnesses, the origin of evil, the reason why people are divided in respect to language. The final and deepest questions of human life he considered and struggled to answer. Thus we have by no means a mere collector or a popular narrator, but a great independent spirit, a personality such as there have been few in Israel, either before or after him.

The Yahwist's work, as we know it, does not now exist separately but as a constituent part of the first six books of the Bible from which it can be separated in its main parts without great difficulty. Thus we are in a position to gain a clear conception of the author.

As one collecting and working over the existing legends, the chief work of the Yahwist was to interpret foreign material for Israel. We remember the legend of the building of the tower, which certainly originated in Babylon; the legend of Sodom and Gomorrah; the struggle of Jacob at Peniel, a story that seems related to Canaan in its origin; or that of the burning bramble bush that belongs to Mt. Sinai. He accepted these legends and many others, but he did not merely copy them as he found them. Certain parts he retained because he treated the material that was handed down to him with the greatest care and reverence, so that many people erroneously believed that he expressed his own viewpoint in these legends with their strong anthropomorphisma. In many cases he worked over the material and gave it new life. Compare his story of the flood with the Babylonian story: in the latter is polytheistic mythology; and in the former a monotheistic one told entirely from the moral point of view. Even in this we see a great and strong personality.

We recognize the true artist, the deep thinker, and the prophetic teacher in this personality; we observe the design of his work and the execution of the details. The creation, sin, increase of evil, the flood, Noah, Abraham appear. Here truly prophetic spirit is evident, most evident in the origin of and the reason for evil, death, birth pangs, and division of nations. In almost all of the oldest narrations, as he retells them, we find such problems considered. In these respects, he is the mental leader and prophet of his people; in his manner of presentation, he is also one of their best artists. His scenes at the wells descriptive of family life are charming idylls; his fall of man and the Abraham and Joseph stories are masterpieces of psychological finesse. The brilliancy of his speech and the vividness of his descriptions can never pale. The charm these tales have exercised upon old and young throughout the centuries can never grow old.

This answers the question whether the work of the Yahwist is that of an individual or of a school. There are but few personalities of such marked originality as that of this man whose will, art, and character stand behind the work. We should seek in vain for a whole school of men extending over decades or centuries as some people believe of the Yahwist or Yahwists. If this very modern theory of the Yahwist has any meaning at all, we may believe that later additions were obviously retained in the author's spirit as shown in this main work. We know that many people believe that in the origin of the Homeric epic various disciples helped the master. This is conceivable only if the disciples have become imbued with the master's spirit and manner of presentation, so that his spirit and will permeate the whole.

IX

REVOLUTIONISTS

When we mentally review the history of Greece, we get two conflicting impressions. Our admiration for the greatness of the Greek spirit and Greek heroism is lessened but not destroyed by regret that the nation on which nature lavished so many gifts failed to establish a permanent government. What might not Hellas have offered the world had she succeeded in establishing an Hellenic state, indeed an Hellenic empire such as Alexander founded later! But a country divided against itself with a tradition that favored division into tribes and tribal groups could never permit the establishment of an Hellenic nation out of the many city states and small leagues which were in constant rivalry. Thus this people was doomed to be remembered in history, not for its great and lasting government, but for its intellectual brilliancy far superior to and more permanent in its attainments than the most firmly founded state.

The nature of the country and the history of Israel seemed to indicate a similar development. Southern Israel, upon which the Judean kingdom was dependent, was mostly pasture land. The capital, Jerusalem, with the surrounding country belonged to the great and rich nobility, and was independent. In the rest of the country, the customs, manners, and standards of living were similar to those of the steppes. Semi-nomadic life prevailed in certain regions. Since ancient times the north had been farm land with separate history, customs, and interests. The country had never been inhabited by one single race. Added to the native population whose origin is uncertain, the country was inhabited successively by people of most varied races and nationalities: Semitic Amorite, Central Asiatic, Hyksos, Hittite who had an Indo-Germanic strain, Semitic or Semitized Canaanite, Aramaic, and Arabian peoples. The Aramaic may have been the chief strain that entered the "Israelite" population in the northern mountain region, while the Arabian was the important addition to the Judeans of the southern mountains. In time these, also, called themselves Israelites, and considered themselves part of greater Israel. Originally they were not Israelite or, at least, much less so than the others. Through the entire period of Judges, they lived apart from the rest.

It is possible that Saul's stern attitude toward David and his numerous invasions into Judean territory were caused by his aversion to Judah's aloofness. We must not be deceived by the chroniclers, who seldom recognize the underlying principles and the deeper connections, and who usually reflect isolated personal viewpoints. At all events, Saul's conduct certainly did not strengthen the bond. Even David himself, whom we consider the founder of united Israel, did not succeed in making the external union of the tribes an internal alliance. Such a unified state would have had greater inviolability because of the lasting union of its parts. Had Israel been a unified whole, it would have been above contradictory and sectional interests, and there would have been effected a real national union in Israel with a degree of national permanency. In this very respect, either circumstances were more powerful than David's otherwise great statesmanship, or perhaps the difficulty lay in certain weaknesses of his home policy which constituted one of the fateful limitations of his remarkable gift as a ruler. Absalom's insurrection, led by the tribe of Benjamin, readily gained sympathizers in the north, and Seba's revolution, furnish noteworthy evidence that David did not succeed in establishing a real union of the North and South.

What David had not accomplished because of his own nature was even less possible for Solomon to do. Apparently Solomon did not even seriously concern himself about the matter. In his many praiseworthy governmental reforms, such as dividing the country into provinces and tax districts, it is noticeable that Judah held a unique position. This does not mean that Judah was exempt from paying taxes and from statute labor, but that it was favored above the others. Solomon seems to have revived and practiced the old principle which Saul frankly acknowledged, i.e., that the kingdom depended upon its own tribe, and in return granted the noble families of the tribe certain offices and privileges. We know that, although the burden of taxes and statute labor pressed heavily upon Judah, across the Judean border it was felt doubly, and this feeling must have increased the tension between Solomon and the North. In addition, Solomon's commercial policy, which has already been mentioned, his building activities, his extravagant court life were of such a nature that they brought material gain chiefly to the inhabitants of the capital and its immediate surroundings. Of what advantage to the people of Shechem or Megiddo were Solomon's luxurious feasting and building of magnificent palaces?

We have already mentioned the heavy burden which Solomon's half despotic rule laid upon the people, and we know that the strained condition ended in violence. It is wrong, however, to believe that the burden of taxes and statute labor were the final causes of the fateful revolution. This resulted from long-repressed ill will among the masses. The real causes lay very deep. It is probable that otherwise the result would have been different. When Solomon died, the people had neither forgotten the old royal period nor the fact that once the Israelite citizens had been free men, in contrast with vassalage in the city states about them; nor had they forgotten the painful fact that in Gideon's time the house of Joseph had ruled in the central country, while in Saul's time Benjamin had ruled. In David's time much combustible matter collected and occasionally burst into flame. Solomon added fuel to this flame of dissatisfaction of the North against the South.

When Solomon died, a rupture between North and South was almost inevitable. Jeroboam, the son of Nebat of Zereda in Ephraim, led the insurgents. He seems to have belonged to the rural nobility of Ephraim. His father had been an independent landowner with the right to bear arms and to train his squires for armed service. Being a widow's son, Jeroboam may have been independent at an early age. He certainly was an energetic, determined young man, whose personality pleased the king who appointed him taskmaster in Ephraim and Manasseh. It was a position of great trust that required ruthless determination. Murmurings and expressions of growing dissatisfaction may long have been prevalent among those who had formerly been free and now were subjected to tyranny. It was a dangerous position for a talented and ambitious young man. After he decided to break faith with his master, he was the natural leader of the working man against the tyrant. Then he was certain of the unconditional support of the oppressed people.

We do not even know whether Jeroboam was truly a great man. His later conduct shows clear vision and good judgment. He also seems to have been a master of intrigue. We know definitely that, even during Solomon's lifetime, he led the revolutionary movement which, however, was suppressed. He escaped to Egypt, there calmly awaited developments, and after Solomon's death returned at once. This is all that the biblical narrative tells us. We can read between the lines and discover that he was not only at hand, but that, during his stay in Egypt, he kept in touch with conditions, and on his return after Solomon's death, he became the soul of the new movement.

Whether Jeroboam himself had a hand in affairs at Shechem through his secret partisans, or whether it was only Rehoboam's folly and Jeroboam's great good fortune that favored him, we can no longer determine. Solomon's son, Rehoboam, ascended the throne in 932. Judah seems to have accepted him, but the northern tribes objected. Jeroboam's revolt was not forgotten, and probably not only Jeroboam, the Revolutionist, but also the agents of the Egyptian Pharaoh supported the people. The Egyptian politicians would have been advised as to conditions in Israel even without Jeroboam, but since he lived at the Egyptian court, they were doubly well informed. They had hoped for the fall of David's kingdom. Because the Israelites did not come to Rehoboam, he was forced to go to them. He went to a meeting of the tribes at Shechem to negotiate with them. This meeting certainly had been preceded by many unsuccessful preliminary discussions with the emissaries. Here was to be set the price for which the northern tribes would join the house of David.

It is significant that the conference was held at Shechem. It was the natural and historical center of central Israel. Abimelech had destroyed it and spread salt over it. After that it was not mentioned. Neither in Samuel's, nor Saul's, nor David's, nor Solomon's time was it prominent or ever mentioned among the district cities. However, it must have been rebuilt in the course of time, and gradually have regained a degree of importance. Its ancient tradition and importance as the center of the Israelite alliance from the time of Joshua had not been forgotten. For these reasons Shechem was chosen as the place for the conference. There was certainly purpose in the choice. Shechem was the seat of an old tribal kingdom; this its very choice was a threat against Rehoboam. If there should be no agreement, then the kingdom of Ophrah and Shechem might be revived.

It is also significant that the discussions were the same as the demands that Jeroboam's revolution had recently called forth against oppression, the burden of statute labor and taxes. We know Rehoboam's answer. Contrary to the advice of his old and experienced councilors, who remembered the days when citizens were free men, he scorned the people's distress and their grievances. "My father chastised you with whips; I will chastise you with scorpions." Instead of the simple rod or whip, the taskmaster should use the spiked whip. This advice was given by the young councilors who had grown up under Solomon's sultan-like rule. These men were the instigators, the enemies of the people, who knew no method other than force to suppress the popular desire for freedom. To them to confer with the insurgents seemed weakness, indeed treason to their sacred prerogatives.

Whether Jeroboam was present and personally conducted the discussions, as our present text leads us to believe, or, what seems probable, whether he was still in Zereba awaiting the outcome is of minor importance. That he had a hand in the matter, that Rehoboam's answer was the one he desired, is certain, and also that he did not act entirely independently but with Egypt's help. Apparently Jeroboam did not desire negotiation but a break with Rehoboam. It is evident there had been a previous arrangement that Jeroboam should be made king of Israel under the Pharaoh's protection. Israel's emissaries had only waited for Rehoboam's answer, and then their decision was immediately made and Jeroboam was at hand.

What portion have we in David? Neither have we inheritance in the son of Jesse. To your tents, Oh Israel: now see to thine own house, Oh David.[1]

This was not a new but an old watchword—the repetition of a well-known password. With it Israel seceded from the House of David. Judah was again the seat of a tribal kingdom as in the days after Saul's death. The real kingdom of Israel returned to the northern tribes. Rehoboam, indeed, had reason to be thankful to have escaped with his life. The people's wrath was unbounded. Their taskmaster, Adoniram, an old man who had held office in David's lifetime, was stoned to death by the enraged masses. The king saved himself only by hasty flight. In his chariot he fled to Jerusalem. Jeroboam was summoned and made king of "all Israel."

This event was of far-reaching importance. In vain we ask whether it was necessary. Isaiah was certainly right when, centuries later, he called Ephraim's secession the hardest blow that ever befell Judah. Jeroboam, now ruler of Israel, did, I believe, all that he could to maintain his country's independence. This, doubtless, explains his wish to become independent of Jerusalem by fitting up the old sanctuaries of Dan and Bethel with new symbols of God. When he erected the golden images of the bull there, he had no desire to leave Yahweh. The bull was only meant to symbolize Yahweh. Like the Aramean weather god, Hadad-Ramman, and the Canaanite Baal, the bull represented the weather god and the god of the fertile fields. In reality, it was far more like Baal worship than like that of the Yahweh of the ark of the covenant and the former tabernacle at Jerusalem. Israel's life as a nation depended mainly upon the peculiarity of its religion. The more it was made to conform to the Canaanite religion, the more it was weakened.

If from the religious point of view, Jeroboam's step added nothing to increase Israel's inner strength in the field of politics, it also seems that there was nothing done to raise its position as a state. Its struggle with Rehoboam and

Judah, who, of course, did not accept without resistance what the revolution expected of them, seem to have brought him little permanent success. As long as he lived, he did not succeed in conquering the enemy. Egypt's promise to help was realized to the degree that Pharaoh Shishak made a raid upon Jerusalem and robbed Rehoboam of his last treasures, the golden shields that Solomon had had made. This greatly weakened his chief opponent, for this treasure constituted Rehoboam's war chest. By experience, Jeroboam learned the old truth that fidelity may not be built upon treason. The Pharaoh faithfully kept his agreement with Judah, but nothing prevented him from treating Jeroboam, his former protégé and ally, as he had treated Rehoboam. Faithful to the old rule, that politics and morals have nothing in common, he unhesitatingly extended his foray over Ephraim. Jeroboam's power was soon so much weakened that, like Eshbaal, he could no longer maintain his capital in the west where it was exposed to attacks from Judah, and was forced to remove it from Shechem to Peniel.

Well as we may understand Jeroboam's revolution from its causes and respect it for its deeper reasons, it brought neither happiness to its promoter nor real gain to the nation. Let us see if we can pronounce a more favorable verdict over Jehu.

We can state in a few sentences what took place between Jeroboam and Ahab, of whom we have already spoken. With all its faults, the kingdom of Judah had the advantage of being indigenous. David and Solomon could not be so easily forgotten. Whatever happened, the house of David stood firmly, and no one ever thought of destroying the dynasty—with one exception of which we shall soon hear. Conditions in Israel were different. After the fall of Saul's kingdom, there had been no hereditary royal family. Thus the crown was tossed from one to another among the leading families and ambitious officers of all the tribes. According to population, power, and traditional rights, Ephraim, Manasseh, and Benjamin might vie with one another for the position; Gilead and Issachar also could claim certain rights. Because of this, the country was never at peace; party struggles and the intrigues of ambitious citizens were always characteristic of the North State. Thus it began and thus it ended. Two dynasties, Omri's and Jehu's, were the longest.

The dynasty of the first Jeroboam ended with Jeroboam's son Nabad. It was characteristic of his time that he should be forced to battle with the Philistines, although David believed that he had permanently conquered them. In 910, during the siege of the Philistine city Gibbethon, the king, was murdered by Baasha, son of Ahiah of Issachar. This seems to have been one of the usual military revolutions incited by an ambitious general who aspired to the throne.

There may have been ground for dissatisfaction with Jeroboam's dynasty. If the father had had little good fortune and had brought nothing to his people, the son did no more. The Moabites, subjugated since David's time, felt the king's weakness and revolted. Conditions were similar to those of modern parliamentary usage; when an administration fails to keep its promises, it is overthrown. The method only has changed. Platforms for public speeches and ballot boxes were not in use then; instead, the murderer's steel worked equally coldly but more quickly. Nabad and his whole house and, probably, his chief partisans were murdered. That was as much a part of an Oriental revolution as "standing up against the wall" is a part of a modern "reign of terror," excepting that psychological justice is greater in the Oriental, for, according to the sacred law of revenge, those of the murdered man's family who remained alive were expected to retaliate. Thus the ruthless murder of the whole family was a sort of protection for the usurper.

Baasha occupied the throne twenty-four years (910-887).
He seems to have been a brilliant warrior and a powerful
prince. He had the courage to move the capital back to
Tirzah, in the west Jordan country. He was one of the
kings of the North State who died a natural death, and
yet his dynasty ended with the first heir. His son, Elah,
fell a prey to a conspiracy in the capital. We understand
the reason when we hear that the struggle for Gibbethon
continued, although the king remained at home and gave
luxurious feasts. Again dissatisfaction arose in the army.
As formerly the house of Jeroboam and Nabad had fallen,
so this time the whole house of Baasha and Elah fell by
Zemri's murderous steel.

The general in command at Gibbethon was Omri. He
was unwilling to surrender Elah's inheritance to a subordinate; therefore he had the army proclaim him king. Then
he marched to Tizrah. Zemri's rule lasted seven days. On
Omri's approach, Zemri set fire to the palace and perished
in the flames. Omri (886-875) was Ahab's father. He
gave Israel a permanent, fortified capital. He founded a
new walled city on the hill of Samaria. Following David's
example, he founded a capital that was not encumbered by
a historical past, either of the nation or of the noble families.
This gave the king freedom to act. Omri, also, renewed
the Phœnician friendship which had been neglected since
Solomon's death. Here is good proof that Israel's prestige
was increasing and its friendship sought after. The marriage of Ahab, Omri's son and successor, with Jezebel, the
princess of Tyre, sealed the alliance.

In the chapter on Elijah, we heard about Ahab and Jezebel. Disappointed and embittered, Elijah is said to have
gone to Mt. Horeb to pour out his soul to the god of Moses.
It is also said that he was commissioned to anoint Jehu,
the son of Nimisas, King of Israel, in Ahab's stead. Elijah
may have received this command, but his disciple, Elisha,

actually carried it out. It is probable that the master suggested it to Elisha.

After the Syrian battle, from which Ahab was brought home to die a hero's death, his son Ahaziah ascended the throne at Samaria. He had the misfortune to be seriously injured by a fall from a window, and died soon afterwards as a result of the injury (853). Ahaziah died leaving no son; his brother Joram, therefore, became king (853-842). The alliance with Judah continued. It supplemented the Tyrian alliance and resulted in the marriage of King Jehoshaphat's son Joram with Athaliah, the daughter of Ahab and Jezebel. Thus protected, Joram apparently ventured to wipe out the disgrace that Israel had suffered at Ramah in Gilead when his father died. He conquered Ramah, but was obliged to fight there again a decade later. The army was at Ramah and the king himself in command. With him, either as an equal or in a subordinate position, was King Ahaziah of Judah, Joram's and Athaliah's son.

Joram followed the good old custom of his father Ahab, of leading his troops in person and exposing himself to the dangers of battle. He was wounded at Ramah. He was taken to the second capital since Ahab's time, to Jezreel, to recover. It was easily reached by way of Bethshean. Ahaziah was now in charge of the army. One day he, too, went to Jezreel to pay his wounded relative and ally a visit. During his absence, the army was commanded by his general, Jehu, son of Jehoshaphat, son of Nimsis. Jehu and Elisha seized the opportunity to shape and carry out their plans.

In a masterpiece of narration, the Hebrew report simply and tersely tells how it happened. As usual we must read between the lines. Elisha sent a messenger to Jehu. Jehu needed to ask only the most necessary questions. He understood at once. Both kings were absent from the army, which fact was apparently a fortunate accident. Later in Jezreel and Samaria, events occurred in rapid succession and with surprising facility and sequence, and Jehu ascended Ahab's throne.

It is evident that all was in readiness, and that the details of the plan were carefully worked out. The technique of revolution is old. Even Jehu and Elisha knew that revolutions must be well planned lest they fail; here everything dovetailed. The king was absent. Even without being wounded he might have been called occasionally to the capital. The second king was visiting him. The country and the capital were without troops. The plan could hardly fail when conditions were so favorable.

We need scarcely ask who originated the plan. Even without the statement that it was an heritage from the great Elijah, we unhesitatingly trace it to him and to his surroundings. Hatred for Jezebel's ambitious and violent deeds, dissatisfaction with Ahab's indulgence toward the overbearing foreign woman, so strongly characterize Israelite tradition that even certain apparent exaggerations which paint Jezebel much blacker than she deserves do not deceive us. Certainly, the people who had confidence in Elijah were convinced that Ahab and his house had forfeited the throne. Samuel and, later, Nathan taught us how little the men of God hesitated to interfere with national affairs when Yahweh's cause demanded it. Trustworthy records tell us that Ahiah of Shiloh supported Jeroboam. Perhaps the real revolutionist, then, was less Jehu than Elisha and his master, Elijah.

The prophet knew well that a change of dynasty necessitated bloodshed. Human life had little value; Samuel had not been sentimental, nor had Jezebel taught her contemporaries differently. However, it would be wrong to hold the prophet and his partisans responsible for all the blood that this insatiable general shed. When, more than a century later, Hosea recalled with terror the bloodshed at Jezreel, we have evidence of how his own people looked upon

Jehu's deeds, probably in his time as well as later. To a man like Hosea, it seemed right that Ahab's dynasty should fall; yet to his contemporaries and to posterity, Jehu's method of bringing this about under the guise of a zealous servant of Yahweh must have seemed contemptible abuse of Yahweh's name and of his prophets.

Knowing how they felt toward Ahab and Jezebel, it is immaterial whether the ambitious general offered his services to Elisha or Elijah, or whether Elisha approached him in the name of Yahweh and Elijah and all those opposed to Baal; even less, who worked out the details of the plan. The plot was carefully prepared by those people who realized that, after Ahab's death, Jezebel's spirit would live on together with that of the Israelite generals, who, since Jeroboam's death almost a century ago, were always ready for everything that a determined warrior who was in command of the army could accomplish with sword in hand, provided he were willing to risk his life. Yet the army must have been dissatisfied with Joram; otherwise Jehu would not have gained the officers' consent so readily. The fact that the king was wounded gives us reason to believe that the war with the Syrians was not going satisfactorily, for when God's anointed succumbed to the enemy's missiles, he was only half a king. What could hinder them from replacing him with another?

The story of the fall of Ahab's dynasty and Jehu's ascent of the throne, as told by one of the best narrators, reads even to-day like a passage from a fascinating story of adventure. The reader is deeply moved by the narration, while the narrator remains unmoved. He merely relates facts. The reader may pass judgment or become indignant. He is as objective as the narrator described above. This is especially admirable because it guarantees the veracity of the narration in its essential facts. Later chroniclers, especially those after Deuteronomy, usually added their own opinions, which makes it more difficult for us to judge impartially.

We were discussing the war at Ramah in Gilead. The king lay wounded at Jezreel; his noble ally was paying him a visit. The kings were separated from the army. This was the moment for action. Then Elisha's messenger, a "disciple of the prophets," as the members of the prophetic guild were called at that time and perhaps even earlier, came to the camp. The officers were gathered about Jehu, perhaps to hold a council of war. The messenger asked to speak to the general alone, and in the inner chamber, according to the prophet's command.[2]

This meant that he came with a message of great secrecy. "I have an errand to thee, O captain." "To which of us all?" asked Jehu. A true revolutionist must be able to deceive. The assembled officers need not know all at once. "To thee, O captain." Only then Jehu followed him. He promptly anointed Jehu with the oil that he brought with him. "With this I anoint thee King over Yahweh's people." The prophet's disciple disappeared as quickly as he had come. He had fulfilled his task; now the new ruler must act. The messenger stood on dangerous ground, and he disappeared as quickly as he had come. Jehu returned to the officers who were annoyed by the secrecy and the urgency of the messenger.

"Wherefore came this mad fellow to thee?"[3] Prophets were holy men, but when they were annoying, people remembered that they, like dervishes and priests, were also poor wretches, and so called them "crazy fellows." Jehu answered in the same strain. He was in no great hurry. "You know the man and his talk," which is as much as to say, "What have I in common with such people? You may know more about them than I do." Every one in Israel knew that they were not the king's friends. Why should Jehu arouse suspicion unnecessarily if the officers did not guess. However, they either knew or suspected more than he thought they did, and they were not satisfied. "It is false. Tell us now." In this way he was finally obliged to tell them the facts. If they would oppose him, this was the time to act. Several officers may have been initiated. They acted promptly, and the others faced an accomplished fact. In a few moments the critical situation was over.

One began by laying his garment on the stairs (probably of the main entrance of the building); a second followed his example. This was an improvised homage, as though Jehu stood beside the steps of the throne. An officer sounded the trumpet as is customary at coronations. Then they all shouted, "Long live King Jehu. Jehu is King." Once again the army had proclaimed a king.

Every one knew what was the next step, for the king still lived. A hasty messenger might cause much harm and confusion. All depended upon quick action before the king learned what had happened or had time to act. Jehu and his officers, who, while the king lived, were also his fellow conspirators, decided to block the road to Ramah, so that neither a messenger nor any of the king's faithful followers with an emergency guard might reach the king at Jezreel. Jehu himself, accompanied by an armed guard, should be the first messenger to the king. Every one knew what his message included. In this situation messenger and executioner were one. Jehu drove in his chariot to Jezreel. The watchman on the tower of the king's castle saw the men approaching and announced them. It was the road from Ramah; the king supposed them to be messengers with reports from there. Was it news of a victory? The king could scarcely await their arrival. He sent horsemen to meet them with the question, "Is it peace? Hast thou to do with peace?" [4] Jehu cried. "Turn thee behind me." A second and a third messenger from the impatient king met the same fate. Then the watchman on the tower announced, "The driving is like the driving of Jehu, for he driveth so furiously," so well known was the conspirator's wild daring.

Now the convalescent king could no longer restrain himself. A dark suspicion drove him from the palace to meet the mad driver. Ahaziah accompanied him.

Foolhardiness and good luck are frequent companions. Jehu could wish nothing better than to have the two kings away from the shelter of their surroundings, and thus unexpectedly in his power. Although Jehu had a group of armed men with him, Jezreel had walls and a fortified castle. Being the second capital of Israel and now the temporary residence of the king and of the visiting king, it certainly was not entirely unguarded. Who could tell what the outcome would be if the guard should rally about the king? A massacre was the least that might be expected. Jehu's extraordinary good fortune, which put the king in his power in the open field, prevented this. When Joram approached him and inquired, "Is it peace, Jehu?" Jehu replied, "What peace, as long as the whoredom of thy mother Jezebel and her witchcraft continue!"

These words express the purpose of the insurrection in the minds of many people and were the flag under which Jehu meant to conduct it. Baal religion was figuratively spoken of as unchastity, although the expressive hints of its real character were not merely figurative. Witchcraft suggests the amulets, talismans, and the secret arts so common to Ashtart worship. Now Joram knew all. He swung his chariot about and warned Ahaziah who followed him.

"Treason, Ahaziah!"

Too late. Jehu had already drawn his bow and sent an arrow through the fleeing king's back. He fell back into his chariot. Jehu commanded his armor bearer, Bidkar, to throw the dead body out of the chariot. They were then just passing Naboth's portion of the field, and Jehu remembered Elijah's prophetic threat. In this·he executed Elijah's will.

Meanwhile, Ahaziah fled not back toward Jezreel, but in the direction of Ibleam where the road turns south. There seemed to be a chance of escape, but Jehu would permit no one to live who might exercise vengeance. The two royal families were related.

"Smite him also," commanded Jehu, after they had pursued the fugitive a while and reached the place where the road begins to rise. His archers struck him, and he breathed his last in the neighboring city of Megiddo.

Now the road to Jezreel was cleared for Jehu. His coming must have been prepared, or the people would not have opened the city gates to him so readily. Nor was it scarcely accidental that Joram drove unguarded to meet this strange man. Jehu entered Jezreel without resistance. Jezebel, the queen mother, still dwelt there. She heard what had happened and knew what her fate must be. She had been proud and dictatorial as becomes a king's daughter, and she would die as befits a king's daughter. In Egypt the ruler greets his guests, who wait in the courtyard of the palace, from a particular window called the king's window. She appeared at the king's window, for she still felt herself a queen. To this day, Oriental women decorate themselves for festive occasions by putting galena on their eyebrows and eyelashes to make the eyes sparkle and appear larger. They apply brilliant red coloring to their cheeks and a dark brown stain to the hair. This is done that they may not look pale in contrast to the brilliant colored garments and scarfs which they wear. Jezebel appeared thus in festive array. With grim scorn she called the king's murderer, who stood in the courtyard below, a second Zimri. That was too much for Jehu in the presence of his soldiers (Zimri's glory had lasted the whole of seven days). In wild rage Jehu called up asking who was on his side. Several eunuchs of the harem guard who stood beside Jezebel favored him.

"Throw her down," commanded Jehu.

The dead queen's blood spurted out upon the courtyard to the palace wall, and Jehu's chariot horses trampled her body to pieces. Satisfied, the monster entered the palace and called for food and drink. Only then he commanded that Jezebel be buried, "for she was a king's daughter." Death demanded respect even from him. Too late! The greedy street dogs had already done their bloody work. Only a few fragments remained.

Jezreel was now in Jehu's power, but the real capital was Samaria. The king's secretaries of state and councilors were there; the royal family was there, and the claimants to the throne, who were also the avengers of the blood he had shed. Jehu knew that all the horses and chariots not in use upon the battlefield were in the hands of the government at Samaria; also the fortified cities and the arsenals. If the government chose to oppose Jehu, it would be no trivial matter. He was anxious to avoid a conflict with them. He trusted to the terrifying news that had reached Samaria from Jezreel. He was not mistaken. "Behold the two kings stood not before him. How then shall we stand?" When he wrote the authorities asking them to take a stand (at the risk of civil war), the captain of the citadel, the commander-in-chief of the city, and the nobles of Samaria replied, "We will not make any man king; do thou that which is good in thine eyes." [5]

What could they do with Jehu in command of the army? They yielded to power. They knew what this meant and Jehu knew also. His answer was a command with a double meaning. As a proof of their devotion, he ordered the "heads" of seventy princes to be sent to Jezreel. Even at this early time, princes had tutors who may have been called their "heads." The following day seventy heads of royal princes packed in baskets arrived in Jezreel. Jehu had them set up in a double row at the entrance of the city. In our day, the Mahdi of Omdurman and the Sultan of Dahomey had the heads of rebels heaped in pyramids at the city gate. Whoever passed through the gate, whoever went to his field or returned from it, knew the fate of those who opposed the new ruler.

This was the beginning of the "reign of terror." To-day auto trucks laden with machine guns drive threateningly through the streets, or a meeting of prominent citizens is called. Together with others I was summoned to the *Alte Börse* by the chairman of the Workingmen's and Soldiers' Council in Leipzig immediately after the ninth of November, 1918. A major of the garrison who had volunteered his services announced that countless cannon and machine guns were being pointed at the city to drown in blood every attempt at resistance. Scornfully Jehu addressed the terrified people (possibly much as the commissioner of the people and the major later addressed us in Leipzig). He admitted that he had murdered the king, but maintained that the plight of the heads was not due to him but to the blind zeal of the people of Samaria. That is as nearly the truth as was the answer of the chairman that November evening to the question, "How about the red flag on the enemies' fleets?" He answered that it was a fact that the red flag had been hoisted on the English and on the French fleets. He had definite information.

If Jehu purposely used "heads" with a double meaning, both he and the others knew exactly what he meant. Indeed he knew more. He had long decided that if he would rest his head in peace, the terror could not end with the seventy heads. The capital still contained people faithful to the old government; at least there were many who were suspected and uncertain. Our information about Jezebel and Ahab, from sources other than the story of Elijah, shows

[218]

that Ahab's dynasty had many partisans. Before Jehu dared enter the city in festive array, they must be killed, at least as many as were necessary to make him safe against surprise. The rest might be done later. First he commanded that all the kinsfolk, confidants, and priests of Joram living in Samaria, i.e., all members of the court and all the adherents of the king, whether they held clerical or secular positions, should be killed to the last man. This suggests Russia and what we read of conditions there and what eyewitnesses frequently told me shudderingly when I was in Kiev and Charkow in July 1918. Not only has the world forgotten none of its cruelty, but it has added to its knowledge.

Samaria was now open to Jehu, but before he finally took possession of the capital and the government, he again marked his path with blood. On the road to Samaria is a place called Beth-eked. It is claimed that by accident he met forty-two princes from Judah there who were on their way to visit the court at Jezreel. The story has been questioned, but there is no good reason for not accepting it. If it is historical, the meeting was scarcely accidental. After King Ahaziah had been killed by Jehu's bailiffs, Jehu had as good reason to murder Ahaziah's kinsfolk as he had had to murder Joram's in Samaria. He probably lured the princes into a trap, and then had them all killed and their bodies thrown into cisterns there. Continuing his way he met Jonadab, son of Rechab, with whom he exchanged greetings, and bade him ride with him in his chariot. All the world should know that every denomination and division of those faithful to Yahweh, together with the prophetic zealots and other sects, (they may have had a large following among the masses) supported Jehu. It was a revolution sanctioned by the church. The church acted as patroness and *temporum ratione habita*, even as the protectress of the revolution and its representatives. This conception is old and yet ever new.

Jehu now entered Samaria and took the reins of government. He scarcely needed to fear opposition. Who was alive who might be called an opponent? Many a house may have been empty, many a street deserted. Still Elisha and Jonadab with their followers looked forward to a final settlement, for Jehu had promised to show Jonadab his zeal for Yahweh in Samaria. Hypocritically, Jehu took on the rôle of a Baal worshiper. This he could do only if his relation to Elisha and the Yahweh worshipers was generally unknown. He invited all Baal worshipers to a great feast in the Baal temple at the capital. When the temple was filled to its last seat, he surrounded it with eighty guards and armed knights. He himself acting as the high priest, offered the sacrifice. Then on a given signal all the people in the temple were massacred without quarter, and the temple together with its asherah and Baal altar destroyed.

Jehu's massacres were disgustingly gruesome and horrible, but we must admit that there seemed to be no reasonable way of freeing Israel from the evil consequences of the worship of Melkart of Tyre as long as Ahab's dynasty continued. Freedom could be accomplished only by violence, by killing the royal family and its favorite creations. However, even Hosea points out the fact that to many of the best people in Israel, the price seemed too high. Although Jehu did exhibit a few chivalrous impulses, such as the rather tardy honor to the corpse of Jezebel, the king's daughter, and the invitation to the Samarian chiefs to make an honest decision, he was a most disgusting personality, a soldier of extreme daring and of ruthless selfishness. At times he calculated cleverly but often more cunningly than wisely. He was frequently cynically hypocritical, wily, and bloodthirsty to a degree unusual even in the Orient. He rendered no service to the state by murdering half of the population of Jezreel and of Samaria; a small state can ill afford such losses. The evil effects were increased by the

fact that in murdering his opponents, he created many enemies. The throne that he believed made firm by bloodshed
was from the beginning unstable. Finally he was forced to
become a vassal of Assyria. This act was his undoing, for
it caused an uprising in Syria with disastrous results for
him. Jehu, like Jeroboam, found little satisfaction in his
own actions.

The inglorious success of Jehu's revolution makes us ask
whether he was suited to assume control of Israel's affairs
at the price of so much innocent blood. I stated above that
the Samarian nobility could hardly have acted otherwise.
This is true, for, as we may say very politely, they were
ready "to yield to power." But suppose they had been determined not to do so? During the German revolution the
author repeatedly had occasion to observe at close range the
surprising degree of cowardice, indecision, and helplessness
of the German revolutionists whenever they faced a man
who stood firmly against threats of violence.* Judging by
these experiences the author feels justified in assuming that
affairs might have turned out differently in Germany if, at
the decisive moment, certain headquarters and governmental
offices had taken a firmer stand in the face of alleged dangers and had followed the praiseworthy example of hundreds of thousands at the front who had unhesitatingly
risked their lives; there should have been less clinging to
this miserable existence. Jehu's personality impresses us as
being in every way similar to that of our modern revolutionary heroes. Who can tell what might have been the result
had Jehu faced virile men? The psychology of terror seems
always to be that when a gun is pointed at a man or when he

* Whenever the representatives of the revolutionists were dissatisfied
with what I did they pointed their guns at me. Much as they wished to
do so they never succeeded in killing me merely because it did not occur
to me to plead for my life. I calmly told them there was nothing to
prevent them from shooting me immediately. This reply apparently
disconcerted them. Evidently they had never heard it before.

sees blood otherwise than at the battle front, all the good genii of courage and power desert him and give place to paralyzing helplessness.

Among the revolutionists in Israel we find a woman, Athaliah, the daughter of Ahab.

In Jerusalem Rehoboam was succeeded first by his son, Ahibiah, and then by his grandson, Asa. The unfortunate civil war, which caused Jeroboam's secession from Israel, continued in both their reigns. Asa brought about a change by making a treaty with Syria. Baasha was forced to surrender Ramah which he had taken; Asa was able to extend his northern border somewhat. This gave Omri and Ahab occasion to look about for allies against the Syrians. An alliance with Tyre and with Judah resulted. Asa's son, Jehoshaphat, was considered the ally of Ahab and Ahaziah. As Omri's son, Ahab, had married Jezebel of Tyre, so in Judah Jehoshaphat's son, Joram, married Ahab's daughter, Athaliah. As we know, the alliance outlived Ahab and Jehoshaphat; indeed it was greatly strengthened by his marriage. Joram, son of Ahab, who ruled Israel after his brother, Ahaziah, and who fought at Ramah, was given chief command. His nephew, Ahaziah, son of Joram, King of Israel, visited him, and the royal princes on both sides exchanged ceremonial visits.

We have already heard the fate of Ahaziah (successor to his father Joram, who died relatively young) at Jehu's hands. He is said to have been made king when twenty-two years of age, and died during the first year of his reign (842). Again the throne at Jerusalem was vacant. Athaliah, early left a widow, was robbed of the influential position of queen mother by her son's sudden death. The influential position of the queen mother in the Orient to this day is well known. On her still rests a reflection of the glamour that surrounded the mother as the center of the family in the marriage relations of primitive times. She held a position second only to the king. Although her mother is not specifically mentioned, Athaliah was both Ahab's and Jezebel's daughter. She apparently inherited her mother's ambition and spirit of violence. The thought that a new king and a new queen mother should enter the palace, that she must then spend her days dully in the privacy of the harem, seemed unbearable to her. Why should her daughter-in-law, Zibiah of Beersheba (this was the queen's name), the simple burgher's daughter of southern Judah, be more prominent than she, the king's daughter?

Her decision was quickly made. To be sure, she could no longer be queen mother, for her son the king was dead. There was another way to retain power and esteem. The ruler was in a position of greater power than the king's mother or the king's wife. The whims of fortune had robbed her of the two latter positions, but the third possibility—that of ruler—remained to her, who was now dependent entirely upon herself. Never before or afterwards did a woman occupy the throne of either Judah or of Israel. The idea was revived only by the late epigones of the Maccabean period. There were cases in early antiquity, however, when a woman sat upon the throne of the Pharaohs, and legend at least tells us that Semiramis of Assyria, a marvelous woman, occupied the throne at Nineveh. This is proof that a woman ruler was conceivable in antiquity.

To a certain degree the country's welfare might excuse Athaliah's ambitious plans. Her royal son, Ahaziah, died when he was but twenty-three years old. His eldest son and heir could have been no more than a mere boy. Jehu had so recently murdered the relations of the royal family in great numbers. Who was left to advise and help the young king? What could his mother, at best an inexperienced Judean burgher's or cattleman's daughter, offer him in experience, wisdom, and regal spirit? Would it not be a service to the state which had suffered such great losses if she who had royal blood and regal experience should aid fate?

On hearing of her son's death, Athaliah promptly acted. She had all the remaining heirs to the throne ruthlessly murdered. There were not many, because Jehu had done his work so thoroughly. They were mainly the king's minor children. If they were permitted to live, Zibiah or another of Ahaziah's wives would become temporary regent. The fact that the children were murdered near their bedchamber points to this. All took place in the palace nursery, and this inhuman woman was capable of sacrificing her own flesh and blood, her unsuspecting grandchildren, to the demon of her inordinate ambition.

Fate willed it that a sister of the murdered king, a daughter of King Joram, thus probably Athaliah's own daughter, Jehoshabeath, married to Jehoiada, the high priest of the temple, was a witness of this bloody scene. Being a royal princess she had access to the palace. She succeeded in saving Ahaziah's one year old son, Jeoash, from the clutches of the hired murders. He was probably the youngest of Ahaziah's children, and the murderers paid the least attention to the babe in the cradle. Jehoshabeath successfully carried him off, and for years hid him in some remote chamber of the temple of which her husband had supervision. She kept him there until the hour for revenge came.

When Athaliah's bloody deed was accomplished, she was free to take the throne. There were no male heirs. The fact that she was the dead king's mother and of royal blood made the people and the nobles consider her claim equal to that of the widowed queen. At any rate, she displayed greater energy than the queen and succeeded. It was her good fortune to be spared from commanding other massacres which would have been inevitable had Jehu not killed the forty-two princes.

Athaliah occupies David's throne six years. We do not

know how much satisfaction she got from ruling. However, her death shows that there must have been a special Baal temple in Jerusalem besides the Yahweh temple. We do not know whether it was on the great square of the temple of Solomon or where else, nor when it was built, nor by whom; perhaps during Athaliah's own reign. It seems more probable, however, that the cult of the Tyrean Melkart (this is what Baal means here) was introduced into Jerusalem by Joram and Ahaziah. The reproach that they both wandered "the path of the house of Ahab" seems to refer to this, because both were closely connected with it through Athaliah.

There is no question that Athaliah was its spiritual founder, just as Jezebel was in Samaria. We take it for granted that she persuaded her husband, Joram, to build a Baal Melkart temple besides the Yahweh temple in the capital, as her father Ahab had done. This temple had a special priest named Mattan who conducted the services there at a special Baal altar and before Baal images. We do not know what this Baal image looked like. We might imagine it was a bull because Baal was often connected with Hadah-Ramman, the Syrian god of the weather and of fertility. But the image of the bull was used for Yahweh in the North State from Jeroboam's time on. For this reason I do not believe that they now used it for Baal. I should rather suppose that by the image of the Phœnician Melkart, peculiar to the so-called Moloch worship which included the gruesome practice of human sacrifice, at least Baal images are meant. The Ashtart images may have corresponded to the nude or nearly nude female figures so frequently found in excavations that represented the goddess of fertility.

Athaliah naturally practiced this cult during her reign. There is no hint that Yahweh worship was abolished or even persecuted. Quite the contrary. Not only had Athaliah's own daughter married the high priest of the Yahweh temple, but the whole conspiracy against the queen is based on the fact that Yahweh worship continued unmolested in Solomon's temple and was protected by the royal bodyguard. Therefore Baal worship was permitted and favored together with Yahweh worship. But this was enough to rouse the old established Zadok priesthood in Jerusalem and all those who clung to the faith of their fathers in the city and, especially, in the country districts of Judah to vow vengeance against Athaliah's reign of violence, not only because of the innocent blood she shed but rather because of the religious objections of the believers. Besides all else, Athaliah's deed seemed to them one of many attempts to gain ground for the objectionable religion in Judah. For that reason alone they felt they must oppose it with every available means.

In fact, a long and carefully planned conspiracy was formed against the power that Athaliah had usurped. It began in the Yahweh temple where the high priest and his wife, Jehoshabeath, kept the embers smoldering until the time came to fan them to a bright flame. Religious zeal for Yahweh against Baal was mingled with moral aversion to the queen's inhuman cruelty toward her own family and the unusual duty of blood revenge on their own blood for their own blood. The nephew's blood still cried to heaven for vengeance against the unnatural grandmother, the avenger's own mother.

For six years the fire was kept smoldering. In the seventh year the flames finally burst forth. The leaders of the body and palace guard, which now consisted of Carites, hirelings from Asia Minor, who had replaced the former Cretans, were secretly drawn into the conspiracy. These and the remaining conspirators were initiated into the secret that the real heir to David's throne had been kept captive for six years in the Yahweh temple. Hidden from the world, the boy had lived under the protection of Yahweh and his priest. Woe to them if one of the queen's spies should get trace of him! The murderous steel of the tyrannical queen would certainly be his lot. Wise consideration, however, bade his friends wait until the child had at least reached boyhood. Then they dared hesitate no longer, for each day might mean the boy's death and the sudden end of their whole plan. Before the time of action, the people in the city and country certainly had heard nothing of the prince. But Jehoiada and Jehoshabeath must constantly have urged their confidants among those faithful to Yahweh (the Levites, priestly acolytes, Rechabites and all other Yahweh worshipers) to be ready for action when the hour of vengeance against Baal should come. It had come to Samaria; it would somehow come to Jerusalem.

It came. The Carite hirelings of the palace and bodyguard were also the temple guard. Every Sabbath the guard changed. The officers took the holy oath by the temple of Yahweh in the high priest's presence to the young prince, whom they now saw for the first time. The moment when the new guard arrived and the old guard was still on duty was favorable for action. There were no troops in the palace then, and the temple was well guarded against surprise. Both in Egypt and in Assyria, the king had a special place where he stood when he took part in the services. The same custom seems to have prevailed in Jerusalem. The king's place beside the great altar was entirely surrounded by troops. Once more the young prince was brought forth, this time in the space surrounded by troops. The priest put him in the king's place, ornamented him with the royal circlet and the bracelet— symbols of royal dignity—and then anointed him. Now the seven-year-old prince was king. All clapped their hands and shouted, "Long live the king!"

Startled by the noise, Athaliah hastened to the temple from her palace. Seeing what had happened, she cried, "Treason!" To avoid desecrating the temple by murder, the high priest had her removed from the temple and then killed. According to another version, Jehoash was proclaimed king in the palace itself, and Athaliah was killed there. In any case the high priest had the people storm the Baal temple, demolish it, and kill the priest, Mattan. The event was conducted as a solemn act of the covenant and as though a real reform had been planned. However, they do not seem to have gone farther than to destroy Baal worship. According to the chronicler, in his later life Joash is reported to have had differences with the priests and prophets because he inclined toward heathen cults. It is even reported that he had Jehoiada's son, the prophet Zachariah, stoned in the courtyard of the temple. We have, however, no proof of this.

X

CLASSIC PROPHETS. AMOS AND HOSEA

PROPHECY surpassed itself in Elijah. But soon after his time, men like the Yahwist surpassed even Elijah. The climax, however, was reached by the classic prophets of the eighth and the following centuries, when the genius of the Israelite people found its purest and most complete expression. In their work we have a phenomenon which no people on earth can equal. If ancient Israel claimed that its religion represented the flower and the crown of all ancient religions, this claim rested primarily upon the high ideals, the greatness, and lofty purity of the devotion of its classic prophets. They were not all equally great, nor is every speech of every one of them a vivid expression of the highest ideals. Yet the devoutness of their best representatives and the work which expressed their very souls may be counted among the purest and highest revelations of divine life on earth.

In this stage, the peculiarity of prophecy first appears formally and psychologically, for the primitive, crude ecstasy of their behavior slowly disappeared. It gave way to spiritual exaltation through contact with God, to the vitalizing radiance of the presence of Yahweh, and to the direction of their thoughts and feelings entirely toward God and His will. The special inspiration and realization of the spiritual life expressed itself sometimes in apparitions or visions, which brought the prophets into the immediate presence of God; frequently, in an apparently entirely conscious state, the inner eye, completely diverted from the outer world, be-

[229]

came active. Frequently in the form of simple encouragement, the prophet heard a voice from above, indeed of God himself, speaking, and the prophet had only to repeat what was told him; this was inspiration in the strictest sense of the term. Finally, it frequently appeared in the form of a simple direction to carry out a commission which came to the prophet without perceptible special meditation, solely as a moral duty, as an inner certainty made known to him by the insistent voice of his conscience.

Among Israel's greatest spiritual attainments belong the idea and the experience of moral monotheism, an achievement unparalleled in history. This experience apparently elevated the prophets more and more above the external means and forms with which their predecessors had worked. The union with God was most significant to the latter as well as to the former prophets, for the more they understood and felt God to be a purely spiritual and a purely moral force, the more the union with God became increasingly a spiritual and a moral process and condition. Ecstasy and ecstatic losing of oneself in the Godhead gradually was transformed to a conscious and voluntary giving up of oneself to God, an absorption in His will and counsel; passive absorption became an active finding of oneself in God. The world-wide difference of this prophetic mysticism from every other mysticism in antiquity is that one ends logically in the surrender of self in oblivion, the passive melting into the Nirvana, while the other only finds its true self in the greatest activity that springs from union with God; in finding one's true self, one discovers also one's greatest moral tasks and capabilities.

Thus it is entirely in keeping with the natural course of events that by conceiving God entirely as the moral director of the world, the classic prophets again found their way back to Moses. With all his strength, he had accepted Yahweh as the moral will which, with inexplicable power, rejected all that was revolting. Thus the prophetic Yahweh was in reality the same as Moses' God of Sinai, brought out again from oblivion, freed from fusion with the heathen Baal and restored to His position of honor. The predecessors, too, of the classic poets, Elijah for example, had had this goal in mind. The more completely Yahweh was again accepted purely as moral holiness, the more strongly and exclusively was the return to Moses recognized as the real means of preventing the spread of the half heathenish spirit and of regaining Yahweh in the old purity.

If with the above discussion we have led the way from the formal characteristics of classic prophecy to the subject matter of this prophecy, we may trace the peculiarity of the subject matter as compared to that of the earlier prophetic messages primarily to the new foreign political situation and the new social-moral attitude.

The period to which the great prophets in Israel lent their names is marked politically by the Assyrian Empire coming into Israel's field of vision. Israel's first intimate connection with Assyria was during Omri's dynasty. Although conflicts had taken place before this time (according to Assyrian inscriptions under King Ahab) the internal disruption in Israel itself and Assyria's advance into Syria were the causes of Jehu's paying tribute to Assyria. The obelisk of Salmansar III mentions the tribute for the year 842. Jehu's terrible massacres aroused so many blood avengers and other enemies in his own country that he needed the Assyrian legions to support his throne. A century later an Assyrian king again reports that he subjugated Israel. After Jeroboam II died, his son was murdered by Shallum, and a month later Shallum himself was murdered by the usurper, Menahem. He, too, like Jehu before him, did not feel himself powerful enough to master his enemies and so made himself subject to Tiglath-Pileser III (IV) who was then invading the country, "that his hand might be with him and confirm the kingdom in his hand." This was in the year 738, scarcely two decades after Amos had appeared.

This marks the political situation as it really was. That most people did not realize it, does not alter the fact that, unless a miracle happened, Israel must sooner or later fall a prey to the advances of the Assyrian Empire. The prophets were among the few people in the country who were not deceived about conditions; and believing themselves the mouth-pieces of Yahweh, they could not remain silent about what they foresaw. They told what they knew with daring frankness, and were therefore suspected of treachery to their own fatherland by the official guardians of statesmanship and patriotism.

We must consider what it meant to these men, who dearly loved their people and their native land, to be obliged constantly to announce its downfall. The disgrace of being considered traitors to their own country was not their greatest sorrow; the anguish at being obliged to foresee the misfortunes of their people and not to prevent them was still greater; to see that the people must become more and more entangled in ruinous actions and surely travel down the road to destruction. Among the greatest achievements known to history in the realm of character and of political morals is this spectacle, continuing for nearly two centuries, of men of undaunted courage making the greatest sacrifices that men can offer for their country. For greater than death in war and battle for one's native country, is life for one's native land, lived in daily disgrace and misunderstanding by one who, knowing the certain destruction of the country, frankly announces it.

With bleeding hearts the prophets rendered this difficult service to their country, not with malicious joy in misfortune, but because they could not do otherwise. They were appointed to announce Yahweh's will. His will was holy. The people's deeds were unholy, for they had fallen away from Yahweh to Baal and had turned from Yahweh to wrong-doing and violence. The one sin, turning away from Yahweh, was old, for the "whoring" with Baal began when Israel entered Canaan. Violence has existed always and everywhere, and so, also, in Israel at all times. At this time, however, it had brought about a condition that filled the prophets with terror. Arrogance and immorality, over-charging, and evading the law had reached a point formerly unknown. Worst of all, increasing wealth and commercial gain had caused a social tension between rich and poor which threatened a violent upheaval. This, however, would not be brought about by the helpless masses, but by God Himself, their champion.

Thus two things worked together for the prophets: because Yahweh is a holy and a just God, religious and moral degradation must lead to collapse; and the Assyrian danger, if a miracle did not happen, would bring about Israel's downfall. The miracle did not happen. It could not happen because God's divine judgment must be pronounced upon Israel. Thus the circle of proof that the prophets worked out for themselves closed with uncanny completeness and logic. In whatever light they might look upon matters, only the terrible Cassandra-like cry remained:

> The virgin of Israel is falling;
> She shall rise no more;
> She is cast down upon her land;
> There is none to raise her up.[1]

And yet this message of judgment could not be the final word of prophecy. It has been repeatedly said that this message was the last word of the older prophets of this time. I do not believe in it. By his judgment Yahweh could not intend annihilation of his people, least of all, religious annihilation. Even the destruction of the state was not intended to destroy the people and to blot them out

[233]

from the face of the earth. Behind the fires of judgment Elijah had already seen the calm rule of the gentle spirit. Thus even this period recognized the work of God's healing powers as the final and real purpose of divine action. The prophecy of salvation reached its climax in the prospect of the Messianic period of blessing.

One of the greatest of the prophets, Amos of Tekoa, gave expression to this newer form of the prophetic proclamation. He was a shepherd, probably the owner of a flock in the Judean highlands. He also earned a living by planting the sycamore, a sort of wild mulberry fig tree. The tree is not native to Tekoa itself, but to lower levels and, especially, to the coast plain. Amos may, therefore, have traveled about sometimes with and sometimes without his flocks. This explains his wide vision, the great fund of information into many sorts of things not belonging to Tekoa itself. He knew about the king's tithe, of mowing grass, of fruit crops, of fishing in the ocean, of the ancestral home of the Arameans, of conquests of the past, and of gruesome war deeds that happened, even of distant lands and cities, such as Hamath and Calneh, and of the stars, and of the great ocean. Although he certainly was a man of the lower class, he knew how to address his comrades impressively and with artistic finish. He was well versed in the style and forms of expression current among prophets and poets. Indeed he seems to have, independently, developed the art of speech. He spoke in threats, in reproaches, in scorn, and in prophecy, in prose, and in lengthy poems, in admonition, in prophetic speech, and in lyric poetry. He used parallelism of parts, rhythm, and refrain. He spoke in bold figures and well-balanced similes; he played sarcastically upon words; he related visions, and filled them with allegories.

We are astonished at the simple shepherd's mental powers, and we ask in vain where this simple man of the people learned all this. Certainly, he may have gathered much in his wanderings with or without his flocks (for Yahweh called him from his flocks). His best came from within; it sprang from his inmost soul and from his intercourse with Yahweh in the great loneliness of the torrid Judean upland, which in many particulars was more like a desert than a pasture land. Hesiod of Askra, almost a contemporary of Amos, and a shepherd like him, tells of himself that the muses at the Helikon taught him their song as he tended his sheep. They bade him hearken to their words in the loneliness of the mountains. "We know how to tell the truth. Thus spoke the daughters of the great Zeus and breathed divine song into me, so that I announce the things of the future and of ancient times." Thus Hesiod spake of himself. Amos tells of himself: "The Lord took me from following the flocks and said unto me, 'Go prophesy unto my people Israel.'" [2]

The loneliness of great silent nature, with only mountains and heath about them, the heavens and the eternal stars over them, awakened in both of these men, as formerly in Moses, the sensation of the nearness of the Godhead. Loneliness turns one's thoughts inward and upward. All that he had seen and experienced in his wanderings and what he had heard in Tekoa, he pondered on and meditated upon as in intercourse with God. Old prophets' speeches, national tales, and many an event that reached his ear when looked at from the viewpoint of the divine will, appeared in a new light. Everything took on a special color; everything appeared in a new light, had a new explanation, and a new meaning when measured by the standards attained by absorption in God and spiritual ideas.

Whoever has been fortunate enough to come in contact with many people of the simpler walks of life, shepherds, peasants, or farmers who gained all their wisdom from contemplation of nature and their God, and whose only written means of education consisted possibly of their Bible and hymn book, such a man may understand, better than many of our scholars at their desks, whence Amos had gained so much knowledge. Whoever comes in contact with people of this type unwittingly gains the impression that absorption in God and in religious life and reflection on the things *sub specie aeternitatis* are capable of bringing about a fineness of feeling and of thinking, a largeness of vision, a breadth of judgment which we consider the indications of true culture. We occasionally find among such people surprising knowledge and capabilities—even a mastery of the poetic form. If Amos had opportunity to hear of men like Elijah, Micha ben Jimla, and their successors, whose names must have been known in his time although unknown to us; if it was his lot to become acquainted with the Yahwist and men of his type of intellect, surely he had opportunity to broaden and enrich his mental life to the brilliant beauty which is reflected in his book.

The strongest persistent impression that Amos gained from the mountains of the plateau of Tekoa, when he let his glance sweep over the landscape before him, was that of ruin and destruction. When he mentally betook himself to the palaces in Samaria and there observed the voluptuous life, or to the royal temple at Bethel and contemplated the sacrifices and the feasts, the one question always came to him: "What does Yahweh say to all this?" The answer that naturally came to him: "All this is only worthy of destruction. Yahweh cannot tolerate these things, neither the morals nor the form of worship of the people can be pleasing to Yahweh." To be sure, Amos' predecessors had already expressed themselves in a similar manner. How Elijah had stormed against the form of worship and the morals of the house of Ahab, and yet what Amos brought to them was something quite new. As far as we know, his predecessors had called the culprits themselves to account. Elijah had reproached the house of Ahab, but former prophets had not reproached the whole nation. Amos did not prophesy ruin for individuals, for he believed that the nation as a whole was liable to Yahweh's judgment. This had never been announced before. It was something entirely new and unheard of. Only he could speak thus, who knew more of God than all the others had thus far known. To all earlier men God had been the God of Israel, the God who clung to his people through good or evil times. True, he judged wrongdoers, but only for the purpose of blotting them out from among his people, to purify his own people, and to be able all the better to help it. The people as a whole were good, and they were God's friends. To Amos the nation itself seemed ripe for destruction, and he must announce it.

Wailing shall be in all the broad ways; and they shall say in all the streets, Alas! Alas! and they shall call the husbandman to mourning, and such as are skilful of lamentation, to wailing. And in all vineyards shall be wailing, for I will pass through the midst of thee, saith the Lord.[3]

An adversary there shall be, even round about the land; and he shall bring down thy strength from thee, and thy palaces shall be spoiled.[4]

Thus saith the Lord: As the shepherd rescueth out of the mouth of the lion two legs, or a piece of an ear, so shall the children of Israel be rescued that sit in Samaria in the corner of a couch and on the silken cushions of a bed.[5]

Here for the first time we see how the consciousness of the inner victory through Yahweh is expressed in the face of the actual political conditions, of social unrest, of the rich oppressing the poor, of dishonest business, and above all, of injustice in legal administration—injustice which had long cried to heaven for vengeance. But the state stood firm; therefore no one expected its downfall. It might deserve destruction, but its time had not yet come. Even men like the Yahwist may have thought this. Now a thundercloud

[237]

from the east rolled toward them. Threateningly it approached. Certain small conflicts and incidents, such as Jehu's paying tribute to Assyria, were only forerunners announcing the approach of destructive thunderbolts.

But no one saw them or wanted to see them except the few who stood guard on the watch towers. They recognized the distant tremors and saw the lightning in the sky. They could interpret the signs of the times. Suddenly Amos knew. What Israel had long deserved was now about to come to pass. It could not be otherwise; the Assyrian advance was God's work, and he did it to punish his people. This made another thing clear. Assyria and all the world were only tools in Yahweh's hand. All people belonged to him, the God of all the world, and "his" people were by no means his people unless they were worthy of their God. This expressed a new and great principle that there is only one God and He is a great, all-embracing, omnipotent God. This God is a God who can will only good. If such a god had decided on Israel's downfall, it was apparent that He could do so only because he saw and punished what the prophet had long perceived: the national religious and moral degradation.

Hear this word that the Lord hath spoken against you, O children of Israel, against the whole family which I brought up out of the land of Egypt, saying, You only have I known of all the families of the earth: therefore I will visit upon you all your iniquities.[6]

Pass ye unto Calneh, and see; and from thence go ye to Hamath the great: then go down to Gath of the Philistines: be they better than these kingdoms? or is their border greater than your border?[7]

Are ye not as the children of the Ethiopians unto me, O children of Israel? saith the Lord. Have not I brought up Israel out of the land of Egypt, and the Philistines from Caphtor, and the Syrians from Kir?[8]

By realizing this and understanding all this, Amos felt he had spiritual proof that he sat in God's council. He knew that he was one with God, and that he must stand with Him whether he would or not. This knowledge can come only to the man whom Yahweh has chosen as His confidant. He was a simple shepherd, neither the son of a prophet, nor in any way a prophet by rank or calling, but now he could no longer remain with his sheep. God had chosen him for higher things. He dared not keep to himself what he knew; he must testify of Yahweh and His will.

Shall two walk together, except they have agreed? Will a lion roar in the forest when he hath no prey? Will a young lion cry out in his den if he have taken nothing?
Surely the Lord God will do nothing, but he revealeth his secret unto his servants, the prophets. The lion hath roared; who will not fear? The Lord God hath spoken; who can but prophesy? [9]

In great trouble of soul people might ask whether there was no way to prevent the fulfillment of that dreadful message. Others, the representatives of the state, especially official church authorities, felt confident. They hoped Yahweh would interfere when the right time should come. They had their altars and their priests who were constantly seeking God's favor for them by sacrifice and religious service. Amos destroyed this consolation, too. To some he seemed a pious, to other a godless delusion, to all a fanatic. The report of the "Day of God" must have long circulated among the people, and the belief that on that great day of judgment Yahweh would call all of Israel's enemies to account, change all sorrow to joy, all darkness to light. How gently and peacefully they rested in this hope in contrast to strange and exaggerated threats of Amos. With a sharp blow Amos rent these hopes asunder.

Woe unto you that desire the day of the Lord! wherefore would ye have the day of the Lord? It is darkness, and not light. As if a man did flee from a lion, and a bear did meet him; or went into the house and leaned his hand against the wall, and a serpent bit him. Shall not the day of the Lord be darkness, and not light; even very dark, and no brightness in it? [10]

Thus came cruel disappointment. The Day of the Lord, of the Lord that Amos knew, was indeed a day of judgment, but the guilty one to be judged was not another one; it was Israel itself. If then one anchor to which Israel had clung was destroyed, there still remained another, and this one could not fail. Yahweh's altars were erected throughout the country, his priests served them and constantly secured God's good will for the people. This, too, was deceit and vain delusion.

I hate, I despise your feast, and I will take no delight in your solemn assemblies. Yea, though ye offer me your burnt offerings and meat offerings, I will not accept them; neither will I regard the peace offerings of your fat beasts. Take, then, away from me the noise of thy songs, for I will not hear the melody of thy viols. But let judgment roll down as waters, and righteousness as a mighty stream. Did you bring unto me offerings and sacrifices in the wilderness forty years, O house of Israel? [11]

It is not historically correct that Israel brought Yahweh no kind of sacrifice during the whole desert period, for it left Egypt to celebrate a feast for Yahweh at the holy mountain; [12] nor is Amos' opinion correct, that as a matter of principle, neither sacrifice, nor prayer, nor hymn should be offered to Yahweh. But when sacrifice and gifts stifled right doing, they should be omitted that right doing be respected. Sacrifice as such was not rejected, but if it assumed a place beside or even above justice and morality, it had failed in its office of serving as a testimony of conviction. Amos did not discard sacrifice, nor did he desire to do so.

[240]

He did limit the significance of the outer forms of religion to such a degree that in theory they were apparently outworn. This was an easy matter for him, because the sanctuaries that he saw in Israel deserved to be called places to worship idols rather than places to worship God.

Come to Bethel, and transgress; to Gilgal, and multiply transgression.[13]
For thus saith the Lord unto the house of Israel, Seek ye me, and ye shall live: but seek not Bethel, nor enter into Gilgal, and pass not to Beersheba: for Gilgal shall surely go into captivity, and Bethel shall come to nought.

Could nothing be done? This thought was unbearable to Amos himself. There was, indeed, one way. Amos modestly hints at it, but even he did not venture confidently to believe in it. It was to return to Yahweh, as he really is, and thus to righteousness and justice.

Seek ye me, and ye shall live:
Hate the evil, and love the good, and establish judgment in the gate; it may be that the Lord, the God of hosts, will be gracious unto the remnant of Joseph.[14]

If Israel did not follow this path, only the last and utmost remained to Joseph: the guilty kingdom must fall, so that Judah and the house of David might not, also, be caught in the whirl and be swallowed up. The ruined heritage from David, the old Kingdom of David, must be reëstablished, but the house of Israel, the north kingdom, must be scattered among all the nations, as one scatters builders' sand with a sieve upon the earth.

It does not seem strange that this message found a poor reception in the northern state. When, presumably at the great autumn feast, Amos himself appeared at Bethel and hurled sharp speeches against Israel and the king, the high priest, Amaziah, made complaint to the king, and he was banished from the country. He was considered one of the many in the prophetic guild, who, if well paid, said what the authorities wished to hear. "Go home to the land of Judah, eat your bread, you may prophesy there!" The priest knew what to expect, for whoever did not speak as he expected him to do was sent away. The priest was mistaken in Amos. He was not a prophet by rank, nor was he the son of a prophet. He did not speak for pay, but because God's voice spoke within him. Without his experience in Bethel, his words, like those of many another, might have been lost to us. He was forced to go away, and to this circumstance we may owe the first book of the prophets. Since he was denied the opportunity of speaking to Israel, he attempted to reach his brothers in the north by writing.

His example and his fate were effective. Probably because of the treatment Amos had received under King Jeroboam II, there appeared during the same reign a successor, Hosea, the son of Beeris. If Amos was only a messenger of truth come over from Judah to Ephraim, Hosea was a native of the state itself so seriously threatened by Amos. From among the natives a man now arose who supported the testimony of the stranger from Tekoa. Hosea seems to have lived through the confusion after Jeroboam's death and through the Syrian-Ephraimite war.

Because of domestic troubles, Hesiod became a poet in Greece. He took to heart the quarrel with his brother. This caused him to turn his thoughts inward. What Hosea tells of himself is similar but told in greater detail. Yahweh, we are told, spoke to him. "Go, take unto thee a wife of whoredom and children of whoredom: for the land 'doth commit great whoredom, departing from the Lord." [15]

He went straightway and married. His wife bore him three children. Their names proclaim misfortune. The son was called "Jezreel" for, because of the massacre of Jehu in Jezreel, misfortune must come over Israel; the daughter, the Unpardoned One, "for I will no more have mercy upon the

[242]

house of Israel." After the daughter was weaned, a second son was born. He said, "Call his name Loammi, not my people, for ye are not my people, and I will not be your God."

To us Occidentals to-day, the soul of the Oriental who dwells under a very different sky and among a people very different from ours, and especially the soul of the Oriental of antiquity is often a sealed book. We cannot, therefore, be too careful to avoid transferring our present Occidental method of thinking and feeling into Israel. But pain and disappointment over disappointed love, anger and embitterment over infidelity, when the flame of true love continues to burn even after the bitterest disappointment, these are feelings native to the universal soul. They can be found at all times, in all climes, wherever human feelings exist. The reader must have these fundamental emotions in mind if he wishes to form an opinion about Hosea's married life.

What Hosea here tells of himself has become a thing so repulsive, so far removed from our own feelings and tastes, indeed so foreign to us, that we are inclined to consider the whole story of his married life not as a real occurrence but an allegory, as a thing only thought to have occurred and to be used for a lesson. When we understand the text correctly, we are not justified in not accepting the marriage literally. Even to an Oriental, Hosea's marriage would be difficult to understand if Hosea had known the character and life of his wife before their betrothal and during the whole period of their marriage. Clearly this was not the case. The names of the two older children refer only to Yahweh's relation to the nation, and thus were, if we will, political characters. Only the third name, which may also be translated "not my clan," has a double meaning and reminds us of the father's personal lot. Thus we may conclude that Hosea discovered his wife's true character during his married life, either at or after the birth of the last child. Then the marriage **relation ceased, even though the man's love** continued.

On his part **then, Hosea's marriage** was founded **on real love** for a woman who, to all appearances, was richly gifted by nature. As Isaiah did later, so from the beginning Hosea put his married life to the service of his prophetic calling. To proclaim ruin to degenerate Israel was his duty as it was to his predecessor Amos. Thus the names of his two older children originated and are not more strange than the names of Isaiah's children.

After the birth of the youngest, the news that he gained from some indication or information, "For years thy wife has been carrying on an infamous profession behind thy back," struck him like a thunderbolt. How could this be possible? How could the depraved woman thus degrade his true love? Above all, how could Yahweh permit such a thing to happen to him? The more he pondered, the greater was the danger of his falling a prey to anger and despair. Then his pondering glance fell upon his calling as a prophet. If Yahweh had already taught him that all the events of his personal life and of his family life were in the service of his calling, perhaps this had been the case from the very beginning—from the day of his being called to become a prophet—and in a very different sense than he had thus far believed. What if the marriage itself and this unspeakably terrible thing that had come to him now, and which he had just learned, what if this were a part, indeed the main part of the subordination of his life to God?

Now Hosea's eyes were opened. It had been intended from the beginning, but he had not understood it until now. Looking back with retrospective understanding, he could preface this strange marriage story with the words, At first when Yahweh spoke through Hosea, he said to Hosea: "Take unto thee a wife of whoredom and children of whoredom." They were not that to him from the beginning. They

[244]

were his real wife and real children. Only later did he know what they were, and for what purpose, and why his God had led him thus. Out of his life's destiny, he now heard God's voice speaking to him and only then understood it. It was God's decree that had directed him from the beginning, that had called him to become a prophet, and whose language he only now heard and understood. His unfaithful wife was the symbol of the unfaithful people among whom he lived and for whom he was destined to work. What it meant to Yahweh to see his own love and fidelity repaid by infidelity and desertion, this the prophet was destined to experience in himself and in his own family that he might become a particularly impressive witness of what he must announce.

Israel had often deserted Yahweh and had broken faith with Him. What Yahweh experienced at the hands of the people He had dearly loved, Hosea now experienced at the hands of his wife. When Hosea expressed this, though, and made it the main theme of his prophecy, he introduced a peculiar figurative language into Israel's religious thought which henceforth belonged inevitably to prophetic speech. Israel was like a whoring wife; Yahweh, like a faithful, loving but duped husband. Deserting Yahweh and serving idols were then often called whoredom and unchastity; reverence for other gods was spoken of as illicit love toward them. This usage was not entirely new, for Jehu is said to have spoken thus of Jezebel and her Baal worship, as we have heard. This form of expression was also used among other peoples, but after Hosea's time the term remained in Israel and became customary. Jeremiah and Ezekiel constantly used it, often in a manner distressing to our sensibilities. It was so familiar to the prophets, because the form taken in real life by Baal worship and other related heathen forms of worship showed them and all the world anew that these expressions were not mere figures of speech. What occurred at the Baal celebrations was of such a nature that these terms, although coarse, called these proceedings and customs by their real names.

Hosea's language was full of figures of speech. His rich fancy supplies them in great profusion. Being a northern Israelite, he was familiar with farm life in all its details. He lived close to nature, but he also knew city life well. He clothed all his observations in figurative speech. He does not seem to have been visionary, but he used expressions of greatest emotion and such as expressed a soul passionately moved. Like Amos, he for the most part threatened and chided his people and their leaders, priests, prophets, and the great among them, yet the note of promise is not lacking. His speech is usually brusque, harsh, and disconnected. His aphorisms and speeches stand like erratic blocks of stone, each one by itself, and frequently in unyielding and fantastic shapes, reflecting the image of his tormented soul. Yet in his inmost soul Hosea was gentle, capable of great tenderness, and of very touching and half lyrical expression. He is the first poet in Israel who was strongly individual. He would like to sit in judgment over Yahweh because he had to stifle his sympathy, but he hardly dared to do this.

Differing from Amos in whose proclamations the social and moral ills play a prominent part, Hosea suffered mostly from the religious degradation of his people. Their abandonment of Yahweh for half-heathen doings, their inclination to Baal worship in the northern state, corresponded to the theme that from his own married life Yahweh himself had given him for his sermons. Israel had deserted its own legitimate spouse and had followed after strangers, the Baals.

Plead with your mother, plead; for she is not my wife, neither am I her husband; and let her put away her whoredoms from her face, and her adulteries from between her breasts;

For their mother hath played the harlot: he that conceived them hath done shamefully: for she said, I will go after my lovers that give me my bread, and my water, my wool, and my flax, mine oil and my drink.

For she did not know that I gave her the corn, and the wine, and the oil, and multiplied unto her silver and gold, which they used for Baal.[16]

It seems that Jehu's abolition of Baal worship brought about no permanent improvement in conditions which might give the prophets of that time cause for rejoicing. This explains the many complaints that Amos brings. It seems that soon after Jeroboam II died and Jehu's dynasty came to a violent end, that the conditions soon returned to the state in which Jehu had found them. The destruction of the former royal family may have demanded this. Utterances like the following may refer to this.

When Ephraim spake, there was trembling; he exalted himself in Israel; but when he offended in Baal, he died. And now they sin more and more, and have made them molten images of their silver, even idols according to their own understanding, all of them the work of the craftsmen. They say of them, Let the men that sacrifice, kiss the calves.

Whoredom and wine and new wine taken away the understanding. My people ask counsel at their stock, and their staff declareth unto them:[17]

They sacrifice upon the tops of the mountains, and burn incense upon the hills, under oaks and poplars and terebinths, because the shadow thereof is good; therefore your daughters commit whoredom, and your brides commit adultery. I will not punish your daughters when they commit whoredom, nor your brides when they commit adultery; for they themselves go apart with whores, and they sacrifice with the harlots:[18]

But Hosea was not only a prophet of human infidelity; he was even more the prophet who proclaimed divine love and fidelity. No one in the Old Testament has spoken more deeply and impressively on this subject than he. The difference between Hosea's peculiarity of proclamation and that of his immediate predecessor, Amos, is most marked in this respect. If Amos was the messenger of divine justice and divine judgment over Israel, Hosea was the messenger of divine love and mercy that would serve the people when the desire for Yahweh was aroused. After judgment should be satisfied by the collapse of the state of Ephraim, repentance and longing for Yahweh would return unto Israel. Then it would say:

I will go and return to my first husband, for then was it better with me than now.
And she shall make answer there as in the days of her youth, and as in the day when she came up out of the land of Egypt.[19]

When this has come about, Yahweh himself will not hesitate to accept the proffered hand.

And I will betroth thee unto me forever; yea, I will betroth thee unto me in righteousness, and in judgment, and in loving kindness, and in mercies.[20]
And it shall come to pass in that day, I will answer, saith the Lord, I will answer the heavens, and they shall answer the earth; and the earth shall answer the corn, and the wine, and the oil; and they shall answer Jezreel (Israel).[21]
And I will heal their backsliding, I will love them freely; for mine anger is turned away from him.[22]

It does not follow that after Hosea had recognized the character of his unfaithful wife and had cast her off, he again married her. Nor does his book say this. Yahweh does this with Israel. What is said of woman in this regard refers to Israel, for which woman is the symbol. Indeed, Hosea went even farther, and he was probably obliged to do so if he wished to portray the future of the pardoned people. He expected Israel to return to Yahweh and to be reëstablished with the renewed Judah. He knew nothing of Judah's destruction proclaimed by the Judean prophets who followed

[248]

him. Compared with his own state, Judah seemed to stand securely. Thus he hoped that some time a second David should appear in Judah who would reëstablish the old realm and would unite the returned Ephraim with the new and great Judah.

XI

ISAIAH

AFTER King Jehoash, who with the help of the high priest Jehoiada had succeeded his unnatural grandmother, Athaliah, to the throne of Jerusalem, came his son Amaziah (797-799). Probably because of unsuccessful battles with the Syrians, his father had fallen at the hands of murderers. The great difference between Judah and Israel is clearly shown by the fact that apparently no one in Judah thought of causing the dynasty to fall with the death of the king, whom they considered incapable. They had no other thought than that Jehoash would be succeeded by his son Amaziah. Indeed, when the latter had ascended the throne, he could bring suit against the murderers of his father and have them executed. The legal proceedings have a special interest for us because here for the first time a new principle of justice of far-reaching significance is mentioned. The old form of justice in Israel had considered it a matter of course that with the criminal his family should be turned over to the judge.

Justice was due the clan, not the individual, just as the old blood vengeance was visited upon the tribe and the commune and not upon the individual alone. In the case of Nabath under king Ahab we still had the old form of justice, but now the people have broken away from it on the basis of a decree which we hear was found in the old Mosaic Law. Therefore Israel and Judah in those days must have entered a new era in the laws of vengeance as well as in other matters. With the new prophecy and the ever-growing

[250]

conception of the moral personality, the conception seems to have gained ground that in matters of justice also every man stands for himself, and no longer should the clan or the family be punished for the wrongs of its chief. To be sure, they were just beginning to use this principle. Only a later period was able to draw further conclusions to be proven by the conception of retribution by divine justice toward man.

It was of great importance for the political development of Judah that Amaziah succeeded in again conquering the Edomites who had seceded after Jehoshaphat's death. A connection with the Red Sea was very important for Judean commerce. This they secured by possessing the seaport of Elath. In spite of this great success, Amaziah died the same death that his father had died. By carelessly provoking Israel under Jehoash, son of Jehoahaz of the house of Jehu, he had brought misfortune upon his country and was murdered.

Again it seems a matter of course for Judah that the succession be continued, and that the son take the father's place on the throne. Then Azariah, or Uzziah, became king of Judah. According to the book of Kings, he ruled fifty-two years, which at least points to a remarkably long reign. He was very young when he began his reign, which lasted approximately from 779-739. A part of his reign, presumably only a few years, however, was also included in the reign of his son and successor, Jotham, who became the regent for Uzziah during the long illness toward the end of his father's reign. The proof that commerce flourished in Judah during Uzziah's most successful period lies not only in the fact that he was able to develop the port of Elath on the Red Sea as a base for his navy, but also in the description that Isaiah gives of conditions then prevalent in Judah. Isaiah reports that the country was full of silver, gold, and no end of treasure; of horses and chariots; likewise of valuable jewels, the spoils from successful cruises. All this admirably suits Uzziah's commercial policy and may, therefore, be looked upon as a sign that he had indeed succeeded in gaining for his country a period of prosperity, and in raising it to power and wealth. He probably also deserves the credit of having expanded Judah territorially at the expense of Israel.

As we have already heard, soon after Jeroboam died King Menahem in the northern state of Ephraim had been forced to buy the favor and help of the great Assyrian king by tribute. According to report, the Assyrian King Pul, otherwise known as King Tiglath-Pileser III, the great conqueror, invaded the land, and Menahem, who was hard pressed by internal dissension, could maintain himself against him and his enemies in his own land only by heavy tribute which he paid to the great king. This was the first time that Assyria set foot on Israel's soil. Clashes had occurred before this time. We know that Jehu had paid tribute, but thus far the people had remained masters in their own land sufficiently to keep the powerful and violent neighbors in the East away from the borders. Now Assyrian legions interfered in Israel itself and maintained order there by subduing Menahem's enemies.

Thus Israel had, as we should to-day express it, entered the field of Assyria's immediate interests, and this through its own doing. They might be sure that when once the Assyrian lion had laid his claws upon Israel's body politic, he would not willingly loose his hold; all the more so since Assyria had procured a sort of legal right to interfere with affairs in Israel because of Menahem's shortsightedness. In this regard antiquity looked upon matters just as our politicians do to-day. If there is no legal right to do violence to one's neighbor or to seize foreign lands belonging to less cultured peoples, even to-day sentiment does not control political necessity. If possible, however, we of to-day shroud the policy of conquest and violence with the mantle of morality to justify it to the world. This mantle may bear the name of chastisement for misdeeds or for war crimes; it may be used to bring about settled conditions, or to make peoples of lesser degrees of civilization susceptible to the benefits of Western culture. The fact is that Assyria had gained a certain right to interfere in Israel through Menahem's request for help. She made good use of this right. We do not know the exact details. This much is clear, however, that soon the complications were so great in Israel that not only Israel was ruined by them, but its neighbor Judah was also caught in the pool, to be swallowed up sooner or later. We may say that, according to human judgment, Judah as well as Israel would finally have succumbed in the unequal struggle. Be that as it may, the fact remains that in the events as they occurred, criminal short-sightedness on both sides hastened, if it did not actually bring about, the end.

Menahem himself was not long a witness to his own disgraceful policy. In all probability this very policy prepared the untimely end of his dynasty. At any rate, but two years after he paid the tribute, in 736, we find his second successor Pekah in power (736-733). He was a usurper, presumably of low birth. His father was a certain Remaliah. What helped him to the throne was simply the fact that Menahem had given up almost the last bit of independence, and any one could be popular who promised to make Israel what it had been before Menahem's time. Pekah counted upon this. To begin with, he was sure of Egypt's sympathy. It, however, consisted more in promises than in deeds, for the land of the Pharaohs was itself in great disorganization so that the Pharaoh, even if he had had a real desire to help Israel, would not have been able to do much. Yet it seems that at all times, true statesmanship—the attitude of the strong toward the weak—has consisted in breaking promises and plans previously made. Rome became great in this way; at this time Egypt constantly applied the principle in its treatment of Israel and Judah, and was by no means a loser thereby.

Much more effective was the intervention of an eastern state, Urartu in the Ararat region. For some time it had taken the stand of an embittered opponent of Assyria and now was again active. Syria, who found it necessary to summon all her strength to ward off once for all the annoying Assyrian invaders, was heartily thankful for every difficulty that Assyria met with from any part of the world. Thus, then, while Tiglath-Pileser (737-735) was occupied in the distant East, Pekah of Israel and Rezin of Damascus, forgetting the former enmity between their countries, united with Urartu and the Phœnician capitals, Tyre and Sidon, in an allied struggle against Assyria.

The undertaking could succeed only if all the Syrian states joined against Assyria. If a number of them stood aloof so that in Syria itself the number of the friends and the enemies of Assyria were equal, then the undertaking was a failure from the beginning, for those friendly to Assyria might at any time attack the enemy in the rear. This was what actually happened. In the north, the remaining Phœnician cities and what was left of the old Hittite state did not join the movement; in the south, Judah, Ammon, Moab, Edom, and a part of the Philistines likewise remained aloof. The undertaking could succeed only if these states, however reluctant or hesitant, could be forced or persuaded to join the movement.

The so-called Syrian Ephraimite war of the year 734 served this purpose. Pekah and Rezin decided to invade Judah to punish it for its resistance, or if possible to break this resistance. This was a desperate attempt to make the anti-Assyrian coalition possible by breaking down the chief of the opposition. We may safely assume that Judah at

[254]

that time was considered the center of the pro-Assyrian policy in Syria. According to what we have heard, Judah's power was strong enough at this time to make it seem a valuable ally. But, because of its proximity to Egypt, Judah may have known well the dangers of a friendly policy toward Egypt and how unreliable this friendship was, and have recommended the greatest reticence toward them. If the politicians of Judah would not voluntarily put aside their disinclination, then there was nothing left to Rezin and Pekah but to force them to do so by violence. King Jotham of Judah had probably negotiated for some time previously with the allied powers. He must have died about 734, for the king who ruled when the assault took place was not Jotham, but his son, the youthful Ahaz, who had now ascended the throne.

It seems that Ahaz was completely surprised by the events. A threat may have been expressed at one time or another during the negotiations with Jotham, but he had not taken it very seriously because the allies themselves were much interested in Judah's peaceful entrance into the alliance. Meanwhile King Jotham had died. The wavering and dependent nature of the young prince, who was to become his successor, may have been known. Perhaps they hoped to make him yield by a strong demonstration; perhaps they already knew the measures he had taken in Nineveh and at the court or in the camp of the great king, and therefore sought to make him harmless even before his measures could take effect. Ahaz and his political advisers seem to have had no idea that the action planned by the allies would occur as quickly as it really did.

Like a thunderbolt from a clear sky, the news reached Jerusalem one day, that the allied armies had already united on the heights in Ephraim and were ready to march against Jerusalem itself to replace the obstinate king with one of their leaders who would be amenable to their rulers. The people of Jerusalem knew that they must be prepared for a siege and the storming of the capital. Considering their own strength and that of the allies, there could be no doubt that the outlook for Judah was very discouraging; indeed its position seemed desperate. We are not surprised, therefore, to read the significant words in the record, "And it was told the house of David, and his heart was moved and the heart of his people, as the trees of the forest are moved with the wind." The King, the court, and the people of Jerusalem and Judah were paralyzed by the terrifying message. A panic, much like the one that occurred in Rome when Hannibal appeared before its gates, seized the court and the capital.

What could be done at this last hour to meet the peril? Could anything be done before it was too late? Naturally the first consideration when an enemy approached the city was to test the walls and fortifications, and then to inspect the water supply preparatory for a siege. By nature, Jerusalem has a poor water supply. At all times in its history the city has suffered under this condition. In case of a siege the scanty water supply that the city had at its disposal in the cisterns and pools had to be carefully estimated, and its distribution regulated. When we first met King Ahaz, he was thus occupied at the water ducts by the upper pool.

King Ahaz knew whatever measures he might take, were insufficient and merely preliminary. They might be useful at the beginning. But could he withstand a long siege? If the united allies should storm the city, could he offer resistance to their united attack? Above all, could he with his Judean hosts venture to offer battle to the combined armies of the two enemies for the purpose of driving them from his capital and his territory? These must necessarily have been Ahaz' thoughts, and to them neither he nor his councilors could give an encouraging answer.

We can thus understand that his thoughts and those of

his councilors turned to Nineveh or to the royal camp of the great King, Tiglath-Pileser. Had not Menahem of Samaria only a few years ago received help and protection there? He had not fared badly in it. To be sure, through Menahem's successor the country was plunged into various entaglements. Yet these entanglements might be considered the natural consequence of forsaking the Assyrian friendship, which Menahem had fostered. Was it not this very friendship with Assyria, and resistance to the inducements of Egypt and its Palestine-Syrian partisans to break away from Assyria, that placed Ahaz in the present painful position? All these considerations may have united to impress upon Ahaz that to claim Assyrian help was wise, indeed the duty of self-preservation, and also his legitimate right.

Thus an embassy from King Ahaz was sent to the great king's camp saying, "I am thy servant and thy son." The great sovereign was both war-lord, to whom one must be subject, and "little father" (czar). Ahaz' attitude was pleasing to Nineveh. The assurance of fealty was emphasized by sending the entire treasure of gold and silver which had been in the treasury in both the temple and the royal palace presumably since Uzziah's time. They had reason to hope that they were not asking in vain when they accompanied the expression of fealty by the request, "Come up and save me out of the hand of the king of Syria and out of the hand of the king of Israel, which hath risen up against me." [1] We can well imagine that such expressions were well received at the court. Doubtless, they had expected the embassy and were relieved when it came. With our mind's eye we can look on and see the Assyrian statesmen assuming toward Ahaz' ambassadors the hypocritical appearance of generous and honest-minded protectors who, for the sake of justice and the good cause, were willing to "sacrifice" themselves by interfering. We are familiar with this attitude. To this day he is no statesman and no politician who is not master of this art. We cannot definitely determine the time of Ahaz' message to the king. It may have been soon after he began his reign, as soon as he saw the danger that threatened from the union of the two northern neighbors; it may have been the result of the approach of the allies against Jerusalem and the threatened siege of the capital.

In reality, Ahaz could have held out for a time with money and troops that Uzziah had left him, even though he could not hope for final success. The position and the fortifications of Jerusalem were probably strong enough to have afforded him protection for a time within the walls of the capital. Meanwhile the great sovereign would have realized that without Ahaz' servility he could not permit Judah to fall into the hands of the allies without abandoning his claim to Palestine. If Judah together with Aram and Israel had withdrawn from the Assyrian influence and gone to the Egyptian side, the Assyrian rights to Palestine would have been buried for a long time to come.

Tiglath-Pileser really had voluntarily to act as he later did, if he at all understood what was to his advantage, but he would have had no right to play the part of master and protector in Judah. History down to the present time has taught us how such "protectorates" usually work out. Ahaz would then have kept his good money and the independence thus far preserved, and the great king would have taken good care, if Ahaz were still in possession of his treasures and his comparative freedom, not to drive him over to the enemy's side through lack of consideration. But Ahaz seems to have been blinded by Menahem's act and the seeming success which his policy of shortsightedness had gained for him. As little as Menahem considered the future of Israel, so little did Ahaz seem to consider what was to become of Judah when once Assyria had the judicial right to interfere and to rule by force, as it had done in Israel since Menahem's time. Thus events took their course, and Ahaz became one of the executioners of his own country. I know that modern scientists have judged Ahaz' conduct differently. They think Ahaz did what any one in his position would have done. He looked about for help, because he was not willing to assume the responsibility of permitting his country to be ruined without attempting everything possible to prevent it. Nor do I doubt for a moment that the majority of our present-day politicians would have done as he did, or as councilors, would have advised such action. Earlier in this account, however, I attempted to show that from a purely political standpoint, Ahaz had little reason to take so hastily the last desperate step, which when once taken he could never entirely retrace. With a little more foresight, Ahaz probably could have avoided sending that embassy to Assyria and thus causing all its evil consequences. Again we must not overlook the fact that the policy of the strongest battalion and of the strongest allies in the world's history has frequently not led to the success expected by their political masters. This policy will always find adherents because it has so often achieved momentary success and seeming gain. Just as often, however, it has had the disadvantage following in its wake that it did not take into account the powerful "imponderables" of which the world is full, and which, contrary to our expectation, frequently influence decisions and finally give to history an aspect very different from that which the political leaders had planned or expected.

This brings us to the man to whom the principle stated above finds special application. From the beginning and with almost passionate severity, Isaiah opposed the political policy of his time. He stood in the very midst of the political life. He took the keenest interest in all that occurred. He experienced the Syrian-Ephraimite war, the fall of Samaria, and the threatening of Jerusalem by Sennacherib, and accompanied them with his prophetic speech. He was the king's councilor and the esteemed teacher of the people. He could not understand, however, how the king and the people could be guided only by what was apparent on the surface, and that they did not attempt first of all to understand conditions fully. To him the foundation of all things was God and spiritual life. He was entirely a man of God, the advocate of religion; he was completely saturated with the great religious thoughts and principles of the religion of Yahweh. Political matters and decisions had a real value for him only when measured by this standard. If they could not stand this test before God, they were vain and could not serve the welfare of a nation and a state, however cleverly conceived and however auspiciously introduced.

> The Lord of Hosts,   and let Him be your fear,
> Him shall ye satisfy; and let Him be your dread.[2]

With this Isaiah acknowledged the principle that moral and religious values and powers which cannot be measured outwardly are vitally at work in things and processes, are frequently even decisive, and should determine the life of the people and the state. When the king and his political councilors did not act in accordance with these principles, Isaiah felt himself to be their opponent. To him God, God's will, and all that resulted from it came first. Everything else, even the apparent welfare of the state, was subservient. In this Isaiah was the diligent disciple of his great predecessors, Elijah and Amos. Fundamentally, this was their desire also. Yet Elijah stood independently and alone. He overtowered all in breadth of outlook, boldness of thought, and power of speech. Few men in Israel so thoroughly impressed their individuality upon their time as did Isaiah. The whole period in which he worked was dominated by his spirit. Neither Ahaz nor Hezekiah nor any of the contemporaries could at all equal him mentally. He overtowered all and stood sovereign above them. The whole period can be understood only as the period of Isaiah.

Isaiah, son of Amoz, was a Judean of Jerusalem and, probably, belonged to the upper class. He dedicated his whole life to the service of Yahweh and his people. He was always ready to direct, by the will of Yahweh, the course of the king, the people, the councilors, leaders, judges, and priests.

When comparatively young he first heard the call of God. It was in the temple, perhaps at a great feast in Jerusalem. He sat lost in reverence in the court of the temple and saw the fire of the altar leaping to heaven. The priests in their white robes were busy at the altar imparting Yahweh's favor to those who offered sacrifice. In rhythmic hymns, the choirs sang the praise of the great God of Israel, and the throng joined their enthusiastic song of praise in a hundred voiced responses. The smoke of the sacrifice mingled with the odor of sweet incense affected the senses, filled the air, and stirred their spirits. All felt that God Himself was present.

Suddenly the young man had a strange feeling. His soul was possessed of the thought of the vital nearness of its God. In place of the earthly temple with the earthly sanctuary of Yahweh, he saw the heavenly sanctuary and Yahweh Himself as the great God of the universe, sitting on His throne arrayed in the royal purple which filled with color the whole of the heavenly throne room. The earthly priests were changed to angelic heavenly forms who hovered about the Lord of the world and tended the heavenly altar fires. The fire of the earthly altar became that of the heavenly altar at which the seraphim offered sacrifice, and choruses of angels praised the Holy One.

When the young man realized what had happened to him, he began to tremble. He had seen the Holy One of Israel,

[261]

although he was of unclean lips and lived among a people of unclean lips. A seraph approached him with a coal from the altar fire and touched his lips with it; now he was freed from sin and made worthy to be in the presence of God. Immediately he heard the voice of the Lord of All, "Whom shall I send?" All shyness and all hesitancy had now left him, and unwavering, an entirely different being from the one he had been a few moments before, he answered, "Here am I; send me."

Thus was Isaiah called and dedicated as a prophet of Yahweh. He immediately received his message. It was, "Go tell the people."

> Hear ye indeed, but understand not;
> And see ye indeed, but perceive not.[3]

A dreadful message! To Isaiah also it seemed too harsh. To his question, how long he must proclaim hardness of heart and when he might finally proclaim mercy, came the answer that his office was to proclaim judgment and again judgment. Only when this was accomplished, as in the root of the felled oak tree, a "holy seed" would again appear as the stock from which a new, better, and happier race would grow up in Israel.

This occurred in the same year in which King Uzziah died after his long illness, and his son Jotham succeeded him to the throne. We have already heard that Jotham ruled alone only for a short time and was soon obliged to pass on the scepter to his son Ahaz. Before this happened, probably while Uzziah was still alive, Isaiah, true to his painful duty, sounded the cry of punishment and threat that Yahweh had laid upon his mouth when He summoned him. What he said gives a very clear picture of Judean conditions as they existed when he first appeared as a prophet, and also of the anxiety with which Isaiah viewed the future of his people because of the evil that he saw.

Woe unto them that join house to house, that lay field to field, till there be no room, and ye be made to dwell alone in the midst of the land.

Of a truth many houses shall be desolate, even great and fair, without inhabitant.

Woe unto them that rise up early in the morning, that they may follow strong drink; that tarry late unto the night, till wine inflame them! And the harp and the lute, the tabret and the pipe, and wine are in their feasts: but they regard not the work of the Lord, neither have they considered the operation of his hands. Therefore my people are gone into captivity for lack of knowledge: and their honourable men are famished, and their multitude are parched with thirst.'

According to the text, there can be no doubt what Yahweh's work and deeds were. They were his judgments. Their cause was the selfish curtailment of rudimentary human rights, which always bitterly avenge themselves on the strength of the nation and of the state. Moreover, vain, love of pleasure and sensuous living are usually attendant phenomena of evil and, together with it, greatly injure the innate strength of the nation. Isaiah dug deeply to the very roots of all problems. He not only saw the evil but its causes. Greed for money and pleasure were the causes of this evil. They themselves were only the result of the false ideals of the Kings, beginning with Solomon, who sought to equal the heathen nations in their share of the world's commerce, in world politics, in feudal and military kingdoms. How fortunate had been the times of the Judges, and even David's time! Once Jerusalem had been a just and faithful city. Now it had become a harlot. Its political life was poisoned by foreign influences and ungodly alliances. Israel's only ally was Yahweh. Its social life was thoroughly unwholesome. In Isaiah we still distinctly hear the note that the Rechabites, who were closely allied to the older type of prophecy, had once uttered.

From whence and by whom judgment was to come, Isaiah did not seem to know definitely at this early period. It sufficed that it would come and, with it, great suffering to Judah. From whatever source it might come, it would bring a day of terror. "A day of Yahweh of Hosts" was destined to bring to a sudden end all the splendor which Judah now so confidently enjoyed. It will come

upon all the cedars of Lebanon, that are high and lifted up, and upon all the oaks of Bashan . . . and upon all the ships of Tarshish . . . and upon all pleasant imagery.
And the idols shall utterly pass away. And men shall go into the caves of the rocks, and into the holes of the earth, even from before the terror of the Lord, and from the glory of his majesty, when he ariseth to shake mightily the earth.[5]

Isaiah had spoken in these terms when that unfortunate imbroglio occurred that threatened to destroy Judah by the alliance of the two states of which each one alone was a dangerous opponent. Isaiah must have suffered bitterly under Israel's policy, as did every man in Israel and Judah who realized what united these states despite their differences. For a time indignation over Judah's internal loss was dulled behind the patriot's anger which saw treason to the common cause in Pekah's alliance with Aram. Thus Ephraim's entire past history appeared to Isaiah as a desertion of Yahweh, a desertion which all Yahweh's former judgments against the country could not prevent. In the face of former judgments, the people of Ephraim and of Samaria still thought with light hearts:

The bricks are fallen, but we will build with hewn stone: the sycamores are cut down but we will change them into cedars. Therefore the Lord shall set up on high against him the adversaries of Rezin, and shall stir up his enemies: the Syrians before, and the Philistines behind; and they shall devour Israel with open mouth. . . .
Yet the people hath not turned unto him that smote them,

neither have they sought the Lord of hosts. Therefore the Lord will cut off from Israel head and tail, palm branch and rush, in one day. . . . For all this his anger is not turned away, but his hand is stretched out still.[6]

This was true of the past when, under the earlier kings, Yahweh had permitted the Philistine and Syrian wars to break out as a punishment for Ephraim. But the judgments failed in their purpose. Yahweh was now obliged to resort to a last decisive measure. Yahweh set up a target and lured the enemy thither from the end of the earth.

Whose arrows are sharp, and all their bows bent; their horses' hoofs shall be counted like flint, and their wheels like a whirlwind.[7]

This is clearly a description of Assyria. Isaiah was certain that the measures of Ephraim and of Samaria were full, their downfall sealed, and he who was to bring it about was none other than the Assyrian king who approached threateningly from the East. From his grasp Ephraim sought to free itself by the unnatural alliance it had just made with Aram.

At the time when Isaiah had thus mentally disposed of Ephraim and its ally, Aram, and had already settled accounts with them, the invasion of the allies into Judean territory and the prearranged attack upon Jerusalem itself occurred. We already know of the paralyzing terror in Jerusalem and at the court; also what measures King Ahaz either had taken to protect his country and his capital or was seriously considering.

From what we have heard, we can well understand that Isaiah was little pleased with his King's plan to call upon the Assyrian king for help, indeed that he looked on with sorrow and indignation as the king's political advisers lured the helpless man upon a course on which Isaiah expected only ruin for both the king and the people. What occurred

here or was planned was the very opposite of what
Isaiah considered right in principle, and the opposite of
what he already knew must surely come to pass. How
could Ahaz commit the crime of buying Assyria's help
when the price was the independence of Judah itself?
How could he be capable of the unspeakable folly of
doing this, when Ephraim's and Aram's days were numbered?

What would become of Judah if this policy of shortsightedness, of headlessness, continued? In his mind's eye,
Isaiah already saw the dreadful consequences. Before his
mental vision appeared the Assyrians who, when once called,
would not relinquish their hold upon the land until it had
been made a desert. The Assyrian king himself appeared
to him like shears which Yahweh had "hired" to chastise
deluded Judah, and with which he shaved clean the people
and the country until all had become *tabula rasa*. Isaiah
felt equally sure of the religious consequences that would
necessarily follow, for where the king of Assyria had
dominion, there the god Ashur also reigned. Only the
king's quick decision to abandon the policy that he had
allowed himself to accept could save Judah. The embassy
to Tiglath-Pileser must not set out, or if it had already
started, it must be recalled lest the worst danger should be
realized.

Isaiah felt sure of God's will and, therefore, approached
his king. He met Ahaz at the upper pool, busy in regulating
the water supply preparatory for a siege. In the excited
manner of the king and of the whole court, he read helplessness and fear drawing them on toward the threatening fate.
Why their fear? Whence this paralyzing helplessness?
Why see sure doom where the definite will of God is clear,
if one has only eyes to see it? To the troubled countenances
and the busy excitement of the king's followers came a message as from another world:

Be calm; you need not fear; your heart is discouraged without reason. You see dangerous fire, but it is not a fire that threatens you; it is only the firebrand still smoldering. Rezin and Pekah, the sons of Remaliah, have already reached the end of their strength; their fire has already gone out. What they are planning will not happen. Yahweh knows and wills it otherwise, and he has command of Judah; not they.

For the head of Syria is Damascus, and the head of Damascus is Rezin: and the head of Ephraim is Samaria, and the head of Samaria is Remaliah's son. If ye will not believe, surely ye shall not be established.[8]

The last words of Isaiah's speech to the king and his followers, ending purposely in a plural, did not conceal the fact that the prophet did not expect immediately to find an echo of his words in the hearts of those for whom it was intended. His message presupposed an eye that could see and a mind that could both understand and follow what he himself had seen in his deep meditations upon God. He knew well that the ordinary human being cannot understand; only he who dwells in God may find understanding. The king's advisers could see that the path they had recommended led to destruction. But they did not wish to admit this because alliance with Assyria seemed to them the only anchor of safety. Thus in spite of all this, they wished to attempt the alliance. What they did not see was that, from the human standpoint, Judah's position was so discouraging that no one but God alone could help them. There was, therefore, only the one means of help: to commit their cause to God's keeping and to have faith in Him. This it was that Isaiah called "faith." He knew it might be difficult for them to rise to this viewpoint, but when he also proclaimed that the enemies were already judged in God's council and their strength already broken, he hoped he might have a hearing. In the spring of 1522 when Luther had returned from the Wartburg and left the safe custody which he found there, Elector Frederick the Wise offered him his princely protection. Luther's answer was a letter that since has become famous.

No sword shall nor can help or save this cause; God must work here and alone without human provision and help. If his Grace the Elector believed, then he would see God's glory, but because he does not yet believe, he has not yet seen anything.

This sounds like Isaiah speaking to the king. Human care or provision was without avail in either case. Judah's prophet was as sure of that as was the German prophet. If anything happened, only God could bring it about; he would do this to show them His greatness if the people had faith enough.

In both cases it was faith upon which all depended. If we add Jesus and Paul to Isaiah and Luther, then we have an unbroken chain of the greatest witnesses for the message of faith. Isaiah's incomparable religious greatness is nowhere more evident than in the fact that the central religious thought, that of faith, had one of its classic representatives in him. For real religion, true living in God, is nowhere more apparent than in faith. The full conviction of the power and greatness of God so completely controlled his whole being that he felt neither care nor fear, and so felt secure in God's protection. This seemed folly to political wisdom, and yet this bold idealism of religious conception has often been worth more than the apparent sober realism of everyday politics. The cause of the unhealthy political life of all nations is the exclusion of God and conscience, and therewith the exclusion of all religious and moral power and strength from political thought. This we call realism. In truth, it is nihilism, which leads only to dissolution of political life into brute violence. For this reason there is scarcely a more unscrupulous calling than politics, and there are scarcely more unscrupulous people than the politicians in all states and parties. Isaiah's conviction did not find a hearing. To-day he would succeed no better. From the icy silence, perhaps from the repellent attitude and gestures of the king and his followers, he realized he was addressing people to whom such a message was too lofty. What he said was above their power of comprehension. What! be calm and fold their hands when the house was already burning! As if that were what he intended! Of course every one must do his part whenever opportunity came, but he must leave the rest to God. What! were they to wage war with Faith? Drive the enemy from their country by faith in God? Only an inexperienced saint could expect that. What could a king and his councilors do with such advice?

Even if all this were not directly expressed in words, Isaiah read their faces. Perhaps a cruder means would finally help him to convince them that he was in the service of a higher power. He offered the king a sign, a wonder, either in the heavens above or in the depth below. If it appeared, they might believe that a god who was capable of giving this was also capable of keeping off Judah's enemies.

We of to-day may ask what would have happened if Ahaz had accepted the prophet's offer and had demanded an eclipse or an earthquake to test Yahweh's strength. This question would never have occurred to Isaiah's contemporaries. For them the prophet of Yahweh was a man of God who was in the council of the Almighty and who, therefore, himself possessed the miraculous power of God. If Isaiah offered the king a marvel, then he, himself, and every one else would know that his God would not desert him. In antiquity there never was a question about this. It was part of the authority of a prophet that the people believed him to possess this power. As the Islamite Marabu can to-day lick red-hot iron or swallow sharp knives without harm to himself, and as the ordeal repeatedly saved people from death in an undreamed of manner, so also the prophet knew himself to be in the ecstatic condition of being filled with the spirit of God beyond the natural laws of cause and effect, and under the especial protection of his God. To this day, these are enigmas that we cannot fully explain. It may be convenient to overlook them or deny them offhand, but this is not worthy of the serious scientist.

Ahaz did not permit the question to come to a practical issue. He did not even have the courage to make the prophet uncomfortable. "I will not tempt God."

Then the prophet's blood surged anew, and in extreme excitement of spiritual emotion, vehemently, angrily, and yet with the passionate enthusiasm of future joy, he uttered the words, "Is it a small thing for you to weary men, that ye will weary my God also? Therefore the Lord of All, Himself, shall give you a sign; behold a virgin shall conceive and bear a child, and shall call his name Immanuel." A strange sign, the pregnancy of a woman and the name of her son! But we must remember that everything was saturated with the miraculous. The "sign" that had been offered the king was not as the word might indicate, a symbol or something similar, but a real miracle. So the sign that he neither wished nor requested was a real miracle; the virgin, a wonder woman; the child, a holy wonder child. Only thus can we correctly understand what Isaiah meant.

What the prophet had just said was not a conception that appeared for the first time. Indeed, it seems to be a law of the religious mental life of humanity, that the highest conceptions of religious thought do not appear at one single time, at a climax as it were, but repeatedly and often, finally culminating in their most complete forms. Thus the idea of atonement and the idea that one assumes sin for another or for many others appears in the sacrifice of animals and in the human sacrifice among peoples of all times. It finally found its highest and finest expression in the purely ethical thought that the sacrifice of one's own life, assumed in voluntary obedience, can secure freedom from guilt for others.

Here and there among the peoples of antiquity we find the conception of the "golden age" as a time of blessing and peace, and with it the hope that this time would return through miraculous intervention of the Godhead to bless humanity anew. It appears in its purest and noblest form in Israel's hope of salvation. The thought of a savior as a child of God, born of a godly woman in a miraculous way and substantiated by marvelous destiny, repeatedly recurred among the nations, until this thought attained its highest and purest expression in Israel's hope for a Messiah, a marvelous king of the house of David. Isaiah found this hope existing. He accepted it, gave it its peculiar form, and presented it to the king.

Israel as well as other nations had long expected a new and great future. Probably even in David's time and at his court they had mentioned that the great King David was, himself, destined to fulfill their expectation. The prophet, Nathan, had expressed this thought by saying that in David's dynasty there would always be one who should be peculiarly favored of God as the son of Yahweh. More and more had Judean affairs shaped themselves, so that they might expect the end of the Judean dynasty. Twice in the immediate past, in Jeoash's and Amaziah's reign, the throne had been made vacant by a murderer's hand. Now the allied enemies desired to exterminate Ahaz and his house by violence. No one could say what plans the Assyrian king had for Jerusalem when once he had power there. Thus they might expect many changes in the royal house in the near future. Disappointment in Ahaz' inability may have nourished this hope in Isaiah. On the other hand, Isaiah must have known the Egyptian beliefs and hopes about a woman of God who should give birth to a child of God, who should bring about the new era and become the future Savior. Isaiah firmly believed that Yahweh would now accomplish this miracle through the house of David. A young woman in David's palace, possibly the king's own wife, possibly another woman there who was just expecting the birth of a child, he believed to be selected to become the bride of God just as, in exalted language and conception in Egypt, the queen was considered the bride of God, and the child that she should bear seemed to him destined to be called both a child of God and Immanuel. In this child the old hope would be fulfilled. His youth might suffer the oppression of the Assyrian invasion, but David's offspring would one day grow to manhood and replace the unstable Ahaz. He would expel the enemy from the country, and then establish the long-desired new kingdom of David as the realm of peace and justice.

When this same child was born (perhaps it was Hezekiah, who later became the king) Isaiah greeted him with the jubilant cry:

> For unto us a child is born,
> Unto us a son is given,
> And the Government shall be upon his shoulder.
> And his name shall be called
> Wonderful, Councillor, Mighty God,
> Everlasting Father, Prince of Peace.[9]

Isaiah did not succeed in restraining the king from his disastrous policy. Ahaz' embassy had no difficulty in accomplishing its purpose. In the year 734 we find Tiglath-Pileser in Syria to punish his unfaithful vassals. He would certainly have done this without Ahaz' request. Pekah lost a considerable part of his territory to Assyria. Damascus resisted bravely, yet it was conquered in 732. The state of

Syria with its capital, Damascus, ceased to be and became an Assyrian province.

From his narrow viewpoint King Ahaz may have triumphed. He was rid of his annoying neighbors. Although Israel existed, it was no longer important. Pekah's murderer, Hoshea, still ruled over the modest state of Israel. It was primarily a vassal state of Assyria, and its territory comprised chiefly the mountains of Ephraim. It was no longer dangerous to Ahaz. Ahaz' gain was, however, as we long have known, only seeming gain. What he had given up of treasure and moral values was lost to him. We conclude from Isaiah's descriptions how the Assyrian armies ravaged the land.

Victorious world powers are usually insatiable. Thus it was natural that all sorts of services and oaths of allegiance followed the first payment of tribute. When, after the conquest of Damascus, Tiglath-Pileser remained there and gathered his vassals about him, Ahaz also appeared to pay his respects to the great king. As part of the proof of submission to Assyria, he expressed his dependence also in the matter of the religious life of Judah. In honor of the great king he removed an altar, which he saw in Damascus, to the temple at Jerusalem. This must have been an altar to the god Ashur. He also introduced the Assyrian star and sun worship into Jerusalem, and he seems to have kept sacred sun steeds at the temple. In keeping with the political dependence upon Assyria which Ahaz voluntarily assumed, he now suffered the religious consequences. Yahweh had not been crowded out of the temple any more than Ahaz had been removed from the throne. But beside Yahweh and frequently above him in rank, Assur and Ishtar ruled as gods of Judah. Only now do we fully understand why Isaiah so violently opposed Ahaz' Assyrian policy. For the present, however, he was defeated and forced to silence.

For years Ahaz continued his reign without fame and

probably without joy, but he lived and was permitted to rule nominally. That was enough for his weak self. In Ephraim affairs moved rapidly. The party that had made Hoshea king of a torso-like state naturally had a hard struggle. The party of the independents in Samaria was strengthened by Egypt, and Tiglath-Pileser's death encouraged new hopes in Samaria. His successor was Salmanassar V (727-722). Soon after his rule began, Hoshea seems to have been forced to a revolt. The great king interfered; he did not immediately conquer the fortified capital of Samaria. But after a three years' siege, it was captured by his successor, Sargon, in 722.

Isaiah had also foretold this deplorable fate of Samaria. In one of his most masterly poems, he mentally saw himself transported to one of the luxurious palaces of the Samarian capital. In the splendid hall of the palace, he saw the drunken revelers tired and wasted after a night of feasting. The wreaths of flowers on their heads were half withered. Morning was approaching when suddenly like a great storm the enemy broke into the city. It is a scene like that of Belthazar of Babylon.

Woe to the crown of pride, to the drunkards of Ephraim, whose glorious beauty is a fading flower, which are on the head of the fat valleys of them that are overcome with wine.

Behold, the Lord hath a mighty and strong one, which as a tempest of hail and a destroying storm, as a flood of mighty waters overflowing, shall cast down to the earth with the hand.

The crown of pride, the drunkards of Ephraim, shall be trodden under foot." [10]

After this misfortune, Sargon led the prominent people of Samaria off captive. This was the custom that Assyria had practiced for some time. This manner of treating conquered nations was new. Apparently the finer feelings of Israel still seriously protested against it. This treatment meant nothing less than the complete and inconsiderate crushing of national individuality. Whole peoples were uprooted from their ancestral soil; entire confederations of nations were brutally crushed. The method succeeded well in its object. The danger of new insurrections was eliminated. A defeated people, whose backbone is broken and whose spinal column is removed, is no longer dangerous.

Isaiah could never forget the kinship of Israel and Judah, that Israel also belonged to Yahweh's people. The barbarism of this procedure wounded him deeply. Henceforth he looked upon Assyria as accursed of God. If before this time Assyria had been God's messenger and scourge to chastise the degenerated peoples, now, because of misinterpretation of its commission and insolent arrogance in assuming God's place, Assyria was itself condemned. Isaiah stands before us here as one proclaiming the moral law. What he announces is the philosophy of history on a large scale; even empires fall if they disregard the eternal laws of divine justice. Assyria had done this when it forgot that it was only a tool in God's hands and, instead of chastising in the name of God, it attempted to destroy nations on its own authority. The way in which Isaiah reaches out here beyond Israel and Judah, summoning the empire, just reaching its zenith, to appear before the forum of his moral judgment shows him in his entire greatness. The boldness and breadth of his vision are such that they compel us even to-day to wonder and to admire.

A tale is current in the capital of one of the few European kingdoms that remained after the war that the crown prince is in the habit of saying, "My business has poor prospects." Almost all the kings of Israel and Judah after David could have said the same of themselves. It is strange, indeed, how few of them reached old age. Almost all, with the exception of the usurpers to the throne who, for the most part, soon disappeared again, succeeded to the throne very young, sometimes too young. The licentiousness of the court and harem life seems to have wasted these undisciplined youths before their time. Ahaz was one of them. We do not definitely know when he died; he survived hardly more than thirty-five years. His son Hezekiah succeeded him (719-691).

Hezekiah had a poor heritage from his father. Politically and religiously the independence of Judah was lost. If Hezekiah would make an effort to rule in the country, he had first to attempt to free himself from the fatal clutches of Assyria. He would fare best if he managed to do this without a real break with the great king. Hezekiah surely knew that a war with Assyria might have the most fatal consequences for Judah. As long as he could avoid this, he could also depend upon Isaiah's help. Much as Isaiah felt estranged in his heart toward the Assyrian kingdom since the fall of Samaria, he could hardly wish that Judah attempt foolish opposition, which might easily result in the loss of all that had thus far been saved with such difficulty.

To appreciate Hezekiah's political measures we must remember that since the fall of Samaria, Judah had become Assyria's immediate neighbor. The boundary which separated it from the world empire now ran only a few hours' journey northward from Jerusalem. In addition, the Assyrian-Ephraimite war and the confusion which had followed it even up to Hezekiah's time, had often brought the Assyrian warriors to and across the border of their country. Everywhere there must have been traces of them in the plundered cities and villages, burned farmhouses, trampled fields, and impoverished people. It was Hezekiah's task to heal and restore, and to bring about security for the future. After he had reigned some time, Hezekiah's treasury and arsenal were so filled that he seemed to King Merodach-Baladan of Babylon a desirable ally against Assyria. This presupposes that he increased commerce, brought money into the country, built fortresses, supplied himself with chariots, horses, and war materials. He also built a new water system in Jerusalem which served a similar purpose of security for the future. Experiences in Ahaz' reign may have taught the people that the lack of a good water supply was one of the weak spots in the capital. Back in gray antiquity, the Canaanite rulers of Jerusalem had attempted to secure the water supply for the city in time of war by building a subterranean passage. The passage was probably in ruins now, and Hezekiah constructed the Shiloh canal and the Shiloh pool which still exist.

Judah had not only become weak politically, but had also deteriorated religiously through Assyrian influence. Religious reforms were greatly needed. We shall discuss them elsewhere. To avoid a complete break with Assyria, it was necessary to exercise greater care in carrying out religious reforms than political ones. Since Ahaz' time, the temple and the entire ritual had been strongly influenced by Assyria. The state and religion were closely bound together. Establishing the worship of Assyrian gods and Assyrian ritual customs was equivalent to acknowledging the power of these gods and of the Assyrian sovereignty. If Judah freed itself from the Assyrian gods and returned to its native Yahweh, the great king's representatives in Judah might become suspicious that further political measures were being planned.

How long Hezekiah succeeded in evading this suspicion we do not know, nor how long he refrained from measures that might justify this suspicion. Of course the break came. It could probably not be avoided as time went on unless Judah blindly made itself a tool of the Assyrian policy. Judah was the only important stronghold that separated Assyria from Egypt, and the ultimate goal of the Assyrian policy in this region must have been the conquest of Egypt.

Isaiah had done his utmost to avoid the break. Ahaz' reign was ever present in his mind, and the painful experiences that had justified the prophet's position. Now his greatest desire was to save the youthful king from the fate of his unfortunate father. It seems that Isaiah had more confidence in the king than he formerly had had in Ahaz, but Hezekiah's advisers were apparently the same men who had counseled his father and had kept the same political principles as in his father's time. Isaiah, therefore, foresaw ruin.

What the politicians of Judah now strove for was much the same as that for which Rezin and Pekah had once striven; namely, to gather all available forces in Palestine and Syria and to drive the Assyrians out of the country with a decisive blow. Of course, Egypt was the instigator of this revolt. The increasing danger had long been apparent to the now aged kingdom of the Pharaohs. Since the fall of Damascus and Samaria, Judah only lay between the two world powers. Thus Egypt had the greatest interest in maintaining Judah and the remaining principalities of Palestine; but Egypt had neither the strength nor the energy necessary to make the sacrifice for this goal. It was satisfied with making promises, and letting others expose themselves to actual danger. In duplicity and intrigue, Egypt's policy at that time was quite equal to that of the great powers who promote the Near East of to-day.

What could a man like Isaiah have in common with such a policy? He could only pity a people who were a prey to its snares, and pour the vial of his bitterest wrath over the masters of that intrigue, whether they were in Egypt or in Jerusalem. He believed they were corrupting his poor people and leading them on to permanent destruction. Isaiah remained true to himself. A generation ago he had sought with all his powers of persuasion, enticements, and threats to turn a young and inexperienced king from a false policy of self-help. Now he took the same attitude toward his son. Once he had hoped great things from Hezekiah; perhaps he still hoped, but he could realize his hope only if the king put his faith in Yahweh and not in men.

Thus Isaiah again became the preacher of faith and God's help. He saw clearly that the calamity which faced Hezekiah might be equal to that which his father had faced. He also saw that in principle the present condition was exactly the same as in his father's time. He knew, therefore, that the help must be no different from that possible in former times. Not human alliance, not earthly machinations, but God alone could help. He did not believe, however, that in the face of troubles the people should fold their hands and, glancing piously toward heaven, expect help from above. But when he considered the existing conditions, when he did not vehemently express, as politicians usually do, the interests of personal vanity or personal advantage attained by human favor, but rather the result of sober considerations of his people's resources and foreign ones, he invariably reached a definite conclusion. It was this. To wage war with Assyria would be a mad adventure. If Yahweh wished to assign a lot to Judah, other than of a modest existence under the Assyrian protectorate, then Yahweh himself would point out the way and would himself champion his cause. Even now to Isaiah the solution was "to be still and wait," and maintain quiet confidence in God alone.

Isaiah had formerly opposed joining Assyria. Now he objected to breaking away from Assyria for an alliance with Egypt. Probably Egypt had urged war with Assyria ever since the beginning of Hezekiah's reign. Indeed, since the fall of Samaria, Sargon had repeatedly made expeditions to chastise the refractory people in the country, first in 720 at Rafia near Gaza, later in 711 at Ashdod. If Judah practiced restraint and thus avoided serious complications, it may have been due to Isaiah's warning. Sargon died in 705. He was succeeded by his son, Sennacherib (705-681), the most ruthless and most greedy for territory of all the conquerors of the Assyrian empire.

It is probable that, from the beginning, the people of Syria knew what to expect from this change of rulers. Internal disturbances in Assyria and Babylon as well as Egypt's enticements had done their part in urging the Syrian-Palestine peoples to renew the old alliances for offense and defense against Assyria. The energetic Tirhakah, later usurper in Egypt, already controlled affairs. For twelve years the objectionable vassal king, Merodach Baladan, acted as ruler in Babylon under Sargon. Immediately after Sargon's death he appeared, and in 702 he even succeeded in securing royal power for himself in Babylon. We know that he had friendly relations with Hezekiah. His ambassadors appeared in Jerusalem and inspected Hezekiah's treasury and arsenals. This meant conferences concerning an alliance, conferences which may have met soon after Sargon's death, at the very latest, in 703 or 702.

Under these circumstances Hezekiah could no longer remain inactive. In the East, Babylonia urged him on to action; in the south, Egypt; in his own country, a strong party of supposed patriots. Near Judah, the Philistine cities of Askelon and Ekron (after Gaza and Ashdod had been eliminated) and, further north, Sidon were all strong centers of the movement. Thus, whether it would or not, Judah was drawn into the whirlpool. During the negotiations, Isaiah made every effort to restrain Hezekiah. In the twenty-eighth and the following chapters of his book, we have a whole cycle of speeches, whose almost exclusive purpose was a warning against an alliance with Egypt.

Woe to the rebellious children, saith the Lord, that take counsel, but not of me; and that cover with a covering, but not of my spirit, that they may add sin to sin. That go to walk

[280]

down to Egypt, to strengthen themselves in the strength of the Pharaoh, and to trust in the shadow of Egypt.[11]

But the power of circumstances was stronger than Isaiah's eloquence. The negotiations ended, the break was made. Now Isaiah had the choice. Should he abandon his country because of the folly of the king and his councilors, or should he support the king and the people in spite of the wrong policy they were pursuing? Never was Isaiah greater than at this time when he conquered himself. Much as he had opposed the break with Assyria, when once the die was cast, he knew his place was at the king's side.

The conviction which he probably had held for years, that the Assyrian empire morally was near its downfall, pointed the way. To him Assyria had long ago changed from a scourge in Yahweh's hand to a defiant, aggressive Titan who must fall by his own arrogance. Now when Assyria began to oppose Yahweh's city and temple, the idea became increasingly clear to Isaiah that the giant must be shattered on the rock of Zion, because Zion was Yahweh's dwelling place. His belief that Assyria would fall in this way was not realized. A long time of grace was granted the Titan. All the more splendidly was Isaiah's prophecy fulfilled, when Sennacherib's attempt to gain power over Jerusalem failed miserably.

Sennacherib could not permit to go unnoticed what had happened in Palestine. Because Egypt had supported the movement, there was much at stake. Sennacherib began by seizing the evil at the very root, but to conceal his purpose by vigorously attacking the old insurgent, Merodach Baladan, in Babylon. He succeeded in conquering Merodach Baladan in 702. Now he was free to turn westward.

In the West, also, Sennacherib proved himself a wise tactician by first proceeding toward the coast of Palestine in order to have a free hand in subjugating the interior. He sought to get possession of the Phœnician coast cities from

Sidon to Accho. Tyre seems to have resisted successfully, but Sennacherib, by the help of a certain Ethbaal who was devoted to him, succeeded in gaining a counterpart to it in Sidon which enabled him to turn southward. There he attacked the Philistine cities Ashkelon and Ekron and gained the former. As he approached Ekron, a relief column of united Egyptians and Ethiopians faced him. At Eltekeh a battle was fought. Sennacherib boasts of a great victory there. He did, in fact, gain Ekron, but he dared not follow up the advantage.

The actual presence of the greatly feared monarch and the terrible punishments that he inflicted everywhere had in the meantime decided a part of the allies of the interior, namely, Ammon, Moab, and Edom, upon voluntary subjection. Only Judah remained firm in its resistance. Thus Sennacherib was obliged to advance against Hezekiah. Doubtless the fact that Sennacherib dared not advance against the Egyptian relief troops had decided Hezekiah to take this course. The king, until then a careful strategist, now had the painful disadvantage, in spite of the Philistine conquest, of still having in the rear a powerful enemy whom he must consider. Hezekiah, probably, had good reason to see in Sennacherib the half-conquered victor at Eltekeh, whose enemy needed only time to gather himself together to strike a new blow.

Sennacherib prepared to advance against Hezekiah. He seems to have been victorious because Hezekiah's troops were incapable. The western part of Judah fell to him. Sennacherib boasted that he had conquered forty-six walled cities and countless villages, and the biblical narrator confirms this statement with the remark that Sennacherib captured and burned all the fortified cities of Judah. Now there was nothing left to Hezekiah but to become subject to the king. He paid the tribute that Sennacherib demanded. At this time Sennacherib broke up his permanent camp at

Lachish and removed it farther eastward. This was certainly not done voluntarily and was equivalent to a retreat from the Egyptians who had not really been conquered. All now depended upon quickly getting possession of Hezekiah's fortified capital. The fact that Sennacherib's dignitaries had first to make a plea for it, proves that its surrender was not included in Hezekiah's subjection.

When the voluntary surrender of Jerusalem was declined, Sennacherib's rabsakehs surrounded it. In Jerusalem the people apparently considered this treason. This increased the embitterment and roused the courage of desperation in the city. Sure of victory, Isaiah, to whom the king had appealed in his distress, is said to have cried out:

Therefore, thus saith the Lord concerning the king of Assyria, He shall not come into this city, nor shoot an arrow there, nor come before it with shield, nor cast a bank against it.[12]

So it happened that Sennacherib did not carry out his plan. What really happened to cause the hasty retreat we shall probably never definitely know. It is reported that news of the approach of an Egyptian army disquieted him, and also that a sudden epidemic that broke out in his army decided him to return. It is possible that both of these causes acted together.

We hear nothing more of Isaiah himself. He had done his life work and might have spent his old age in peace. As long as Hezekiah lived, Isaiah certainly enjoyed the highest honors. If he lived to see Manasseh's rule, it is possible that the deserving old man experienced ingratitude and persecution in his old age. Legend assumes this. It even has the renowned old man translated to heaven, and when later he related what he saw there, King Manasseh is said to have had him sawed alive into pieces.

XII

REFORMERS

A GREAT man's work is seldom carried on by a long line of successors so, too, with Moses. Possibly the peculiar conditions under which he worked were responsible; however, under different conditions, he might have had the same fate. Neither Joshua nor any of his successors, as far as Samuel, impress us as being capable of leading Israel, even without the special difficulties of the entrance into Canaan.

These difficulties proved a drawback to Israel's development. Their nature we know. The Israelites took possession of Canaan either with the voluntary or the forced cooperation of its former inhabitants. In only a few cases did the Canaanites go and leave Israel in possession. In most cases they remained, and Israel had to come to terms with them. Even where they were destroyed, as is reported of Jericho and a few other cities, taking possession of the country necessitated agreement with the Canaanites. The Israelites could not cultivate the soil without knowing its peculiarities and the customs of centuries, the location of the springs, the manner of irrigation, or the time and manner of planting in the different localities. Such matters the farmer does not know instinctively and must be told them. "His god taught" him how to till the soil and also to control the yield of the springs. The products of the soil, of the field, and of the fruit trees were the gifts of divine powers that reigned in them. To cultivate the soil and make it productive was a part of the religion of the ancients, and, therefore, of the Canaanites.

When Israel took possession of Canaan, it accepted with the secular customs the religious ones and adapted them to the religion which Israel had brought with it from the desert. This means that the Mosaic Yahweh must replace the Baal who was so prominent in the Canaanite religion, as the protector and patron of the soil, distributor of its fruits, and instructor of the farmer. We have already stated that it was Israel's historic misfortune to lose Moses at the time when the Yahweh of Sinai with his people was about to enter Canaan. Moses was obliged to leave to others less skilled than himself the task of leading his people into Israel, of guiding them, and watching over them to make sure that the religion of the steppes should become the religion of Canaan. In many instances, Israel's post-Mosaic religion had to seek a contact and agreement with the Canaanite religion without the help of a great creative genius to settle the disputes in such a way that Yahweh and Israel would not suffer.

Israel's religious development after Moses' death was a constant struggle with Canaan. In the period of the judges and early kings up to Solomon's time, Baal repeatedly threatened to supplant Yahweh. There always were some people who cherished as a valuable heritage the Mosaic tradition which Israel must cherish. The danger increased when Jeroboam I founded the northern state. The people felt the effect of separating the agricultural districts from the southern part nearer the steppes. This effect was increased by introducing the bull, as a symbol, into the national worship. Jeroboam's national religion remained the religion of Yahweh, although it contained more Baal elements than formerly. It was not necessary but natural that at some time an attempt be made to replace the half-heathen religion by complete heathenism expressed in the Baal or the Phœnician Melkart. Jezebel and Ahab did this in Samaria, and Athaliah, in Judah for a short time.

Even before Athaliah's time there were several such attempts when, after Solomon's death, Judah separated from Israel. This change was the result of Solomon's great tolerance toward foreign religions. Even though these efforts were not nearly as widespread or as aggressive as Jezebel's actions, they prove that Baal attracted the Judeans and indicated what might occur if those faithful to Yahweh failed to be constantly on guard. The time came, however, when this danger, which was never entirely overcome, became but one of many similar dangers from the increasing political power of Assyria and Babylon.

After Samuel's and Nathan's time, Yahweh's seers had led the movement to restore the Mosaic Yahweh to his rights. Although Yahweh was acknowledged as the god of Israel, he was never the undisputed God of Israel. He never completely ruled Israel and the Israelites. After Samuel, and especially after Elijah, the one object of prophecy was to make Yahweh the sole ruler of Israel. After Elijah the prophetic movement was a great reform movement to make Yahweh supreme in Israel. It was supported by the Brotherhood of the Rechabites, the order of the Nazarites, by scattered Levite clans who had remained faithful to Yahweh, later by the priesthood of the temple, and by the kings who favored either the priesthood or the prophets. The strongest support was from the prophets who, from the time they began to serve Yahweh, remained the chief champions of his cause. At this time their object was to combat Baal, but they did not always limit themselves to this. In the course of time, political conditions changed their task. Yahweh's will remained their sole interest. Disloyalty to Yahweh was not expressed alone in favoring Baal or other gods. The prophets always combated this tendency. All religious reforms in Israel and Judah which strove to establish and advance Yahweh worship were in some way connected with prophecy and its champions.

Jehu's attitude in Samaria toward Baal worship and the abolition of it in Jerusalem together with Athaliah's fall may be considered a reform movement. In both cases, however, dynastic interests were too much in the foreground. Jehu's chief interest was to seat himself upon Ahab's throne, even if prophecy, which supported him, was far more interested in the religious question. In the fall of Athaliah, interest in the legitimate dynasty of David was the chief concern, and abolishing Baal worship only a phenomenon, however much desired and well planned. We shall, therefore, not take these two cases into account. There are a number of cases of similar nature in which the religious interest in restoring and retaining the purity of the worship of Yahweh seems to have been the motive force. These are reforms in the real sense. Priestly, hierarchial, or political interests may have existed in them, also, but were never the true driving force and, certainly, not the only factor.

The Book of Kings reports that Solomon's son, Rehoboam, erected high places, pillars, and asherim on every towering hill and under every green tree in Judah. There were even sodomites; all the heathen abuses seem to have been practiced. The narrator traces this to Rehoboam's mother who was an Ammonite and so belonged to the heathen, foreign women in Solomon's harem.

"High place" was the general term for the Canaanite place of worship, which might be innocently adopted for Yahweh worship as Samuel had done. The pillar or monument was originally a drift block turned upward. Gradually the stone was hewn to a point and became a stone pillar. People believed it had a soul and was the dwelling place of a divine being; therefore the sacrificial oil and the blood of the slaughtered animal were poured upon it. The simple blood sacrifice, such as Saul commanded for special occasions, needed no altar. Where there was no special altar to serve as the sacrificial table for food or for the burning of certain

parts of the sacrificial animal, the pillar replaced it. Therefore, there probably was no objection to the pillar in the
early time. The more the altar became the real seat of God,
particularly after the burnt sacrifice came into use, the more
the pillar was superfluous and was scorned. This usage may
have begun in Rehoboam's time, for the building of Solomon's temple does not mention a pillar besides the altar.
Thus it seems that the seat of God and the objects used in the
ritual had already been combined in the altar.

This was not so with the asherah, for it was the symbol
of the goddess of the same name who was closely related to
Ashtart, the goddess of fertility. It was the sacred pillar,
an imitation of the fruit tree. Nowhere in the Old Testament do the patriarchs mention it or recognize it in any way,
doubtless because it presupposes Ashtart worship. This
was directly opposed to the worship of Yahweh which never
included a female counterpart of Yahweh and, therefore,
never recognized the sodomites. They belong to Ashtart
worship and represent the lowest degree of religious aberra-
tion of which nature worship is capable. In holy places,
women and even men sold their bodies in the service of the
goddess of fertility and gave the proceeds to the temple
treasury. This practice was now established in Jerusalem.
It proves better than all else that this worship had begun to
ensnare the people (at least those about the queen mother)
in the meshes of the nature religion. The statement that
Rehoboam and Abijah brought idols to Jerusalem agrees
with these conditions. We are not told of the nature of the
idols nor what they represented, but the description fails to
make of them Yahweh images.

Since our information about Rehoboam comes from the
later editors of the Book of Kings, we have no absolute
guarantee that it is correct. Yet we do not question the
nativity of Rehoboam's mother, because other information
about Solomon makes this fact seem probable. As Solomon's

wife, the Ammonite princess, undoubtedly, had freedom of religious worship. With her son's accession to the throne she rose to be Sultana Walide, the first lady of the empire, and her rank was second to that of the king. If the king permitted, who might hinder her from continuing her native religious practices? It was natural, also, that if the noble lady attached importance to this form of religion, many in the princely household and at the court as well as in the city and country would follow her example.

Rehoboam's son, Abijah, is said to have reigned only three years and then to have passed on the throne to his son, Asa. This grandson of Rehoboam and great grandson of Solomon seems also to have been the son of a heathen or semiheathen mother. Like Rehoboam's Ammonite mother, and perhaps her son and grandson she, too, strove to gain a foothold in Jerusalem for Canaanite heathenism. She seems to have had no difficulty, for only a few years had passed since Rehoboam's reign, and she needed only to support what he had created. Both Rehoboam and Abijah appear to have been friendly to these efforts. For a long time, apparently, no change occurred. All objects that suggested the Canaanite nature religion in the so-called high places, the pillars, the asherim, and images of all sorts, remained untouched. The sodomites continued their evil practices at the sacrificial places, and all with the special sanction of the highest authority after the king. Indeed the practice was given special prominence when the queen mother used a splendid utensil or a valuable adjunct of some sort, probably intended to add great splendor to the Asherah worship. We have no exact description of it. The ancients supposed it to be some obscene representation, such as was connected with a similar worship in various places. Be that as it may, the worship gradually took on such an objectionable character that the king was obliged to interfere.

Because of the great esteem which the queen mother enjoyed, it may not have been easy for Asa to take this step against his mother. The chronicler clearly infers that it was very unusual for the state authorities to take action against the queen mother. But greater interests were at stake for Asa. When we review these events to-day in the light of history, we must admit that Asa was guided by a correct feeling. He, apparently, felt that Israel's individuality was threatened. If people in Jerusalem continued as they had been doing since Solomon's death, indeed had begun to do during his lifetime, Yahweh would soon be supplanted by Baal and Ashtart. By giving up Yahweh they gave up what distinguished them as a nation from the Canaanites, for Israel's nationality depended upon its faith in Yahweh.

The more the Israelite religion in the northern state was made to conform to the Canaanite religion after Jeroboam's time, the more pressing was the need, so it seemed to Asa, for Judah to retain her pure Yahwist faith. History must give Asa credit for this insight, although in political matters he was very shortsighted and, for temporary gain, permitted himself to be persuaded to summon Syrian aid to conquer his enemy, Baasha of Israel.

Asa began by driving all the sodomites out of the country. Every respectable person who had an interest in the dignity of the worship of Yahweh must have rejoiced over this ruling. Even though we may not judge by our present standards, there can be no doubt that the finer sensibilities instilled by the worship of Yahweh were shocked even in those days by the degradation of woman and of marriage which the Canaanite practices brought about. The Israelites felt keenly that these religious practices had forced them upon a wrong path. The lower instincts of the masses always favor him who persuades them that they serve God, or civilization, or advancement, or freedom.

The many images of God that had been made during the

reign of the later Judean kings were destroyed. Yet the most important action was that which Asa took against his own mother and her favorite creation, the "abomination" or shameful image, as the text calls it. The image which was probably carved of wood may have stood beside an altar. Now this was hewn down and burned in the Kidron valley. The queen mother was divested of her high rank, her legal right. Because this could be done only by bringing a lawsuit against her, we can see the great importance which Asa and his confidants attached to the matter. It implies that removing and burning the image was a solemn act of state in which the king and the people participated. Had the chronicler wished to give more than a mere summary, he could have told us that King Asa, like the priest Joiada and the later King Josiah, embraced the opportunity to make a covenant with his people, i.e., to solemnly pledge himself and his people to serve only Yahweh in future.

Reviewing the whole matter, we feel no doubt that the reform in Judah began with King Asa. It seems like a prelude to the time of Hezekiah and of Josiah. This is verified, I believe, by the statement added to the narrative that Asa caused the votive offering of silver, gold, and costly vessels, gifts from him and his father, to be carried to the temple. We ask where they had been before this time. They must have been gifts to different sanctuaries, especially to the one which had the asherah image mentioned above and which was located probably in the Kidron valley. It is possible that Asa had been influenced for a time by his mother.

If this was the case, it is evident that even at that time the temple was superior in rank to other sanctuaries. Especial emphasis is given the fact that Asa did not interfere with sanctuaries; he merely purified them or part of them. By taking away the images and votive offerings, which decorated them and increased their maintenance, he reduced their influence so much that they were, for a long time, no serious menace to the temple.

It is not likely that Asa made this far-reaching reform on his own responsibility. We have every reason to believe that the priesthood of the temple supported this measure as did also much of the Judean population and the prophetic men who worked in the spirit of Nathan and Ahiah of Siloh. We have no statement that the abuses mentioned entered the temple itself. To be sure, it was in the interest of the priesthood to increase the prestige of the temple, but they did not advance the temple's interests solely through ulterior motives. The temple priests, or most of them, were Levites. The fact that Jeroboam appointed non-Levite priests in his sanctuaries proves this. Since the days of Kadesh Barnea, the Levites preferred to dwell in Judah, and we have good reason to believe that they and the Judean population, particularly those living in the steppes, were more devoted to the Mosaic traditions than the rest of the Judean people. We may take for granted that the rural population of Judah, the Levite priesthood of the temple, and the prophets of Judah were those who influenced Asa in his decision.

In imagining the course of events, we assume that for a time King Asa continued in his father's and grandfather's ways, and may even have outdone them in permitting his mother freedom of action. He showed himself their equal in giving votive offerings to the different sanctuaries. Later, the prophets and priests who were about him persuaded him that this course would lead to Judah's ruin. Conscious of the king's responsibility, he interfered effectively, brought the temple into prominence once more, and purified the sanctuaries at the high places. Thus the man whose political shortsightedness we lament takes on a more favorable aspect by what he did in the religious field for his country.

Asa was succeeded by his son, Jehoshaphat, who seems

to have continued in his father's ways. If certain reports in the Book of Chronicles are true, he even outdid him in certain respects. The text is somewhat obscure, however, and we prefer at present to make no definite statements. This much is certain, Asa had only made a beginning in the struggle against the nuisance of sodomites, both men and women. Much remained for Jehoshaphat to do. The fact that he did it gives him a place among the reform kings. Whatever may be the truth about the report in the Book of Chronicles, we know he continued the course his father had begun.

Jehoshaphat was the father of Jehoram, who was the husband of Athaliah, Ahab's daughter. She is reported to have helped to restore the Baal priests to favor in Judah. Ahab was succeeded by his son, Ahaziah, who died early at Jehu's hands. He was followed by his ambitious mother, Athaliah, whom we have already discussed. Even before she officially took the throne, her native religion, that of the Tyrean Baal, Melkart, had been reëstablished in Jerusalem, apparently due to her influence. All the things that Asa and Jehoshaphat had abolished may have returned with the Melkart worship. However, these heathen objects do not seem to have entered the temple as in Asa's time. Athaliah seems to have respected the Temple of Yahweh. A special temple after the pattern of the Samarian temple was built in Jerusalem, perhaps at the place where Asa's mother had set up her "abomination" for Asherah and where the foreign idols had formerly been. This temple had its own priest, altars, and images of the god. No change seems to have been made in the Temple of Yahweh other than to protect it by a special guard against a possible attack by the queen's followers.

The votive offerings which, under Athaliah's influence, Jehoram and Ahaziah had presented to the Baal temple, seem to have been removed to the Yahweh temple by Jehoiada. We know for certain that in Joash's time the temple had a

[293]

great treasure of gold which consisted in part of votive gifts from the kings, Jehoshaphat, Jehoram, and Ahaziah. This treasure Joash sent to the Syrian King, Hazael, to bribe him to withdraw from Jerusalem.

In important matters, Joash's successors, Amaziah, Ahaziah, Uzziah, and Jotham, seem to have followed the course outlined by Joash in the abolition of Athaliah's rule of violence. Conditions changed only with Jotham's son, Ahaz. We have already heard of his disastrous policy and its results. Quite apart from Isaiah's general attitude toward the question of foreign alliances and political promises of the Judah of his time, apart from the political disadvantages which he foresaw, was his religious reason for objecting to Ahaz's policy. He realized that political dependence upon Assyria would cause religious dependence.

The altar which Ahaz saw in Damascus and later brought to the temple (certainly a sacrificial altar for the god Ashur) proves that as soon as Ahaz became the political vassal of Assyria, Judah's religion was influenced. Another proof we find in the sun steeds which he brought to the temple to honor the god Ishtar. I have purposely mentioned repeatedly that, as far as we know, the temple had, up to this time, been either entirely or almost entirely spared. Canaanite heathenism and the worship of the Tyrean Melkart had, it seems, been satisfied with the old "high places" and numerous locations in and about Jerusalem. Even Athaliah had spared the temple. Up to this time the foreign gods had been introduced by their own people. Now a change took place. Ahaz had become the vassal of a foreign power which exercised its authority, not only over the King of Judah but also over his God, Yahweh. This marks a new and different situation. Ashur now entered the temple.

Naturally, the ancient Canaanite and related symbols and images were restored. If Ahaz tolerated the Assyrian religion, in justice he could not object to the various forms of Baal and Ashtart worship which formerly had been either suppressed or restricted. Thus not only the high places, which had continued unmolested, resumed their influence and were furnished with many scorned images of Baal and Ashtart, but also the objectionable Asherah and Ashtart images, which we have frequently observed in King Asa's time, were reëstablished in Jerusalem. Ashtart and Ishtar were so closely related that it is quite possible that Ahaz treated this old image as an Ishtar image. Child sacrifice, the important feature of Melkart (Moloch) worship, was now introduced.

The need of reformation was again great. Ahaz died about 720 (probably 719). He was succeeded by his son, Hezekiah. Shortly before Hezekiah ascended the throne, the last barrier separating Judah and Jerusalem from Assyria had fallen. With Samaria's fall, Judah became the immediate neighbor of the world empire now so greedy for territory. If Hezekiah wished to remain at all independent of Assyria, he must make every effort to free himself from the fatal Assyrian embrace voluntarily taken on by his father against Isaiah's advice. Yet he dare not (especially at the beginning of his reign) risk a complete break with Assyria. Even a decade and a half later when the separation took place, Hezekiah's strength was still entirely inadequate and he could not face the situation calmly. In the early part of his reign the breach would have been folly.

This indicated Hezekiah's plan of action. We have heard of the political side of his activity. Now we are interested only in the religious side. The Second Book of Kings reports Hezekiah's reforms, and emphasizes that he was the first of the Judean kings who took serious action against the sanctuaries on the high places. If we read carefully in the Book of Kings the short descriptions and the author's comments about the different kings after Solomon, we find concerning every one after Rehoboam this remark, "that which was evil in the sight of Yahweh" or "that which was right in the sight of Yahweh." With the latter remark, which designates those who were devout kings, we find without exception the remark, "howbeit the high places were not taken away." Hezekiah is the king who is said to have begun this work.

It has already been stated that the expression, "high place" (bamot) merely means the native Canaanite place of worship and sacrifice. These places may formerly have been in the open, provided with the pillars and asherah, the seat of God which gradually became the symbol of Baal and Ashtart. In an earlier period they probably were provided with an altar for a sacrificial table. In time, temples and halls were built, or at least temple-like buildings which were called temple houses. When Israel came to Canaan, the high places were taken over and many of them were used for Yahweh worship, either for Yahweh only or for Yahweh and Baal. Each different high place naturally had a different development. Where Yahweh alone was worshiped, the Asherah, or some other image, may have vanished or may have lost its signifiance, for it belonged only to the Ashtart-Asherah worship and never to Yahweh worship. At the high places where the worship of both Yahweh and Baal was carried on (i.e., Gideon's ophrah in Judges), we find Ashtart and the asherah beside Baal, also sodomites and the ritualistic orgies associated with the goddess of fertility. The idols, statue-like images of Baal and Ashtart to which we constantly refer, may have been placed at the already existing high places or near Jerusalem. We read frequently of one asherah, which must have been a very valuable, very unique, and probably an objectionable image of Ashtart, placed there.

It is not probable that the reform kings before Hezekiah were indifferent to these sanctuaries. If their efforts to purify the worship of Yahweh were sincere, the kings surely were not indifferent. Yet the chroniclers tell us that the people still offered sacrifice at the high places, and the kings abolished neither the high places nor the pillars. This means they were not destroyed but somewhat purified by the removal of the images, the sodomites, and probably some of the most obnoxious asherah. To the narrator, however, the high places were still a source of danger. In the course of time the expression, "high place," became very elastic in Israel-Judah, and was as varied in use as was the relation of Yahweh to Baal. Sometimes worship at the high place was very similar to pure Yahweh worship and permitted only a pillar, which was regarded as the seat or symbol of Yahweh; sometimes it differed greatly from the Yahweh ceremonial and seemed similar to that used in Baal worship. The ceremonial depended upon the principles that prevailed at the given time. A high place was different from the temple. It was more than the mere rival of something having an equal value. The difference was that, from the very beginning, the temple had been built as Yahweh's Temple and had never been a Baal sanctuary. The high places had first been places for Baal worship, and they constantly lured the people to backslide to Baal.

Hezekiah wished to overcome this danger completely. We have reason to believe that King Asa was very tolerant toward Baal worship at the high places and elsewhere, as were, e.g., Athaliah and Asa's mother. Daily, Hezekiah had opportunity to see the devastating effect upon Judah of the spreading of the Assyrian national religion. He could not hinder it without rousing the Assyrian king's suspicion. He was so near the Assyrian border that every movement he made was observed. The Assyrian king had many agents and "watchmen" in Judah. We know that the rolling ruble, the Napoleon, the sovereign, the talent, or the mines was as effective in those days as now.

Since Hezekiah was limited in the scope of his reforms,

he devoted himself all the more zealously to that part of the worship over which he had power. The Assyrian was not interested in Baal and Ashtart, in high places or in asherim. He was satisfied if the Assyrian worship remained unmolested in Jerusalem. Hezekiah, therefore, decreed the abolishment of the high places, destroyed their pillars, and cut down their asherim. This made the sanctuaries at the high places of no use. We assume (although this is not definitely stated) that he also prohibited the use of images of gods and similar appurtenances. The report is so brief that much must be supplied to complete the picture. Only one object of worship is mentioned, evidently because of its importance. We read that he shattered the brazen serpent, called Nehustan, which Moses had made and to which the Israelites had offered burnt offerings up to this time. The image of a serpent (probably of a healing nature) similar to the one which legend tells us Moses erected in the desert to heal snake bite had been in Jerusalm for some time. It had probably been spared thus far because its use was traced to Moses. It is not stated nor is it likely that this image was placed in the temple. It may have been in the Kidron valley near the Serpent Stone or Dragon Springs. Now it must fall as a proof of the seriousness and thoroughness with which Hezekiah did his work.

Modern criticism doubts the historic truth of Hezekiah's reform, but without reason. I never believed the theory, and now that we have learned to look upon Hezekiah's and Josiah's work more clearly in the light of general world conditions than we formerly did, I am even more convinced than formerly of the error of this theory. Let it suffice here to refer to a statement I shall make later that Manasseh's counter reform would have been impossible without Hezekiah's reform before it.

Hezekiah's reform was more thorough than that of his predecessors. The situation was far more critical than ever before. Jerusalem's future was at stake. If Hezekiah did not act when he still had freedom to do so, there was danger that Jerusalem and Judah would become heathen territory in a short time. Yahweh was threatened on one hand by the god Ashur and on the other by Baal. What would become of Yahweh unless strong and effective measures were taken? Without them Yahweh would soon belong only to history. His position was already endangered. Ashur and Ishtar had already invaded the temple, although it still belonged to Yahweh, and sacrifice to Yahweh was still permitted. When the high places were abolished, the people who had formerly worshiped and sacrificed at them had to go to the temple. Thus Yahweh and not Ashur worship increased at the temple.

This proves the hypothesis that the ruling about the temple was due merely to the priests' desire for gain. There were far greater interests at stake for Hezekiah and his advisers than securing for the priesthood proceeds from votive offerings and sacrifices.

We know the outcome of Hezekiah's political struggle with Assyria. The break came after Sennacherib had ascended the throne, near the end of the century. Sennacherib returned to Assyria without having full control over Jerusalem. Now Hezekiah might remove Ashur and Ishtar from the temple. Here was the climax of his reform. This cannot be definitely stated, however, because the text tells us nothing of Hezekiah and Judah after Sennacherib's departure. The principal source of information is the account of Manasseh's counter revolution, an account so detailed that it throws the necessary light upon Hezekiah's later reforms. Manasseh, we learn, had to begin, as it were, at the beginning. Thus Hezekiah must have done his work with great thoroughness.

It is not difficult to understand why Manasseh, Hezekiah's son (691-638), undertook this far-reaching counteraction to his father's measures. Those people who had suffered under Hezekiah's reform may have been partly responsible. No reform is ever made without friction or protests from those who lose by it. When we make restrictions upon hotels, the keepers object; when we consider restricting places of amusement, the owners of cinemas and other places of amusement complain that their business will suffer. The priests and other officials of all the abolished sanctuaries struggled for a living, and probably considered the change of rulers a favorable opportunity to bring forward their protests. The many who favored the joyful national religion which had been practiced since olden times rather than, what seemed to them, the Puritanic severity of prophetic circles, may have influenced the young king and his advisers. It suggests to us that the Puritanic tendencies of the Wahhabites were for a long time sharply rejected by the rest of Islam. In Egypt, too, the national popular religion early opposed reforms. The great god was too far removed from the masses; they again sought their little "helpers."

These considerations certainly entered into the matter, but political conditions were far more important to Manasseh and his supporters. To be sure, Sennacherib had withdrawn from Jerusalem, but he had captured and destroyed Babylonia. His son and successor, Ashurhaddon (681-669), succeeded splendidly in achieving what his father had failed to do. He not only forced Manasseh and other Palestine princes to pay him tribute, but he reached the goal of Assyrian aggression in the west, the conquest of Egypt. After Ashurhaddon's death, his son, Ashurbanipal (669-626), made new conquests. Manasseh and other kings sent him auxiliary troops. He conquered Tirhaka and captured Thebes in 666. This was the zenith of Assyrian power.

To the ancients, this meant that the Assyrian gods were superior to other gods, including Yahweh. Manasseh must accept this fact. The Assyrian party in Judah had never been entirely subdued, and now it became more daring. Because Assyrian policy had triumphed so completely, Isaiah and his friends and, after his death, his disciples and their anti-Assyrian policy seemed to be forgotten.

In the edict of the King of Assyria we find the simple but significant statement: "I made them, the conquered people, responsible for the sacrifice to the great god Ashur." Manasseh was forced to comply to this canon, whether he chose to do so or not. If we read what the Book of Kings relates of Manasseh, we understand the meaning and the importance of his measures.

For he again built places which his father Hezekiah had destroyed; and he reared up altars for Baal and made an asherah as did Ahab, King of Israel, and worshiped all the hosts of heaven (He built altars in the Temple of Jehovah . . .) and built altars for all the most of heaven in the two courts of Jehovah's Temple. He made his son to pass through the fire . . . and set up a graven image of the asherah that he had made, in the temple.[1]

Canaanite and Assyrian idol worship was completely reestablished. Baal and Ashur again reigned, and with Ashur probably also Ishtar under the name of Asherah. Conditions were the same as under Ahaz. The tribute of gold was followed immediately by that of honor and worship of the foreign god. The people seem to have sought diligently to wipe out every trace of the effort to free themselves of Ashur and Baal. How thoroughly Hezekiah must have done his work if all these things must be rebuilt. In one respect Manasseh seems to have outdone Ahaz. He set up in the temple the image of the Asherah, so often mentioned. Until then no one had done this. It may have been a statue of the Ashtart and Ishtar type, strongly emphasizing sex, as we know from excavations. Introducing the image into the temple must mean that it now represented Ishtar and, together with Ashur, represented the queen of heaven. This may also be the reason why groups of sodomites now settled in the temple precincts.

Even the greatest empire has its limit. The end of the Assyrian Colossus came sooner than people expected. The subject nations had grown weary of unreasonable slavery. Enemies appeared on all sides, and the mighty empire fell under a united attack. Isaiah's prophecy about Assyria's fate had long been forgotten; now the time came when the people remembered it. Prophets such as Zephaniah and Nahum revived Isaiah's thoughts. The world seemed to shake in its very foundations as if something strange and new was about to happen.

In Ashurbanipal's time (about 645) Psammetichus of Egypt shook off the Assyrian overrule. The Medes in the far East seceded and founded an independent empire. The Scythians, an eastern nation of swift horsemen who are said to have overrun the Near East at times, followed their example. Ashurbanipal died in 626, at the time when all this was occurring. His son and successor, Ashuretililani, immediately lost Babylon, always an unwilling vassal. The Chaldean prince, Nabopolassar, declared his independence in 625. When Sinsharishkun ascended the Assyrian throne in 620, the Medes joined forces with the Babylonians and Scythians for a decisive battle.

Egypt had not foreseen this turn of events. People now realized that it was a question whether Asia should be ruled by the Semitic or Indo-Germanic powers, for the Medes and Scythians had nothing in common with the Semites. Then Egypt deserted her traditional policy and sided with Assyria. In 614 the Medean King, Cyazares, and Nabopolassar of Babylonia began the decisive attack upon Assyria. Nineveh fell in 612. For a time, the Assyrian torso state continued and was governed at Harran by Ashuruballit who was supported by Egypt which had already fought Nabopolassar. In 609, Pharaoh Necco, who had ascended the throne the year before, advanced with an army to assist Assyria. His reward was Syria.

Soon after 640, and after a long reign, King Manasseh died in Jerusalem. The short interregnum of his son, Amon, was followed by Amon's young son, Josiah in 638. The spirit of Hezekiah or, better, of Isaiah was awakened in him and his councilors. The Assyrian star was already waning when he began his reign. Assyrian enemies were already active in various places, and faint whispers of hope were heard among the nations. In the twelfth year of the young king's reign (627-626) Ashurbanipal died. The following year (625) Babylonia seceded.

It is not accidental that the Book of Chronicles sets the beginning of a great reform in Jerusalem in exactly the twelfth year of Josiah's reign. After Ahaz's and, particularly, after Manasseh's time, the Assyrians oppressed Judean religious life so greatly that every change in the political situation necessarily affected religious life. Hezekiah had long been forced to exert the greatest care in avoiding a break with Assyria, but from the very beginning Josiah, probably, had far more freedom of action. After Ashurbanipal's death, Assyria was so busy with itself and its own problems, as the newly found Babylonian chronicles recently taught us, that it was in no position to concern itself with the lesser western vassal which occasionally overstepped or transgressed the laws.

It seems reasonable that with the change of rulers in Assyria, Josiah at once should take certain steps. We recall that after Ahaz's and, more especially, after Manasseh's time, two attacks different in kind were simultaneously made upon the Yahweh religion. At this time the political situation called for the Assyrian religion to be established in Judah. A long time before this, the Canaanite Phœnician religion appeared and constantly demanded recognition. It had often been repulsed but never completely driven out. If the

Assyrian religion was permitted for political reasons, then this religion could no longer be kept out of Jerusalem. Thus Josiah had a double task before him, as Hezekiah also had had.

It is not probable that he faced the two tasks separately. When Ashurbanipal died, the political situation was such that he could unhesitatingly make a law against Ashur and Ishtar. His councilors were under the spiritual influence of Hezekiah and Isaiah, and thus opposed to Baal and Ishtar and everything connected with them. In the Book of Kings, these two reforms are not recorded separately.

The objects that belonged to Baal worship, the asherah and the heavenly hosts, were removed from the temple and burned in the Kidron valley. The heathen priests, appointed by Manasseh, Ahaz and others for his worship, were dismissed. The asherah itself (this may again refer to that particular image so frequently mentioned), we may call it the Hebrew Ishtar, was taken from the temple, burned in the Kidron valley, and its ashes scattered. The sodomites were cast out of the temple precincts, and their dwellings destroyed. All the priesthood of Judah was assembled; the high places and all that pertained to them where sacrifice had been offered were defiled. The priests were given a share of the gain from the sacrifice, but were not permitted to minister at the altar. The high places of the satyrs at the city gates were destroyed. The place of the child sacrifice in the Hinnon Valley, called Tophet, was defiled. The horses of the sun were abolished, and the chariots of the sun god were burned. The altars to the sun on the roof of Ahaz's upper chamber and the altars of Manasseh in the two entrance courts were destroyed. The shrines which Solomon had built for his foreign wives to use to worship their gods had remained unmolested until now, perhaps because they followed common custom. They were now defiled and destroyed. The pillars and the asherim were broken, and human bones were scattered over the ground. Jeroboam's place of sacrifice at Bethel was destroyed, and the asherah burned.

Now the country was in the state Hezekiah had striven for, at least as Hezekiah's predecessors after Asa had desired, although none of them had ventured to destroy the high places of Yahweh. Apparently the sad experiences after Ahaz's time were necessary to convince the kings that the high places, too, might become a danger when circumstances permitted. The natural result of defiling the high places was that the people now brought their sacrifices to the temple, at least the obligatory ones. For occasional special sacrifices they were permitted to use altars that they themselves had built, but not the altars that had recently been defiled and which were under suspicion because of much abuse. What was to become of their priests was for the time an open question. By performing lesser services at the altar they became assistants of the temple priests as long as they remained in Jerusalem. As Ezekiel shows, further changes were natural. He, too, formally declared them subordinates of the Zadok priests.

Because of these regulations, based as much upon national as upon religious considerations, after 626 a gradual change may have taken place in the form of the religious services. The enumeration is dry and schematic and in disconnected sentences, so that we have no clear conception of the chronological sequence. New regulations did not appear in rapid or simultaneous succession. Many of them were far-reaching and required time for fulfillment; others were easily carried out.

Either while this reform was in progress or after it had brought about a temporary effect, an event occurred which caused a great stir among the people. In the eighteenth year of the king's reign, six years after the reform movement had begun (the king is said to have been twenty-six years old) there was handed to him a book of laws which the high priest Hilkiah claimed to have found in the temple, perhaps during building operations. It proved to be a book of the laws of Moses, more exactly a book of the covenant. Both the king and the people were conscience stricken because its teachings had not been followed; they feared God's wrath. The king and Judean people made a solemn covenant with Yahweh, promising in future to comply with the laws in the book of Yahweh. The king commanded a feast of the Passover based on the book of the covenant, a feast such as had not been kept since the days of the judges. On the basis of the book of laws, the king abolished "all them that had familiar spirits and the wizards" and all objects left in the city and the country such as teraphim, idols, and other heathen things.

Unfortunately, we have no report of how the Passover was celebrated. The one remark, however, that it took place in Jerusalem while the people were gathered there from the country, gives us some explanation. The only Passover regulation which lays the greatest emphasis upon the feast's not being celebrated in the dwelling place but at the sanctuary, we find in Deuteronomy. Thus the book of laws that was brought to Josiah (which we therefore may call the Book of Josiah) must in some way be connected with Deuteronomy.

All the reforms which Josiah had projected, but not completed, he now continued with renewed zeal. Certainly his greatest desire was to do all in his power to carry out all other regulations given in the book of laws. Prophets like those already named may have supported him. The decline of Assyrian power, once invincible, encouraged him. Unmolested, he now ventured to reach beyond the Judean border, first to Bethel, then to Samaria, in order to enforce reforms. Certainly it is not by accident that his narrator boasts that no king before him or after him had been so devoted to God and faithful to the law as was Josiah. This was his opinion as well as that of his contemporaries. Josiah's ideal was to be a second David and, if possible, to exceed the first one. He was convinced that Yahweh would support him if the time ever came to reëstablish the old kingdom of David in Jerusalem.

The time did, indeed, seem at hand. When the book of laws was found, or soon after 620, Assyria was attacked by its united enemies. Egypt then sided with Assyria, for it much preferred weakened and oppressed Assyria for its neighbor in Asia, to a successor to Assyria who was beginning his career with fresh vigor, whether it be Babylon or Medea. In spite of this, Nineveh fell in 612. There was still a king of Assyria, and it was of the utmost advantage to Egypt to support him. In 609 Pharaoh Necco set out against Nabopolassar and his allies, the Medeans. If his plan succeeded, the country west of the Euphrates would be regained for Egypt, but this would thwart Josiah's hope to renew the kingdom of David. To prevent this, there was but one thing for Josiah to do. Conscious of his just right and of being Yahweh's representative, for he believed he had thus far served Yahweh well, he met Necco in battle at Megiddo. Josiah fell. How could it have been otherwise? He was sacrificed for political aspirations encouraged by his reforms.

The grave of his hopes was also the grave of his reforms. Jerusalem sincerely mourned Josiah's death, but was forced to become subject to the Pharaoh Necco and, later, when he was conquered by Nabopolassar's son, Nebuchadnezzar, it became subject to him. Thus Josiah's work was destroyed. Although political ambition repeatedly blazed up and inextinguishable desire for freedom constantly kept the masses of Judah uneasy, religious zeal was lacking among the masses and, especially, in the king who ruled them at the time. The movement had no religious background and, therefore, did not lead to religious reform.

XIII

LAWGIVERS

LIKE many other countries, Israel had both a secular and an ecclesiastical law. They sometimes overlapped, for even in secular matters the final decision rested with the deity under certain conditions. They left the oath, the ordeal, and the judgment of God to deity. This occurred when the ordinary proofs (witnesses) were not convincing. With this exception, these secular and ecclesiastical laws were independent of each other.

If one man had a lawsuit with another in times of the clan and tribal government, the chiefs of the clan or of the tribe or a majority of their elders were the natural judges. The case was brought before them, and they decided according to their best judgment.

We are told that Moses and a number of representative men whom he had appointed made the legal decisions in this way during the desert period. This very ancient.method of passing judgment was continued both in name and in deed for a long time. In the Canaanite Carthaginia and in Israel at a comparatively late date, the community leaders, or part of them, were called judges—suffeta, schofet, and also quasin (root contained in Kadi) Kadesh. At a much later time, the expression, "he judged" Israel, was said of a man in times of peace because judging seemed the leader's most important duty.

When Israel entered Canaan, the blood ties naturally developed into local alliances. District, village, and city ties gradually replaced clan and tribal bonds. In the earlier period, the clan was ruled and judged by the clan leader, but later the community was governed by a number of noble families. This method, or one similar to it, had long been in use in the Canaanite city states. The Israelites adopted the system of aristocratic oligarchical community government from the Canaanites. Their representatives were the large landowners, the landed nobility of both the city and the country which supplied the armed knights in times of war, and supervisors and judges, called sarim and mechqequn, in times of peace. They carried a staff in token of their office. Perhaps the entire community held the office of judge, and these noblemen or elders were merely their representatives. After the kingdom was established, the judicial authority naturally passed into the hands of the king and his officials. However, in simple cases the elders of the village, occasionally even the elders of the clan or certain free men of property and prominence, may have been called upon to act as judges. This was usually called a "legal dispute." The plaintiff and his opponent faced each other in debate.

By what standards did they judge? In the primeval period, certainly the standard was the best judgment of the chieftain or whoever else was appointed to judge, sometimes few and sometimes many persons. A precedent with certain definite principles was gradually established. Due to the wisdom and the fairness of their decisions, certain tribal and, later, certain district judges or groups of judges may have gained favor and influence above others. Other judges adopted their principles which thus became standards of justice. In time these standards were put in writing, probably first as private law books, a sort of compendia, collected from the practice of the noted judges or groups of judges for their own later use. Their reliability caused other judges to adopt them, and they thus gained further recognition. In the period of Kings, the judges probably based most of their judgments on such law books, for we seldom hear of a personal royal edict that interfered with legal procedure. We have but one instance in the time of King Amaziah. Even then a standard in a book of laws was taken for granted. The standards and decisions of such lay judges were called statutes and judgments, mischapatim and chaqqum.

We believe that ecclesiastical law had a similar origin. If a man wished to know his duty toward Yahweh, or to make amends for a wrong he had committed, or to regain his lost right to participate in religious services, he appealed to the priest. In Greece the priests also guarded the sacred tradition. They were expected to know the laws concerning sacred matters, because the service of the gods demanded a devout mind and religious experience. Teaching the divine law is called tora. Tora regulates the sacrifices of the firstlings of the flocks, the obligatory sacrifices, the atonement sacrifices, the holy seasons, and the purifying and taboo rites. The important sanctuaries naturally had a distinguished priesthood. Other sanctuaries followed their usage. Gradually this usage was put into writing and became the standard for their own sanctuary. It was sometimes adopted by other sanctuaries as well, either unchanged or altered to suit their conditions. The standard of this usage was either the wisdom of the priesthood, divine revelation of the priesthood, or tradition which was faithfully preserved in the sanctuary. The priests of "Dan and of Shiloh cited Moses and his Egyptian priesthood." The ecclesiastical laws or tora collections may first have been the private possession of the priests for use in certain definite sanctuaries. They became common property only gradually and in a much-revised form.

The question had often been asked whether Moses was really a lawgiver. Unfortunately, tradition had ascribed the whole volume of laws contained in the five books of Moses to Moses himself. This has caused further misleading conclusions. As soon as the tradition was recognized to be erroneous, many scientists believed the very opposite tradition, namely, that Moses was not a lawgiver.

From the very day, however, when he decided not to lead the Israelite tribes back to Egypt, he must have considered their future: first in the desert, then at the oases, and later in Canaan (in case he intended to lead them there). Later, he must have taken certain steps to impress upon them the decisions he had reached. Whether we call the expression and formulation of such principles and the regulations and provisions for their practice the work of a lawgiver, or whether we ascribe it differently, it is a fact that Moses did this work. Moses' work was the economic, social, and religious adjustment of the people who came from Egypt. This could not be done without certain laws. Unless the adjustment were left to accident, it could be done only by making legal provisions. It was necessary to regulate by law living conditions and worship.

Many modern scientists believe that Moses was the exponent of a religion free from ritual. They believe the spiritual nature of the religion he founded would have suffered had he introduced a ritual. This conception may be thoroughly modern and advanced, but it is entirely unhistorical. In exaggerated individualism, modern Protestants may seek to withdraw from public worship and from congregational activities, and may prefer to worship privately in unusual forms which they have discovered for themselves, or in a service they planned for themselves without a ritual. We must not forget how much the seemingly stereotyped ritual means to many Catholic Christians and to many northern and non-German Protestant Christians. The ritual completes the sermon and is often a welcome substitute for it. All preachers are not brilliant speakers, and to make devotion depend entirely upon preaching is dangerous. If this condition is true of many Western countries to-day, how much more in the East, in Islam, and especially in the Ancient Orient, to believe he opposed the ritual I consider a crude misconception of Moses and his religion.

If Moses found a ritual in use among his people and continued to use one, it could only be done by making laws to regulate it. As far as we know, the deities that Israel brought from Egypt consisted of a harmless polytheism that found expression in certain Elim. To these may be added the Syrian weather god, Hadad, symbolized by the bull and the female Baal, Hathor (images of her have been found on the Sinai peninsula); also many spirit beings, spirits of the dead, of the fields, or desert demons. There were many ceremonial rites to ward off these spirits. The Passover was an important feast at which the blood of the bullock (usually of firstlings) was spread on the doorposts of the dwellings, that these spirits would spare the people. These old tribes may have celebrated the feast of the Mazzoth, unleavened bread. This is not a harvest feast but an ancient atonement feast for some deity. The omission of the leaven symbolized purification.

All the deities and spirits were supplanted by Yahweh. "Thou shalt have no other gods beside me." This commandment compelled Moses to explain their customs, so that they might either be continued now in the service of Yahweh or discarded because they were opposed to Yahweh worship. The feast of the Passover was kept. The blood now belonged to Yahweh who protected man and beast. The Israelites celebrated the Passover and the feast of the Mazzoth to commemorate their deliverance from Egypt. Perhaps the two feasts were already celebrated together at this time. The blood rites, formerly intended for the demons and the Elim, were also retained. Blood was taboo and must not be eaten. This conception remained, but the blood now belonged to Yahweh.

Moses must have made these and similar laws. Since he

wished to unite his people in a religious congregation, certain congregational laws had to be made to govern them, or the congregation would soon break asunder. A religious center was necessary for these laws. Tradition tells us that this center was the Holy Tabernacle where Yahweh revealed himself. As long as the congregation remained together, the sacrifices had to be brought to the Tabernacle because they belonged to Yahweh only. Equally important were certain laws pertaining to property rights, personal protection, certain limitations of the laws of blood revenge, and other matters pertaining to community life in the steppes and in Kadesh-Barnea, and later on, even more in Canaan.

From what we now know of the age of writing in Palestine and in the surrounding territory, there can be no doubt that, if ecclesiastical and judicial laws existed, they could be put in writing and were put in writing when the need arose. The only question is whether Moses intended the laws only for the immediate present or also for later use in Canaan.

This question seems of minor importance to me, for it is certain that Moses laid the foundation and thus gave his people standards, not only for religious ritual but also for social and judicial affairs in Israel. The answer to the question whether that was all or whether, in certain cases, he had Canaan in mind is not essential. It is apparent that he intended leading his people into Canaan, and we know definitely that he could easily gain sufficient knowledge of conditions in Canaan to enable him to prepare certain laws to govern the people on their entrance into Canaan. We have no proof, however, that he did not leave the legal details to the generations that followed him.

To-day there are three principal books of laws which may be traced to Moses himself: the so-called Book of the Covenant in Exodus xx. 22-xxiii. 19; the Deuteronomy in the fifth Book of Moses; and the so-called Priests' code in the last third of the Book of Exodus, in the Book of Leviticus, and in a part of Numbers. We need no special proof to show that this claim is not correct. Whether any parts of all three of them may be traced to Moses is quite another question. In this case later generations accepted, revised, and expanded to suit their own needs, until centuries later they finally gained their present form, a remarkable monument to the mind which originated them. This is the spirit of the great lawmakers of Israel, both secular and ecclesiastical. The fact that we do not know their names detracts nothing from their greatness.

In the Book of the Covenant there is evidence that parts may be traced to Moses. The very beginning, the law of the altar, takes for granted that the instrument with which the altar stone was hewn was called chireb, a word which usually means sword. This points to the time when the chisel and the sword were not very different, i.e., the stone age. This altar law assumes that the stone had life, or rather that it was the dwelling place of a deity. To hew the stone might injure the deity; to mount it might injure its feelings. This certainly is not the conception of the Mosaic Yahweh, but of pre-Mosaic, ancient Canaanite spirit beings. The law originated in a pre-Mosaic time; Israel adopted it and transferred its application to Yahweh.

The same applies to the law of the human first-born. It reads: "Thou shalt not delay to offer the abundance of thy fruits and of thy liquors. The first born of thy sons shalt thou give unto me. Likewise shalt thou do with thine oxen and with thy sheep." The Septuagint explains the obscure words in the beginning as "the firstlings of thy threshing floor and thy wine press." Therefore, firstlings refer to the obligatory sacrifices to the sanctuary. The closing clause refers to the firstlings of the flocks; the middle clause, to human firstlings. As far as we know, the law was not followed in this crude form as Exodus xxxiii shows. Probably in the Canaan of Moses' time an animal or some other sacrifice was already substituted for the man child. This substituted form is taken for granted in this law. The law, however, could not possibly have been made in post-Mosaic Israel, for it is only possible as an Israelite law if it existed in pre-Mosaic Canaan (to which the Baal (Melkart) worship with its child sacrifice belonged), and was adopted by Israel at that period.

From this example we conclude that Canaan, like other nations, early had a fully developed ecclesiastical law which was probably fostered by the priests at the important sanctuaries. Bethel, Shechem, Peniel, Megiddo may have been the seats of such priesthoods.

Besides the ecclesiastical law, they doubtless had a secular law. Since the discovery in recent times of the Code of Hammurabi, we realize with increasing clearness that all the countries of the Near East, as far as the old City State of Sumaria, had definite codes of laws in written form well formulated and arranged in paragraphs. Besides the Code of Hammurabi we know the Sumarian, the Hittite, and the old Assyrian laws sufficiently well to be sure that they placed the welfare of their citizens upon a firm legal basis. It is an interesting fact that none of these laws were made much later than Moses' code of laws. We can definitely place the Sumarian and the old Babylonian laws long before Moses' time, the Code of Hammurabi at about 2000 B.C. Although the date of the other two is indefinite, we know that they were made either before or very shortly after the Mosaic period.

We know that many cities and district states of ancient Canaan (certainly after the sixteenth century) had well-established civilizations. They produced works of art, carried on commerce, produced literary documents, and maintained archives. This would hardly be possible without a definite code of laws. We know certain legal principles which point to a definite code of laws. This as far as I know, is still undiscovered. Because of Canaan's close proximity in the Amarna period and its unbroken communication with remnants of the old Hittite and Amorite states, it naturally profited by the many laws which they saw their neighbors use successfully. There is every reason to believe that in the Mosaic and pre-Mosaic period Canaan, as well as Sumaria, Babylonia, the Hittite state, and perhaps ancient Assyria, had a well-developed system of laws. We have instances in which the same law appears in all the existing codes of laws. This suggests that lawgivers or groups of lawgivers gladly availed themselves of the great mass of laws already existing. They probably had the laws in writing and adopted them according to their best judgment and their local needs, changed or unchanged.

The biblical Book of the Covenant in Exodus xx to xxiii is a code of laws which (now that we have the Hammurabi Code and other Oriental laws) must be examined in connection with contemporary codes of law. In doing so we observe, especially in the Code of Hammurabi, a remarkable, at times almost a verbal similarity, of certain analogous provisions. This necessarily calls for an explanation of the relationship.

How and when did contact occur? If it were a question mainly of the old Hittite or old Assyrian law, we might suppose this contact had been the time of the Israelite kingdom. Uriah, the Hittite of David's army, and David's campaigns against his northern neighbors suggest that there was much intercourse with the southern part of the old Hittite kingdom after David's time. After Omri and even more after Menahem, Assyria's influence over Israel increased constantly. We can imagine that the Assyrian law might have been brought to Israel and have influenced the biblical Book of the Covenant.

But there is much evidence to the contrary. There is much in the Book of the Covenant to suggest that the date of its founding was earlier than that of the Israelite kings, particularly of the later ones. It is worth noting the chief influence was neither Hittite nor Assyrian but ancient Babylonian. Of non-Israelite influence the Code of Hammurabi is the greatest. We now know that Babylonia greatly influenced pre-Israelite Canaan from antiquity. Its influence was great during the Egyptian control and greater during the Amarna period. If, as we have shown, there probably were independent codes of laws in the Canaanite states during the pre-Israelite period, these codes were probably much influenced by the Babylonian law of Hammurabi during the pre-Israelite period rather than in the monarchial period. The Hittite and the Assyrian law might have influenced Canaan and Israel during the monarchial period, but not Babylonian law, for Babylon had long been outstripped politically by Assyria.

Therefore it is probable that when Israel entered Canaan, the Canaanite city states already had their own code of laws which was strongly influenced by the old Babylonian law of Hammurabi. This throws light upon the origin of the Book of the Covenant. We have already spoken of Shechem, Bethel, Peniel, and Megiddo as examples of Canaanite cities to be considered here. We know that Shechem worshiped a special god called the god of the covenant, god of contracts. Together with his other duties, this god guarded over contracts that had been made, protected them, and avenged any injury done to them. Of course contracts in the sense of legal documents presuppose a code of laws. Therefore it is possible that there were certain legal provisions which both the Israelites and the Canaanites in Shechem observed in worshiping this god and in making contracts in his name.

The statement near the end of the Book of Joshua, that

Joshua gathered his people at Shechem and made a covenant there for his people and gave them statutes and ordinances which he wrote into a book is very significant. A remarkable statement indeed. "Statutes and ordinances" are what Moses is reported to have given his people in Kadesh-Barnea. Thus Joshua followed in the footsteps of his great predecessor, the great lawgiver. This, too, was the very city in which the people worshiped the god of the covenant, where we suppose certain legal ordinances to have existed. It was in this city of the god of the covenant that Joshua made a covenant for his people and wrote its provisions in a book. "Making a covenant for his people" can only mean that Joshua made a covenant or contract with Yahweh in which he represented the people and conducted the ceremonies in the name of all the people.

Summing this up, all evidence points to the conclusion that after Moses' death Joshua made a covenant between Yahweh and Israel in Shechem, which we know had a large Canaanite population. The covenant was a code of laws that was written in a book. What name could the book have had other than The Book of the Covenant? Since it was drawn up and confirmed by oath in Shechem, what could it contain other than an agreement between Israel and Shechem, i.e., between the Israelite and the Canaanite law?

Thus we have an account of the origin of the biblical Book of the Covenant or of one similar to it. There is no reason to question the historical nucleus of this account, for everything which we might expect, independent of the account, actually took place.

We now know, also, why the biblical Book of the Covenant is so strongly reminiscent of the Hammurabi Code; it is based upon Israel's adopting Canaanite laws, and the ancient Canaanite laws had probably already adopted much of the Babylonian law. Therefore it is immaterial whether Joshua made the agreement (as the narrative tells us) and thus was the author of the Book of the Covenant, or whether it was some one else a generation or two later. The essential fact is the proceeding itself, which may have occurred as described here, or in some similar way.

If we examine the content of the document, we find it is an excellent piece of legal work. It is not a complete whole, for there probably were interruptions in the work of framing the laws. The religious ritual probably did not have exactly the same origin as the part relating to the purely judicial law. The one was framed by the priests, the other by judges. Otherwise there is an element of unity in both parts. It throws light upon many considerations, events, and experiences that led to making these laws. There must have been a store of traditional religious, moral, and judicial standards which had been preserved since Moses' time. With these the authors of the book of laws approached the existing Canaanite laws and Israel's needs in Canaan. In this way the book of laws, which we call the Book of the Covenant, must have come into being. The second of the larger codes of laws, Deuteronomy, is contained in our fifth book of Moses.

The twenty-second and twenty-third chapters of Second Kings state that in the eighteenth year of King Josiah's reign (621-620) a book of laws was brought to the king. The priest, Hilkiah, is reported to have found it in the temple. When the Book of Laws appeared, the king had probably already spent years trying to reform the Judean religion which had gradually come under foreign influences. The newly found book made a deep impression upon the king because he felt that, in the past, Judah had not been obeying the will of Yahweh as taught in this book in detail. We are not told what these details were. Only one point is strongly emphasized: the Passover feast, which was celebrated as prescribed in the newly found book of laws. It was the first celebration of its kind since (or immediately after) Israel entered Canaan. Apparently, Josiah had good reason zealously to resume his work of reform.

What was the book of laws found in Josiah's time? We have already stated that the feast of the Passover which Josiah celebrated in Jerusalem presupposed the law we have in Deuteronomy. Thus we conclude that Josiah's book was either Deuteronomy itself or a book similar to it.

The present Deuteronomy is a very intricate structure which gained its present form only after repeated editions. It was not brought to Josiah in this form, but we can imagine a simple form, a preparatory stage of the present book, which was the basis of the covenant with Yahweh, the binding agreement which Joshua made for his people by promising in the future to obey strictly this law. Josiah's book may have been such an early form of the present book. Can we definitely determine this with the evidence we have?

The usual belief is that the special characteristic of Josiah's book and Josiah's reforms based upon this book was to centralize the worship at the temple at Jerusalem. The law that only one place which Yahweh had chosen was acceptable to Yahweh, they naturally interpreted as the temple at Jerusalem. They, therefore, believed that the most important law in the book was to abolish all places of worship other than the temple. This is correct to the extent that by carrying out this law, all the idolatrous places of worship still existing were destroyed and all others were ranked below the temple. It is not true that, as a matter of principle, the law prohibited bringing the so-called private sacrifices to other altars than the one at the chief sanctuary.

We conclude, therefore, that the distinguishing feature of Deuteronomy and, especially, of Josiah's book of laws is not (as has almost universally been accepted since the time of de Witt) that all sanctuaries except the principal one must be abolished, but that heathen places of worship must be abolished, and the great obligatory sacrifices must be made at the place designated by Yahweh. Occasional sacrifices were permitted at altars in different parts of the country, just as they had formerly been permitted in the steppes. Josiah's book contained other laws. Among them was the feast law contained in Deuteronomy xvi. Evidently this is important because it is especially mentioned in the Book of Kings. Its mention may be accidental, the time may have been that of the feast of the Passover, and therefore their first duty was to celebrate the Passover according to the law. There is no reason why we should not ascribe a large part of Deuteronomy xii to xxviii (all that bears no trace of later revision) to the older book.

This reasoning brings Josiah's book relatively near the Book of the Covenant. There is no fundamental difference in the two books concerning the holy place. If it should be true that other ritualistic or legal provisions had common points with the Book of the Covenant, we may connect the entire Book of Josiah in point of time with the old law book. To understand better the book of laws, we must remember that in the olden time, law books were probably kept at the principal sanctuaries. Many of them may have had their origin there; people liked to keep them under the protection of the deity. If, as we believe, the Book of the Covenant originated at Shechem for the needs of the central country (it may have been taken to Shiloh later), we can readily imagine that Josiah's book originated in Judea. If it was discovered in the temple at Jerusalem, it may have been brought there from a Judean sanctuary, perhaps from Hebron.

There are many indications that Josiah's book contained numerous old laws which, in point of time, seem to bring it close to the Book of the Covenant.

We know that when King Amaziah punished his father's murderers, he vigorously objected to having their families killed also. His chronicler refers to Moses' book of laws which states this principle. It is possible that Amaziah knew nothing of this law and acted upon his own impulse, while his chronicler, who lived later, added this remark after the book of laws became known. Yet this does not tell us when this principle was established in Israel. To-day we know that the old Hittite law of the fifteenth century and, after it, paragraph two of the Assyrian law contains this principle. This justifies us in concluding that this law was incorporated into the Israelite book of laws in the period after Moses and before Amaziah, and with other provisions, e.g., that of the Feast of the Passover, it had long been forgotten.

A good example of the great antiquity of certain provisions of the book is the frequently cited case of a murder committed by an unknown person. The law provided that a calf must be killed, and the elders of the nearest city (thus the most suspected one) must wash their hands over it in token of their innocence. This is a very ancient atonement rite, a death sacrifice for the spirit of the murdered man, to prevent it from disturbing those in the region where he lived. By calling upon Yahweh for forgiveness and having the Yahweh priest conduct the ceremony, the sacrifice for the dead became a sacrifice to Yahweh. This change in the ceremony may have been made immediately after the Israelites came to Canaan, for they needed only to exchange tribal elders for city elders. The Hittite law, which contains similar provisions, seems to substantiate our conclusion that this was the probable time.

Other parts of our law book also indicate great antiquity, especially the judicial part in chapters xxi-xxv. The law that slaves and fugitives from other countries should not be turned over to their masters for vengeance is found in a similar form in the Hittite law. The law about rape of a betrothed or married woman is similar in the Hittite, the Assyrian, and the Hammurabi codes to the biblical law. In each of them the man alone bears the guilt; in each case it is taken for granted that violence was done the woman. In case both parties are guilty (when death for both parties is ordained), the law of Hammurabi and the Assyrian law are based upon the same principles as Deuteronomy.

There is no reason to believe that these and similar laws in their simplest form originated much later than the Mosaic period. We are justified, then, in believing that the book found in King Josiah's time was a code of laws similar in many respects to the Book of the Covenant; also that it was near it in point of time, but intended for a different part of the country, probably for Judah. Judah and Israel were often independent politically of each other even in the olden time, and may have been in the matter of laws also. The great fundamental principles were the same in both countries. Both belonged to the congregation of Yahweh that had gathered under Moses' leadership. Therefore they both followed the standards which Moses set, but each had its own central holy place chosen by Yahweh; perhaps even its own sanctuary. Those in the south had the tabernacle; in the north, the ark. Later the ark also had a tabernacle.

Judah certainly had well-intentioned farsighted men, disciples of Moses, who, perhaps for a long time, may have been making ecclesiastical and secular laws for their people, laws that would permit the people to worship Yahweh of Moses in the new country, and yet maintain their position as equals in manners and customs with the Canaanites. The fact that we do not know their names should not prevent us from honoring them as benefactors of their people and builders of the future.

How it happened that their book of laws disappeared and all trace of it was lost until King Josiah's time is an enigma which he may never solve. Yet this is no reason why we should consider the report of its discovery in Second Kings as a romance in which the high priest, Hilkiah, played the unworthy rôle of a crafty falsifier or cheat. It has almost

[323]

become the fashion in our textbooks and commentaries to believe that Hilkiah "found" the book, i.e., that he himself had a sly hand in the "discovery" and succeeded in duping the credulous king. Because a very crude forgery (immediately discovered) was once connected with the name of the lawgiver, Numa, and because the Sibylline books (probably without good reason) are declared by modern scientists to be a forgery, it was promptly decided, therefore, that Hilkiah's discovery was also gross forgery. There is no real evidence to prove that a pious or impious deceit was practiced on Josiah. The assumption of forgery may be one of those hypotheses which, once set up, is so often repeated that finally every one believes it has been proven. Then one seems ultra-conservative and unscientific not to believe it. Who, nowadays, would take upon himself the odium of being behind the times when so many government bureaus and so many professors are so ultra-modern?

The old Judean law could not long survive in the form in which it was found in Josiah's time. Although Josiah attempted faithfully to carry out its requirements, even when it was found, its spirit pointed beyond itself in many respects. Thus it was thoroughly revised and expanded before the exile and, probably, again during the exile. In this way the book soon took on a very modern appearance, so modern as to mislead us as to the real age of its oldest nucleus.

The third and largest book of laws contained in the Old Testament is the so-called Priests' Code of the Pentateuch. It is a much-revised collection of groups of laws and separate laws that originated in very different periods. It took on its present form at a relatively late period, and then served the post-exilic congregation as the basis of their religious ritual. The interpreters of the law gave it its present form during the exile and the early post-exilic period.

This fact has often led people to believe that the book originated at this late period and was compiled at the time of the Second Temple. Count Wellhausen's entire theory, which the scientific world had accepted and used in textbooks for the past half century, is based upon this belief. Speaking for all branches of science, we may say that a hypothesis which has stood for half a century has done its duty. Measured by this standard, Wellhausen's theory is as good as the best; however, there is increasing evidence that it has had its day, and that those scientists who, from the first, expressed serious doubts of it are right.

We cannot enter into the question here. Suffice it to say that the belief is constantly growing that much of the great volume of laws was intended for use by the priests of Solomon's preëxilic temple. Indeed, we may even go a step farther and say that of the many strata of legal work collected in this so-called Priests' Code, some probably reach much farther back than Solomon's temple. There are sacrificial regulations and ceremonial provisions which, to all appearances, were not at all intended for Jerusalem and its temple, but which Jerusalem adopted from other sanctuaries. Like parts of the Book of the Covenant and of Deuteronomy, they may go back to the early period of the Mosaic congregation of Yahweh; from there have been adopted by some sanctuary, and then have been taken over by Solomon into the temple.

I shall give a few examples to verify this. The first to seventh chapters of the Book of Leviticus (third book of Moses) explains the ritual of a sacrifice, and gives minute directions for the procedure of the priests and their assistants in the different sacrifices. Traditional theory makes the origin of such sacrificial laws seem possible only in exile and for use in the post-exilic temple. Only during and after the exile was it understood "how the sacred practice of former times now became the subject of theory and writing." The present form of the ritual may be late, but close examination shows that it is made up of late, earlier, and even very early parts. Again, according to every analogy with other nations, especially with the Egyptians and Canaanites, a sanctuary as important as Solomon's temple and the other large sanctuaries could not exist without a well-defined sacrificial ritual. Indeed we can easily prove that in their original form, these sacrificial laws and many ceremonial provisions of the Priests' Code were intended for any sanctuary and its priesthood, and only later (when they were to be adopted for the temple at Jerusalem) were they provided with the characteristic that pointed to Jerusalem and the Aaronite priesthood.

In their simple forms, these laws may have existed long before Solomon's time. They prove anew how diligently the priestly lawgivers worked. A fixed usage for sacrifices may have been established at the most prominent sanctuaries when the Israelites settled in Canaan, after the earliest post-Mosaic period. This usage was encouraged, and so gradually developed into set forms by the priesthood. The same is true of certain purifying and taboo rites mentioned in Leviticus x to xv and elsewhere. After the Mosaic period, all this gave rise to many torot or priestly regulations, which were collected at an early period and may have been put in writing. When they were adopted for use in the temple, the Zadok priests of Jerusalem naturally took over the material and made additions and revisions suited to their needs. Because the priests at the temple were named after Aaron, the laws were changed accordingly. Thus they were in a constant state of reconstruction until a late period. This alters nothing, however, as to their origin or in regard to their connection with early Israelite tradition.

The same is true of the place of worship. When the law of the Priests' Code mentions the Tabernacle or the Tent of Revelation, the belief now is that it meant Solomon's temple, if not Zerubbabel's. It is quite true that in Jerusalem and at the temple this expression referred to the temple. How could they explain it otherwise in the days of temple worship? It is wrong to believe this was the primary meaning and the real purpose of the lawgiver. Many laws show that they might formerly have belonged to any of the great sanctuaries. It is also wrong to believe a single sanctuary was intended for all Israel. To be sure, only one was mentioned, but this one does not by any means refer always to Jerusalem. The lawgivers might have had anyone of the local sanctuaries in mind, e.g., Shiloh, Bethel, Gilgal. Each one of these cities had a district sanctuary to which the people from that district made pilgrimages and brought sacrifices. We know there were such district sanctuaries long before the temple was built. Therefore these provisions are no indication that they were made when the temple was built. They probably existed long before that time.

The result is even clearer when we dismiss another error with which modern criticism has struggled. Every one agrees that the description of the so-called tabernacle in the Second Book of Moses cannot be the correct description of the desert tabernacle. It is the picture which pious and admiring fancy painted of Moses' tabernacle. On the basis of this knowledge it is easy to go a step farther and to decide that the tabernacle never really existed except in the pious imagination of later Israel. Yet it is a part of the knowledge which has been confirmed in recent times that in Moses' day and during the desert wanderings there was a sacred tent (Tent of Meeting) which was the religious center of the desert congregation and the place where Yahweh revealed himself to Moses. The Priests' Code constantly enjoins the people to make the tabernacle the center of religious services. There is no reason why we should believe that this·expression originated at a later time. We should rather look upon it as an old, very old expression, which only later referred to the temple after the tabernacle was replaced by the temple.

Viewed from this angle, many laws in the Priests' Code,

which we are inclined to attribute to a later period, appear in a new light. The Law of Feasts found in Leviticus xxiii is much revised to-day, but we can still find certain provisions which indicate the earlier form of the law. We may take for granted, therefore, that the author of the Priests' Code incorporated older laws which he revised and provided with additions suited to his time. Omitting the later ones, we have a law of feasts extraordinarily similar to the oldest laws in Exodus xxiii. The Passover was combined with the Mazzoth, a procedure which probably dates back to Moses. Its purpose was to modify as much as possible the superstitious customs connected with the Passover. Besides the feast of the Mazzoth there were two other pilgrimage feasts, the Harvest (wheat) Feast or Feast of the Weeks (seven) called Pentecost, and the Feast of the Tabernacle. The Mazzoth was not a harvest but an atonement feast much like the Passover. These feasts did not at all presuppose Jerusalem and the temple, for they were probably celebrated at any of the larger sanctuaries of the premonarchial period after Joshua.

The whole passage to which this law of the feast belongs (Leviticus xvii-xxv) is usually called the Law of Holiness. It probably contains the oldest part of the entire Priestly Code. Chapters xviii and xx contain laws regarding chastity and marriage which have parallels in the laws of Hammurabi and of the Hittites, and thus evidently are of no great antiquity.

More important, it seems to me, is the fact that this very book of laws and the documents most closely connected with it contain many instances that reflect the pre-Israelite, old Canaanite belief in spirits. This is sometimes done by denying the belief, i.e., a custom connected with this belief may either be forbidden or reinterpreted or referred to Yahweh, and thus retained. In every case these laws contain very ancient customs. The only question is in which period these customs were taken for granted, were either forbidden, or so interpreted that they were possible for Israel. The answer can be only that they were either pronounced heathen or were interpreted to suit the Israelites of the time when Baal was replaced by Yahweh at the different sanctuaries, i.e., these laws are the result of a desire (immediately after Israel entered Canaan) to substitute Yahweh for Baal at the important Yahweh sanctuaries, such as Shechem and Bethel. This fixes the time. Most of them date from the time of Israel's first clash with the Canaanite religion, i.e., the early post-Mosaic period. In their oldest form they merely express the standards Moses set, especially the commandment, "Thou shalt have no other gods before me."

Finally, Leviticus xvii is one of the most remarkable parts of the whole law. Verses three and four state, "What man soever there be of the house of Israel that killeth an ox, or lamb, or goat in the camp, or that killeth it without the camp and hath not brought it unto the door of the tent of meeting to offer it as an oblation (Korban) unto the Lord before the tabernacle of the Lord, blood shall be impugned unto this man; he hath shed blood; and that man shall be cut off from among his people." In verse ten we read, "Whatsoever man there be of the house of Israel or of the strangers that sojourn among them that eateth any manner of blood, I will set my face against that soul that eateth blood, and I will cut him off from among his people." [1]

Beginning with the second statement, all depends upon the idea that blood is taboo. This conception is certainly ancient. Before Moses' time, the Israelite tribes conformed to it as did other tribes. Their deities were considered bloodthirsty, and they pacified their gods with the blood of animals they slaughtered. This explains the Passover. Some deities dwelt in the fields or on the steppes and were supposed to be demons in the form of rams (seirim). When the Israelites accepted Yahweh, they abolished these deities

[329]

but retained the blood rites. To eat blood still violated religious feeling, but now the blood belonged to Yahweh. It was "the life of all flesh" [2] and this life belonged to Yahweh.

This was the period when these laws might have been made, indeed must have been made according to the ideas we have discussed. When Yahweh entered the Israelite religion, the other deities were naturally forced to give way. Thus we conclude that only Moses could have formulated these laws, and that they seem to have been intended first for the desert wanderings. We used to believe that the desert camp was mentioned only to give the law artificial desert coloring. This belief is unfounded. If the law suits the actual conditions of the Mosaic period, especially the time when Israel accepted Yahweh worship, why should we not ascribe it, in its simplest form, to Moses?

The same is true of the law that no animal may be slaughtered without Korban, a sacrifice, at the holy tent. The context indicates that the sacrifice means only the blood, and according to a later interpretation, perhaps the fat. The law is the immediate result of the preceding law. For if the blood belonged to Yahweh, it must be brought to him. During Israel's wanderings and in the early Canaanite period, this was done at the holy Tent. This, according to the preceding discussion, was during the early period of the congregation of Yahweh. The same applies to the law in verses eight and nine of the same chapter (xvii), which prescribes that burnt and meal offerings must be brought to the tent.

There are few parts of the Old Testament which have been more thoroughly misunderstood and misconstrued by their expounders than this one. We are all guilty to a certain degree. The chief reason for the misunderstanding is that we overlook the fact that verses three and four speak only of slaughter, not of sacrifice in its real sense. Further, that they sometimes speak of "profane" slaughter and, again, of the combination of slaughter and sacrifice. Both are inaccurate. We should speak of semiprofane slaughter, and combination of slaughter and semisacrifice in contrast to complete sacrifice, for the so-called profane slaughter also had a sacrificial character in that the blood was Korban, i.e., a sacrifice to Yahweh. Complete sacrifice required burning certain parts or the whole of the animal upon the altar. In this sense, slaughter was not real sacrifice.

Bearing this in mind, both Leviticus xvii and the basis of Deuteronomy xii fit best into Moses' time. We must give up every attempt to place them at a later period. These very laws show how earnestly the men of the entire post-Mosaic period were engaged in continuing Moses' work and adapting it to their time. The period of wandering, with its transitory camp which the Book of Joshua correctly takes for granted, was about to end. With it the tabernacle ceased to be a wandering tent. It still changed its location at times, but it also remained in the same place for a space of time. The wandering sanctuary became a district sanctuary. Great obligatory offerings still had to be brought either to Shiloh or Nob or Gibeon or other district sanctuaries that had become important in the meantime. They continued to use crudely made altars of earth or stone, which are taken for granted in the altar law of Exodus xx, besides the larger ones for occasional sacrifices.

What became of the half-profane slaughter during this period of the district sanctuaries? If a man wished to kill a lamb or a goat, and the sanctuary was two or three hours' or a half day's journey from his home, he could not go there merely to pour the blood and then return with the meat. Consequently, in relatively early times the law must have been changed so that people who lived a long distance from the sanctuary were permitted to kill the animal at their homes, provided they poured the blood upon the ground.

Later no difference was made between those who lived far away and those who lived near the sanctuary; they might all slaughter under the same provisions.

Another example of laws which developed throughout the centuries is the code of laws of feasts. We decided above that Leviticus xxiii is fundamentally the same as the law in the Book of the Covenant and the old laws of Deuteronomy. It is equally clear that the laws for the three feasts, the Passover Mazzoth, Pentecost, and the Feast of the Tabernacle, were not only enlarged by numerous provisions which prescribed the sacrifices for these feasts, but the number of feasts was increased by the Sabbath, New Year, and the Day of Atonement. We cannot here explain when these feasts were added nor when they originated. We wish to emphasize one point only: the celebration of the feasts and their sacrifices may have received their ritual then. There is no evidence that the ritual was first intended for the post-exilic congregation. It is far more probable that it consisted of priestly laws of the preëxilic period of the kings. In Numbers xxviii and xxix we find the laws expanded by a detailed account of the sacrifices provided for the different feasts. This version of the law is one of the latest ones of the Priests' Code and shows how the Zadok priesthood continually revised the old laws.

Let these examples suffice. We might examine many more without causing any change in our conclusion. Evidently Moses laid the foundation of Israel's ecclesiastic and secular laws. Every period after him by elaboration of the laws continued the great work of legally regulating life in Israel according to the needs of the time. At first, the modification was done in the principal district sanctuaries in both the North and the South; later, mainly at the temple in Jerusalem; after Jerusalem's fall, in the place of exile. The work went on in early post-exilic times. In every period there were men in Israel who devoted themselves to this great work. They did not always do it without opposition; in the time of the great prophets especially, they were opposed by the leaders of the prophetic movement. The priests, however, like the prophets, were convinced that in their work they were doing a great service for their people.

XIV

JEREMIAH

JEREMIAH was the greatest of the great prophets of Israel. He looked deepest into the heart of God and into his own heart. This insight made him a man, prophet, speaker, and poet of special excellence.

Jeremiah's home was the little town of Anathoth, two hours' journey north of Jerusalem in the territory that formerly belonged to the tribe of Benjamin. It is the present peasant village of Anata, whose houses we see peeping out among fig trees and grain fields as we look from the northern end of the ridge of the Mount of Olives. The name of the place has a strange sound. It is a plural formation and signifies the plural of Anat, exactly as the name of a place Ashtarot means the plural of Ashtart, for Anat like Ashtart was a Canaanite goddess. Therefore, since the days of gray antiquity, there may have been a sanctuary there with several Anat images. In the village sanctuary or weli, traces of that old sanctuary may still be preserved. There from his early childhood, Jeremiah had an opportunity to observe at first hand the life and ceremonies at the heathen or semi-heathen sanctuaries of the high places. What deep impressions they made upon him we hear from his own lips.

Jeremiah was the son of a priest. His father belonged to the priestly family at Anathoth. This does not mean that he was one of the priests at the high place of his native town; nothing indicates this. We do know from other sources that Anathoth was counted among the priests' cities, and that not all the priests of the temple had their dwelling in Jerusalem, but that some of them lived in the country and came to the city only for their temple service. Jeremiah's father, Hilkiah, may have been one of these. We know that long before this time Solomon had banished the high priest, Abiathar, to his estate at Anathoth. Even at that time a few priests of the capital may have dwelt permanently or temporarily in the villages of the neighboring country. Jeremiah's family were landowners there. It is entirely probable that the priestly descendants of that Abiathar in the time of the kings after Solomon were again granted service at the temple, even if they were not made equals of the sons and grandsons of Zadok. Possibly Jeremiah was a descendant of one of the priestly families of the Abiathar line, who dwelt in Anathoth and who did service at the temple in secondary positions. If our assumption be true, it would be very pleasant to imagine this most serious, thoughtful, brilliant son of the priest as the descendant or relative of that genius already mentioned, the gifted delineator of the latter part of David's life. One must not allow fancy more play than to speak of interesting possibilities.

The time of his birth may have been during the fall of the Assyrian empire. From his early youth, the wide-awake mind of the mystically clear-sighted boy was aware, from what he had heard from his father and from the people of the nearby Jerusalem, of the approaching fall of the Titan, Assyria. In the thirteenth year of King Josiah, in 627-626, Yahweh called the youth to the office of prophet. He himself speaks of himself as a boy. "See, I have this day set thee over the nations and over the kingdoms to pluck up and to break down and to destroy and to overthrow; to build and to plant." [1]

A tremendous, indeed for him, even a really uncanny commission! To uproot and to build up kingdoms! What wonder that the young man trembled and hesitated. But it was Yahweh's hand that came upon him, his word that commanded and compelled him to act. He might hesitate, but he must obey. For him now his own word was God's word, and God's word was power and truth. Such was the dreadful greatness of his office that he now felt he had the power to give nations and empires their fate—such a fate! More than once his tender heart felt it must break under the burden.

It certainly was not accidental that the year 627-626, when he was called to prophesy, was also the year in which the great King Ashurbanipal lay down to die, and that his death gave the signal for the opening of the final chapter of Assyrian history. The priest's son of Anathoth knew what it meant to the world when, at this time, he was considered worthy to announce the fate of the great Empire and to act as the viceroy appointed by God. He knew what it meant to him that, with the fate of the Empire, that of its vassal state, Judah, was also most closely connected. Its days, also, were numbered, and he himself was the messenger and the agent also of its fate. Often, indeed, he shuddered to the depths of his soul because of his task.

We have reason to believe that immediately after King Josiah had begun his reign, which was at nearly the same time as that of Jeremiah's call to the prophecy, King Josiah broke his vassalage to the great empire and began to abolish heathen services. At this Jeremiah's heart rejoiced. What he had observed all the years of his youth, probably even in his native town, certainly in Jerusalem, while King Manasseh and King Amon ruled, must have disturbed him greatly. It is quite possible that the severe censure with which he criticized the ugly doings in Judah was intended directly to influence the proud young king in his decisions. With this in mind, read poems like the two following:

The children gather wood
and the fathers kindle the fire,
and the women knead the dough,
to make cakes to the queen of heaven
and to pour out drink offerings unto other gods,
that they may provoke me to anger.
Behold mine anger and my fury shall be
poured out upon this place.[2]

Clearly this is the description of a feast for the Assyrian Ishtar, the goddess of heaven, also the Mother goddess, worshiped throughout the whole Orient, the favorite and protectress of women. The threat of God's wrath is connected with her. Involuntarily we remember the terrible curses which soon afterwards again frightened King Josiah. He knew very well what the root of this heathen activity was. It was the stifling, sensual service of the Oriental worship of fertility.

For of old time I have broken thy yoke and burst thy bonds; and thou saidst I will not serve; for upon every high hill and under every green tree thou didst bow thyself, playing the harlot. . . . Thou art a swift dromedary traversing her ways; and a wild ass used to the wilderness that snuffeth up the wind in her desire; in her occasion who can turn her away? All they that seek her will not weary themselves; in her mouth they shall find her.[3]

Thus he designated his people and their form of worship. We have already learned what this means. He had long been certain that Yahweh had decided to uproot nations and kingdoms, and this judgment, therefore, could not fall upon Assyria alone. Judah, too, was long ripe for judgment. Whether in his mind's eye he saw the Scythians advancing toward them, or the Babylonians and the Medeans, is of no consequence to us. It suffices that, from the beginning of his career, Jeremiah saw in a clearer vision an enemy from

the north storming them. Its armies swept over the country
and carried out God's judgment on Judah itself. The idolatrous, luxurious life in the country had richly deserved all
that. He says:

And the word of the Lord came unto me the second time,
saying, What seest thou? And I said, I see a seething caldron;
and the face thereof is from the north.

Then the Lord said unto me, Out of the north evil shall break
forth upon all the inhabitants of the land. For, lo, I will call
all the families of the kingdoms of the north, saith the Lord; and
they shall come, and they shall set every one his throne at the
entering of the gates of Jerusalem, and against all the walls
thereof around about, and against all the cities of Judah.[4]

Behold a people cometh from the north country; and a great
nation shall be stirred up from the uttermost parts of the earth.

They lay hold on bow and spear; they are cruel, and have no
mercy![5]

For every young man in the Orient, to-day as in olden
times, it is a matter of course that when he reaches the proper
age, he look about for a wife, or rather his father or one of
the nearest relatives do it for him. Nature and custom demanded this; so did the young priest's son of Anathoth. But
Yahweh taught him differently. A prophet of God is not a
man like others. Isaiah had put his family life at the service
of his calling. Hosea had had to sacrifice his marital happiness to his calling. Jeremiah must do this also. He should
not marry a wife, nor have sons and daughters. They would
be born only to misfortune. For the fathers and the mothers
of the country—

They shall die of grievous death; they shall not be lamented,
neither shall they be buried; they shall be as dung upon the face
of the ground; and they shall be consumed by the sword and
by famine.[6]

Here appears, already in the very early part of his work,

the special characteristic that distinguished this prophet from his predecessors and placed him in advance of them. The older prophets simply did Yahweh's bidding. What they saw and heard they passed on. They spoke Yahweh's word and nothing more. Jeremiah reflected upon what he received. God and his commission became the object of his reflections. He himself observed, examined, and came to a decision. Indeed, he felt himself directly commissioned to be a tester of metal as to whether it was pure or dross. For him it was a moral necessity not to express judgment that was not fully substantiated. Every one should know that Yahweh is a just and morally holy God, that not passion but holy seriousness guides Him. Thus he continually carried on conversations with God; he struggled with Him and with himself. Discussion and absolute clearness were a mental necessity to him. In this way he was constantly brought nearer to the soul of man, to the soul of the people, and to the soul of separate individuals among the people, indeed to his own soul. While he was wrestling with God for his own soul—although he wished to drag away from Him, yet stayed by compulsion, although he wished to plead for his people but might not, although he wished to weep over the fate of his people but could not—he became the discoverer of the religious ego of his personal self. He became a religious thinker who kept even in the face of God Himself his own personality. But when overpowered by God and brought to sacrifice his personal will and even his national will, he likewise became both a martyr to his calling and a martyr to God. He was to become the martyr to mankind.

Meanwhile King Josiah's work of reform had continued and entered a new stage when the book of laws was found. Jeremiah's book does not mention all these things directly. Thus the question has always been asked: "What attitude may he have taken?" We should like to connect a few of Jeremiah's utterances with the newly found book of laws, but their interpretation is not entirely above reproach. I shall limit myself to one of them. Jeremiah speaks of the "words of this covenant," and says that every one is accursed who does not obey them. But a "conspiracy" led Judah and Jerusalem again to follow other gods in order to break the covenant. I believe that when we think of the expression, "word of the covenant," and the curses connected with the book of Josiah, that indeed we may not understand these words other than that Jeremiah expressed his indignation that Josiah's work of reform was ended by a public act of state which he called a conspiracy, an act of high treason, a revolutionary act, by which the old worship of idols was again introduced as legal.

We already have heard of Josiah's later history, and know that, probably by his very confidence in his work of reform, he was misled to attack Pharaoh Necco who was hastening to the assistance of Assyria. He died in Megiddo in 609. His younger son, Jehoahaz, occupied the throne a short time; then at Necco's command, was followed by his older son, Jehoiakim. With Josiah's death, the whole work of reform crumbled. His successor, Jehoiakim, hastened to buy the favor of the overlord by immediate subjection; first, to Pharaoh Necco and, after the latter had been conquered, to the son and successor of the Chaldean King, Nabopolassar, and to Nebuchadnezzar, the great king of Babylon. That the surrender signified not only the payment of tribute and acceptance of political direction, but also the establishment of the great king's religion, we know from former references.

This explains how Jeremiah came to speak of a conspiracy or of a revolutionary act by which the worship of strange gods was again introduced into the country, making it thus impossible to live according to the "word of the covenant." Jehoiakim undid everything that his father Josiah had accomplished for the Yahweh worship. Now the old heathen and semi-heathen religious customs again flourished. The horses of the sun and the chariots of the sun must have returned. Women again baked cakes "according to the images of the queen of heaven, Ishtar"; they brought drink offerings and were happy in so doing. The severe and stern Yahweh existed only for their important or most important requests and, as a recent expounder of Jeremiah says, Yahweh was far too much a man to concern himself about their little everyday wishes and their secrets. Naturally, the Canaanite Baal and Ashtart altars and the Asherahs and all that belonged to them also reappeared.

All these doings and what prompted them, i.e., Jehoiakim's whole foreign policy in religious matters, naturally called Jeremiah upon the scene again. Since Josiah's early years, after a short prophetic activity, Jeremiah had been able to be reticent in public, because much of what he strove for was accomplished by the favorably inclined king. This circumstance and Jeremiah's shy and hesitant nature explains why we have relatively few speeches from him before Jehoiakim's time. The judgment that he first announced over Judah he may have considered avoided or, at least, postponed by Josiah's work of reform. He was all the more obliged to raise his voice, now that matters took a new turn, unexpected even by him. He, like many others in Jerusalem, was greatly shocked and probably greatly disappointed by Josiah's death.

The time of Jeremiah's real martyrdom now began. Aside from his political attitude, Jeremiah had only words of wrath for Jehoiakim. He called him a conscienceless despot and splendor-loving petty tyrant "that buildeth his house by unrighteousness and his chambers by injustice," and he prophesied for him a death without a lament: "he shall be buried with the burial of an ass . . . drawn and cast forth." Jehoiakim himself felt that Jeremiah and he naturally repelled each other, and his base nature did its part in making life hard, in humbling Jeremiah to the utmost, even in torturing him.

Soon after the king was appointed by Necco, even before Jerusalem came under the rule of Nebuchadnezzar, he had made an attempt to take Jeremiah's life. At the coronation festival, probably the new year's celebration of 609-608 when the people were gathered in the temple, and while the death of Josiah and the misery of the present (at that time it was the Egyptian oppression) were in all their mouths, the leaders of the people comforted the discouraged masses with the words: "Here is the Temple of Yahweh"; as much as to say, "We have the temple and thereby the seat of Yahweh; it shelters us. Misfortune will turn aside, for Yahweh must acknowledge his abiding place." Isaiah had once thought thus in his greatest distress concerning Sennacherib, and had been proved right. It is possible that the people remembered this. But this same Isaiah had left no possible doubt that he did not hope for Yahweh's favor because of Judah's merit or because of Judah's rich sacrifice. What assured him of Jerusalem's protection was Yahweh's wrath over Assyria's boldness in forcing his way even into His holy place. Judah's sacrifices counted for naught unless they came from clean hands and pure hearts. The message now deluded the poor people into thinking that they were sure of divine protection because of the temple and their sacrifices. We may imagine the shout of relief which this message called forth. Jeremiah turned indignantly upon them and, into the midst of the festive rejoicing and delusion of safety, shouted the fearful threat: "Will ye steal, murder, and commit adultery—and come and stand before me in this house which is called by my name and say, We are delivered . . . therefore will I do unto the house which I gave to you and to your fathers as I have done to Shiloh?" The Philistines had destroyed it in Eli's day.

That was too much for the spiritual leaders of the people,

the priests, the prophets, and for the deluded masses themselves. They seized Jeremiah. A mob demanded his death. To announce the downfall of the city and of the temple was high treason and blasphemy. The authorities took up the matter; the city leaders and elders of the country held council in the courtyard of the temple with the masses; the representatives of the clergy were the accusers. The king kept aloof. If he had wished, he certainly could have spoken a strong word in Jeremiah's favor. What he actually wanted and doubtless what he told his people to strive toward, became apparent later in the prophet Uriah's case.

Reverencing truth Jeremiah now stood before his accusers and the angry masses, in lonely grandeur and with the courage of death. What he said was Yahweh's message. "Improve your conduct; then perhaps He may relent. I am in your power. Do what you think right, but know you will spill innocent blood, for this was Yahweh's message."

Here was a defense such as we should like to hear at every judicial court with power over life and death. The accused, proud, unshaken, with no fear of death, his every word a blow of a hammer upon the consciences of his judges, with no plea for pardon, no turning and twisting of his former words, speaks only of justice, their consciences, and God's message. In all ages men have stood before their judges—whether these were priests and elders, national courts, or courts for disciplinary offenses—men to whom truth, God, and the future of their nation or community were worth more than life or the comforts of life. And at all times they found people who understood them, as well as those who mocked and derided them.

His appeal to their consciences was not in vain. What his own comrades, together with the priests in office, had with blind zeal killed in themselves, was still alive in the masses and in the elders. The voice of conscience told them that no man guilty of high treason would speak thus. The holy seriousness of his words, pointing to moral improvement as the means of saving themselves from the present distress, seemed to them to deserve rather gratitude than punishment; his voice seemed indeed the voice of God. Then several elders of the country remembered that long ago under Hezekiah the prophet Micah had been permitted to speak similarly when in similar peril. Thus the voice of reason and moral seriousness conquered, and Jeremiah was acquitted.

When we consider how Jehoiakim dealt with one who held the same views and also perhaps was a disciple of Jeremiah, namely, the prophet Uriah of Kirjath-Jearim, who said the same things as did Jeremiah, then we doubly respect the verdict of the tribunal. Jehoiakim wanted to kill Uriah at once and, when by fleeing to Egypt Uriah evaded the execution, the king sent his bailiffs after Uriah and had him brought back and executed before his very eyes. If this was the attitude of the king and the court, then we clearly recognize a contrast between them and the masses who, together with their elders, had decided Jeremiah's fate. Here were blind rage and passion; there was the voice of calm fairness on the basis of serious moral consideration. To be sure, for a time both the people and the elders had been carried away by a few unscrupulous people, but finally Jeremiah's impressive speech prevailed. It seemed almost as if he might have been able to remind them of former periods of harmony between him and them. An undertone of his speech may have carried this thought. Formerly, under King Josiah the "word of the covenant" had still been powerful and the desire to do Yahweh's will was the rule of conduct for the lives of many. Could all this have died away? The note found an echo, and the misled masses found their way back to their own better selves.

The question has often been asked why so few of Jeremiah's speeches from Josiah's time have come down to us.

In part the answer may be in the aforesaid. The success of his speech with the assembled masses on that decisive feast day may be, as I should like to believe, a proof that a bond that had existed between Jeremiah and his people may have been loosened by the recent misfortunes and by the delusion of the masses with falsely conciliatory words, but not entirely severed. The bond still existed because it had once been firm and enduring. In other words, Josiah and Jeremiah who, for a long time, pursued a common course, had found an echo in their people. For some time the prophet could devote himself to something besides faultfinding and threatening speeches.

The disastrous influence of the new king, however, and those who agreed with him increased constantly. The people gradually lost power and inclination to support what Jeremiah considered right. Misfortune dulls the senses, those of a nation perhaps even more than those of an individual. Jeremiah's speech on that coronation day against absolute faith in the temple had made the priests his bitter enemies. From the very beginning the weak point in Josiah's reform had probably been that it gave the temple and, with it, the priesthood added significance. Every great idea converted into hard reality is in danger of leaving the pure atmosphere of ideals and of burdening itself with the commonplace and with the soil of the dust of earth. Here, too, the unselfishness and the idealism of the priesthood were sorely tried. For the people, the principal religious services, now relegated to the temple, might easily become mere meaningless performances, and for the priesthood, a source of gain and of priestly power. The course of events proved that the priests succumbed to this danger; Jeremiah had raised his voice against it and thus remained their enemy.

Like a chapter from the description of the conspiracy and the fanatic hatred of the Pharisees and Sadducees against Jesus in the Gospels, read the prophet's statements how the rage of the offended priesthood persecuted him and tried to lay him low like a hunted stag. Jeremiah must have spent years in untold suffering and bitterest mental anguish.

Among the most painful of all his experiences must have belonged the discovery that he was chosen as the sacrifice of a malicious conspiracy in his own home and among his own kinsfolk. Unsuspecting "as an innocent lamb" he had come to Anathoth, and was to be killed secretly by poison mixed with his food, probably at a festival. Anathoth was a city of priests; his "brothers and kinsfolk" were the priestly families there. There is scarcely a doubt that Jeremiah's public speech against the temple had not been forgotten after his acquittal. If the accusation did not succeed in silencing him, then other means must be used. The rage of the injured and threatened priests was boundless. It spread to his home and kinsfolk. It may have ruptured the peace of the village and family. Every means was welcome. Among even the "brothers" of the poor victim, traitors were found who served as executioners. How deeply this devilish plot wounded his spirit we gather from the terrible curses that he hurled against these malicious friends. We understand them. Although we may know that Jesus would have spoken differently, we will attribute Jeremiah's words to his deeply wounded spirit.

When this plan, too, failed, his enemies seem to have sought new means to be rid of him. We know his undaunted courage. Speeches like those that had almost cost his life he perhaps continued to make. It was necessary only to hear them, to seize upon and to use them for a new lawsuit. His enemies would see to it that the number of his friends and protectors, dating from Josiah's time, should not be sufficient this time to save him again. They watched him in order to use every suspicious word toward an indictment. Indeed, the infamy and the malice of his enemies were used freely to poison the good will of his friends, as formerly was done to his food. His friends and confidants were incited to spy upon his confidential words, to betray him, and to deliver him over to his accusers.

Knowing the baseness in the struggle against him, the reader of the book of Jeremiah will have more tolerance for the terrible outbreaks of righteous indignation, although they seem excessive. The pious man of the Old Testament frequently knew no other way of expressing his indignation and his injured sense of justice than by a cry for revenge. The law of blood revenge, the law of retaliation, was so firmly rooted in him that he could not entirely free himself from it. The noble Jeremiah fell a prey to it in the shock of the cruel experiences which he had suffered. Perhaps the idea that only by the downfall of the unworthy could betterment and restoration for the masses be achieved was also determinative.

But even this did not exhaust the measure of Jeremiah's sufferings under Jehoiakim. There is a question as to the time, but probability indicates this very time. Again it seems to be a feast day. All the people were assembled in the court of the temple. Jeremiah used the occasion to remind his deluded people of their terrible condition. He invited representatives of the elders and of the priesthood to go with him to the gate of Harsith in the south of the city where the refuse of the city was dumped. He himself carried a new clay jug in his hands, and upon arriving there, shattered the jug, saying, "Even so will I break this people and this city." The city and the state were to be shattered and cast upon the refuse heap. Then he returned to the temple and repeated the threat. Either he himself or those who accompanied him immediately reported the occurrence at the heap of débris.

What the prophet did was far more important than the words that he spoke. To be sure, his words were God's verdict and not man's word and, therefore, had uncanny power, but the threatening act had a much greater effect. It was not merely a symbolical action that illustrated his words; the belief of his time was that whatever a man of God did was inspired, was carried out by divine power, and counted the same as an act by a god.

We do not wonder that pale terror and wild indignation seized upon those who had seen Jeremiah's act or heard of it. Their leader was the over-steward of the temple, Pashur. It was his office to keep order in the widespread area about the temple and to supervise the great numbers that were present during feasts. It was his office to prevent or to punish unseemly behavior within the holy precincts. Even to-day the holy precinct in Jerusalem is under the supervision of a special sheik. North of the temple precinct in connection with the gateway that afforded entrance to Benjamin was the prison for those who disturbed the peace, for those who disgraced the sanctuary, and for similar culprits. Pashur had Jeremiah seized and scourged with whips. After this treatment he was locked into the stocks to spend the night in pain. This may have been the customary punishment for serious wrongdoing. When on the following morning Pashur had him released from the stocks, he probably hoped that Jeremiah would relent and withdraw his threat. How astonished and frightened he must have been when Jeremiah repeated the threat, only in a far more definite form, by naming the King of Babylon now as the agent of destruction and stating that Pashur himself should especially suffer.

Here, too, physical torture and abuse were not the worst for Jeremiah. Far worse was the mental torture. Misunderstood and despised, he sought to help; scourged and abused, he sought to heal; scorned and wounded, he sought to comfort. Without hope of improvement, in the midst of surroundings that grew constantly colder and more forbidding, opposed by powerful enemies who hated him fiercely—

all that was too much for a man standing entirely alone without family and almost without a friend.

We are surprised and amazed that this man under such conditions could hold out to the end and could preserve, in writing, his different mental states. His exhaustion and mental depression, his distress and longing to get away from the torturing position that sapped the strength of body and soul, the torment of his soul, his hopes—all this he committed to paper. Here are monologues, effusions of soul, confessions of such frankness, depth, and beauty as are seldom to be found in the world's literature. They reveal the inmost life of a very unusual man with a spirit of great tenderness and purity, gentleness, and depth of feeling, and almost unequaled strength of character. We owe this man almost more for the insight he has given us into his own soul than for all he did and said. We do not know for whom he wrote. He had neither wife nor child, and hardly any friends. Apparently it relieved him to put in writing what he felt and what troubled him, whether it found readers or not. He did not know the relief of discussion, because he had no one to share his feelings; he, therefore, chose the method of writing, and thus he did an immortal service to the world's literature and all people who love to meditate upon the souls of the great men of the past.

Most of all, he wished to flee where no person would follow him. Elijah had done this in his deepest anguish by escaping to Mt. Horeb. Jeremiah felt as he did.

I sat not in the assembly of them that make merry, nor rejoiced; I sat alone because of thy hand; for thou hast filled me with indignation: [7] Oh that I had in the wilderness a lodging place of wayfaringmen; that I might leave my people, and go from them. [8]

But he was obliged to remain. Then he poured forth bitter complaint. Mockery and scorn tormented his soul. God

compelled him, and he had not the power to withdraw from
God. He complained, he writhed, but he could not survive
without God. He was fettered to him and could not free
himself.

O Lord, thou hast deceived me, and I was deceived: thou art
stronger than I, and hast prevailed: I am become a laughing
stock all the day; every one mocketh me. For as often as I
speak, I cry out; I cry, Violence and Spoil: because the word of
the Lord is made a reproach unto me and a derision all the day.
And if I say, I will not make mention of him, nor speak any
more in his name, then there is in mine heart as it were a burning fire shut up in my bones, and I am weary with forbearing,
and I cannot contain.[9]

It is touching to see how Jeremiah cannot leave God. As
a lover sighs for love which makes him unhappy but without
which he cannot do, so he would like to free himself from
Yahweh's service but cannot. His lot with Yahweh is
hard, but without him he is in danger of pining away.

Thus driven hither and thither by contradictory feelings,
he was in danger of utter ruin. Life became torture, and
he longed to cast it off or never to have had it.

Woe is me, my mother, that thou hast borne me a man of
strife and a man of contention to the whole earth! I have not
lent on usury; neither have men lent to me on usury; yet every
one of them doth curse me.[10]

Cursed be the day wherein I was born: let not the day wherein
my mother bare be blessed. Cursed be the man who brought
tidings to my father, saying, A man child is born unto thee;
making him very glad.

Wherefore came I forth out of the womb to see labour and
sorrow, that my days should be consumed with shame?[11]

But it seemed that he himself must have been alarmed by
such wrangling with God. In reality, a man of Jeremiah's
type could not be comfortable in his outbreaks of ill humor,
wrangling with God in wrath and passionate desire for re-

venge. In his subconscious self there was a note of shame. When he expressed self-condemnations and even hurled the reproach against God that he had deceived him like a "deceiving brook," i.e., a brook of the steppes that deceived the thirsty wanderer when he hopes to quench his thirst, then the voice of his conscience became the voice of God within him, and he heard Yahweh Himself.

If thou return, then will I bring thee again, that those mayest stand before me; [12] and if thou take forth the precious from the vile, thou shalt be as my mouth.

He was on the wrong road; he must about face! Ignoble are wrath, revenge, wrangling with God; not of God, but leading away from him. Whoever would be the mouthpiece of God must have a pure heart and pure speech. Self-reproach and reproach of God mingled and led the great Godfearing man back to wisdom and to God.

At the very time when he was farthest removed from God, he felt most keenly what he had already expressed, that he could not leave God. He could not do this because God did not leave him. In his greatest distress he recognized that the way of God was the way of obedience; that true religion is giving one's self to God. In this he again found God, so that he could never lose him. He remained exalted above mere human desires. Thus in the deepest misery of his wounded soul he could reach out his hand to God.

Heal me, O Lord, and I shall be healed; save me, and I shall be saved: for thou art my praise. [13]

Thus he took up his life again and bore his burden to the end. He even decided in the fourth year of Jehoiakim's reign to see whether written speech to his people would not have a greater effect upon Judah and Jerusalem than the spoken word. He had his scribe Baruch write and read the message aloud publicly at a feast of penance in the court of the temple. All seemed moved. The day when the people were in a mood to do penance had been especially well chosen. We do not know the occasion, but hardly err in presuming that the collapse of Necco had become more evident, and that Nebuchadnezzar had begun to make felt his brazen fist. Then the people turned to Yahweh. But the king and those about him already feared the increasing influence of the prophet and his preaching, even before he began to be active. The king demanded the scroll, had it read to him, slowly cut it to pieces, and threw the pieces into the hot coals in a brazier that stood beside him. This was in the ninth month; therefore, in the late fall. In vain, some of his courtiers with better judgment sought to restrain him. They had recognized the great value of the unique book. The king would have preferred immediately to turn Jeremiah and his scribe Baruch over to his bailiff, but they were warned in time and found a refuge.

It seems that henceforth as long as Jehoiakim lived, Jeremiah could live only by remaining in hiding. Thus what he had sometimes desired when he was dissatisfied and discouraged now came unsought to him for a time and much sooner and in a quite different way from what he had expected. Now he might remain silent for a time, might withdraw from his calling, and live very quietly and in secret. It is also possible that mental exhaustion and confusion, which his laments betray, made this time of quiet a pressing need. Perhaps in this way only could he gather strength enough to hold out to the end, for Jeremiah still had a long and thorny path before him.

The fifth year of Jehoiakim in which the reading of Jeremiah's book and the warrant for the arrest from the king came was the year 605-604. We have long heard nothing of Pharaoh Necco. Even before the ruinous defeat by Nebuchadnezzar came, it seems that all were prepared for him as the successor to Assyria. The Book of Kings ascribes an eleven years' reign to Jehoiakim, saying that in his day King Nebuchadnezzar, King of Babylon, had come, and Jehoiakim had been subject to him for three years, but after that he had turned and rebelled against him. It announces also that "the king of Egypt, Necco, came not again any more out of his land; the king of Babylon had taken from the brook of Egypt to the river Euphrates all that had pertained to the king of Egypt."

Pharaoh Necco was considered conquered. Nebuchadnezzar was the ruler of the world. Jehoiakim, apparently, had long expected this change, but he did not like to suffer from it and wished to keep a free hand; therefore, aside from all other reasons, Jeremiah's message was discomfiting. He feared it would foster a spirit of subjection which he himself could not escape. The "enemy from the North," of whom Jeremiah had spoken so much formerly, now was tangibly present. Why Jeremiah deserted him later we do not know but can guess. At first Nebuchadnezzar had not appeared personally in Judah or Syria. The statement in the Book of Kings telling of his approach in Jehoiakim's time may not be interpreted in this way; it refers to the latter part of his life. Nebuchadnezzar was satisfied to advance against Necco and to receive the allegiance of the vassals through emissaries. For years he remained away from Judah, occupied in the East with more pressing matters. This may have made Jehoiakim hopeful, especially as a new Pharaoh, Psammetik II, now appeared in Egypt from whom he might expect help. Even now the great king did not come himself. He had other means to bring rebels to obedience. He set the other vassals, Arameans, Ammonites, and Moabites, against Jehoiakim. They had always been jealous neighbors of Israel. Their "interference" by burning and plundering was just as effective as the coming of the enemy's army.

Not even against these lesser enemies did Egypt once bestir itself to help Judah. It was fortunate for the sorely tried country that the wretched King Jehoiakim died just then. Only thus was the capital temporarily saved from the worst. Apparently the great king was already on the way. Soon after Jehoiakim's death, he appeared before the city. Even before his arrival in the city, it seems to have been surrounded by the vassal troops summoned against Jehoiakim. When he himself approached, they are reported to have stormed the city at once. After Jehoiakim's death, his eighteen-year-old son, Jehoiak or Jeconiah, ascended the throne. What could he do but surrender to Nebuchadnezzar encamped before the city gates? Three months after his father's death he, together with his mother, his wives, and his court, became the captive of the great king and surrendered the city unconditionally. In addition, the great king demanded the surrender of 7000 wealthy landowners capable of bearing arms, and of 1000 ironworkers. They with their king and his court were carried away to Babylon, and with them he also took a part of the sacred vessels. Among those taken into exile was the prophet Ezekiel. The royal youth languished in Babylonian prisons thirty-seven years, until finally he was set free by Evil-Merodach. Jeremiah composed a stirring lament for him.

It was a severe calling to account, but in comparison with Samaria, Jerusalem had been treated mildly. Probably Nebuchadnezzar considered that the chief culprit, Jehoiakim, escaped vengeance by his premature death. Thus he decreed captivity as punishment. The Babylonian Captivity began in 597. Jerusalem was not destroyed; the country round about was not, as in the case of Samaria, settled with foreign colonists. The state itself continued to exist. The captives, too, were permitted to take with them what they could of possessions.

At the head of the government, Nebuchadnezzar placed a son of Josiah and uncle of Jehoiak, or according to other reports, his brother, Mattaniah, under the name of Zedekiah.

He had a bad inheritance. He ruled from 597-586. This youth of twenty-one years does not seems to have lacked good will as much as did Jehoiakim, but he lacked insight and energy. To be sure, the untold difficulties that now faced the Judean ruler required an almost superhuman measure of these qualities. The small measure of freedom which the Judean kings had thus far preserved was now gone. All of the country's valuable possessions, its intelligence and established traditions, were carried away to Babylon. In all positions of trust there were new men, mostly ambitious and selfish upstarts who almost without exception faced new and unaccustomed tasks. Under these conditions, the work of rebuilding, we realize, was a Sisyphean task under which a stronger man than Zedekiah might perhaps have failed. Failure was inherent.

Difficulties doubled with political strife. In the background Egypt enticed them to rebel. Whoever wished to gain favor with the masses did well to speak evil of the reign of the great king and to promise the return of the old freedom. Even though, as every sober-minded person must have seen, the only wise thing to do at the time was to submit calmly to the Babylonian overrule and, under its protection, internally build up new strength, the blinded fanatics and, even more, the ambitious politicians were not satisfied with this modest task. Modest tasks, however necessary and morally obligatory, have always seemed insignificant in the world's history to that class of people who harm the public and whom, to this day, we see everywhere in the shape of ambitious politicians.

The fall of Babylon, revenge for their lost freedom, and similar phrases were the catchwords that promised popularity, honor, and gain with the masses, although thereby the party leaders might plunge the country into even greater distress and confusion. Among the party leaders stood the helpless young man who was supposed to rule the state, but who, in truth, was only the tool of men of power and of party leaders.

With the downfall of Jehoiakim, Jeremiah had again attained freedom. Zedekiah treated him with respect and good will. The prophet's position was clearly defined. If among his colleagues, the would-be patriots, often in honest fanaticism, could not do enough in calling for divine vengeance upon Babylon and in announcing the early return of the captives and of the stolen sacred vessels, Jeremiah was placed in the painful position of opposing them. To be sure, their feeling appealed to his sympathetic soul. He was far too devoted a son, too warm a friend of his native soil, not to rejoice inwardly at such wishes. But higher than his own wishes he respected duty and truth gained from divine instruction which left no doubt in his mind that Yahweh's wrath was not yet appeased and the exile would still last a long time; the "pride of Judah," its best men, would perish at the Euphrates.

In these days Jeremiah found as his strongest opponents the political prophets. Since olden times they had confused religion and politics. In the days of Samuel and Ahab they had upheld the national movement and the belief in Yahweh connected with it. At that time they had done many a service for the good cause. But what had marked Samuel and Elijah, i.e., an understanding of the deep moral seriousness of the Yahweh religion, most of them lacked. Thus their patriotism now became unscrupulous chauvinism, exaggerated nationalistic fanaticism. This caricature of true patriotism becomes increasingly dangerous when it is carried under the banner of moral pathos or religious zeal, because it assumes the support of ideal powers for its mundane desires.

We understand how, after the struggle against such opponents was now forced upon him, Jeremiah became like his great predecessor, Isaiah. As formerly in times of political strain addressing the king and people Isaiah had placed the eternal spiritual truths above the political wisdom of the politicians of the confederacy, so now Jeremiah was the advocate of Yahweh's will, even where he opposed the favorite views of the masses and their flatterers. Isaiah had once insisted on patience and faith in God. Jeremiah now preached simple fidelity even toward the heathen lord, for Yahweh had appointed him, and under his rule also Judah could do God's will, i.e., be sufficiently active morally and religiously to fortify itself with new strength for the future.

At this time Jeremiah must have been well along in years. His hair may long ago have grown white from care and suffering, his back bent by the burden that for decades had rested upon him. His few friends and those well disposed toward him may have wished him peace. Instead, new struggles awaited him, and suffering of various kinds, both of body and soul.

A sharp disagreement came with Zedekiah a few years after his ascent of the throne, probably in 594. The insidious policy of Egypt seems to have roused the same voices that resounded from the political dervishes in Judah, also heard elsewhere in Syria and finally causing a general agitation against Babylon. Everywhere they expected the fall of Babylon and that they could shake off the foreign yoke. As formerly in Zedekiah's time, so now, also, foreign embassies were sent to Jerusalem to encourage an insurrection. Edon, Ammon, Moab, Tyre, and Sidon offered to become confederates. On the whole, they were the same "faithful neighbors" who only a few years ago had overrun Judah as Nebuchadnezzar's executioners. But passion and delusion have poor memories. Now these neighbors seemed welcome friends, and great excitement prevailed in Jerusalem when they appeared. The foreign dress and foreign faces of the magnates together with alluring prospects fascinated the people of Jerusalem. They even dreamed of the return of their brothers and kin, long banished in Babylon.

The only one who remained calm seems to have been Jeremiah. In a strange garb he took his place among the astonished masses and appeared before the foreign ambassadors. He had laid a yoke, such as is used for oxen when plowing, over his shoulder. The wood was fastened to his body with ropes. Thus he entered the room, probably in one of the palace buildings, where the ambassadors were holding council. "What does this strange-looking man want?" This question that was certainly in every mind was just what he desired. He was ready with the answer which was an expression of great political wisdom and deep religious insight. Jeremiah let Yahweh say: "With my great strength I have made the earth, the man and beast, and I give unto whom it seemeth right to me. Now I have given all these lands into the hand of the King of Babylon, and all peoples shall serve him until the time of his own land come, and great kings and powerful nations shall serve themselves of him." He closed with the words which might be intended for Zedekiah as well as for the emissaries: "Bring your necks under the yoke of the King of Babylon. Why will ye die by the sword, by the famine, and by the pestilence?" With these words Jeremiah accompanied his strange action. Others may have been said later, but these splendidly express his meaning— that God had brought about conditions as they were and knew what he wished to do. Thoughtful insight into the political situation and attentive devotion to God's will would lead to the same result. The people must be calm and await better times.

Whoever had considered the Egyptian policy of the last century and compared the despotic power of Babylon with that of the lesser Syrian-Palestine states must, from a purely political standpoint, read the same conclusion that Jeremiah did. What history proved was true of Isaiah, that also was true of Jeremiah, namely, that his attitude showed far more political insight than that of his opponents.

Jeremiah's action seems to have caused great excitement. It was increased by the fact that he wore the yoke about his neck for weeks whenever he appeared in public. By doing this he wished to emphasize his speech as long as seemed necessary. Then one day a prophet, Hananiah of Gibeon, halted him in the precincts of the temple and violently pulled the yoke, a strong and broad piece of hard wood, down from his neck and broke it with a powerful blow. He then cried out Yahweh had spoken to him: "Even so will I break the yoke of the King of Babylon from the necks of all nations!" He had already announced as God's verdict that the sacred vessels should be returned within two years. Jeremiah reproached him by saying that he was no messenger of Yahweh: "This year thou shalt die." After two months, we are told, Hananiah died.

Jeremiah's bold stand seems to have again brought him many friends. It is quite possible that for a time he enjoyed peace and increasing favor. He seems actually to have prevented the alliance and thus momentarily to have saved his country from endless disorder. It would be strange, had not at least a few unbiased ones, among them presumably the king himself, come to realize how much the country owed the man whom they had so scorned. On the other hand it was almost inevitable that what had recently happened at Jerusalem should become known both at Babylon and at the court of the great king. It was also very probable, because of the close contact with Babylon, that the movement that had been started in the homeland might also affect those in exile. They were the ones most concerned, and many of them may have languished in Babylonian prisons as did King Jehoiachin.

Only when we consider all this, do we fully understand what a great service Jeremiah had done his country by preventing the uprising. The exiles were hostages in the great king's hands. What would have been their fate in case of an uprising in the west? Zedekiah himself considered it wise to offer the great king proofs of his vassal fidelity. Doubtless, this was the only possible way of saving the country from a campaign of punishment. He sent a commission of atonement to Babylon. Jeremiah used the occasion to send a letter to his exiled fellow countrymen by the embassy. That Zedekiah knew of the letter and that his embassy carried it is indicated by the fact that Jeremiah acted as the confidant and the one commissioned by the king. Apparently Zedekiah himself was convinced that Jeremiah's deed was correct. Doubtless, the letter was also intended for Nebuchadnezzar and, more than the speeches and the gifts of the embassy, may have served to bring about the embassy's object, for the great king had a keen interest in keeping peace among the Judean captives. In impressive forms the letter urged them to build houses in Babylon, to bring forth children, to seek the welfare of the country, and to be warned against false prophets who urged them to an uprising.

In this Jeremiah expressed not only great political wisdom and true national spirit, but from another point of view his letter was also very significant. Until then the heathen country had been unclean territory. The Israelites shuddered at the thought of living in such a land and doing without the many religious customs that connected their everyday life with the deity. Jeremiah also realized the hardship expressed in this thought, but in this guidance he recognized Yahweh's will and thus he knew that a way out must be found. He had long realized that the city and the temple must fall. He was equally certain that they still had God, and to have Him, to serve Him was the essence of all religion. A way must be found to serve God without a temple, without sacrifice, and without the ritual. "Ye shall call

[360]

upon me, and ye shall go and I will hearken unto you."
Jeremiah applied this in stating that one could seek and find
God in Babylon as well as in Canaan. This consecrated the
exile, and the foundation was laid for the building of the
Babylonian Kingdom of the Jews so historically significant.
From now on Babylonia might be considered the second
home of the Jews. From this it followed that Jeremiah
urged his exiled countrymen to pray for Babylon and to look
upon its welfare as their own. This, too, was an unheard
of thought of immeasurable significance. What wonder
that among the men holding the older viewpoint, it caused
surprise and indignation. Doubtless, it had a relieving and
calming effect among the exiles. In truth it gave the first
Jewish community in a foreign land the right to a higher
existence. By it Jeremiah became the father of religious
cosmopolitanism, of the conception that religion is super-
national. A citizen has a fatherland; religion has none. The
world belongs to religion.

We lack information concerning the events between the
time of the commission to the beginning of the last act of the
tragedy with which the fate of Judah was sealed. There
may have been disturbances in Egypt even under Psammetik II who ruled from 594. At any rate the situation
changed with the beginning of Pharaoh Hofra's reign, 589-
588. Hofra again took up Egypt's old claim upon Syria.
The war party in Jerusalem, whose desire had always been
to shake off the foreign yoke and who, although repressed,
had never been entirely at rest, now became alert. Hofra
seems to have succeeded in again rousing the Syrian minor
states or part of them to a common advance. All this meant
nothing to Jeremiah. But his king was a chip of another
block. He did not dare resist when all were united: a strong
party at home, the great Egypt, and the neighbors. Thus
the die was cast.

Nebuchadnezzar knew the seriousness of the situation

when it was backed by Egypt. He marched to Syria and
made his camp at Riblah on the Orontes. From here he
sent an army to Tyre; he himself led the main army in the
winter of 588 against Jerusalem. After all that had been
clear to him for so long, Jeremiah could not be in doubt
about the result. All the more did the zealots in the city hope
for Yahweh's and Egypt's assistance. When the Chaldean
hostile armies suddenly entered the country, Judah became
helpless. Zedekiah sent messengers to the prophet, asking
him to plead with Yahweh to oppose the enemy. Now Jeremiah said what he always had said. Either now or a little
later, he even went so far as to direct this proclamation to his
fellow citizens.

He that abideth in this city shall die by the sword, by the
famine, and by the pestilence; but he that goeth forth to the
Chaldeans shall live, and his life shall be unto him for a prey.[14]

It seems that the city was not so firmly shut off but that
the people might go over to the enemies' ranks. The meaning of his proclamation is that, since those in power were not
willing to surrender the city, any might go voluntarily into
the enemy's captivity. Jeremiah has often been reproached
for calling upon his countrymen to do this. But we must
remember that he himself remained and held out to the end,
and the reproach that was made of him, that he was a de-
serter, he indignantly reputed for himself. Since he with
clairvoyant clearness saw the end beforehand, should be add
to the misery of the besieged? Should he agree to the zealots'
blinded conscienceless lack of reason which should plunge
thousands into misery, only to hold to a point a while longer?
Was it not his duty, especially toward the noncombatants,
to save all whom he could save.

In the meantime, Pharaoh Hofra had at least sent out his
army as a relief army to Jerusalem. As a matter of fact, the
Chaldeans preferred to give up the siege for a time. Zede-

kiah sent a commission to Jeremiah to plead for God's intervention. Jeremiah answered the same as before: the Babylonians would return, and matters would take their course;
thus Yahweh had decreed. The indignation of the war party
reached its climax. To the leaders in the city Jeremiah's
speeches had long had the reputation or appearance of high
treason. While the siege was lifted, Jeremiah wished to
make a business journey to his home. The country's being
overrun by the enemy and the confusion of the times were
reason enough for him to wish to attend to his affairs. Immediately he was arrested under the accusation, which at
this very time seems rather foolish, that he wished to escape
to the enemy. He was put in prison without examination
and without proof. Already the terror of despairing ones
who were losing everything had done away with the customary procedure of right and justice. No longer did anyone concern himself about the king's wishes. The prisons
above ground seem already to have been overflowing with
suspected people and unreliable soldiers. Therefore they
thrust the old man mercilessly into the cistern pit under the
palace of one of the prominent men. Jerusalem, which has
a dearth of water, normally has a cistern for every house.

We are told that the poor man languished many days in,
the damp, dark place. Finally Zedekiah ventured secretly
to send for him, for he still hoped to get a favorable oracle
from him. Again without success Jeremiah, tortured almost
to death, stood by what Yahweh had announced to him. He
did, however, make use of his visit at the palace to make a
request—we may imagine the tortures he suffered—for a
more dignified prison. It was the least that he could ask,
and the king did not venture to grant more. He then was
placed in the court of the guard and was granted a small flat
cake daily. What must he have received in the cistern?
Probably the king placed him in the garrison of his bodyguard where he was at least protected against gross wrongs.

The Babylonians returned just as Jeremiah had expected. To those in power he now seemed even more dangerous. He had gained favor. What could they expect of the soldiers in the besieged fortress if he told his now well-known opinion to every one who would listen. At any time such a man would not be well treated. Martial law! The directory which was the ruling committee of the government demanded his execution. The weak king openly expressed his powerlessness and permitted them to act. Jeremiah was thrown into a pit of mire in the court of the guard. There he was to sink into the mire and silently to vanish. He certainly would miserably have choked to death here if a black eunuch had not had a more tender heart than Jeremiah's own people had, and taken pity on him. After receiving the king's permission to free Jeremiah, the eunuch, with the help of a few strong men who used ropes, succeeded in drawing him out. Thus he was again in the court of the guard as before.

Zedekiah again had a conversation with Jeremiah in which the latter again urged him, almost successfully it seems, to surrender to Nebuchadnezzar, but the king could not summon the necessary courage. It is characteristic of the weak man. When he had no other reason left to object, then he claimed that he feared the scorn of the Jews who had already gone over to the enemy. He broke off the interview and only asked Jeremiah to keep the subject matter of the interview secret from his councilors, and should they press him, to give a false report. Jeremiah agreed. Often in the past and even to this day, this has been held against Jeremiah. He had long shown that fear of his persecutors could not move him. If this almost fanatical devotee of truth made this sacrifice of truth, he must have had reasons greater than the fear of his own life. In fact, he fought a great battle to know whether he should sacrifice the king and himself to the rage of the fanatics, or the truth. He sacrificed the truth in order to save himself to his people. The truth was certain death for him. He certainly had the courage but not yet the right to die. God still needed him.

Zedekiah paid dearly for his stubbornness. After a siege of eighteen months, Nebuchadnezzar succeeded in breaking through the city wall. Zedekiah, too, now saw the end approaching. He ventured a sally and succeeded in escaping as far as Jericho with a group of faithful followers. There he was overtaken. His sons were executed before his eyes, while he himself was then blinded and taken in chains to Babylon. The city was plundered and destroyed. The inhabitants who remained in the city were taken into captivity.

For the few who remained, a new period of confusion began. The distress of the time and the terror of the siege had long loosened all bonds. Thus the noble Gedaliah who attempted to build a little community upon the ruins could accomplish but little. Soon he was the victim of fanatical murderers. Those still remaining preferred to escape the vengeance of the great king by migrating to Egypt. They pressed Jeremiah to follow them thither. When the city was captured, he was still imprisoned in the courtyard. The victors took him and brought him in chains with the other prisoners to Ramah, before the general of the guard of Nebuzaradan. The latter had his chains removed, and permitted him to choose between going to Babylon under the king's protection or remaining in Jerusalem. He chose the latter. After Gedaliah's murder, the leaders of the Judean remnant begged him for a word from God concerning their future. They planned to migrate. He was still in such high esteem that they wished to have him on their side. He answered to the contrary. Yet they insisted and took Jeremiah and Baruch with them. Here, too, he continued his office as witness for God. He had great reason to do so, for Jerusalem had scarcely fallen when the people believed that Yahweh had failed them and that the gods of Babylon and Assyria had carried off the victory. They believed that all the misfortune that came upon them resulted from Josiah's removing the foreign gods. Thus they returned to their old practices, as Manasseh and Jehoiakim had done, and hoped for good fortune in the future.

So the old man's struggle in the end was the very same one that he had begun as a young man. He may have succumbed to the struggle, for after that he was silent.

His own time scorned and tortured him greatly. Posterity, however, recognized what he had been to his people. When Jesus asked his disciples whom people considered him to be, beside Elijah, they named Jeremiah as one of the greatest and best of the olden time. And Judas the Maccabee had a vision of a noble man with gray hair and a marvelously fine form. "That," said the high priest, "is Jeremiah, the prophet of God who loves his brother, and prays much for the people and the holy city." Michelangelo has painted him, an old man, bewildered and broken, sitting on the ruins of the devastated city, his noble head resting sorrowfully on his hand and bowed down so that he may not see the misery about him. His burning love for his people was never extinguished.

All in all, the world has seen few greater than he. It has seen many who have had greater worldly success, many with greater prosperity and more joy, but few men of greater and finer will power.

XV

SECOND ISAIAH AND THE GREAT SUFFERER

In 597, when Nebuchadnezzar had carried off to Babylon much of the population of Judah, there were two centers of Judaism, Judah and Babylon. By the destruction of Jerusalem and by the transference to Babylon of a part of the people who had remained in Judah, the Babylonian Jews gained new strength. If the most prominent Judeans had been taken at the first captivity, after the second one there remained in Judah only very few people of any special ability, and the greater part of this modest group left the country soon afterwards. Then for the time being the future of the nation rested entirely upon the Babylonian Golah, as the exiles were called.

Their material conditions were, as a whole, not unfavorable. To be sure, they were captives! They were not as formerly free men in a free state on hereditary soil. They were in a foreign country among people of another tongue, other customs, other religion, and a different mental attitude. In those respects they felt themselves strangers for a long time in the new country. Nor were King Jehoiachin and, later, King Zedekiah the only ones among them who languished in Babylonian prisons. There may have been many others among the leading men of Judah who shared their fate. We have hints that the Babylonian authorities ruthlessly condemned individuals who caused disturbances to cruel death by fire! Many exiles may have suffered under the victor's severe laws in this or some other way, for doubtless the victors, both the authorities and the populace, did not fail constantly to remind them that they were conquered and were captives carried off from their homes.

But aside from these almost natural consequences of their fate, they seem to have had comfortable living conditions. Although they speak occasionally in pronounced rhetorical language of "torturing" and humiliation, or of plundering, or of caves in which they hid, probably there were actually only a few such cases. It seems the exiles were not all scattered among the Babylonian population, but they dwelt in groups, had elders, and must, therefore, have been permitted to form a sort of community which was governed by its own members, similar to their former clan government. Ezekiel had his own home. It may have been modest, yet it was spacious enough for the people to gather there. Since in his well-known letter to the exiles, Jeremiah urged them to build houses and plant gardens, it is evident that they were permitted to acquire property. It seems that when they went into captivity, they were permitted to take with them what possessions they could carry. Many of them had hastily sold their land and taken the proceeds with them. When we consider that among the captives were those highest in rank and wealth and also many of the greatest artisans, we can understand that many of them, especially those living in cities, soon attained prominent positions and accumulated riches due to thoroughness and commercial ability. In the early period of the restoration they were able to make large contributions of money to Jerusalem. In spite of this, it is conceivable that at first, before they had accustomed themselves to conditions, they sometimes had little, and that certain ones among them even had to have food meted out.

Proof that they were treated with a certain degree of leniency is the fact that they were permitted to have much intercourse with their homeland. We have the impression that messengers constantly traveled back and forth, which fact made it possible for every one, who wished, to keep in touch with his family at home. Letters were sent back and forth; they quarreled with the home people. Jeremiah was absolutely informed about the most intimate occurrences in Babylon. Jerusalem's destruction probably did not change this condition, for it is quite out of the question that all who had remained in Jerusalem later migrated to Egypt. Assembling at the waters, as described in Psalm one hundred thirty-seven, "by the rivers of Babylon, there we sat down," and gathering in Ezekiel's house presuppose a degree of freedom of motion and activity, which, even if there were a few exceptions, do not have the appearance of petty restriction or of police interference. Even proselyting seems to have been permitted. Conditions were probably no worse than those of the Germans in the territory occupied by France after the Peace of Versailles.

As is always the case in a large community, their mental adjustment was not equally happy. Certainly, there were many doubtful characters among the large number who, during the siege of Jerusalem, went over to the enemy and then on to Babylon, and were no addition to Golan. They were hirelings, men with neither national nor personal pride, miserable fawning people seeking their opportunity. For them it certainly was an easy matter speedily to forget the homeland, to discard quickly their nationality and their religion, and to acknowledge unconditional allegiance to their new country. There may have been many others who thought as they did, but did not completely discard their nationality and their religion, because they disliked to appear as renegades before their former compatriots. At heart, however, they sympathized with the former group. The struggle between Yahweh and Marduk and Ishtar was settled against Yahweh by the conquest of Jerusalem. They were sure of this. Why not draw the conclusion? Before this time, they may have belonged to the many who, after Josiah's death, thought and acted unfavorably to Yahweh, or they may have been faithful to Yahweh to the last; at any rate, the time now seemed to have come when they must no longer permit themselves to be misled.

Thus Ezekiel found occasion, when the elders came to him to hear Yahweh's word, to reproach bitterly even them for worshiping idols. They denied neither Yahweh nor Judaism. In special cases they even came for help and advice. Perhaps because of their heathen surroundings, perhaps because of their own inclination, they considered it advisable to take part also in the Babylonian worship. If in their hearts the elders, the leaders of the nation, had partly broken away from Yahweh, what could be expected of the common people? Apparently conditions were the same in Babylonia as in Egypt, and after their government had fallen, some of the Jews again turned to the old heathen ways.

There was another group apparently in striking contrast to this one. Despite the contrast, they had common ground. In his letter to the exiles, Jeremiah had already mentioned prophets who contradicted his message and who, like those nationalistic nabi or dervishes who caused him much annoyance at home, continued their practices among the Golan. They felt sure that Babylon would soon fall, and Jehoiachin and the captives would soon return home in triumph. Ezekiel even turned against prophetesses, women with the prophetic gift, whose object it was "to capture souls" and who, for a few handfuls of barley and a few bits of bread, killed souls outright, i.e., snatched them forcibly from Yahweh. These women were not prophetesses of a foreign god, but women who spoke in the name of Yahweh. Doubtless they had their origin in the ranks of the nationalistic nabi; perhaps they still belonged to them; but the heathen characteristic which, even in olden times, existed in the sort of prophecy given in return for a "bit of bread" drove them, at least religiously, to the other side. Ezekiel looked upon their doings as pure heathenism; they enticed souls away from

[370]

Yahweh and killed them. Ezekiel plainly states how they did it. They sewed bandages for the wrists and made veils or kerchiefs for the heads of those that they drew to themselves and, thus, away from Yahweh. Thus it was with net, knot, and tying magic that they bound the people, especially the women, to themselves. They intended no open break with Yahweh. On the contrary, in the name of Yahweh their victims were to be initiated into their interpretation of the fall of Babylon and the return of the exiles. Babylon was the home of all sorts of magic and witchcraft, and the conduct of these prophetesses shows clearly that they had learned their art solely from the Babylonian priests who taught those secret arts.

But as has already been said, we must not get a wrong impression from these complaints. They are the striking cases that occurred not singly, but which characterized many groups of the exiles. Yet they represented only one side of the life and thought of the Golan, and probably in compass, certainly in importance, the lesser. We have sufficient evidence that the representative people of the Golan, at least in point of numbers, not only remained faithful to their old religion and their homeland, but that many of them looked upon the hard fate that befell them and the nation as a punishment from Yahweh. They recognized that distress should teach them the lesson that, from its present distress, Israel should develop a deeper and more vital religious life.

The prophet, Ezekiel, pointed out the way in this direction. At least it is from him that we have the first testimony to which we can definitely ascribe a date. In the seventh year of his exile, before the destruction of Jerusalem (it was in the year 591-590), he gave the elders who had gathered at his home a retrospective view of the history of his people. As a climax, he pointed out that worship at the high places was falling away from Yahweh and breaking faith with him, and thus was the cause of all the misfortune at the time. He drew one conclusion himself; if they should return into those evil ways, then the present and the future generations would surely share the fate of their fathers. He left it to them to draw the other conclusion; if they desired a better future than the past and the present, the return to Yahweh must be preceded by a spirit of earnest penance and loyal obedience to his will. This is the spirit of Deuteronomy and of the sermon-like expansion which later characterized the book of Josiah.

Such was the tendency of a spiritual movement among the Babylonian exiles. Because of its origin we usually call it the Deuteronomic movement. We know it mainly from the literature it produced. In keeping with the ideas that Ezekiel had expressed concerning the past, these devout exiles now also seriously turned their attention to the history of ancient Israel. They studied past events from the point of view that if you do not turn away from the deeds of your fathers, then you and your children will share your ancestors' fate; if you would gain a better lot for yourselves and for your children, then you must see to it that you are not minded like your fathers. The second chapter of the book of Judges and the introductions and conclusions of the various stories of the Judges and Kings give typical examples of this attitude. It is not history but philosophy of history. It is a religious moral pragmatism which throws light on ancient history, always with the purely practical object that the grandchildren do better those things that the grandparents failed to do well, that they may, therefore, have a better lot. This entire literature furnishes evidence of a proceeding almost unknown in history. A nation, or at least the dominant factor of it, consciously turned away from its past usage because it realized that it had followed wrong ideals. It plowed a new field, consciously brought forth a new spirit, the spirit of self-examination and understanding of themselves. It is the greatest example known to history of the renaissance of a nation from within. It was this spirit of humiliation and remorse, whether we praise it or not, which produced Judaism. This kept the nation alive in Babylon and inspired it with the strength to rise from humiliation and collapse. It may be called the father of Judaism. It stamped it with the absolute, often fearful and petty, indeed slavish but constant fidelity, to the laws of their fathers, which they considered the will of Yahweh.

All this occurred in Babylon, and this is the proof that the tendency to backslide to heathen ways, even though there was much of it, by no means permeated the whole people. The attitude which finally dominated and characterized the nation was a very different one. Jeremiah's frank statement that the Jews in Babylon seemed to him the better part of the whole nation is in keeping with this. He compared the two sections of the nation with two basketfuls of figs: the one useful; the other, not. Much as Jeremiah felt he must criticize his people, he knew that among those of high station there were capable men devoted to Yahweh. This comparison refers to them and their influence.

Those Babylonian Jews, to whom simple faith in Yahweh and the renaissance of the nation through Him were vital matters, were convinced that Babylon was not their real home. They longed for Jerusalem and the Holy Land, for Zion was and continued to be the real seat of God to them. A deep feeling of homesickness overcame them and a longing to merit Yahweh's permission to return to Jerusalem. Although they may have learned from Jeremiah that they might find God and serve Him without sacrifice and without a temple, under the conditions we can fully understand that their feelings toward Zion and the temple were quite different from what Jeremiah had supposed them to be. To be sure, they might now serve God in the foreign land but the thought of their return home necessarily awakened the

[373]

thought that their religious services would have far greater sanctity in Zion and in the rebuilt temple.

The hopes of Jeremiah and Ezekiel encouraged them. Their hopes, their longing, and their confident expectation ever increased. Jeremiah confidently expected, at sometime, not only the return of Judah but of Ephraim and, especially, the restoration of Jerusalem. Rachel, the tribal mother of Ephraim, wept over her captive sons, but Yahweh comforted her.

"Refrain thy voice from weeping, and thine eyes from tears: for thy work shall be rewarded, saith the Lord; and they shall come again from the land of the enemy.[1]

At that time they shall call Jerusalem the throne of the Lord; and all the nations shall be gathered unto it; neither shall they walk any more after the stubbornness of their evil heart." [2]

Then Jeremiah also felt that the time had come when Yahweh could make a new covenant with his people. When man bears God's will in his heart, the good becomes natural to him. That thought Yahweh would give to the new Israel.

"Not according to the covenant that I made with their fathers" . . .

"But this is the covenant that I will make with the house of Israel" . . .

"I will put my law in their inward parts, and in their heart will I write it" . . .

"And they shall teach no more every man his neighbor." [3]

Ezekiel took up this hope and carried it forward. Now Israel was a great field of the dead, but Yahweh showed him a vision in which the bones of the dead took their places and became living bodies; the nation, now dead, should again be awakened to new life. When that was done, Yahweh would restore the old Kingdom of David. It would be a nation under one ruler, the resurrected David. There God's will would prevail, and therefore Yahweh would make an eternal bond of peace with it. It was self-evident that the people, the citizens of this new kingdom, would do God's will without force or threat of punishment. God's will would be written in their hearts, because through his spirit God had created new people with new and contrite hearts.

In these surroundings and in this spiritual atmosphere, a man grew up who became the leader of his people whom we have accustomed ourselves to call the Second Isaiah. No book tells his name, his birthplace, his home place, or his life. Because his book was outwardly connected at an early period with that of Isaiah, it gave this "great unknown one" this emergency name. His book proves unmistakably that, like Ezekiel, he was an exile who lived in Babylon. Whether, like Ezekiel, he had lived in Jerusalem or whether he was born in Babylon is an open question. His book leads us to believe that King Cyrus of Persia had already captured Lydia. This occurred in the year 546. As far as we know, Ezekiel did not make public utterances after the year 571. Thus there were twenty-five or thirty years between Second Isaiah's coming and Ezekiel's disappearance, and at least forty years between his coming and the destruction of the holy city. If we assume that the prophet received the call to prophesy at forty years of age, he must have been born about the time of the destruction of Jerusalem or soon afterwards. But it is far more probable that he was called by Yahweh as a much younger man. Then he would have been born in 570, at the time when Ezekiel ceased to be active. Then he would have grown up completely under the influence of the work of his two great predecessors and with vivid impressions of the thoughts and the feelings of the exile community mentioned.

✓This period between the victory of Cyrus over Crœsus and the fall of Babylon, between 546 and 538, or in round numbers about 540, was the time of Second Isaiah's activity as recorded in his book. It shows a poet of great talent, who wove a great many single poetic gems into a garland of rare beauty found in chapters forty to fifty-five of the book of Isaiah. Its sparkling beauty proves the author to be a truly great artist. He was also a good public speaker. The reflective attitude which Jeremiah introduced into prophecy and the irritations caused by unfriendly factions among his hearers, which the many controversies prove, may have been the reason for this. He remained, however, a poet with a lofty flight, with strong and often stormy passion, capable of tender love as well as glowing hatred, who often used inimitably beautiful figures of speech. His speech often indicates great mastery of language and poetic form.

Second Isaiah was a man whose thoughts were all-embracing. The highest things, God and creation, humanity and its history, and how God leads it to its goal and the past, present and future of his people in the light of divine guidance, occupied him constantly. He was a man of both rich and warm emotions who felt keenly the sufferings of his people, but God's guidance seemed greater, and led to future splendor that Yahweh had decreed for his people and for humanity. His idealism knew no bounds. He looked upon all things with the spiritual eye, with his vision fixed upon God's great and eternal purposes. Israel's faith in God would conquer, and thus God himself. That was his object. To proclaim this he had at his command a fertile and vigorous mind and a poet's soul. Sometimes he uttered soft, lyric, almost flattering words of the gentlest style, again he was capable of pouring forth the thoughts of his agitated soul in mighty notes of solemn pathos.

Through his poems we are enabled to look deeply into the eyes and the soul of this nameless one of unknown origin. He was a man gifted with a great love for his people and his God, and a passionate hatred for Babylon. He was an unusual prophet. Even though he never mentions them, he was familiar with the work of his great predecessors, Jeremiah and Ezekiel; he may have been well read in their books. He was also familiar with the older prophets. He knew what he owed them, but he was sustained by the feeling that he lived in a new era with new tasks and a new proclamation from God. He knew and was filled with the consciousness of the knowledge that his people, although they were now crushed and downtrodden, should some day rise, indeed soon, and that God himself would visibly appear and take his place above other gods, and call all the world before His judgment seat; and He would bring salvation to all the world. In inconceivable boldness of faith, in a flight of thought never before attained he ventured to say that every knee should bow before his God, and that every one who had fled from judgment in all the world would find refuge and salvation in Him. Thus the climax of his prophecy was that Yahweh would at last be victor; to acknowledge and to worship Him would be the religion of all the world, and his people. Israel would thus be the center of all the world.

We see that our prophet had much in common with the prophet who preceded him, and yet he was quite different. Whence did Second Isaiah gain this world-wide vision and this eagle's light of faith?

The answer gives us a glimpse into the history of the period. Scarcely had the Babylonian kingdom begun to assume its Assyrian inheritance when it showed signs of an early decay. Nebuchadnezzar reigned until 562. Shortly before his death he had humbled Egypt (568) and made it powerless for a long time to come. His death signified the passing of one of the greatest kings of the ancient world. He developed the Babylonian kingdom which he had inherited from his father into a world power, and the capital, Babylon, to one of the most strongly fortified and most beautiful cities of the ancient world. He was succeeded by his son, Evil-Merodach, or Amel-Marduk. If we may be-

lieve the accounts of the ancients, he, quite the opposite of
his father, was a man of unbridled morals and unjust dealings. It is possible, however, that this verdict was influenced
by party politics which thus early afflicted the state. Certain
it is that the national strength was exhausted with Nebuchadnezzar. Of special importance for us in Evil-Merodach
is the fact that in 560, after thirty-seven years' imprisonment, he freed Jehoiachin-Jechonja, the captive king of the
Jews, and elevated him to higher rank than the other kings
at his court. Thus he·seems to have distinguished him with
special honors. What does this signify? It must mean a
particular political attitude that he took, and it is possible
that the king's early death was in some way connected with
this. His action was certainly criticized. His brother-in-
law, Neriglissar, son-in-law of Nebuchadnezzar, succeeded
him, and after Neriglissar's early death in 556, came his
young son, Labashi Marduk, who immediately fell prey to
a conspiracy. It seems that the Chaldean party, which was
responsible for Babylonia's greatness, now sought to stay
the threatened fall of the empire, and perhaps hoped to resurrect the spirit of Merodach-Baladan, Nabopolassar, and
Nebuchadnezzar. Naboned (Nabunaid) ascended the throne
in 555-539.

This was ·at the time when the Medes and Persians were
beginning to be a serious danger to the newly founded empire. In the struggle over the Assyrian succession, the
Medean King, Cyaxares, was apportioned all the territory
east and north of the Tigris, a part of Iran, and parts of
Asia Minor as far as the Halys. During the rule of Asty-
ages (Ishtuvegu), Cyaxares' son, his vassal, the Persian
king, Cyrus (559-529) succeeded (550) in securing the
sovereign rule. The Achæmenid Persians, who thus far had
ruled over one of the main provinces, now became the overlords of the Empire. It seems that the weak and unwarlike
King Naboned, for whom the Medes had long been an un-

comfortable neighbor, was pleased with their humiliation. Naboned devoted himself entirely to his antiquarian interests and estranged the priesthood of the capital by neglecting the temples and the religious services. It seems that soon afterwards they proudly called themselves Chaldeans. When Naboned himself or others recognized the danger, they entrusted the command of the army to his son, Belshazzar. In fact the Persians made an attack. At first in 547-546, Cyrus turned toward Asia Minor by crossing the Tigris at Arbela. Crœsus, King of Lydia, had formed a protective alliance with Naboned and Pharaoh Amasis, but he was defeated by the rapid advance of Cyrus (in the fall of 546) before help could reach him from his allies. In a very few years, all of Asia Minor became a Persian province. Now, Babylonia's fate also was sealed.

The Babylonians called upon the gods for help but nothing decisive happened. In the general helplessness, great bitterness seems to have come over the inhabitants, especially the real Babylonian party who felt themselves oppressed by the Chaldean party. It seems that the Akkadians among them had joined forces with Cyrus. When Cyrus' troops gained a victory in 539, the Akkadians did not hesitate to surrender the capital to the Persians. Soon afterwards, in October 539, Cyrus himself entered the city and was jubilantly received by both citizens and the priests; thus Cyrus became the ruler of the great empire. He immediately considered himself the rightful successor of Babylon, and believed that Bel, Nebo, and Marduk had called him because Naboned had not served them as they wished. He made good what the latter had neglected and restored the ruined temples. This made him a real Babylonian. He did not come as a conqueror but as a protector and bringer of peace.

We see that a time had again come like Jeremiah's time, when the maker of history strode powerfully through the land to give the world a new aspect. Thrones rocked, empires collapsed like frail tents shaken by the storm, and new rulers and new thrones were established. All the world stood at attention when the victorious hero appeared on the horizon like a brilliant morning star; with the greatest interest, it watched his extraordinary victory. Those whose insight was keenest, saw with seer's eyes what the meteor's course would be.

In the field of mental achievements, also, the world was about to take on a new aspect. Solon, whom posterity considered one of the wisest men in the world, is reported to have been at the Lydian court of King Crœsus in Sardis. He preached moral seriousness and wise moderation to counteract the struggle for power and gold which excited the world. From the nearby Miletus came Phocilides who coined clever mocking speech about the fall of Assyria, ever greedy for territory; from Smyrna came Mimnermos to whom the following statement is ascribed: "Life brings only care and distress even for the gods, to say nothing of poor mortals." From Miletus came the great Thales who predicted an eclipse in 585 and thus showed an understanding of the laws of the heavenly bodies. This was the beginning of a new conception of the world that based the planetary system upon laws. In its native Greece, the Orphic religion had for sometime been seeking to fathom the nature of God and of the world and, from them, to deduce the fate of the human soul. It promised the believer release from bodily bondage and from death also, and purification of the soul. Pythagoras of Samos in Magna Græcia had similar views. He, too, taught punishment after death, and demanded purity; but he associated reflections on the laws of numbers and the measurement of space with these ideas. This, again, also disturbed the old conception of the world. To him knowledge was the soul's freedom from bodily bondage, while to his opponent, Xenophon (born about 565) knowledge meant freedom from delusion and superstition. "One God is the highest among gods and men." How much of a monotheist he was in our sense we cannot say, but he believed that a unified power permeated all creation and the Greek Olympus of the gods was a fable.

A new light also dawned in the far East, whence came Cyrus. The great prophet, Zarathustra, broke away from the old tradition, and taught a new way of thinking of God and the world. He announced a gospel of light opposed to the powers of darkness, of order and work opposed to brutality and laziness, of purity and good intentions opposed to lying and deceit.

I do not believe that Second Isaiah personally knew any of the great people who were intellectually so important for the period. It is not even probable that he had definite knowledge of their teachings. Yet means of communication were far better developed in antiquity, especially in the Persian Empire, than we are usually inclined to believe. It is probable that messengers constantly went hither and thither between Ecbatana and the Persian capitals and to Cyrus' camp at Halys, in Sardis and in Lydia. Warriors and merchants constantly traversed the same road. Nor was there dearth in the Babylonian army of Greek hirelings. Even if the new ideas did not come directly to Babylonia or to the home of Second Isaiah in Babylon, the mental atmosphere of the time might reach anyone who was mentally alert, either directly or at second, third, or fourth hand. Thus we can understand whence Second Isaiah had his world-wide flight of thought.

We have heard the expectations that the Babylonian exiles cherished on the basis of the prophets' proclamation. Naturally they entered about King Jehoiachin who still languished in prison. As long as he lived they might hope. Nebuchadnezzar apparently had good reasons for constantly disappointing Jewish hopes. It was his successor at last who fulfilled them after his ascent of the throne. Why did Evil-

Merodach do this? It seems that with the change of rulers a change of policy also took place, as is so often the case. The son did not share the father's hesitation. As we have already suggested, party differences may have entered into the question, perhaps even the influence of Jews who had prominence at court. At any rate, the new king did not share his father's ideas. He not only released Jehoiachin, but he granted him special favor at court. Whether we look upon this as the legal acknowledgment of the Judean kingdom and thus the formal cessation of the exile, as had been done recently, or more correctly merely as an act of most friendly advance, the real difference is not great. What Judaism had passionately longed for and anxiously expected for decades now became a fact. This fact, however, gave occasion and reason to expect more and to exert greater zeal to attain the next goal. To all those who had expected and brought about the king's release, the honors he received at court seemed only a first step toward the release of his subjects and their country. What was the king without a people? And what were king and people without a country? Thus hope was fulfilled and the first tension broken only to give place to a second and greater one. Now their watchword was the return to and the restoration of their country and their kingdom.

This was in the year 560. Ten years later, in 550, the Persian King Cyrus appeared on the political horizon. His movements were watched with intense interest. Four years later, in 546, the "little vassal," as Naboned had scornfully called the aspiring hero, astonished the world by the fall of Crœsus. The world was terror-stricken. From the Nile to the Pontus the people were confronted by an enigma, and wondered, bewildered, to what the astonishing feats of this bold barbarian might lead. When the rest of the world trembled in confusion and perplexity, the exiled Jews trembled with joyous excitement. Since Jehoiachin's release and honors, their goal was the return to and restoration of their country. They could hardly have expected an early fulfillment of their hopes because of the opposition of those who represented Nebuchadnezzar's policy. Now, contrary to all expectation, came a tragic event: the despot, the ally of the defeated Crœsus was suddenly vitally attacked, shaken to the marrow, and threatened with ruin. We may imagine the feelings of the exiles in the villages and at the meeting places when they received this news. How the tension they had long felt may have changed to ecstasy, to loud or restrained jubilation. Now it was certain: if victory only remained faithful to the daring hero, Babylon's fall from its height was assured. If once the hated despot fell, then they must do their part to help the victor continue the work which one of the despots, Evil-Merodach, had already began. Then deliverance was at hand.

This news passed from mouth to mouth among the Jews of Babylonia who were consciously loyal to their people and its hopes. Thousands may have thought and expressed them thus. Like tinder ready to burst into flame, this igniting spark fell on one of the many whose souls were filled with these thoughts and hopes. The spirit of Yahweh had seized upon him and awakened the flame of prophetic enthusiasm. This was Second Isaiah. The time of his proclamation is obvious.

The voice of one saying, Cry, And one said, What shall I cry? All flesh is grass, and all the goodliness thereof is as the flowers of the field: the grass withereth, the flower fadeth; because the breadth of the Lord bloweth upon it: surely the people is grass. The grass withereth, the flower fadeth: but the word of our God shall stand forever.[4]

It was clear that God's word, Yahweh's promise, should remain though the earth trembled and her empires fell. This message was put into the prophet's mouth in the hour of his calling. What the older prophets had long proclaimed should

[383]

now come to pass; such was the theme of his own proclamation.

What had God's word long ago proclaimed?

The voice of one that crieth Prepare ye in the wilderness the way of the Lord, make straight in the desert a high way for our God. . . . And the glory of the Lord shall be revealed, and all flesh shall see it together: for the mouth of the Lord hath spoken it.[5]

This was the subject matter of that proclamation, and this the content of his message: God himself would come, his glory, his majestic radiance, which he had long withheld, would at last reappear, and with it would come the salvation of the world and the millennium; with it the kingdom of God and salvation. Isaiah had promised it, Ezekiel had hoped for it; now finally it had come! Yahweh had already set out and was on his way. They must receive him worthily. As one prepares the way for a royal visitor, removing stones and boulders, so now valleys should be leveled to plains and hills, to flat lands, for he who should come was a wondrous king.

With this great and last fact as the theme of his proclamation, there was no longer cause for suffering and mourning; for here was everything that Judaism might wish: forgiveness, return to Jerusalem, comfort, and assured future. Thus the prophet's proclamation was consolation in contrast to what the older prophets had been obliged to announce.

Comfort ye, comfort ye my people, saith your God. Speak ye comfortably to Jerusalem, and cry unto her that her warfare is accomplished, that her iniquity is pardoned; that she hath received of the Lord's hand double for all her sins.[6]

Second Isaiah clearly states the occasion of his hope and prophecy.

Thus saith the Lord to his anointed, to Cyrus, whose right hand I have holden, to subdue nations before him, and I will loose the loins of kings; to open the doors before him, and the gates shall not be shut; I will go before thee, and make the rugged places plain: I will break in pieces the doors of brass, and cut in sunder the bars of iron: and I will give thee the treasures of darkness, and hidden riches of secret places, that thou mayest know that I am the Lord, which call thee by thy name, even the God of Israel.[7]

The prophet did not think of declaring Cyrus to be the promised Messiah as is sometimes assumed. He merely designated him as the man chosen of God and endowed with the spirit of God's divine confidence. Cyrus had achieved thus far what was Yahweh's work, and Cyrus' future undertakings would, therefore, be successful. As Yahweh had driven Crœsus from the throne for Cyrus and opened the gates of Sardis for him, so, also, he would open the gates and treasures of Babylon for him. All this He would do to prove to Cyrus and all the world that He alone is God.

Cyrus' victory meant not only the fall of Babylon but also the release of Jerusalem, the assembling of the scattered Israelites, and finally, the salvation of the whole world. In Yahweh's name we read of Cyrus.

"I have raised him up in righteousness and I will make straight all his ways: he shall build my city, and he shall let my exiles go free. . . .

"even saying of Jerusalem, She shall be built; and to the temple, Thy foundation shall be laid." [8]

When Jerusalem should be restored, it should be repopulated as formerly. Its scattered sons would again have a home; Yahweh would gather them from all parts of the earth.

"I will bring thy seed from the east, and gather thee from the west! I will say to the north, Give up; and to the south, Keep not back; bring my sons from far and my daughters from the end of the earth." [9]

[385]

With this Yahweh reached out into all the world. His world-wide activity might mean revenge upon Israel's enemies, especially upon Babylon. This thought was included.

However, Second Isaiah was not a preacher of judgment but of salvation. True to his calling as a comforter, he brought comfort not only to Israel but to all the world.

Attend unto me, O my people; and give ear unto me, O my nation; for the law shall go forth from me, and I will make my judgment to rest for a light of the peoples. My righteousness is near, my salvation is gone forth, and mine arms shall judge the people; the isles shall wait for me, and on my arm shall they trust.[10]

As in the beginning of the second chapter of Isaiah all peoples set out for Zion because "direction," i.e., the true revelation of God came forth from Zion, so here, too, they received direction, justice, and salvation. They are all the same, and Yahweh's arm is the power that brings about everything. Thus all peoples to the most distant seacoasts await the salvation that goes out from the God of Israel.

There could be no higher conception of Yahweh. The whole book of Second Isaiah is really one great song of triumph of the incomparable greatness and sublimity of Yahweh. To this favorite theme the prophet devoted his highest and fullest notes. Yahweh's glory, Yahweh above everything, above all gods and peoples. In words of rebuke, in sarcastic songs, in hymns, and controversy, the prophet reverted to Yahweh's incomparable greatness. There must have been an undying faith in Yahweh in this man's soul. Therefore ever and anew his soul almost involuntarily overflowed in the praise of Yahweh. He could not mention Yahweh without an outburst of rejoicing. A fire of mighty enthusiasm burned within his soul which he wished to kindle in the souls of his compatriots. Everywhere he strove to

[386]

gain practical results, to comfort, to admonish them to have faith, to sustain them, and to help them.

We would like to know whether this faith in Yahweh was equally great from the first. His book gives a contrary impression. When he never tires of admonishing, rebuking, and arguing with those who doubted Yahweh's omnipotence and greatness, we remember this was a time when there was much doubt of the traditional conception of God. What our prophet fought against when he refuted secret doubts and skeptical thoughts almost gives the impression that he himself had had a similar experience. Before he gained his form of faith, he may have fought out in his own heart the doubts and fears that he now refuted. At any rate there may have been some among his hearers who were influenced by the prevailing doubts.

Little as we know of the origin, name, or time of death of our prophet, so little also do we know of his life. We may only safely assume that he was one of the exiles and lived among them in Babylonia. How he worked among them, we can conjecture from his book—a book which is a paradox. We seek in vain for continuity of thought, and we cannot make the later editor responsible for the lack, as has been done of the books of Isaiah and Jeremiah. In this regard it is like Hosea's writings, with the great difference that in this anonymous writer not only the types of speeches vary greatly, but great repetitions occur. Consolation, rebuke for lack of faith in God, controversies over the question who knew beforehand of Cyrus' coming, and similar subjects long after they occurred, are common, constantly restated in words, but with little new subject matter. We explain this only by the fact that the same speech, whether oral or written, was intended for a number of small intimate groups among whom the prophet worked. The speeches were naturally quite similar in content and were written, probably only partially, and collected in the book. We shall hear why his addresses were of this nature.

We notice also that, when Second Isaiah speaks of Cyrus, of the fall of Babylon, and especially of Israel's future, he expresses himself in general and indefinite terms. Frequently he does not go beyond mere hints to the effect that Cyrus drives kings from their thrones, forces gates and locks, and carries out God's plans as he will perhaps do in Babylon. But what he will accomplish in Babylon is not told. Only once there is a shy hint, that He will carry out Yahweh's plan for Babylon and the Chaldeans. He often speaks of Yahweh's mighty and destructive deeds against His enemies. The luxurious daughter, Babylon, is described in bold, figurative language as a woman greatly humiliated; Babylon's gods are described as having fallen. The conquest of Babylon itself is mentioned only once, and there only possibly, for the text is very unreliable. Even more remarkable is the fact that a man in our prophet's position and surroundings, familiar with the definite mercies of David and Yahweh's eternal bond of peace and thus with his predecessor's high hopes of the future, especially those connected with David's dynasty, nowhere mentions the Messiah, and yet is writing soon after Jehoiachin's release and elevation to high honors.

We can explain this only as intentional silence. Only political considerations can have caused his reticence. We know how harshly Nebuchadnezzar checked attempts of the Jewish exiles to resist the Babylonian rule. The Babylonian national policy did not change, even if Nebuchadnezzar's successors were personally less severe or less inclined to violence or were restricted in their actions by party struggles in the country. Even Jehoiachin's restoration to position, much as it proved a new spirit in the king's palace, changed nothing in the policy. As long as the Jews remained captives in Babylon, the governors and their subordinates were obliged to have a care that every attempt to change conditions should be suppressed with iron firmness. Thus Jehoiachin's very release might signify rather increased severity of the Jews' condition than the contrary, for the more they themselves interpreted the king's release as the forerunner of general freedom and perhaps used it as propaganda, the more severe the authorities were obliged to be and to insist that, before the king himself had spoken, no practical conclusions might be drawn from Jehoiachin's freedom if they did not wish to risk danger to themselves.

Thus the natural explanation must be that the prophet was reticent, not voluntarily, but for fear of violent interference by the Babylonian authorities. He was satisfied to hint in terms clear enough to be understood by his compatriots, and yet so general as to avoid indictment by the authorities.

There is every indication that Second Isaiah not only took a prominent part in the life of his compatriots and knew well their cares, their hopes, and also their weaknesses, but that he was also familiar with court life and, therefore, was in a position to know the attitude of the authorities. He was familiar with the Babylonian gods and the Babylonian form of religious services. He knew the priests who explained the omens and astrology, he knew well the workshops of the goldsmiths and the factories where the idols were made. He knew and even used the language of the Babylonian religious texts, and that of the priests when, in the servile manner of the court, they tendered the king their devotions, and used it particularly in speaking of Cyrus, surely with the definite purpose of making the victorious hero favorable to his own and his people's hopes. The thought has often been expressed that Second Isaiah never addressed his people orally but always as a writer through his book.

The nature of his book and the above described political conditions of the exiles suggested this assumption. It seems improbable to me, for the author of this book is very much

[389]

the public speaker. In many sections we can clearly see him standing before his audience. The above assumption is correct only in so far as he did not, like the older prophets, speak publicly before the assembled people. Much that he said was of such a nature that, even if the authorities could not attack him, they would not have permitted such speech in public. But we assume that Second Isaiah spoke to trusted men among his people in private and in small groups, of the things of which his heart was full and which he hoped might serve his people. In this way he spoke now here, now there; hence the repetitions. He spoke now on this topic, now on that one, whatever lay nearest his heart at the time; therefore, the many disconnected sections. He sometimes wrote himself; sometimes his disciples wrote this section or that one for him, and then he added something at the beginning or the end; hence the free, almost playful change of address. What he wrote may have circulated secretly as lengthy single sheets, loose leaves, in the homes of the captives, before it was collected into a book. Perhaps it was not collected in book form until after the master's death.

Second Isaiah was not a prophet in the old sense. A new type of prophecy began with him, brought about somewhat by Jeremiah's method of reflection. The older prophets repeated what they saw and heard. Their personality was fully absorbed in the subject, and they received what they spoke directly from God. "Thus spake Yahweh," was the full truth for them. The religious thinker began with Jeremiah, who reflected on what he heard. Our prophet went a step farther. His subjectivity was so strongly apparent (remember his words when he was called to the prophecy) that in time there seemed to be a barrier between him and Yahweh. In Zechariah Yahweh no longer spoke, but a special angel who was a mediator between God and man. In Second Isaiah it is a "voice" from heaven that proclaimed what God had to say to him.

SECOND ISAIAH AND THE GREAT SUFFERER

If, in spite of being nameless, the great anonymous one seems a living and tangible personality to us, in what we thus far know of him, this is even more true when we consider his relation to another anonymous one, whom we know only through him. This is the Great Sufferer, whom Second Isaiah introduces as the "Servant of Yahweh." Here the old proverb, that we may judge a man by his associates, is again corroborated.

A number of sections with a special character and special significance are interpolated in the book we have just discussed. At all times they attracted the greatest attention of their readers and of devout people, because the mysterious Servant of God, who suffered punishment and martyrdom for the sins of others, is portrayed in the final section in chapter fifty-three of the book of Isaiah. Even the New Testament and Christian exponents of all periods have considered this portrayal to be the description of the long-hoped-for Messiah or Savior in a new form, namely, in that of the Sufferer. Others contradicted this explanation and believed the "Servant of Yahweh" to be the people of Israel itself, called by Yahweh, by its suffering in exile, which it bore for the welfare of the other nations, to bring about its own salvation and that of the whole world.

In recent years this explanation has been widely accepted because it seemed the simplest solution to all the difficulties. But in spite of contrary appearances, there has always been an objection that pointed to the weak spot of this "collective" theory, and constantly called attention to the fact that certain remarks concerning the Servant of Yahweh can be understood only as spoken of a definite individual.

In the course of time a complete literature grew up concerning the question of the *ebed* of Yahweh, or the Servant of Yahweh. It is still a live question, and presumably will continue to be for some time to come. I cannot present the whole question in detail, but shall merely give the reader the result of long years of personal research. From this the reader may draw his conclusion as to the correctness of the statement expressed above, that Second Isaiah and the Servant of Yahweh, called the second great anonymous one, were contemporaries and had a close personal relationship.

We must assume two things that for the present cannot be proven in detail here. But if what I am about to say gives a satisfactory general impression, they will be proven by it. The one is that the Servant of Yahweh must be looked upon as a definite individual, a person of flesh and blood like the rest of us. He is neither the people nor a mere idealistic figure, but a tangible historical person, a great martyr for a great cause. The second assumption is, that the sections dealing with the *ebed* or Servant of Yahweh belong neither to the real book nor to the first main proclamation of Second Isaiah. They are entirely independent fragments of a separate work written as a proclamation, and were included later in the book of Isaiah (chapters xi-lv). I believe they were written by Second Isaiah himself; the striking similarity of style of the *ebed* sections and of the book prove this.

There is no doubt that the thought of the approaching period of salvation and its personal mediator, a ruler of the House of David, in short what we are accustomed to call the Messianic idea, whenever it may have originated, already existed in the exile. Consequently, Second Isaiah was familiar with the certain mercies of David by which he surely must mean these promises. He suppressed this thought for reasons that we already know. We must remember the emotions of the Jewish exiles when Jehoiachin was set free and again when Cyrus appeared. The first event, even more the second one, revived the long-cherished but long-deferred hopes of the Jews. It is possible that many of the people believed the king of David's house who languished in prison was the long-promised one, whose coming they had long expected. We can safely say that when the king was released and elevated to high honors by the magnanimous decision of Evil-Merodach, the Jews in Babylon were greatly encouraged.

We realize that in this there was a certain danger for the peace of the country. The newly awakened hope of the Jews, of which Babylonian authorities certainly knew, involved, if taken seriously, the collapse of, or at least a great upheaval in, the empire. Even though they did not generally speak of these matters (already we have heard how carefully Second Isaiah expressed himself), yet Evil-Merodach's pardon had created a feeling of unrest and, thus, of disturbance to the peace of the state.

This was sufficient reason, especially after the king's early death, for the authorities to be on their guard. Even before Cyrus came, the Medes had become a danger to the safety of the empire. After Cyrus' coming the danger was multiplied. Disturbing factions within the country were therefore dangerous. In addition, Nebuchadnezzar's policy of the iron hand was still popular in the empire. To the many internal difficulties brought on by the rise of the Chaldeans in place of the Babylonians formerly in power, were added the fears of those who opposed Evil-Merodach's policy of clemency. In his policy they saw a weakness that might become dangerous to the empire. Events in the north seemed to justify this opinion. When the authorities met every serious movement among the Jews which seemed a result of Jehoiachin's elevation to power with iron severity, they did nothing surprising either for their time or for ours.

Under these conditions, as we have already heard, Second Isaiah became a prophet and worked among his fellow exiles in the manner above described. One day his attention was called to a man whose personality, whose deeds, and whose experience were of the greatest interest to him. There was something about the man so remarkable that Second Isaiah felt drawn to him. Step by step, the better he knew him and the deeper he sought to penetrate the other's being and his ideals, the higher he esteemed him; the more he bowed in admiration before this extraordinary personality. Outwardly unattractive, almost unnoticed by his contemporaries and fellow countrymen, his greatness unrecognized, he possessed great qualities of soul which attracted Second Isaiah to him. Gradually he rose above the level of ordinary human beings. The thought came to Second Isaiah, "Could he not be the long-sought-for and longingly expected one?" The better he knew him, the deeper he sought to read into his soul, the more certain he was that Yahweh had decided to fulfill His promise in this man. He should bring the mercies promised to David, and as the Messiah, should bring the kingdom of peace and the eternal kingdom of God to Israel and all the world.

Then the seer's eyes were again opened, and his poetic mind had a new flight. He approached his hearers and announced what Yahweh himself had shown him.

Behold my servant whom I uphold; my chosen, in whom my soul delighteth: I have put my spirit upon him; he shall bring forth judgment to the Gentiles. He shall not cry, nor lift up, nor cause his voice to be heard in the street. A bruised reed shall he not break, and the smoking flax shall he not quench: he shall bring forth judgment in truth—I the Lord have called thee in righteousness and will hold thine hand, and will keep thee, and give thee for a covenant of the people, for a light of the Gentiles; to open the blind eyes, to bring out the prisoners from the dungeon. . . . Behold the former things are come to pass, and new things do I declare; before they spring forth I tell you of them.

This was a judgment of God. Yahweh himself spoke and introduced His "Servant." That he spoke of him thus, gave him this title, which the trusted servants and viziers of rulers bore, and not the name of king or anointed one, as we might expect of the Messiah, was due as we long since know, to a good reason. But like the Messiah, he was filled with the spirit of Yahweh, and like him, he should bring peace, justice, and freedom. The fulfillment had already begun. Jehoiachin had been freed, Cyrus had risen as the avenger. Now came the second stage; the avenger himself had appeared. Yet he brought them something entirely new. He brought freedom and salvation not only to Israel, but he brought light, justice, and alliance with God to all mankind; he freed all peoples from fetters of slavery.

With his mind's eye, Second Isaiah saw all this embodied in the man whose appearance in the service of God and in unselfish modesty and merciful charity he followed with wonder. Occasionally he may have called attention to this man and sought to gain favor for him among people by hints and words which his fellow countrymen, who were interested, well understood. He labored among his compatriots to lighten the Servant's work. But the fate of all prophets at all times was also the fate of this one for whom Second Isaiah sought to gain the hearts of his fellow countrymen. From the very beginning his work, to direct the souls of Israel and of the nations to Yahweh, met sharp resistance among his own people. Then his herald again spoke—this time in the name of the protégé himself. He introduced him by speaking in his name; or perhaps the new prophet spoke similar words to his countrymen, and Second Isaiah wrote down his words, incorporated them among his own speeches, and then gave them publicity with his own writings. He may have hoped thus to secure wider circulation for them.

Listen, O isles, unto me; and hearken, ye peoples, from far: the Lord hath called me from the womb; from the bowels of my mother hath he made mention of my name; and he hath made my mouth like a sharp sword, in the shadow of his hand hath he hid me; he had made me a polished shaft, in his quiver hath he kept me close: and he said unto me, Thou art my servant; Israel, in whom I will be glorified. But I said, I have labored in vain, I have spent my strength for nought and in vain, yet surely my judgment is with the Lord, and my recompence with my God. And now saith the Lord, that formed me from the womb to be his servant, to bring Jacob again to him, and that Israel be gathered unto him (for I am honorable in the eyes of my Lord, and my God is become my strength) : Yea he saith, It is too light a thing that thou shouldst be my servant to raise up the tribes of Jacob and to restore the preserved of Israel: I will also give thee for a light to the Gentiles, that thou mayest be my salvation unto the end of the earth.[11]

His own fellow citizens, whom he wished to help to rally about Yahweh, not only to secure a material return to Jerusalem but also for a spiritual return, seem to have opposed the Servant of Yahweh; he was greatly discouraged for he feared that his work was in vain. But the misunderstanding of the people and the failure to succeed could not permanently discourage him. Yahweh, who had called him and who had put the prophetic word, sharp and cutting as a sword, into his mouth, would protect him and secure him justice. Yahweh himself considered him worthy and would, therefore, be his strength and reward. He would prove that his sharp words were justified, and he would bring to a climax this justification against his enemies by giving him a still higher calling than the one entrusted to him who restored Israel. He was again assured of his calling as a missionary to lead the nations from the ends of the earth to light and salvation in the alliance with God. His triumphant faith in God and his confidence in having God as his support were stronger than all temptations.

But opposition because of misunderstanding and ill will roused by sharp reproof increased, until it took the form of outright maltreatment. Here, too, it was the "tongue of the disciple," therefore, the reproof of the prophet that caused the enmity of his fellow countrymen.

The Lord God hath given me the tongue of them that has taught, that I should know how to sustain with words him that is weary: he wakeneth morning by morning, he wakeneth mine ear to hear as they are taught. The Lord God hath opened mine ear, and I was not rebellious, neither turned away backward, I gave my back to the smiters, and my cheeks to them that plucked off the hair: I hid not my face from shame and spitting. For the Lord God will help me; therefore have I not been confounded: therefore have I set my face like a flint, and I know that I shall not be ashamed. He is near that justifieth me; who will contend with me: let us stand up together: [12]

Again the Servant himself spoke. He had daily revelations from God himself. Perhaps they came to him in prayer; they always gave him new strength. Even when he spoke sharply, the words came from a tender heart. His intention was not to wound feelings but to comfort the weary and heavy laden. His reward was misunderstanding and ill will. He would have liked best to withdraw from Yahweh's calling, but as Jeremiah had formerly done, he remained faithful to his duty to glorify Yahweh. Those who beat his back, pulled his beard, spat in his face, met with no resistance. Without a murmur, with faith in God, he faced his tormentors, indeed, he confidently challenged them to justice before God. He knew that God was with him. Indeed, Yahweh "is near"; therefore it could not be long until all should be fulfilled, and the Servant would be recognized as the Messiah and the end should come. Thus the Servant thought; thus, doubtless his herald also.

Then events occurred, of which we know only in a general way, but we can understand them clearly. If the unknown one, whom our prophet calls the Servant of Yahweh, was so sure of his goal and of his calling that he could not be diverted from it by the greatest ill will and maltreatment, as thus far seemed to be the case, and if by wisely avoiding every Messianic title or similar term, he did not conceal the fact that his message was to lead his people and all peoples to light and to freedom, it would be strange if the Babylonian authorities did not watch him. They might have done so of their own accord. They may also have had their attention directed to him by his own countrymen. The latter were capable of anything; if we judge by what we have just heard of them. The rest is told in the great final section in which Second Isaiah again speaks.

Who hath believed our report? and to whom hath the arm of the Lord been revealed? For he grew up before him as a tender plant, and as a root out of a dry ground: he hath no form nor comeliness; and when we see him, there is no beauty that we should desire him. He was despised and rejected of men; a man of sorrows, and acquainted with grief; and as one from whom men hide their face, he was despised, and we esteemed him not.

Surely he hath borne our griefs, and carried our sorrows; yet we did esteem him stricken, smitten of God, and afflicted. But he was wounded for our transgressions, he was bruised for our iniquities; the chastisement of our peace was upon him; and with his stripes we are healed. All we like sheep have gone astray; we have turned everyone to his own way; and the Lord hath laid on him the iniquity of us all.

He was oppressed, yet he humbled himself and opened not his mouth; as a lamb that is led to the slaughter, and as a sheep that before her shearers is dumb; yea, he openeth not his mouth.[13]

Later, Second Isaiah was himself surprised at his proclamation concerning the Servant. He considers it almost natural that he found little following, when he recalled what sort of man he was, through whom Yahweh had revealed himself. He appeared insignificant of figure, uncomely in appearance, weak and unmanly. Little wonder, after all, that no one wished to accept such a man as the one chosen of God. When, finally, suffering and painful illness afflicted him, belief in his divine mission was completely destroyed. Such

[398]

people were supposed to be marked by God as sinners. How could he, whom God had visibly stricken, be His messenger? This caused many people to consider it quite natural and well deserved when men attacked him, indeed even wounded, and finally killed him. His fellow countrymen could not have done this. He seems to have been tortured outright and his body cruelly mutilated. Such a death could be inflicted only by the authorities. In astonishment, the song tells of the patience and the silent resignation with which he bore pain and suffering. Whence came this superhuman strength and greatness of soul? This question puzzled Second Isaiah a long time. Only the Servant's death made clear the fact that he suffered and died as a martyr for the welfare of others. Only his suffering and death could atone for the world's guilt.

> By oppression and judgment he was taken away; and as for his generation, who among them considered that he was cut off out of the land of the living? for the transgression of my people was he stricken. And they made his grave with the wicked, and with the rich in his death; although he had done no violence, neither was any deceit in his mouth.
> Yet it pleased the Lord to bruise him. . . . When thou shalt make his soul an offering for sin, he shall see his seed, he shall prolong his days, and the pleasure of the Lord shall prosper in his hand.[14]

Here it is stated more clearly than before, that not his fellow countrymen but the authorities were his torturers. Probably he had long been suspected, and now the judges sentenced him to be tortured, mutilated, and finally to be executed. Even his dead body was maltreated. Without mourning and without a proper grave, he was given a criminal's burial, or a burial like that of the very poorest and the homeless about whom no one concerns himself. This was his lot, the innocent one, who knew neither reproach nor crime. Second Isaiah again faced a difficult, unsolved question. The mass of countrymen and contemporaries passed it by. Who has not often experienced such a case? A terrible accident, a gruesome crime, a base injustice has occurred. It becomes the sensation of the hour. Soon there follows a new sensation which is taken up, and the first one forgotten. The cares and pleasures of daily life demand our interest. Of the incident we may say, "Who among our contemporaries remembers it?" One man, however, could not cease thinking of it until he found its solution—Second Isaiah.

The course of his life, his calling, his death, and the character of the second one of the two great unknown ones (who concern us here, is sufficiently before us. A prophet among the exiles in those days of great political tension and religious national hope felt himself called by Yahweh to introduce the era of glory. He would bring Israel freedom, help justice to conquer. He would do far more; he would bring the light of the true knowledge of God and the blessing of alliance with God to all nations. He was marked neither by heredity, beauty, nor a noble figure. Like a slender twig on the arid heath, he was insignificant from his youth up and burdened with illness; but as a recompense, God himself had endowed him with His own spirit. It was not the spirit of power or of fame; it was the spirit of gentleness, of humility, of mercy. He would neither conquer nor rule; but would comfort and heal. Even where his testimony was like a sharp sword that must be drawn against human folly or malice, there, too, it was the spirit of meekness that guided him. His deeds were service for the weary and heavy laden.

To be sure, it is not usual for the broken reed or for the weary and heavy laden to use violence to procure justice for themselves. But it is the manner of those who break the reed and trample upon it and those who like to give the weary the death blow. Before the people had a proper understanding, salvation could not come to them. But they did not desire understanding and justice; they clung to their unrighteous deeds which brought them gain and honor. This caused the opposition which led to open enmity, to scorn and maltreatment. Now the cheerful helper whose only desire was to help gain salvation for his people and for all the world became a submissive sufferer. For a time he seemed to grow weary, his spirit seemed broken by ingratitude and ill will, but Yahweh supported him. If Yahweh championed him, that was sufficient reward. Daily communion with Yahweh in prayer and revelation gave him power vigorously to defy all resistance. Full of faith in Yahweh he continued his work, confident of results with Yahweh's help.

(It was not to be so. Did his followers commit the same folly that those of Zerubbabel did openly, to proclaim him the promised Messiah? Did he, himself (which would seem foreign to his nature) forgetting caution and reticence, allow himself to be carried away to ill-considered acts? Did his enemies carry their aversion, perhaps their fear of him, to the heathen tribunal? Or did the state authorities themselves observe him?) At all events)a suit was brought against him. It could have been only for high treason. Severe flogging and various kinds of torture were the usual punishment for high treason. It was customary to make each case a warning to others. In silent greatness of soul, he overcame the scorn of those who mocked him as one abandoned of Yahweh, and bore the bodily torture without complaint. Released from physical and mental torture by death, he, who had never done wrong, who had practiced only love, humility, and mercy was humiliated even as a corpse. He received a criminal's burial. An unparalleled tragedy; the life and death of the great Martyr! Of his own free will and at Yahweh's command, the noble man paid the price with his blood of being the savior of his people and the world.

This is the story of the second unknown, the "Servant of Yahweh." But the story of the first unknown one, of Second

Isaiah, whom we called his herald, does not end here. He rounded out his inner life and completed his character by seeking to solve the enigma which the tragic death of the other one presented to him and to his period. This developed an entirely new mental attribute in him. He was no longer a prophet, a seer, a preacher of consolation, penance, and hope of Yahweh's great deeds, but a theologian who carefully reflected on religious experiences. In the capacity of theologian, he at once gave the world a thought of historical significance, for if at any time or in any place the truth was verified that thoughts make history, it was here. Second Isaiah's explanation to himself and to his countrymen of the tragedy of the Great Sufferer introduced a cycle of ideas into history by which the tragedy of another life and its sufferings can be understood, i.e., the greatest drama that the world has ever seen, the tragedy of Golgotha. Whatever we may think of the latter and from whatever angle we may view it, there can be no doubt that in his sufferings and death the Jesus of Nazareth of our Gospels was greatly influenced by the tragedy of the martyrdom which Second Isaiah described and explained.

We have already stated the result of Second Isaiah's meditation over the Servant's fate. Because the great Sufferer was entirely innocent, his sufferings and death could be explained only by the fact that he suffered and died for others as an atonement for them. How did Second Isaiah grasp this remarkable and difficult conception?

If, as is evident, Second Isaiah believed in the special mission of the Servant, if he looked upon him not only as a prophet such as he himself was, but as one elected in a special sense, indeed as the mediator of the great salvation for Israel and the world, chosen and endowed by Yahweh, then his fate must have been a cruel disappointment to Second Isaiah. Where was Yahweh? Where His justice? Where His promise? Or, was it, after all, not true that the person executed was chosen and anointed of Yahweh? Had he only assumed the rôle, and were these people in the right who had formerly explained his illness and now his ignominious death as the just punishment of God? In short, what he had just experienced might have completely upset his mental equilibrium and put to the severest test his faith in God, in himself, and in the moral world.

How could he regain clearness of judgment, poise, and equilibrium? Whenever Second Isaiah considered the life, and especially the sufferings and death of the Servant, he could not imagine him a dishonest man or a dreamer who had deceived himself. A man who devoted himself in humility and in loving kindness to the suffering and the oppressed, who sought only to heal, to help, and to sustain the heavy laden, who was faithful to his duty for Yahweh's sake, although despised and scorned, who accepted without resistance the lot of one punished by Yahweh, who bore the anguish of torture in silent patience and greatness of soul, and who remained faithful to his duty and to himself unto death, he could be neither a criminal nor a dreamer.

But if he was the chosen one of Yahweh and His Messiah, how, then, could Yahweh allot to him this fate? The answer was this: it was possible only if Yahweh had a special purpose for him. Such a fate must have had a reason, such terrible punishment must have had its origin in God's justice. For such a fate there must also have been sin. Such suffering was not without cause; it came from God's hand as a punishment. If the sin were not in him who suffered and died, it could be only with the living. He did not endure it for himself, but for others, for all of us. "All we like sheep have gone astray . . . he was bruised for our iniquities . . . and with his stripes are we healed." His suffering and death were, therefore, not atonement for his own guilt but a vicarious atonement for others.

We have already treated the fact that, in exile, during the

severest suffering that came to Israel, a feeling of great guilt came over the people. From antiquity the belief had existed in Israel that sin could be atoned for by sacrifice and various deeds of atonement. Sufferings and, especially, death might be considered such atonement. As they considered sufferings that came to the individual or the people as a punishment for special sins, conversely great suffering and even death might atone for guilt. Second Isaiah himself stated that Israel atoned for its guilt in the sufferings of the exiles.

Thus suffering as a means of atonement was well known to Second Isaiah. The idea of atonement through mediation or vicarious atonement was equally familiar to Israel from ancient times. Because Saul had committed a crime against the inhabitants of Gibeon, David had the surviving members of his family killed after Saul's death. In Saul's stead they atoned for his sin. When Jonathan, Saul's son, was to be executed, he was "ransomed" either by a slave or an animal which was killed as his substitute.

From this it is clear, that because Second Isaiah knew that the Servant of Yahweh suffered and died guiltless and because he was familiar with the idea of atonement through suffering and death as that of vicarious atonement, the conclusion was obvious to him; the Great Sufferer suffered and died for the welfare of others as an atonement for Israel's sins. This reassured him that the Great Sufferer was the long promised Messiah; but a new and marked factor had entered into his conception of the Savior of Israel and of the nations. Formerly the promised Savior had been a victorious king; now he became a Suffering Servant. He had always been a prince of peace; now he attained the kingdom of peace, not through violence but through humility and suffering. The exile had broken Israel's pride and taught it to place humility among the virtues.

A further deduction naturally resulted from this one. If

the innocent dead had died as the Suffering Servant in the service of Yahweh, indeed if he was the one chosen by Him to bring salvation, it was evident that human malice and folly could not hinder Yahweh from finally carrying out his purpose. If, then, we read above that at last he should "live long and Yahweh's plan should succeed through him," these words can be only an expression of the definite hope of his resurrection. To be sure, he succumbed to his adversaries, but Yahweh was not overpowered. Yahweh would still carry out his plan for him. He must return, must be brought forth from the grave, and resurrected; he must complete his work.

This was indeed a bold conception, but not too daring for the period and for the thoughts of Second Isaiah. The myths had long ago taught that gods may be taken from the lower world and returned to the living. Osiris and Tamuz had been resurrected. In Egypt people could become Osiris and live on in the beyond. Why then should not one dead be able to return to this world as an exception? In the thirty-seventh chapter, Ezekiel describes a vision he saw according to which a whole field of bleached bones again took on flesh and blood and returned to life here on earth. He thought of his people. When this thought was once expressed and the figure created, what was to hinder a daring thinker with firm faith from going a step farther? The marvelous translation to Yahweh of Enoch and Elijah were accepted as facts. Why should not the marvelous return to earth be possible for the Servant of Yahweh? Soon afterwards, in their boldness of faith in Yahweh, one or more contemporaries of Second Isaiah ventured to rend the veil that separates the here and the hereafter and to believe in the return (as an exception) of the especially devout. Everything is in favor of the fact that Second Isaiah shared their belief.

This completes the portrayal of the great man. He was not only a poet and prophet of an unusual type, but through his great contemporary, he became a theologian greater than others, who discovered the idea of vicarious atonement and of the suffering and resurrection of the Savior.

XVI

EZRA AND NEHEMIAH

WHEN Cyrus entered Babylon in October of 539, he was received by a large part of the native population with great rejoicing, but the joy of the captive Jews must have been far greater and more genuine. The hope which the prophets had fostered since the beginning of the captivity, which the release of King Jehoiachin twenty years before had seemed to establish and which Second Isaiah at the first appearance of Cyrus had proclaimed with even greater assurance, now at last seemed to be fulfilled. Babylonia, the enslaver of nations, Judah's tyrant, had finally been conquered. The way was open for the liberation of the Jews.

If we assume that certain of Second Isaiah's speeches were intended for Cyrus, the latter probably understood their meaning and acted accordingly. It is not necessary, however, to assume this, for with the new ruler a new spirit had come over the great empire. Herodotus praised the Persians for their justice and leniency. The Achæmenes were especially farsighted and humane, as is shown by their treatment of subject nations. As far as possible, they adapted themselves to existing conditions and respected, as best they could, the sacred traditions of subject nations. They were especially tolerant toward religions. Cambyses and Darius offered sacrifice to native gods in Egypt and in Babylonia; Cyrus introduced himself to the Babylonians as a better servant of Marduk than Naboned had been. Indeed the Persians used the religion of their subject nations as a support, and sought favor with the priesthood by giving them power and influence. Cyrus' dealings were much the same in Jerusalem as in Babylonia.

Cyrus, apparently, desired to grant the Jews their wishes. In doing so, he introduced a policy, especially in religion, which his successors continued, and which was most significant for Judaism and other nations and civilizations. In 538, in a decree issued from Ecbatana, Cyrus commanded the return of the sacred vessels which Nebuchadnezzar had taken from the Jews, the rebuilding of the Temple at the expense of the national treasury, and granted permission to the Jews, who so desired, to return to the land of their fathers. Large numbers of all the tribes gladly returned to their native land. A list made after their arrival shows that there were about thirty thousand men and over seven thousand slaves, male and female. Cyrus set out evidently ahead of the caravan, and appointed as governor Sheshbazzar of the house of David. Sheshbazzar, as ruler of the Persian subprovince of Judah, was responsible to the satrap, who was probably stationed at Damascus. The leader of the caravan was Zerubbabel of the house of David, the high priest, Jeshua, assisting him. At first religious services were held at the altar in Jerusalem, now long restored.

We are mistaken if we believe that Cyrus was actuated merely by humanitarian motives. Syria had always been dangerous ground for the empire, and southern Palestine was so near Egypt that Cyrus, as a man of foresight and wisdom, must have realized the great political value of a well-regulated state, grateful to the emperor, and situated upon this bridge between Asia and Egypt.

The Jews probably returned from Babylonia through Mesopotamia and across Tadmor over the Syrio-Arabian desert. Hopes were high; one promise of their prophet had been gloriously fulfilled in Cyrus' gracious decree. They dared hope that other prophecies would also be fulfilled: that the valleys would be made smooth; the mountains and hills, an easy road; the desert as easily crossed as a field; and the land of their fathers, a garden of God for them. And yet none of this seemed to come to pass. They probably bore patiently the difficulties and hardships of the desert journey, for they hoped all the more for rich recompense in their homeland. There, however, new disappointments awaited them.

The country with which nature had not dealt too lavishly had been deserted by its best inhabitants for fifty years. To be sure, it was not depopulated. Certainly, many people remained even after those had departed who dragged Jeremiah with them to Egypt. The intellectual and energetic people, however, had been taken captive. Doubtless, many formerly well-kept estates and farms were now deserted. Those who returned found much uncultivated and deserted land which required hard labor, privation, and hardship for the farmer before he could expect returns. Then, too, much of their native land was now in the hands of strangers. When Judah fell, her neighbors—the Edomites, the Moabites, the Ammonites, and the Philistines—who had long been casting wistful glances across the border, had taken possession of the deserted estates. Pushed on by the Edomites, the people who formerly dwelt in the southern steppes (members of the old tribes of Caleb and Jerahmeel) now settled in the region about Bethlehem and Jerusalem.

All this caused much confusion. The returning Jews, who gained possession of their old or of new lands, found hard work and privation instead of comfort and enjoyment. This, perhaps, may have been the fate of only a very few of them at first. Most of the estates, indeed entire sections, had completely changed owners. Who was empowered to expel the new occupants? Who could decide the rightful ownership in every case?

This was the difficulty not only in regard to ownership of land but also in regard to means of livelihood as well as trade, now at a complete standstill in this half-deserted and disputed country. But the question of ownership of land and gaining a living were not the principal nor the outstanding difficulties. The Jews had learned to live rather as a religious community than as a nation. To be sure, they had much to learn, but they had made a beginning. The religious question was vital to them. Doubtless, most of those who returned came because of the temple and the holy city. Here again they were disappointed. The Deuteronomists, Second Isaiah and Ezekiel, had labored among the exiles and had changed the spirit of the exilic people completely, as we have already heard. Thus the people who returned from Babylon had a very different spirit from those who went into exile. There was no similar movement among the people who remained in the homeland—at least we find no traces of it. The Jews who returned found an attitude different from their own among the native Jews and among those who had immigrated to the country, even though the latter acknowledged Judaism. What the Jews of Palestine called Yahweh worship, although similar in some respects to the national religion which Jeremiah had attacked, seemed sheer heathenism to those who had experienced the clarifying influences of the exile. When the newcomers looked to the north, the territory formerly occupied by the ten tribes, they must have felt their difficult position doubly and triply. There they found a mixed race, the descendants of the seven hundred and twenty-two who had remained in the country with the Assyrian inhabitants whom Sargon and his successors had forced to settle there, and several tributary Assyrian states. Formerly, indeed, a marked difference between Israel and Judah existed. Now it was greatly increased by the mingling of the inhabitants of Samaria and Shechem with the heathen near by. The mixture was not merely of blood but of religious faiths and religious forms. If the newcomers respected themselves, the purity of their blood, and their religion, they could have nothing in common with these people. If the latter sought to associate with them and were repulsed or felt lack of cordiality, tension which might lead to new complications was inevitable. We do not know exactly when or how antagonism between the Jews and Samaritans came about. Doubtless, its roots lay in the early period of the new congregation in Judah.

Under these conditions more than a decade and a half passed before the new colony made visible progress. The upper class of the priesthood, the leaders of the clans, and the wealthy landowners may still have been in and about Jerusalem, for the city had certainly long been partially repopulated. The governor and his officials were there, of course. Those having means could buy property or make arrangements with the people living in the country, or could gain a living by trade or some other branch of industry. But the majority of the people of limited means among both the priesthood and the laymen, and particularly among the slaves, had a very difficult position. When crop failure or drought or annoyances from unfriendly neighbors came, their condition was sad indeed. The city had no walls and, therefore, was exposed to attack. No one ventured to think of rebuilding the temple, although the edict of Cyrus was issued for this purpose. The people lacked courage and means to do it, and the unprotected city was insecure.

In the meantime two prophets had appeared, Haggai and Zechariah. Unlike the old prophets, however, they lacked the great passion for the stern all-powerful Yahweh in spiritual matters. They spoke the everyday language of crop failures and hard times, and believed conditions would improve when the temple was rebuilt. There was a passion within them, however, reminiscent of the older prophets, which proves to us that the old promise that the great kingdom should come through one on David's throne was only delayed in fulfillment and not forgotten.

After Cyrus' death in 529, his son Cambyses ascended the throne and, in 525, subjugated Egypt. He was called back by an insurrection in Persia, instigated by the Magian Gaun.ata (Smerdis). Cambyses lost his life in Syria in 522. Darius, the son of Hystaspis, murdered the Magian in 521 and himself ascended the throne. Only after many hard struggles could he enjoy his rule. Rebellion broke out on all sides: in Medea under Phraortes; in Persia, where a second false Smerdis appeared; in Babylon; in Elam; and in Armenia. The walls of the kingdom shook to the foundation and threatened to break asunder. What wonder that the old hope was again awakened in Judah and its prophets. Could this be the promised end of the tyrant's rule and dawn of the long expected new era? Would Yahweh now fulfill his promise and end the misery of his people? The first governor, Sheshbazzar, had been replaced by Zerubbabel, who was also of the house of David. Perhaps Zerubbabel exaggerated the hopes of many Judeans more than did his predecessor; at any rate, the Messianic hope awoke in him. In the latter half of the year 520, the prophet, Haggai, summoned the people to rebuild the temple and, at the same time, pointed out the great upheavel that Yahweh would cause to come in heaven and earth and among all peoples and kingdoms.

I shall overthrow the throne of kingdoms, and I will destroy the strength of the kingdoms of the nations; and I will overthrow the chariots and those who ride in them; and the horses and their riders shall come down, everyone by the sword of his brother. In that day, saith the Lord of hosts, I shall take thee, O Zerubbabel my servant . . . and I will make thee as a signet, for I have chosen thee, saith the Lord of Hosts." [1]

Thus he proclaims Zerubbabel as the promised Messiah, the king of the approaching kingdom of God. Under these exciting impressions, the cornerstone of the temple was laid in December 520. In February of the following year 519, Haggai's successor, Zechariah, continued this dangerous line of thought and, through the contributions of wealthy Jews in Babylonia, had a crown made and laid ready for Zerubbabel. With feverish tension the people awaited the news of Darius' fall and the collapse of Persia. For as soon as this should come, Zerubbabel would mount the throne of the great ruler. But this was not to be. In 521 Darius successfully suppressed the rebellion in Babylonia; in 520 he advanced against the remaining rebellious nations; and in 519 became master of the Persian Empire and remained this until 486.

And so it was that the Judean dream of ruling the world was ended for the time being. We do not know what became of Zerubbabel. He disappeared. The Persian government may have quietly killed him. It seems that, after these experiences, the office of governor was not again filled. The government had no desire to repeat the experiment with a Davidite. The satrap, Tattenai or Uschtanni, who governed Syria must have come to Jerusalem about this time. After what had happened he had good reason to wish to set affairs in order. He saw the Jews were rebuilding their temple. If he had heard that the Judean prophets believed that, when the temple was completed, the Messianic kingdom would begin, it is reasonable to assume that he opposed continuing the work. When the Jews cited the edict of Cyrus, the satrap decided to ask his king for instructions in the matter. If the edict existed and Darius acknowledged its validity, the satrap's responsibility ceased. Darius did not share the satrap's fears. He upheld Cyrus' generous and politic views, and generously supported the undertaking. The temple was completed in three or four years. At that time Darius was fighting in Egypt. Perhaps the conflicts that began at the turning of the century, first in Asia Minor and later with the native Greeks, were casting their shadows ahead. The far-sighted ruler may have considered it good policy to grant the Jews this modest request.

The expectations of the prophets of the period as a result of the building of the temple were not fulfilled. On the contrary, after Zerubbabel's failure enthusiasm waned. Our reports of the following decades are few and unreliable. Yet the little book, bearing the name of the prophet, Malachi, and perhaps certain parts of the supplement to the Book of Second Isaiah, probably belong to the period between Zerubbabel and Ezra. They suggest that conditions grew steadily worse. In spite of the temple, the community did not flourish. Their burdens were heavy. They had no native governor to intercede for them. Crop failures, grasshopper plagues, and heavy indebtedness made living conditions unfavorable. Religious zeal and interest in the temple worship decreased perceptibly; foreign religious practices gradually gained favor. Many Jews married foreign women without compunction. The unsatisfactory relations with their northern and southern neighbors, especially with the Samaritans, continued. In short, all we know about this period (until about 460) shows clearly that their condition grew steadily worse; disintegration had set in, which suggests that the return of the captives from Babylon and the attempt to refound a Jewish community was a great mistake, and that every trace of it would soon be blotted out.

It is probable that the colony would have failed completely and have gradually disappeared from history but for Ezra and Nehemiah. Neither was a really great man; neither was a real genius, nor had unusual greatness of soul or great religious zeal. On the other hand, both prove to us how great is the value to a distressed community of one man or a very few men endowed with energy and wisdom in action. Whether we praise or blame Judaism as it has emerged in history (both opinions will always find champions), the fact remains that its essential characteristics were due to these two men whom, together with the Deuteronomists and Ezekiel, we may justly call the fathers of Judaism.

Both Ezra and Nehemiah had weaknesses. Both were masters of political intrigue. Yet the great love for their people and their passionate striving to raise it to their ideal of the greatness and vitality of Judaism inspired them and gave zest to their deeds and a certain greatness to them. Ezra was entirely the priest and the champion of the priestly hierarchy. The religious community, the church, was everything to him; the state, nothing. For him the church rested entirely upon the law. It was an institution for the welfare of humanity. Because people were incapable of understanding what was for their good, they needed the gentle pressure of the law. Nehemiah as a layman was convinced that these principles were correct, and he defended them unreservedly. He was decidedly the superior political advocate of the hierarchy, a character such as we find in Windthorst and Reichenberger, possessing political skill and being ready to make the utmost sacrifice, but with such naïve egotism as to remind even the deity of his own merits.

We have repeatedly stated that after the fall of Jerusalem the real development of Judaism was not in the homeland but among the exiled Jews. There the great men had labored with their people; there the spiritual rejuvenation of the nation took place. There, even before the edict of Cyrus, the Messianic hope had experienced an important change, which meant denying the political power of the coming savior. The first few decades after their return in Cyrus' reign brought them the bitter disappointment about Zerubbabel. They may then have expressed for the first time their complete abandonment of plans for Israel's political future. Many of the Israelites had already attained wealth and position by successful commercial enterprise in the cities; others held high governmental positions. They had no desire for new political experiments, either in Palestine or in Babylon, for the latter might react upon them also. As faithful Israelites, they had the greatest interest in supporting Judaism and their faith in Yahweh. To these they owed everything and, even in the midst of their foreign surroundings, protected them from threatened collapse. If the national political splendor could not uphold Judaism, spiritual sovereignty of their faith and their religion must do it. They could not practice the religious cult in the foreign country as their fathers had done and as Ezekiel had taught them to do. Therefore, they must do it all the more in the Holy City and at the temple now long rebuilt. Their thoughts centered about Zion; they longed for it, for it was the seat of the God of their fathers, who to them had long become the great God of heaven and of all the world. They had long been sending contributions to the temple. In the course of the decades, thousands may have made pilgrimages to Jerusalem to worship and to sacrifice to the God of their fathers at the holy place. And now misfortune befell them, for everything in the homeland, even religion, was at the lowest ebb, and as a result, the people had as little interest in keeping their religion pure as in retaining the pure blood of their fathers. Unless a change came about, there was danger that the temple and the Holy City, instead of being objects of longing, would soon become objects of heathen abhorrence, because they were no longer the places of pure Judaism and pure faith in Yahweh. They must do all in their power to prevent this.

Judah and Babylon still had the old law. We do not know how it was acknowledged either in the homeland or in Babylon. The fact that Ezekiel sought to direct the religious services and religious life in the new community by perfecting the existing laws, fixes one of the few definite dates that we have. It is very probable that the priesthood of the exiled Jews and the newly founded congregation (since 538) at home did their best to meet present demands by elaborating the existing laws. In keeping with what we have already said, we have reason to believe that the work of expanding the law zealously continued in Babylonia. The so-called law of holiness took on its present form, or one very similar to it, by the revision and expanding of the older laws. Here, too, Deuteronomy received the form which it has for the most part to this day. At this time the Judean congregation may already have possessed many of its laws, while other laws may still have remained in the possession of the priests and the devout people of Babylonia. Nevertheless, it is worth noting that the few definite evidences we have of the early post-exilic period, which are contained in the Books of Haggai and Zechariah, scarcely mention the law of Moses. We are certain that they knew it, but it seems equally certain to us that it was not so much the standard of religion or of life as it was after Ezra.

There seemed to be no other means of helping and strengthening the prostrate congregation in the homeland than to give it definite standards for life and ritual. Gifts of money had proven useless; nor had political aspirations been of service. The leaders of Babylonian Judaism may long have looked with concern upon the growing neglect at home and the decline of national pride before those of other faiths. It may have been not only their dearest wish but also their reputation among other nations which demanded that conditions be changed. The respect which was shown them rested upon the esteem in which other nations held the God of heaven whom they proudly served. If religion died out in the homeland or Yahweh worship stagnated or was stunted in the homeland, what would become of them, their standing, their position, and their esteem in Babylonia?

Political means had failed; only religious ones could serve them. The older prophets would have considered inner change, a conversion of heart and life, a circumcision of the spirit and not of the flesh. The new generation of the exilic period had long realized that happiness for their children and children's children could be gained only by entirely forsaking the path of their fathers. Ezekiel taught them, more than his predecessors, the way to attain this. In Babylon they had a splendid ritual constantly before them, and they had gradually learned to differentiate themselves from their heathen surroundings by certain rites and ceremonies, especially by circumcision and by celebrating the Sabbath.

This pointed the way. The law, expanded and enlarged since Ezekiel's time, had gradually reached a perfected form at the hands of the priests and scribes of the Babylonian Judaism. It must become the standard for ritual and life in the homeland, in so far as the Jews still controlled the latter. Doubtless they believed that they were following the teachings of the old prophets in this. By giving up all claim to worldly power, martial success, and the desire to rule, they believed they were satisfying spiritual demands, not realizing that they thus seemed to interpret morality and piety by mere concrete acts. Existing conditions must cease. They had a law of God, but after all every one decided for himself to what extent he would obey it. What certain rulers had formerly accomplished for parts of the law by pledging the people to obedience must be repeated for the law in its present form, for the benefit of the present and for all time.

This could be done only with the help of the Persian government. The former ruler now gave way to the imperial government. If the Jews could interest the empire, their success was assured. We do not know how they gained the favor of the king and the government. We frequently do not understand the secret power of royal confessors at the courts of Christian rulers. Acts of state, royal edicts and proclamations, the wills and the final requests of the dying are affected by these influences and, frequently, the secret is buried with those concerned. The influence of Jewish confidants and councilors was equally great upon princes and rulers of ancient and modern times.

During the Middle Ages and later, Jews often either supplied funds or negotiated for them; but in antiquity they gained position and importance by their skill, versatility, and mental superiority, as well as by the imposing superiority of their religion. Both Ezra and Nehemiah occupied positions of trust with Artaxerxes I. The stories of Judith, Esther, and Mordecai prove that high positions were not unusual.

How strongly the nationally conscious groups in the homeland felt the danger of worldliness, of indifference to ritual, and of contaminating their blood is shown in the anonymous little book of the prophet called Malachi. It probably appeared a short time before Ezra's coming. It must have been a common occurrence for Jews to marry women of the Ammonite, Moabite, Philistine, or Samaritan tribes. This of itself endangered the purity of the race and the religion. Jews seem to have had no compunction in breaking faith with "the wife of thy youth . . . of thy covenant" to marry "the daughter of a strange god," i.e., they abandoned their native wives for foreign ones. It is probable that they settled property problems in this way. The returning Jews found the best lands in foreign hands, and an unscrupulous marriage may frequently have been the easiest solution of the problem. Worldliness and lack of reverence for Yahweh and his worship existed even among the priesthood. They did not hesitate to offer inferior animals in their sacrifice to Yahweh, animals they would not have ventured to bring to the governor. The priests failed in the lofty task of being messengers of the truth; their judgments were biased. Thus they caused many to stumble, and they forfeited the respect of the people for themselves and their calling.

These were the feelings of only a small minority, and they gradually died out. The masses and the majority of the ruling classes became indifferent to these dangers. The Jews in Babylonia knew this, and therefore the leaders felt justified in interfering with home conditions.

We do not know who Ezra was except that he was sometimes called priest and sometimes scribe. His life shows that he was prominent in the Babylonian Judean priesthood. He may have been the leader: certainly he was one of the prominent members of the group, interested in collecting and editing the written laws as a means of reform in the homeland. His life also shows that he occupied a position of trust at court with the emperor himself. This is all that we know of him, but it is enough to give us a fairly clear picture of him as a man of his time.

Artaxerxes I was the successor of Xerxes (465-424). When he began to reign, the great Persian campaigns in the west were by no means ended. The terrible defeats which Xerxes suffered from the Greeks were continued in the battle at Eurymedon in the year 466, shortly before Artaxerxes ascended the throne. With the first decisive Greek victory, the Persians had passed the zenith of power. Insurrections against which Xerxes had probably already struggled were contributing causes. At all events, Xerxes' younger son, Artaxerxes, had a difficult position from the first. In addition to his heritage of annoying Greeks, there were rebellions in various places, the worst one in Egypt where the Lybians, aided by the Athenians, pressed him hard. The Athenians first conquered Cyprus, then reached out toward Egypt, destroyed the Persian fleet, and threatened Memphis. Even the Phœnician coast was no longer secure.

These campaigns and defeats were at the very time when Ezra was preparing his expedition, and they continued during the early part of his work in Palestine. There is no question that his coming was the result of years of labor and careful planning in his immediate circle and at the king's court. Under these conditions, Artaxerxes and his councilors may not have wished a decadent nation so near Egypt and on the Phœnician coast which was already unsafe. When in his day Cyrus published his edict of pardon, Persian policy had an interest in having a province near Egypt which was faithful to the empire; at this time, Artaxerxes and his councilors may have been actuated, not by humanitarianism and tender heartedness, but by motives of political wisdom which caused them to realize the importance of having an obedient and faithful province on the bridge between Egypt and Asia.

Thus the imperial interests and the wishes of Babylonian Jews fortunately coincided. We thus understand why the representative of the Babylonian Jews found an opportunity to bring his petition to the emperor and was received graciously. Ezra and his friends succeeded in getting a royal edict which sent Ezra back to the homeland well supported by royal authority "to inquire concerning Judah and Jerusalem, according to the law of thy God which is in thine hand." Ezra was given power to appoint officials and judges in Syria whose duty it was to see that the law was obeyed and to sit in judgment over those who scorned it. The people who worshiped the God of heaven were permitted also to proselyte. "Whosoever does not do the law of thy God and the law of thy King shall be punished by death or imprisonment, fines or banishment." This made the Mosaic law equal to the royal law, and established it as the imperial law for the Jews in Palestine.

Because of its far-reaching authority and of certain expressions in the document which indicate its Jewish origin, the whole document was pronounced a bold Jewish forgery of a later period. When we consider how many important proclamations in the course of history up to the present time have not been written by the ruler himself, but by one of his confidants who was entrusted with the matter, we can understand both the phraseology that suggests that it was written by a Jew and the extensive powers it gave. If, according to a well-known remark at a historic moment by Bismarck, a chamade (that is a mere signal for a parley) may become a flourish of trumpets under the pen of a scribe, all that baffles modern expounders may have entered the edict by Ezra's pen. That he or some one appointed by him was the author of the document is evident under the circumstances.

This power was given Ezra in the year 458, the seventh year of the king's reign. Early in the year he set out with a caravan of one thousand seven hundred and sixty Jews which reached Jerusalem after five months. Of course, as already stated, Ezra was well informed of the conditions there. That he did not act and judge alone by what he had heard at a distance proves his wisdom and justice. He spent four months studying conditions and receiving reports of the situation. There was a group, naturally a minority, who favored his plans. It may even have been greatly responsible for his coming. It was the group to which the so-called Malachi belonged. Prominent members of his group reported to Ezra. The question of mixed marriages was an important one, and one which seems to have been considered the root of the evil, because the upper classes were most guilty. Nehemiah's report, made a little later, throws strong light upon this question. Even the high priest's family was related by marriage to Sanballat, the chief of the opposition. This caused many difficulties and dissensions. Even the Jewish language was threatened by the foreign mothers.

Before he exercised his other powers and insisted upon strict compliance with the law, Ezra decided to seize the evil by the roots and so destroy the cancerous growth. He believed drastic measures necessary. Apparently he did not wish to use violence but public opinion to reach his goal. Then because of a demonstrative report, he created a carefully considered scene which really expressed his feelings and was also calculated to make an impression upon the masses. This was part of his plan. Deeply moved by a report, he rent his clothing and his mantle as if in mourning, tore his hair and beard, and sat motionless upon the ground. His adherents gathered about him. In the evening he arose and addressed them; then falling upon his knees with outstretched arms, offered a touching prayer of penance in the name of his people. The group that gathered about the prostrated, royal, wailing ambassador grew larger and larger. All were moved with him and wept. One of the bystanders expressed what gradually filled all their hearts: "We have trespassed against our God and have married strange women of the people of the land. Now let us make a covenant with our God to put away all the wives and such as are born of them. . . . Be of good courage and do it." This was what Ezra wanted. He pledged the leaders of the priesthood and the people by an oath. Then still fasting he withdrew for the night into a chamber of the temple. A few days later he called a mass meeting of the people in the temple court. It was the twentieth day of the ninth month, counting from the spring, and therefore in the depth of winter. Ezra repeated his demands, and the people approved them. They were ready to submit the whole matter to a committee. By the new year all was settled, although an influential minority, including a representative of the Levites, opposed his reform.

We now understand fully that, although there was no other way to purify their blood and their religious practice, this method was very radical, for repudiation of their wives and children ruthlessly tore asunder thousands of tender bonds. This naturally created much ill will, injured feelings, and caused bitterness. Our sources are so inadequate that we do not clearly know the further developments. We are certain, however, that this protest of the minority was not the only act of the opposition. The foreign peoples—the Samarians, the Moabites, Ammonites, and Philistines, whose prominent families were injured—certainly opposed the measure in every possible way. Their object was partly revenge and partly desire to force Ezra to retract. There may have been serious threats of force which Jerusalem could not meet because of her ruined walls. We can understand that Ezra might have been persuaded to overstep his authority and to begin to rebuild the wall for Jerusalem's protection. At any rate this report reached the overlord's ears. Its object, of course, was to bring Ezra in disfavor with the king. Even if, as is quite possible, it was mere calumny, the enemies of "Judah and Benjamin" had touched a tender spot in the government at Susa, when with threats they pointed out that, since the Jews were restless and formerly had always been inclined to insurrections, it might be dangerous to give Ezra great power and, perhaps, cause the subprovince of Judah to secede.

To understand conditions we must remember how much the king's power had weakened in the west because of the outcome of the campaigns in Greece and Egypt. True, the Persians gained an important victory in the year 456 over Inaros, of Lybia. A few years later, however, the satrap, Megabyzos, raised the banner of mutiny in Syria and gained several victories; the whole province, it seems, was seriously threatened. Such matters are usually carefully planned. Thus the officials, who made the above-mentioned report to the emperor of Ezra's real or alleged intentions, may have had reason for warning Artaxerxes. We can understand that, because of general world conditions, the emperor became suspicious. Ezra was deprived of his authority and he was probably recalled. We do not know the date.

Thus Ezra's mission had temporarily failed. To begin with, many of the forced divorces from foreign wives were probably pronounced null and void. In the face of strong opposition at home and at the court, others would have given up all hope. Ezra's tenacious persistence and cleverness did not allow him to become discouraged. To save the nation and its faith was to him a goal so lofty that he sought new means to attain it. He was not the only Jew who was a favorite at court. He knew Artaxerxes was a weak character who could be managed, if one knew how. His envious opponents had now succeeded in Palestine, but another might succeed later, especially if women and wine played a part.

Fortune had placed a Jewish cupbearer in the emperor's harem. A cupbearer must be both handsome and cheerful. Once when the king and a beautiful lady were drinking wine which Nehemiah served, the king noticed his careworn expression. The Jewish eunuch, who knew well that the king and the beautiful women favored him, may have expected the king's question. He reported that recent arrivals from the homeland brought depressing news of the great misery in the unprotected city, of ruined walls and burned gates.

It was the twentieth year of Artaxerxes' reign, hence 445-444. If Ezra had been in Palestine five years, by now eight years must have elapsed since his return. We are not quite sure what was meant by the ruined walls. If Ezra had really begun to rebuild it, this meant that it was again ruined. The frequent attacks by armed bandits may have caused them constantly to mourn over the ruined condition (since 586) of the city wall.

The king was in a happy mood and, "while the queen sat by him," unhesitatingly granted Nehemiah's request to go to the city of the graves of his fathers to rebuild it. The king furnished him with letters to the governors, and with a military escort. He set out immediately, taking Ezra with him. One night soon after his arrival, Nehemiah rode out to investigate the condition of the ruined city wall. Then he approached the leaders of the people and of the priesthood. He demanded that the wall be immediately rebuilt, and presented his royal authority. His demand met with approval and the work began. The inhabitants of both the city and the country supported him enthusiastically. With few exceptions, notably the nobility of Tekoa, the landed nobility and the population without land gathered in local unions; the artisan guilds in the cities took part in the work, which was completed in fifty-two days.

Nehemiah had to expect considerable resistance. The leader of the opposition was Sanballat, the governor of Samaria, who was related to the family of the high priest of Jerusalem and to a prominent Ammonite named Tobiah, who was, in turn, closely related to the nobility and the priesthood of Jerusalem. He was scornfully called "slave," probably because he descended from a family with a trace of negro blood. All these neighbors of foreign tribes, who had already strongly opposed Ezra, saw their efforts defeated and, naturally, strained every nerve to thwart Nehemiah. Because of Sanballat's official position, we question their committing violence, although Nehemiah's report seems to imply this. They seem rather to have used chicanery and intrigue to hinder the progress of the work and to cause Nehemiah's downfall. Nehemiah even expressed a suspicion that they wished to lure him into an ambush to kill him. When this failed, they threatened to report to the king that he was planning to play the rôle of Zerubbabel or Megabyzos in order to proclaim himself King of the Jews. Nehemiah does not appear to have been guilty of the charges. Perhaps Zerubbabel's fate was a warning to him. We must not overlook the fact that if the governor was faithful to the king, the fortification of Jerusalem might prove a strong bulwark for Persia. Thus Persia herself might be interested.

Nehemiah had to exert all his strength to control in his own ranks dissatisfaction nurtured from without. Because he was continually obliged to arm half of his laborers, it seems that the arms were intended to protect those in his own ranks who were willing to work, rather than to guard against an enemy from without. The excessive burden of the work seems to have led to the ruin of Judah, but here, too, Nehemiah proved himself equal to his task. He led them in making generous gifts, believing he might expect others to make sacrifices which he believed necessary to improve conditions and to complete the work. Nehemiah prided himself that he and all his official assistants personally took part in the rebuilding of the wall, although he was not obliged to do so for he was not a landowner; that he daily kept open house for a great many people according to the custom of the Persian officials, without taxing the overburdened people; that quite contrary to the custom of governors, because he "feared God," for many years he voluntarily waived his claim to the large income to which his office entitled both him and his assistants. This enabled him to face the nobility, creditors of the poor, who were again hard pressed by statute labor, and to demand general remission of all debts. By this act, Nehemiah not only prevented internal and external dangers, but gained valuable assistance for his future plans. Naturally his praises resounded everywhere.

Nehemiah now ventured to take the last step in which Ezra had failed. On the first day of the month of Tisri (445) in the fall of the year he proclaimed a great mass meeting of the people, and at that time called upon Ezra to read from the Book of Law. What they heard made so great an impression upon the people that the clan leaders came to Ezra on the following day asking to hear more of the book. They found a law which stated that in the seventh month tabernacles must be made of foliage and placed on the roofs of the houses and in the courtyards, and the people should live in these tabernacles during the feast. They now kept the feast for the first time since "Jeshua the son of Nun." On the twenty-fourth of the month, the final celebration, the climax of the feast occurred. The people, preceded by the governor and the leaders of both the priesthood and the laymen, solemnly pledged themselves by signing a solemn vow to obey the law henceforth.

This was the funeral dirge of the oldest type of Israelites, of the old national religion, and of the religion of the prophets. The latter two survived, but as substrata, as it were; the state belonging to olden times now consciously relinquished every claim to political power (it was relegated completely to future hopes) and became a religious community under a foreign government. In return the governor, as the representative of the empire, promised the Jews the right to control their internal affairs, and especially their right to worship in the manner desired by Babylonian leaders of Judaism. Thus that share in the government which fell to the Jews was put into the hands of the high priest and the priesthood. Their chief office was to make sure that all the provisions of the law were strictly obeyed whether of greater or less value from a moral standpoint. The Jewish community became a church state with a religious law for its standard of living in all matters not purely affairs of state.

All this was not accomplished without opposition. The great restrictions, which violently suppressed many natural emotions and forced civic and religious life into a definite mold, could not be accomplished without a strong reaction. Strict observance of the Sabbath interfered with commerce. Violent dissolution of family ties caused friction and could not be carried out as strictly as they had been planned. Even the prominent priesthood were unwilling to accept the advantages of their new positions at the price of former freedom. A grandson of the high priest, Eliashib, preferred banishment to leaving his wife, the daughter of the Samaritan chief, Sanballat. Nehemiah settled many problems on his second visit; other matters were settled as time went on. The strong opposition did not prevent Ezra's and Nehemiah's final victory.

The transformation from the old state into a church state continued. The people gradually became a community faithful to the law. Even proselytes and strangers became Jews as soon as they submitted to the law. It was no longer blood but faith or, rather, fidelity to the law that characterized the Jew. Everywhere in the world where Jews dwelt, they recognized one another by observing the law, and felt a common tie. In time the blood tie played no important part; acknowledgment of the law made the Jew. As the church state replaced the national state, as the history of religion replaced the political history, so religious civilization replaced the national civilization. Spengler is correct in this fact, although his term magic is incorrect. Apparently this change proclaims the broadest universalism: whoever reveres the one God, the Creator and God of Heaven, is a true Jew. What the prophets had already proclaimed, however, was still true. All that ever happened in the world and all that was now happening occurred for Yahweh's sake and for his people's sake. When empires rose and fell, Israel was the center of the world's history and in it "all people are blessed." Religion relapsed, however, into narrow particularism. When everything happened for Israel's sake, and Yahweh's laws were made to signify a worship according to rites, such as circumcision, and according to the various food laws, there was created a narrow particularism and legal formalism which could not possibly claim world recognition but made its adherents exclusive, although composed of a large congregation of believers. This caused a world of contradictions and internal tragedy. Noble and truly religious creative works, such as Job and many of the best Psalms, could only lessen the contradiction but not wholly overcome it

We can best understand the importance of this separation of religion and state, really the work of the Persian empire and extending to all religions of the Near East, by the fact that Christianity, Islam, and many religious cults of the period of the Roman Emperors, also, had therein their origin.

[429]

XVII

JUDAS, THE MACCABEE

It was inevitable that the burden of the law should seem unbearable to many Israelites. No doubt some had long felt the burden of religious formalism without being able clearly to express the feeling. Through Alexander and his successors, the Israelites came in closer contact with Greek culture, a new world to them. The freedom and scope of Greek spirit now showed many Israelites the narrowness of their former life, and caused a conflict whose peculiarity and acuteness drew them into the great conflict of world powers. The struggle for power in the Orient and the conflict between the orthodox Jews with the modernists, who favored Hellenism, brought Israel into the world's arena as in the days of the Assyrians and Babylonians. In the homeland the Jewish congregation, which had long been leading a retired and peaceful life, was thus suddenly transformed into a host of armed warriors. For a short time it even again became a state.

When, in 333, Alexander had crushed the Persian Empire in the battle of Issus, the Jews of Palestine without resistance became subject to his general, Parmenio. Whether their overlord was a Persian, a Macedonian, or a Greek was a matter of indifference to them and, as far as we know, no one in Judah thought of resistance. After Alexander's early death, Ptolemy, the son of Lagus, the governor of Egypt, occupied Palestine. With few interruptions Palestine remained in the hands of the Ptolemies until Antiochus III, called the Great, gained southern Syria for the Seleucids in the battle of Panias at the source of the Jordan. That was in the year 198-197. The Seleucids had reigned over Babylon and the eastern provinces since 311, and considered themselves executors of the heritage from Alexander. The Ptolemies in Egypt fostered the national spirit of Egypt, while the Seleucids were all the more eager to introduce Greek civilization into the Near East. The Jews had long been in touch with Greek civilization, first in foreign lands and later in the homeland.

For some time Jewish communities had been established in different places. Great numbers of Judeans had gone to Egypt long before Judah ceased to be a state and before Jerusalem fell. After Jerusalem's fall the number increased. Nebuchadnezzar brought great hosts of Jews to Babylonia. A high birthrate and lively propaganda soon increased these numbers so greatly that, in spite of the return of the Jews in Cryus' and Ezra's day, large Jewish communities were established in Babylonia and in Egypt, and soon in Persia and in Mesopotamia, in Cyrene, in Asia Minor, and in many other places. Strict compliance with the law brought about the segregation of the Jews from the peoples among whom they dwelt. Industry and skill in commerce frequently brought them wealth in foreign countries. Because they kept themselves aloof from the inhabitants and because of their skill and cleverness, the kings frequently considered them valuable and chose them to help in governmental affairs. Because of their imageless religion and their strict laws of purification, other peoples believed they had something mysterious and worthy of respect. Their faith in God, their observance of the law, and their many pilgrimages to Jerusalem to celebrate the feasts, especially the Passover, kept them in close touch with the mother church. But in spite of their clannishness and aloofness from the "heathen," they were influenced by Greek culture, which had now spread everywhere where Alexander had reigned. The Hellenic

[431]

spirit greatly influenced the language, customs, and ideals in all Jewish communities in Babylonia, Asia Minor, and Syria, and especially in Alexandria.

This influence was felt in Palestine also. Constant intercourse between the homeland and Jewish settlements in foreign countries was sufficient to introduce Greek culture. Yet this influence would have reached Palestine eventually even if it had not been brought from the Diaspora. Geographically, Palestine was on the bridge between Asia and Egypt and, therefore, was the object of many disputes between Alexander's heirs. This naturally brought contact with Hellenism. The Book of Koheleth, called Ecclesiastes, is doubtless a reflective Jewish document, strongly influenced by Hellenism, and written in the period between Alexander and the Maccabees. When power seemed to be on the side of the Seleucids who favored the Greeks, the Jews were immediately ready to support them. Not only did the Seleucids realize the rising power of the Jews, but they understood better than the Ptolemies how to gain the sympathy of the Jews and how important they were as a political factor.

In his efforts to keep the blood and the ritual pure, Nehemiah had to struggle against a prominent Ammonite named Tobiah. Tobiah was closely related to Sanballat, governor of Samaria and one hostile to the Jews, to the high priest Eliashib, and to other prominent Jewish families. Through the high priest he had even obtained an influential and lucrative position in the Temple. Nehemiah opposed him. After the appearance of Hellenism, Tobiah's descendants and partisans naturally showed their objection to orthodox Judaism by favoring Hellenism. We find descendants of Tobiah among the Seleucids, men who held prominent positions in the Temple and, at the same time, favored the Seleucids. This justifies us in concluding that they maintained their old antagonism toward orthodox Judaism, which was so narrowly prescribed by laws; also that this former semi-heathen and worldly-minded opposition, which now favored Hellenism, favored the Seleucids for party reasons. I shall say as little as possible about these party interests, also about their personal interests which they sometimes pursued in a most shameless manner. Nor is it necessary to elaborate this subject, for up to the present time party and personal interests are common the world over.

At that time the temple funds were bartered to the rulers for well-paid offices. To-day leading politicians provide for themselves by accepting positions on boards of directors and by receiving concessions. Because of the great influence that the Tobiah party of enlightened aristocrats had over the people for a time, the cleverness of the Seleucids and the stupidity of the Lagidic (Egyptian) policy seem readily to have induced Judah to adhere to the Tobiahites. After the battle at Panias, when Antiochus III was fighting Ptolemy V and had occupied Jerusalem, the Jews joyously accepted him. He acknowledged their acclaim with many tokens of favor and by the bestowal of many privileges.

Of course there was opposition from those who remained faithful to the law. They now joined the Egyptian party of the Lagids. Thus it happened that Judaism was again tossed hither and thither by the two great powers of the East and of the Nile, just as it had formerly been by the Assyrians and Babylonians. The Seleucids gained power and, with them, the worldly-minded party, the liberals, who sought freedom from the restraint of the law. This sealed the bond between the Seleucids and the liberal Jews who hoped Hellenism would free them from religious narrowness.

These were the conditions in the year 175 when Antiochus IV, the illustrious Epiphanes, ascended the throne of the Seleucids. Antiochus had great and varied talents, and was energetic and zealous to raise to its old position the newly acquired empire which for several decades had suffered greatly from the wars. Hellenism was to help him in this. Following in the footsteps of his great predecessors, Seleucides I and Antiochus I, he founded Greek cities in many parts of Asia and granted many privileges. He tried to gain their complete devotion by giving them privileges and by extending great generosity toward them. He was inclined, however, to be eccentric and moody, had strange ideas, and was stubborn and overzealous. In spite of the great services he rendered his country in both peace and in war, he lacked the stability and breadth of view necessary to permanent success in a great empire.

Like many cities, such as Antioch, Epiphania, Seleukia founded by him and his predecessors, Jerusalem was to become a Greek city. Antiochus believed that unity and security were possible only if each nation gave up its customs and worshiped the great Zeus who had taken on human form in Antiochus, for the term Epiphanes means the visible God. He asserted the very principle which the enlightened Jewish aristocrats who clamored for reform had long desired.

In those days came forth out of Israel transgressors of the Law, and persuaded many, saying, Let us go and make a covenant with the Gentiles that are round about us, for since we are parted from them, many evils have befallen us. And the saying was good in their eyes. And certain of the people were forward herein and went to the King, and he gave them license to do after the ordinance of the Gentiles. And they built a place of exercise in Jerusalem according to the laws of the Gentiles, and they made themselves uncircumcised and forsook the holy covenant.[1]

This refers to Onias, the high priest's brother, Jesus or Jason as he called himself according to the custom that was now coming into use of assimilating Hebrew names into foreign ones. He was the leader of the Jewish reform party and had communicated with the king and offered to be his tool. Thus the Tobiah party by no means stood alone. The new party now extended to the Aaronite priesthood. As a reward for entering into the king's plans, Jason asked for the lucrative office of high priest and offered the king 440 talents in return for the appointment. He was ready to pay the king 150 talents more for the privilege of selling to citizens of Jerusalem citizenship in Antioch, in which citizenship was included participation in the Greek plays. The king gladly granted Jason's request, and Jerusalem seems to have become a real Greek city. Now Jason was high priest and hastened to introduce Greek customs. His first object was to educate Jewish youth in the Greek spirit.

He built a gymnasium at the foot of the citadel. Now that the new fashion was made official, young men of prominent families eagerly took part in athletic contests. They came in broad-brimmed Greek hats and covered the traces of circumcision. Even the priests left their altars to enjoy the games and discus throwing and to win Greek honors. "And thus there was an extreme of Greek fashion and an advance of an alien religion in Jerusalem," a chronicler sorrowfully reports. A meeting of delegates to games at Tyre called themselves "Antiochites from Jerusalem." Naturally, Jewish law was not binding for the Antiochites and for those who no longer were subject to the law of the temple, and as a result the temple treasury was not sacred. Thus Jason easily gained the king's consent and favor by offering large sums to him.

Now after a space of three years, Jason sent Menelaus . . . to bear the money unto the king and to make reports concerning some necessary matters. But he being commended to the King and having glorified himself by the display of his authority, got the high priesthood for himself, outbidding Jason by three hundred talents of silver.[2]

Menelaus was a Tobiahite and, therefore, belonged to the energetic and businesslike Jewish Ammonite family, whose very ancestry and history pointed to foreign and Jewish reform tendencies. He was jealous of Jason's laurels and even more of his financial success. Without scruples, he replaced one rascal by another, nor was he conscience stricken because Jason had trusted him. Business was business. Fine fellows indeed! Jason deserved to be outdone by Menelaus in rascality. Our text does not tell us what were the pressing matters Menelaus was sent to discuss with the king. However, we can read between the lines. If Menelaus succeeded in representing himself as an influential man, there must have been much discord and opposition. When we consider the great upheaval which the king's decrees had already caused, we easily understand that the mass of the faithful in the city and country who clung to the customs of their fathers looked askance upon the strange new life which had recently come into vogue in Jerusalem. Those who clung to the old faith and those who carefully observed the laws gradually sought to express their indignation; soon all was in a ferment. The ruler must prevent a revolt. Menelaus succeeded in presenting himself as belonging to an old reputed liberal family long established in the nation, in contrast to Jason, the Aaronite, whose family was after all bound by tradition to the law. A frank overbid of three hundred talents gave the necessary emphasis to his reasons, and Aaron's seat was his.

Menelaus did not pay the money he had promised. How could he, for the votive offerings and other temple treasures had doubtless been pillaged. Then the king called upon him to justify himself. Meanwhile his brother, Lysimachus, acted as his deputy. To raise money, Lysimachus robbed the temple so shamefully that it caused a rebellion in Jerusalem in which Lysimachus was killed. Again the king called Menelaus to account. By bribing one of the king's confidants, Menelaus succeeded in being acquitted while his accusers, three emissaries of the high council, were executed.

"But Menelaus through the covetous dealings of men in power still retained his office, cleaving to wickedness, as a great conspirator against his fellow-citizens." [3]

In the year 169-168 Antiochus fought with Egypt. The report spread in Jerusalem that he had died. Immediately the banished high priest invaded the city and committed terrible massacres among the partisans of Menelaus who had fled to the citadel. Thereupon, Antiochus hastily set out from Egypt. He felt he must subdue the insurrection of the Jews who were already embittered because of the contemptible execution of their envoys. He occupied the city and ordered a new, even more terrible massacre. Led by Menelaus who had been reinstated, he forced his way into the temple and carried off the golden vessels and everything upon which he could lay his hands.

A year or two later, in the summer of 167, after Antiochus had had bitter experiences with Egypt because of Rome's interference, he continued his measures against Jerusalem. The more insecure his position became in Egypt and in Rome, the more he felt the need of a firm hand in Palestine. Only thus did he feel able to attain his ideal of unity in the Seleucid empire. An officer of a Myser regiment, named Apollonius, was entrusted with carrying out the king's commands. He did this in the most treacherous and barbarous manner. The papers report that the English High Commissioner of Bagdad laid hands on a troublesome official of King Faisal of Irak by inviting him to a tea. The unsuspecting official was taken captive surreptitiously and carried off to Ceylon on an English man of war. In the spring of 1925 during the insurrection of the Druses, the French invited to Damascus five prominent Druse chieftains for an interview. They came, suspected nothing, were arrested, and carried off to Palmyra and other distant ports.

Apollonius appeared before Jerusalem and gave the Jews assurance of his friendly intentions. The people, suspecting

[437]

nothing, believed him and celebrated the Sabbath. He waited until the next Sabbath when he knew the Jews would be celebrating and, profiting by their lack of suspicion, he invaded the city and instituted a massacre. As in later years, leading French politicians believed there were several million more Germans than necessary, so Antiochus and Apollonius believed there were too many Jews in the world. Those they did not murder, they carried off captives. Only the king's partisans were spared. While the city was being partially destroyed, a new section with a citadel, the Akra, was built for them south of the temple court. "And they were a sinful nation, transgressors of the law." That is to say, that really only gentiles or the apostates among the Jews who favored the gentiles were to inhabit the city. This completed the ideal of a Greek city.

There was but one thing lacking, and Antiochus attended to the matter. An edict of the king required that "all should be one people and that each should forsake his own laws." Accordingly, the usual sacrifices were forbidden, the Sabbath and the feasts were canceled, the holy places defiled, circumcision and food laws abolished. In their stead heathen customs were introduced. Idols and heathen worship were again in use in the country. The temple was filled with riot and revelings by the heathen who dallied with harlots and had to do with women within the sacred precincts and, moreover, brought thither things that were not befitting. The king's birthday was celebrated each month. Instead of the Sabbath and the feasts, the Jews were forced under penalty of death to partake of the sacrifice for the king and to wear wreaths at the Bacchus feast in honor of Bacchus. Two women who circumcised their children, "when they had led them publicly round about the city with their babes hung from their breasts, they cast down headlong from the wall." Eleazar, an aged scribe, was executed because he would not eat swine's flesh. A group of people who had assembled in a cave to celebrate the Sabbath were burned or stifled to death by fire. Those who were found possessing the scroll of the law were punished by death. In December of 167 the Temple of Yahweh was transformed into a Temple of Jupiter Olympus.

Now all was done that a government stricken with blindness could do to revive a movement already dangerous and one it wished to suppress. In the meantime the pressure of the religious formalism, which had survived so much, and the struggle among the aristocratic families for power and lucrative positions had already caused great internal dissension. The desire for freedom among the reformed Jews and the desire for support from the Seleucid government helped to retard the orthodox movement and to support Antiochus' wishes fully to incorporate Judaism into the unified Hellenic state. If Antiochus had been wise enough to be satisfied with what he could attain, he might have been very successful and have come relatively near the goal he had set for himself. The influential people of Jerusalem and the country would, for the most part, have completely gone over to the new Hellenic party, for the orthodox and those who clung to the law had gradually dwindled to modest numbers. The very lack of initiative, which was the spirit of the law, obedience, and silent submission, keeping the Sabbath, and acceptance of the priests' demands would tend to make of them a quiet group. Had they not been roused, they would not have disturbed the apparent victory of Hellenic culture over the part of the world in which Antiochus ruled. Great persecution and torture did not change their passive attitude. When, in the early period of their persecution, they were attacked on the Sabbath, they refused to battle on that day and preferred to be massacred rather than break the law. A thousand people are said to have met death at one time in this way.

Now the measure was full. The oppression was so great that unless help came, Judaism was doomed. Then the head of a simple priestly family, the aged Mattathias, who lived in the modest village of Modin on the road from Jerusalem to Joppa, opposed the royal commissioners, who had set up an altar, and urged the people to offer sacrifice. Mattathias refused to listen to their flattery and promises, and when an unfaithful Jew was about to offer sacrifice at the altar, the priest rushed toward him, drew his sword, and killed him. Then he killed the commissioner, destroyed the altar, and caused the proclamation to be made in the city: "Whosoever is zealous for the law and maintaineth the covenant, let him come forth after me." Upon this he and his sons fled into the mountains. This was the first stroke; the time for silent suffering was past. A group of men with the courage of death drew their swords; insurrection was declared; the stone was set rolling. What would the end be? The aged priest was the father of Judas Maccabæus.

We see that great stupidity of action was necessary to rouse the party faithful to the law to action. Antiochus and his helpers succeeded in doing this. They considered these quiet sufferers like the people with whom they were accustomed to deal, who had proven themselves cringing cowards and avaricious, ambitious politicians. Antiochus and his friends may have looked down upon the narrow dependence of ritualistic law as a sign of weakness and limitation which could easily be mastered by a firm hand. They did not realize that the martyr's blood is the best seed for a spiritual movement, be the movement petty or sublime, to make it bear tenfold fruit. Still less did they realize that the Jewish God was a different God from the Phœnician Baals or the Asiatic deities that they had so easily overcome; that the laws of this God, petty as they seemed to them, possessed vital power far greater than a superficial glance suggested.

Now the real weakness of the new movement came to light. Unfortunately, ambitious men were appointed as leaders who sought only personal gain. The rank and file of particularly honest people among them were keenly disturbed. There certainly were many who honestly sought to rise above the narrowness of the law. Perhaps these idealists believed that Greek culture was what they needed. Perhaps they hoped to attain a religion of free and noble humanity through Greek culture. The result was much the same as had been the case elsewhere, when religion sought to ally itself with the culture of the period. Real religious life was in danger of being sacrificed to culture. There is every indication that this movement toward enlightenment lacked deep religious feeling, the living spark kindled by the deity which is necessary to every religion, and without which no religious movement can produce new religious life. Thus the Hellenistic movement in Judaism from the very first lacked the innate power without which, like many similar phenomena, it was doomed to religious decline and final extermination in shallow enlightenment.

A new phenomenon appeared in the opposing party simultaneously with this one. When Ezra and Nehemiah had successfully completed their work, they could rest in peace, feeling they had given their people a law of life which would carry it through life's trials without struggle or anxiety. He who obeyed the law, kept the Sabbath, obeyed the law for circumcision, and the laws prescribed for food and for purity, might calmly go about his business and face God at home and abroad with a clear conscience. Neither Ezra nor Nehemiah had been truly religious. None of the fervor of the old prophets inspired them. They had no personal relationship to God. Their religion was sane and practical, a sort of good bargain between God and man. If you keep Yahweh's laws, he must care for you.

Yet the Israelite prophets had not lived in vain. Although Ezra and Nehemiah had not been baptized with prophetic fire, the prophetic spirit survived and could not be exterminated. It lived on beside the law and made a covenant with it.

We have much testimony that, at the time of the new congregation and even during the period when law reigned after Nehemiah's time, there was true religious zeal. The poem of Job and a number of Psalms, which preach a form of piety entirely free from the law and far above any sort of religious formalism, give evidence that the teachings of the prophet were not forgotten. They may have been pushed into the background by Nehemiah's reforms, they may have disappeared from the surface of the official and dominating church life, but they lived on below the surface like an undercurrent which seldom reaches the surface, yet exists and has an influence. In certain pious circles after Nehemiah up to the time of our story, true piety found expression in such Psalms as the seventy-third. If man has God and communion with him, if man has access to God and certainty of God's favor, he has all that the world and the period can give him. Zeal for the law is not the highest ideal, but to have God in our hearts.

Even where the ritual and the law seemed the greatest good, many people attained a degree of piety which rose higher than cold formalism and dead justification by works. Zeal fulfilled the requirements of the law, not duty and, therefore, the people did not consider the practice an irksome compulsion or hard yoke about their necks, as the less zealous did. On the contrary, they looked upon it as a blessing, and heartily thanked God for it; they not only proudly obeyed the law because it led them to a morality higher than that of the heathen, but they felt it was a fine and noble means of approaching God, to gain his favor. One day in the forecourts of Yahweh was better than a thousand; to share in the splendid services of the Temple, perhaps during a pilgrimage, gratefully to rejoice in the presence of the Almighty was a great blessing and comfort to the pious. Law and ritual reigned. But the law was stripped of all harshness and sternness which it had for those who served reluctantly. It was a benevolent helper, a kindly guide to God; it "refreshed the soul." This is not the religion of the prophets, but this piety through the law went far beyond itself in honest souls who sought more than rites and narrow formalism. Because these honest people sought piety, and through piety, God himself, piety half unconsciously made a connection in them with the old prophetic piety, and the memory half forgotten and yet not forgotten, that Israel had formerly had greater possessions.

Mattathias and those about him may have been such people. When they took up arms, they doubtless did it quite contrary to their inclination and their original intention but as an act of extreme desperation. Death meant nothing to them; but Yahweh worship must not die and, for its sake, to maintain it, the nation must live. This was the reason they resorted to arms. At first they sought to harmonize their resistance with the law. The experience of the thousand who were massacred and burned in the cave on the Sabbath taught them that halfway measures were useless. The villagers seem to have accompanied Mattathias. Soon many fugitives rallied about him who stood by the law. Many of them belonged to the already-organized party of the Hasidæans or Chasidim, those who clung to the old faith. Thus began one of the bitterest and most disastrous religious wars which history has known. Not only the heathen oppressors but all who did not strictly uphold the law were considered enemies. They soon treated those who had formerly shared their own faith with the same ruthless and often brutal cruelty as their heathen oppressors. The "miserable" or "oppressed," whom the Greek translation designates as the "meek," were soon entirely changed. They seemed more like tigers than men.

Mattathais must have quickly gathered a large following with whom he traversed the country. They gave violence for violence. Those who did not uphold the law, they killed; they overthrew the new altars and circumcised the children.

Those who would not comply might flee. The aged priest soon died. His bequest to his followers is reported to have been: "Take ye unto you all the doers of the law, and avenge the wrong of your people. Render a recompense to the Gentiles and take heed to the commandments of the law." His son Judas, called Maccabæus, the Hammer, became their leader in 166.

For an armed force of several thousand men to attempt to oppose a kingdom that extended from the Egyptian border to Armenia and the Iran was indeed a bold venture. But each man of them was ready, not only to give his life which he had already forfeited, but to sell his life most dearly. The father had realized what his sons after him also realized, that raids for revenge and punishment of their fellow countrymen were not enough; they must face the king's armies.

Then the governor of Samaria, Apollonius, and the governor of Syria, Seron, marched against the bold leader. With the courage of desperation his band overran Apollonius and killed him. Judas fought his later battles with the sword he had captured in this battle. He attacked Seron unexpectedly and scattered his army, "and every nation told of the battles of Judas." These bold strokes brought Judas sudden fame.

Antiochus was then making a campaign to the eastern part of his kingdom where he had heavy battles in Armenia and Babylonia against the Medes and Persians. He left part of his army under the leadership of Lysias, whom he appointed regent in the west. He had him rout the rebels and carry out drastically his old plan. The value of the newly established fortified Greek part of Jerusalem, called Akra, as a base for the governmental troops was now proven. Lysias sent out an army to conquer Judah. The enemy came from the coast and camped near Emmaus, called Nicrompolis by the Greeks. This was three miles west of Jerusalem. From there they intended to advance upon Jerusalem. Men from the citadel Akra were their guides. The assurance which the superiority of their numbers gave them is shown by the fact that a host of slave dealers followed the army. They felt certain of large spoils. Rome needed men, and the king needed great sums of money to indulge his wishes and to pay his debts. Gorgias, one of Lysias' generals, planned to take Judas' camp by surprise. Judas, however, succeeded in skillfully evading him, and while Gorgias was searching for him, Judas attacked his camp. The fact that Judas' army left the spoils of the surprised camp to conquer Gorgias, who was returning from the mountains, proves the courage and the severe discipline of his army.

Then Lysias set out in person in the fall of 164 with a large new force. He approached from the south. Again at Bethsura, twenty-five kilometers south of Jerusalem on the Hebron road, Judas won a glorious victory. Now that he had conquered the auxiliary troops from both sides, there was nothing to prevent him from attacking the capital. He occupied the temple precincts on Mt. Zion, but the Grecian quarter of Akra withstood. "And they saw the sanctuary laid waste, desolate, and the altar profaned, and the gates burned up, and the shrubs growing in the courts as in a forest . . . and the priests' chambers pulled down." ' We imagine what bitterness they felt on seeing this and upon hearing of the reports of a frightful punishment planned to avenge the injustice. They purged the defiled sanctuary and rededicated it. They removed the desecrated altar stones and placed them without the sacred precincts until a prophet should come to decide their fate. They destroyed all the heathen altars and places of worship. They erected a new altar of unhewn stones and replaced the ritual vessels. On the twenty-fifth of the month of Chislev in 164 the feast of dedicating the temple was celebrated. This is said to be the anniversary of the very day on which it was desecrated. This feast, retained permanently, is called Chanukka, or the Feast of Dedication, or "Feast of Light" to celebrate the returning of daylight. Bethsura and the restored temple were strongly fortified, the former as a defense against Edom, the latter to protect them against the Grecian settlement at Akra.

Lysias now realized that he could not hope to suppress the movement by violence. Thus he began negotiations with the Jews in the year 163. The king was favorable. Antonius had appointed his son Eupator as co-regent. Judas was also willing to negotiate. Two ambassadors, John and Absalom, presented a document from the high council containing suggestions for an agreement. Thereupon the king wrote to Lysias:

We having heard that the Jews do not consent to our father's purpose to turn them unto the customs of the Greeks, but choose rather their own manner of living and make request that the customs of their law be allotted unto them . . . we determine that their temple be restored to them and that they live according to the customs that were in the days of their ancestors.

To the high council itself he gave assurance "that the Jews use their own proper meats and observe their own laws, even as hithertofore."

In reality, the government had retreated along the whole line in the absence and hardly with the consent of the real king of whose great sufferings Lysias and Eupator certainly knew. Perhaps they knew also of his defeats in the East. This seems to suggest that the ruling class about Antiochus Epiphanes was doubtful of this policy of suppression. Even Rome shared this feeling. This shows that the personal intolerance and stubbornness of Epiphanes himself added a keen edge to conditions. He displayed these same traits in the East and caused great bitterness by violently suppressing traditional religion, and therefore suffered great defeat.

We assume the Jews were satisfied with the agreement, but conditions were not definitely regulated. What was to be the fate of the still hostile neighbors? What that of the Jews lately become Hellenists and apparently cowardly traitors to those who remained faithful to the law? These and many other questions were unanswered. Above all, the deep-seated hatred that every war engenders, and most of all a religious war, had not been extinguished. Nor did the generals seem satisfied with this solution that brought little honor either to them or to their absent king. They were interested in continuing the strife. Little wonder that the peace was short-lived. Here and there we find hostile deeds and spiteful cruelties toward the Jewish minority which constantly forced Judas to resort to arms. The revival of Judaism, which they believed stifled, was a thorn in the flesh to the Edomites, the Ammonites, and the people of Gilead. There were constant conflicts which extended as far as Galilee and Phœnicia, and soon the religious war was fiercer than ever before. Both sides committed the greatest cruelties and deeds of fanatical hatred which gave this new phase of the war an especially disgusting aspect: surreptitious murder of peaceful groups on the one side; banishment and slaughter of whole communities on the other. The slaughter was so unspeakable that the adjoining lake, which was two furloughs broad, appeared to be filled with the deluge of blood. Even if the numbers, ten thousand killed, are exaggerated as was common, the scene was one of utmost cruelty —a bloody religious war in which all moral ties were broken and men became beasts. The group of the meekly pious of former times had long ago become a band of wild or half-wild animals by becoming accustomed to war which unleashed all the passions, by the brutality of their opponents and hatred of the accursed backsliders from their own ranks and, too, by acquiring various revolutionary spirits. Again Judas proved himself a brilliant and successful leader, bold and skillful in his plans. Together with his brother, Jonathan, and an army of eight thousand men, he succeeded in a campaign against Timotheus. They destroyed the celebrated sanctuary of Atergatis, the former Ishtarte in Carnaim in the Hauran region, and triumphantly brought the endangered Jews who lived there back to Jerusalem by way of Bethsean. His older brother Simon did the same for the Jews of Galilee. They pillaged and devastated the land of the Edomites, Hebron, and the Philistine territory. Occasional defeats which the fortunes of war brought them, such as the unsuccessful campaign into the Philistine territory against Gorgias, did not shatter Judas' ardor and determination to conquer. Now he might even venture to allow the people to return to their peaceful tasks; to distribute the lands of those who had forsaken their faith among his adherents; and to reorganize the priesthood which, in a large measure, had failed him. This was the reëstablishment, in a modest degree, of an independent Jewish state.

To rule the country completely Judas must conquer the citadel of Akra at Jerusalem which was still occupied by soldiers. This fortified citadel was a constant menace to him. He attacked it in 162. Lysias gathered a large force and again advanced from the south. His numerous elephants with towers and his heavily armored foot soldiers were Judas' undoing. Bethsura fell. Judas was forced to retreat to the Temple Hill where he suffered greatly for want of food, for it was a Sabbatical year. In spite of this condition, Lysias was willing to make peace because of the unsettled conditions in the empire. Of course he could state the peace terms now. The Jews gave up Zion but kept their property and religious freedom. The king himself sacrificed in the Temple to the God of the Jews, but the sacrifice for the king was reinstituted. This signified the establishing of the royal overrule. The high priest Alcimus, however, was made ruler over the congregation. Judas was unmolested, but his influence was eliminated.

We see the empire had got the lion's share. Therefore the orthodox Jews could not possibly be satisfied with this peace. Tension increased, if for no other reason than that Judas and his company refused the high priest, who was established in the Hellenistic citadel of Akra, access to the altar and the Temple in the Jewish quarter which they had established on Zion. Since Alcimus was an Aaronite and the Hasidæans had acknowledged him in spite of their misgivings, Judas and his followers were put in a difficult position. Attempts at conciliation failed or were unsatisfactory. The condition was made even more critical by Alcimus' treacherous acts of vengeance toward Judas' partisans and by cruelties which the hostile general, Bacchides, committed. The main reason, however, may have been that Demetrius had meanwhile ascended the throne. He had killed Eupator and Lysias. Since the Romans had not yet acknowledged him, he must do his utmost to bring about speedily settled conditions in Palestine. This drove Judas to arms. Religion was pushed more and more into the background. The struggle between Alcimus and Judas was for power. A former commander of the elephant division, named Nicanor, was sent to restore peace. In March of 160, a battle was fought near Modin northwest of Jerusalem. Judas conquered and triumphantly occupied Zion and hanged the head and the arm of the fallen Nicanor on the walls of the Akra This was by the spring of 160.

Judas had long had the support of Rome whose policy was to do all it could to weaken the Seleucid empire. After the victory, or more probably before it, Judas even sent messengers to Rome who succeeded in making an alliance with the senate. Under its protection, Judas hoped soon to be unquestioned ruler in Judah. In the meantime, Demetrius recovered his strength, so that he was able to send Bacchides in the spring of 160 with a large army against Judas. With it was the high priest, the legitimate representative of true religion to many of the people. Rome did not follow up its alliance with action, and Judas had to face his opponent with only a small army which had grown weary of war. The real object of the war had long ago been changed, and his men had slowly lost their former zeal. The armies met west of Jerusalem; Judas' army was overpowered, and he himself fell in battle. He was buried in the family burying ground at Modin. The hope of the independent Jewish state he had tried to found was buried with him, and the power of the Seleucids which he had hoped to overcome was established. Years later Jonathan and Simon (notably Simon) succeeded in reëstablishing, for a time, an independent Jewish ecclesiastical state. The ideals for which the Maccabees had fought vanished; the priestly purple lost its splendor.

With Judas Maccabæus passed the last of the great men of Israel. Judas' tragedy was that he did not recognize the hour of destiny. War for God and religion gradually changed to war for self and for power. Where was the limit? And when the turning point of time? Perhaps Judas was aware of them but could not seize them because of the malice of men and circumstances. Be that as it may, his glory has been remembered by his people.

And he got his people great glory, and put on a breastplate as a giant, and he was like a lion in his deeds and a lion's whelp roaring for prey—and the lawless shrunk for fear of him, and all the workers of lawlessness were sore troubled—and his memorial is blessed forever. And he went about among the cities of Judah and destroyed the ungodly out of the land and turned away wrath from Israel: and he was renowned unto the utmost parts of the earth, and he gathered together such as were ready to perish.[1]

He who said this is right. Without Judas Maccabæus in the homeland, Judaism would have succumbed to violence both in the homeland and later, of course, in the Greek cities of the Diaspora. Where small groups held their own, they would have been forced for safety into remote places. Judas is responsible for Nehemiah's work continuing throughout the centuries. Although he died in defeat, his life was a victory.

XVIII

EPILOGUE

HERE and there in this book, the reader may have come upon remarks referring to a period as late as the present. In this material, he may note that I have asserted a conviction that, although humanity may have increased its knowledge somewhat, have gained certain refinements of life, and have acquired partial control over matter, in the essentials of life itself, in the growth of the spirit, in the purifying and ennobling of moral life, humanity has advanced but little if at all. Thus far religion has not brought about ideal morals, partly because, in critical times, religion has failed to realize the opportunity, and partly because one of the contradictions in history seems to be that religion is fated to have but limited control over opposing forces.

Far be it from me to fail to appreciate that religion has brought about the elevation of woman and a combat against slavery, that, in what Bismarck calls practical Christianity, much has been done to assuage social distress, and that the unselfish labor of noble individuals and organizations has accomplished much. Yet the strain in business morals as well as political ones, destructive class distinctions, and above all, the continued raging of the great scourge of humanity—war, with changed but more cruel methods toward combatants, prisoners, and non-combatants, regardless of age or sex—prove how little we have advanced. Neither the oft-repeated saying that politics and business are a law unto themselves, nor the famous theory of the gradual development of mankind by the standards of the gospels, assure us of a final solution. Whether the present Protestant ecumenical movements will succeed in bettering conditions, the future must show. They may do much good. This is the sincere wish of all well-intentioned people and my own firm conviction. Yet I fear they will not exterminate the egotism of the masses.

Should egotism and want of public spirit triumph over nobler impulses, the optimist should not be discouraged. He who knows his duty will always be able to hold his own in his immediate surroundings. People must learn to master themselves and their surroundings before they attempt to better the world. God will do the rest without them.

Then, although generations be swallowed up by hatred, although the earth pass away without having seen the perfection of which many of its inhabitants dreamed, the ideal for which millions of the finest spirits have striven for thousands of years cannot vanish in the sea of forgetfulness.

As I write these final sentences, it gives me special pleasure to find similar thoughts verified by a friend and coworker, Johannes Volkelt. They are the result of a long life of careful research in matters of the ultimate meaning of life. The object of this book, however, has not been to answer the question of the why of things, but to establish the facts.

BIBLICAL QUOTATIONS

I. MOSES

[1] Ex. iii. 16
[2] Ex. xix. 6
[3] Gen. xxxi. 42

[4] Ex. xx. 5, 7
[5] Ex. xix. 18
[6] Ex. xv. 25

Read the book of Exodus.

III. DEBORAH

[1] Deut. xxxiv. 5, 6
[2] Judges v. 8
[3] Judges v. 4, 5
[4] Judges v. 9, 11
[5] Judges v. 13, 14, 15, 18

[6] Judges v. 20, 21
[7] Judges v. 19, 22
[8] Judges v. 25, 26, 27
[9] Judges vi. 22
[10] Judges iv. 9

Read Judges iv and v.

IV. JERUBBAAL—GIDEON

[1] Judges vi. 4, 5
[2] Judges vii. 15
[3] Judges viii. 1, 2, 3

[4] Judges viii. 6
[5] Judges vi. 16
[6] Judges ix. 54

Read Judges vi, viii and ix.

V. SAMUEL AND SAUL

[1] I Sam. xi except verses
12 and 13

[2] I Sam. xv. 35

Read I Samuel.

VI. DAVID

[1] Amos vi. 5
[2] I Sam. xxix. 4

[3] II Sam. iii. 38
[4] II Sam. i. 25

Read I Samuel and II Samuel, I Kings v, II Kings,
Elijah and the other religious enthusiasts.

VIII. GREAT NARRATORS

[1] Judges viii. 20

Read Judges xvii and xviii, I Kings i,
II Samuel x, xiii, xix.

IX. REVOLUTIONISTS

[1] II Sam. xx. 1
[2] II Kings ix. 5
[3] II Kings ix. 11, 13

[4] II Kings ix. 18, 22
[5] II Kings x. 5

Read I Kings xi, xii, xiv, xv, xvi, II Kings ix, x.

X. CLASSIC PROPHETS. AMOS AND HOSEA

[1] Amos v. 2
[2] Amos vii. 15
[3] Amos v. 16, 17
[4] Amos iii. 11
[5] Amos iii. 12
[6] Amos iii. 1, 2
[7] Amos vi. 2
[8] Amos ix. 7
[9] Amos iii. 3, 4, 7, 8
[10] Amos v. 18-20
[11] Amos v. 21-25

[12] Amos iv. 4
[13] Amos v. 4, 5
[14] Amos v. 4, 15
[15] Hosea i. 2
[16] Hosea ii. 2, 5, 8
[17] Hosea iv. 12
[18] Hosea iv. 13, 14
[19] Hosea ii. 7, 15
[20] Hosea ii. 19
[21] Hosea ii. 21, 22
[22] Hosea xiv. 4

Read the books of Amos and Hosea.

XI. ISAIAH

[1] II Kings xvi. 7
[2] Isaiah viii. 13
[3] Isaiah vi. 9
[4] Isaiah v. 8, 9, 11-13
[5] Isaiah ii. 13, 16, 18
[6] Isaiah ix. 10-14, 17

[7] Isaiah v. 28
[8] Isaiah vii. 4, 8, 9
[9] Isaiah ix. 6
[10] Isaiah xxviii. 1-3
[11] Isaiah xxx. 1, 2, 3
[12] II Kings xviii. 32

Read II Kings xiv, xvi, xix, xx, Isaiah i to xxx,
especially ii, v, vi, vii, viii, ix, x, xx, xxx.

XII. REFORMERS

[1] II Kings xxi. 3-7

Read I Kings xiv, xv, xxii, II Kings xi, xii,
xviii, xx, xxii and xiii, I Samuel ix, xiv.

XIII. LAWGIVERS

[1] Exodus xxii. 29   [2] Levit. xvii. 11

Read Exodus xv, xviii, Judges x, xi, Deut. xii.

XIV. JEREMIAH

[1] Jer. i. 10
[2] Jer. vii. 18, 20
[3] Jer. ii. 20, 23, 28
[4] Jer. i. 13-15
[5] Jer. vi. 22, 23
[6] Jer. xvi. 46
[7] Jer. xv. 7
[8] Jer. ix. 2
[9] Jer. xx. 7-9

[10] Jer. xv. 10
[11] Jer. xx. 14, 15, 18
[12] Jer. xv. 19
[13] Jer. xvii. 14
[14] Jer. xxi. 9

Read Joshua xxi, Nehemiah xi, 20, and St. Luke i, 39f.,
I Kings ii, II Kings xxiii, xxiv, Isaiah xxx,
and all of Jeremiah.

BIBLICAL QUOTATIONS

XV. SECOND ISAIAH AND THE GREAT SUFFERER

[1] Jer. xxxi. 16f.
[2] Jer. iii. 17
[3] Jer. xxxi. 32-34
[4] Isaiah xl. 6-8
[5] Isaiah xl. 3-5
[6] Isaiah xl. 1, 2
[7] Isaiah xlv. 1-3
[8] Isaiah xlv. 13, and xliv. 28
[9] Isaiah xliii. 5, 6
[10] Isaiah li. 4, 5
[11] Isaiah xlix. 1-5, 6
[12] Isaiah l. 4-8
[13] Isaiah liii. 1-7
[14] Isaiah liii. 8-10

Read Jeremiah xxix, II Kings xxiv, Ezekiel viii, xiii, xiv, xxix, xxxi, xxxvi, xxxvii, Isaiah xl to the end.

XVI. EZRA AND NEHEMIAH

[1] Haggai ii. 20ff.
[2] Ezra x. 2, 3

Read the books of Ezra and Nehemiah, Haggai i, ii.

XVII. JUDAS, THE MACCABEE

[1] I Maccabees i. 11-14
[2] II Maccabees iv. 23, 24
[3] II Maccabees iv. 50
[4] I Maccabees iv. 38

Read I and II Maccabees.

CHRONOLOGICAL TABLE OF CONTENTS

CHRONOLOGICAL TABLE

CHRONOLOGICAL TABLE

CHRONOLOGICAL TABLE

CHRONOLOGICAL TABLE

INDEX

[459]

INDEX

Ethical power of religion, 41.

Exiles, returned, found Palestine in great confusion, 409; land ownership, 409; religious conditions in Palestine, 410; make slow progress, 411.

Ezekiel, gatherings at his home, 369; preaches Yahweh, 370; gives a history of his people, 371; vision, 374.

Ezra, 407; character, 414; priest, scribe, prominent position in Babylon, 420; sent by royal edict to homeland, 421; causes the people to dissolve marriages with heathen women, 422; takes a caravan of Jews to Jerusalem, 422; deprived of authority, 424; ill will toward him, 424.

Feast laws, 332.

Federation to shake off Babylonian yoke, 357.

Foreign wives, 162.

Gedaliah, attempted to rebuild Jerusalem, 365; murder, 365.

Gideon, pursues enemy in forced marches, 71; captured the chieftains, 72; surprised the enemy, 72; large booty, 72-73; revenge, 73; ruler in Israel, 74; attitude toward religion, 76; demolishes Baal altar, 79; had ephod made, 80; religion, 80; ruled over Shechem, 80.

Great Narrators, 175.

Great Sufferer, the, 367.

Greece, its leading spirits, 2; Hellenic spirit, 3.

Greek culture, 441.

Habiru, who they were, 15; their relation to Canaan, 16.

Haggai, 411.

Hebrew, 17; general term, 21.

Hebron, built, 10.

Hellenic spirit, 431-432.

Hesiod, 242.

Hezekiah, political measures, 276; prosperous, 276; begins religious reform, 277; political attitude, 280; vassal of Sennacherib, 282;

reform, 295; decree, 298; reform questioned, 298; reform, reasons for, 298-299; reform—its climax, 299.

"High place," 287, 296.

Hilkiah, finds the book of laws, 306; "found" the book, 324.

Historical narrations, 177-178.

History of pre-regal heroic period, 187; of King David's latter life, its excellency, 189-190.

Hittites, 12.

Hofra, his policy, 361.

Hosea, his family, 243; eyes opened, 244; language, 246; prophet of divine love and fidelity, 247.

Hyksos, 5; rule in Egypt, 7; period, 10; tribe, 17.

Ibn Sa'u, 128.

Immigration, from Sinai to S. Palestine, 22.

Isaiah, 250; reports great wealth, 251; opposed the political policy, 259; religious views, 260; call to prophesy, 261; family, 261; message, 262; sounded cry of punishment, 262; suffered under Israel's policy, 264; foresaw religious consequences, 266; tried to dissuade King Ahaz, 266-267; demands faith in God, 267; offered a miracle, 269; prophesies birth of a Savior, 270; foretold fall of Samaria, 274; urged Hezekiah not to break away from Assyria, 277-278; again preached faith in God, 279; political attitude, 279; remains faithful to the king, 281; later life—legend, 283; his spirit revived, 303; Isaiah, second, 367, 375; his writings, 375-376; mental superiority, 376; message, 384; preacher of salvation, 386; "salvation" for all peoples, 386; his life, 387; political considerations, 388; nature of his book, 389; prominent position in life of his time, 389; new type of prophecy, 390; believes the Suf-

Jews, 361; urges the people to desert to enemy, 362; goes to his home on business, 363; imprisoned in cistern pit, 363; cast into mire and then rescued, 364; sacrifices the truth, 364; "one of the greatest and best of the olden times," 366; letter to Babylonian captives, 368; believed Yahweh would make a new covenant with his people, 374.

Jeroboam, flight, 154; insurrection, 154; introduced the bull into the official worship, 157; 203; demands, 205; had Egypt's support, 205; erects golden bull, 206; king of all Israel, 206; political situation, 206-207; dynasty unsatisfactory, 208.

Jerubbaal, legend, 65; summons his vassals to arms, 66-67; raid upon the enemy, 67; victory, 69.

Jerubbaal-Gideon, 61; meaning, 65; national hero, 69; Jerusalem, threatened, 255; water supply, 256; subject to Pharaoh Necco, 307; Jerusalem, siege of, 362; its restoration, 385; a Greek city, 434, 435.

Jewish, feasts, 328; ideals, 441.

Jews, not racially pure, 6; returned to foreign gods, 366; longed to return to Holy Land, 373; establish a church state, 428; not blood ties but observance of the law, 429; massacred, 438-439; persecuted, 439; roused to action, 440.

Jezebel, goal, 163; her character, 163; religion, 164.

Jonathan, bravery, 102; murdered the governor, 102.

Joram, wounded at Ramah, 210.

Joseph, 7; in Egypt, 20.

Josephus, 169.

Joshua, 44; statutes and ordinances, 318.

Josiah, reform, 304; death, 307; ideal, 307; book (Deuteronomy), 320; reform, 339.

Judah's short-sighted policy, 264-266.

Judaism, its two centers, 367; its development, 415.

Judas, the Maccabee, 430; many victories, 444; attempts to gain the Akra, 448; had the moral support of Rome, 449; quarrel with high priest, 449; fell in battle, 450; last of Israel's great men, 450.

Judean commerce strengthened, 251.

Judgment upon the nations, 337.

Kadesh-Barnea, 34; sanctuary, 41; springs at, 41; statute and ordinance, 41.

Korban, 330.

Lapaja, his rule, 14.

Lawgivers, 308.

Law of Holiness, 328.

Laws, books of, 313-314.

Lysias, negotiates with the Jews, 446.

Malachi, report of conditions, 414; shows contamination of blood, 419.

Manasseh's counter-reform, 299-300.

Maritime Peoples, 26, 31, 49.

Mattathia, resistance, 440; violence for violence, 443; zeal, 443.

Megiddo, battle of, 307.

Melkart of Tyre, 164.

Menahem, pays tribute to Assyria, 252.

Menelaus, 435.

Meneptah, immigration in his time, 23; his monument of victory, 26; boasts that he subjugated all Palestine, 47.

Mental achievements of the period, 377, 380.

Metrical speech, 178.

Meyer, Edward, 189.

Midian hordes plunder the country, 62.

Midianites, object of, 64; kill Gideon's brothers, 70; return to plunder, 70.

Migration of nations, 4, 18.

INDEX

446